CLARENDON'S

HISTORY OF THE REBELLION AND

CIVIL WARS IN ENGLAND.

MACRAY.

London

HENRY FROWDE

Oxford University Press Warehouse

Amen Corner, E.C.

THE

HISTORY OF THE REBELLION

AND

CIVIL WARS IN ENGLAND

BEGUN IN THE YEAR 1641,

BY

EDWARD, EARL OF CLARENDON.

RE-EDITED FROM

A FRESH COLLATION OF THE ORIGINAL MS. IN THE BODLEIAN LIBRARY,

WITH MARGINAL DATES AND OCCASIONAL NOTES,

BY

W. DUNN MACRAY, M.A., F.S.A.

In Six Volumes.

VOL. V.

(*Books XII–XIV.*)

Oxford

AT THE CLARENDON PRESS

Oxford University Press, Walton Street, Oxford OX2 6DP

Oxford New York Toronto
Delhi Bombay Calcutta Madras Karachi
Petaling Jaya Singapore Hong Kong Tokyo
Nairobi Dar es Salaam Cape Town
Melbourne Auckland
and associated companies in
Berlin Ibadan

Oxford is a trade mark of Oxford University Press

Published in the United States
by Oxford University Press, New York, New York

This edition first published 1888
Re-issued 1992

British Library Cataloguing in Publication Data
Data available

Library of Congress Cataloging in Publication Data
Data available

ISBN 0–19–820372–1

Printed and bound in
Great Britain by Biddles Ltd,
Guildford and King's Lynn

A TRUE HISTORICAL NARRATION

OF THE

REBELLION AND CIVIL WARS IN ENGLAND.

BOOK XII.

And now ye purpose to keep under the children of Judah and Jerusalem for bondmen and bondwomen unto you: but are there not with you, even with you, sins against the Lord your God?—2 CHRON. xxviii. 10.

Woe to the multitude of many people, which make a noise like the noise of the seas; and to the rushing of nations, that make a rushing like the rushing of mighty waters.—ISAIAH xvii. 12.

The Lord hath poured out upon you the spirit of deep sleep, and hath closed your eyes: the prophets and your rulers, the seers hath he covered.—ISAIAH xxix. 10.

1 [1]. WHILST these tragedies were acting in England, and 1649 ordinances formed, as hath been said, to make it penal in the highest degree for any man to assume the title, or to acknowledge any man to be king, the King himself remained in a very disconsolate condition at the Hague. Though he knew the desperate state his father was long in, yet the barbarous stroke so surprised him, that he was in all the confusion imaginable, and all about him were almost bereft of their understanding. The truth is, it can hardly be conceived with what a consternation this terrible news was received by all the common people of that country. There was a woman at the Hague, of the middling rank, who, being with child, with the

---

[1] [*Life*, p. 389.]

1649 horror of the mention of it fell into travail and in it died. There could not be more evidence of a general detestation, than there was amongst all men of what quality soever. Within two or three days, which they gave to the King's recollection, the States presented themselves in a body to his majesty, to condole with him for the murder of his father, in terms of great sorrow and condolence, save that there was not bitterness enough against the rebels and murderers. The States of Holland, apart, performed the same civility towards his majesty; and the body of the clergy, in a very good Latin oration, delivered by the chief preacher of the Hague, lamented the misfortune in terms of as much asperity, and detestation of the actors as unworthy the name of Christians, as could be expressed.

2. The desperateness of the King's condition could not excuse his sinking under the burden of his grief; but those who were about him besought him to resume so much courage as was necessary for his present state. He thereupon caused those of his father's Council who had attended him to be sworn of his Privy Council, adding only Mr. Longe his secretary, who before was not of the Council. All which was done before he heard from the Queen his mother; who, notwithstanding the great agony she was in, which without doubt was as great a passion of sorrow as she was able to sustain, wrote to the King that he could not do better than to repair into France as soon as was possible, and in the mean time desired him not to swear any persons to be of his Council till she could speak with him; whether it was that she did not think those persons to be enough at her devotion, or that she would have them to receive that honour upon her recommendation.

3. The King himself had no mind to go into France, where he thought he had not been treated with excess of courtesy; and he resolved to perform all filial respect towards the Queen his mother, without such a condescension and resignation of himself as she expected; and to avoid all *éclaircissements* upon that subject, he heartily desired that any other course might be found more counsellable than that he should go into France. [He]

himself lived with and upon the Prince of Aurange, who sup- **1649**
plied him with all things necessary for his own person, for his
mourning, and the like: but towards any other support for
himself and his family, he had not enough to maintain them
one day, and there were very few of them who could maintain
themselves in the most private way.   And it was visible enough
that they should not be long able to reside in the Hague, where
there was at that very time an agent for the Parliament,
Strickland, who had been there some years, but pretended at
that time to reside there with his wife, who was a Dutch
woman [1], and without any public character, though he was still
under the same credentials.   And their advertisements from
London assured them that the Parliament had nominated one
who was presently to be sent as their ambassador or envoy to
the States, to give them an account of their affairs, and to
invite them to enter into an alliance with them.   So that it
was time to think of some other retreat for the King; and
none appeared then so reasonable in their view as Ireland;
from whence they heard that prince Rupert was arrived safely **1649**
at Kinsale with the fleet; that the lord Inchiquin had made a **Jan. 29.**
cessation with the Irish before the Lord Lieutenant came **1648 May 20, 22.**
thither, and the Irish had deserted the Pope's nuncio, who was **1649**
driven away, and had embarked himself for France; that the **Feb. 22.**
marquis of Ormonde was received by the lord Inchiquin with
all the obedience imaginable, by which he became entirely
possessed of the whole province of Munster; and that the **1648**
confederate Catholics had invited him to Kilkenny, where he **Oct. 28.**
had made a full peace with them; so that they were preparing **1649 Jan. 17.**
an army to march under his command against Dublin.   This
news made them hope that every day would improve it so
much, that it would be fit for the King to transport his own
person thither in the spring.

   4. In this conjuncture there arrived a gentleman, one sir **Feb. 6.**
Joseph Douglasse, with a letter from the Privy Council of
Scotland, by which they sent him word that they had pro- **Feb. 5.**
claimed him King of Scotland, and sent him the proclamation,

---

[1] [Anna, d. of Sir Charles Morgan, governor of Bergen-op-Zoom.]

1649 and wished that he would prepare himself to repair into that his kingdom, in order to which they would speedily send another invitation to him. And that invitation arrived at the same time with some commissioners deputed by the Council, and three or four preachers sent from the commissioners of the Kirk. The proclamation indeed declared, that, for as much as the late King was, contrary to the dissent and protestation of that kingdom, removed by a violent death, by[1] the Lord's blessing there was left unto them a righteous heir and lawful successor, Charles, who was become[2] their true and lawful King; but upon condition of his good behaviour, and strict observation of the Covenant, and his entertaining no other persons about him but such as were godly men and faithful to that obligation. A proclamation so strangely worded, that, though it called him their King, manifested enough to him that he was to be subject to their determinations in all the parts of his government. And the commissioners, both laity and clergy, spake no other language; and, saving that they bowed their bodies and made low reverences, they appeared more like ambassadors from a free state to an equal ally than like subjects sent to their own sovereign. At the same time, though not in the same ship, arrived likewise from Scotland the earl of Lanricke and earl of Latherdale; the former not knowing till he came into Holland that he was duke Hambleton by the slaughter of his elder brother. But they two were so far from having any authority from their country, that they were fled from thence as proscribed persons and malefactors. The earl of Latherdale, after his departure from the Hague in that discontent that is mentioned before[3], bent his course for Scotland, but before he came thither he was informed that the state of all things had been reversed, and the Engagement declared unlawful, and to what penalties himself was liable if he should be taken. Whereupon, without suffering his ship to go into any port, he found

---

[1] ['that by,' MS.]

[2] [The words 'that for as much—who was become' are substituted for 'that by the death of his father, which they mentioned as if it had been by the course of nature, he was become.']   [3] [Book xi. § 91.]

means to send on shore to some friends, and so to concert all **1649**
things, that, without being discovered if himself did go on
shore, the earl of Lanricke and himself, and some other persons
liable to danger if they were found, put themselves on board
the same ship, and arrived in Holland about that time when
the other messengers from the State and from the Kirk came
from Scotland, and when the news came of the execution of
duke Hambleton.

5. Whereupon the new duke kept his chamber for some
days, without so much as waiting upon the King; who sent a
gracious message to him to condole for the loss of his brother;
and all the lords, and other persons of quality about the King,
made their visits to him with all civility.   This duke was not
inferior in wisdom and parts of understanding to the wisest
man of that nation, and was very much esteemed by those
who did not like the complying and insinuating nature of his
brother.   He was a man of great honour, courage, and sincerity in his nature, and, which was a rare virtue in the men
of that time, was still the same man he pretended to be, and
had very much to say in his own defence for the errors he had
run into; which he acknowledged always with great ingenuity,
and abhorred the whole proceedings of his countrymen, and at
this time brought a heart and affection clearer, and less clogged
with scruples and reservations, for the King's service than any
other of them did.

6 [1]. Though Cromwell, at his being in Scotland, had left
Arguyle in the full possession of the government there, reduced
and disbanded all those who were in arms against him, and
promised him all necessary assistance to subdue those who
should rise up in arms against him in that kingdom, and
thereby compelled the Committee of Estates to convene and
summon the Parliament to assemble, which they had authority
to do; and so he had suppressed the party of Hambleton,
driven the earl of Lanricke to hide himself in some obscure
place, and condemned the Engagement as unlawful and sinful,
and all the persons who advanced and promoted it as deserters

[1] [*Hist.*, p. 1.]

1649 of the Covenant, and so to stand excommunicated, and not to be capable of serving in Parliament or in the Council of Estate[1], so that he was sure to find no opposition in whatsoever he proposed; yet after the Parliament had served him so far, when they heard that the Parliament in England was broken, and their freedom and privileges were taken from them by the insolence and power of the army, (which they perfectly hated and detested,) and all those sects and liberty they heard [were[2]] introduced in religion contrary to their Covenant, which Cromwell himself had promised should be strictly observed, they began to examine what the obligations were which were incumbent upon them even by the Covenant itself. The delivery of the King's person into the hands of the Parliament at Newcastle had been, in the instant it was done, the most unpopular and ungracious act to the whole nation of Scotland that it had been ever guilty of, and to the army they had then on foot, which took itself to be deeply wounded by the infamy of it, and was therefore quickly disbanded by the wisdom of Arguyle: and the general indignation for that action was the principal incitement to that general Engagement with duke Hambleton, that the honour of the nation might in some degree be repaired or redeemed. And it was a gross oversight in the Hambletonian party, and discerned then to be so by the earl of Lanricke, that, upon that popular advantage, in which he would have found an universal concurrence, Arguyle himself and all his faction had not been sacrificed to the redemption of the honour of their country. But the duke's politics did not lie that way; and, so he might return to his old post of favour in England, of which he made little doubt, he was not willing to give a new beginning to those bloody enterprises in Scotland, which he knew well used not to be shortlived in that climate after once begun, but had always fresh sacrifices of blood to perpetuate the memory of them.

---

[1] [An Act of the Scottish Parliament of Jan. 16, 1649 established previous Acts to the above effect of Sept. 22, Oct. 4, and Nov. 9. *Acts of Parl. of Scotl.* 1872, vol. vi. part ii. p. 136.]

[2] ['was,' MS.]

7. They no sooner heard of the erection of a High Court of **1649** Justice, and of a purpose of trying the King for his life there, than, notwithstanding all the artifices Arguyle could use, they were all in a flame. As well the Assembly of the Kirk as the Parliament renewed the sense they always had of the reproach in the delivery of his person, of which the present danger he was in was the consequence. And the marquis of Arguyle had had too deep a share in that wickedness to endure the shock of a new dispute and inquisition upon that subject ; and therefore gave not the least opposition to their passion, but seemed equally concerned in the honour of the nation to prosecute a high expostulation with those of England, for the breach of faith, and the promises which had been made for the safety and preservation of the King's person at the time he was delivered up ; and therefore proposed that commissioners should be forthwith sent to the Parliament at London, to require the performance of what they had proposed, and to enter their dissent and protestation against all their proceedings against the King, in the name of the kingdom of Scotland. And the earl of Lothian and two others[1], who were known to be most zealous for the Covenant, and most enraged and incensed against the proceedings of the army, were made choice of, and presently sent away, that they might make all possible haste to Westminster, and were immediately upon their arrival to demand permission to wait upon the King, wherever he should be, and to receive from him such farther directions as he should judge necessary for his service.

8. Thus far Arguyle could not oppose, and therefore was as zealous as any man to advance it ; knowing that the particular instructions must be prepared by a less number of men, and not subjected to the examination and perusal of so many; and in those he was sure to prevent any inconvenient powers to be granted to the commissioners, with whom he had credit enough,

---

[1] [Sir John Chiesly and William Glendoning. Chiesly had been first accredited as sole commissioner by a letter from the Estates of Oct. 17, presented in Parliament, Oct. 26. The others appear to have been sent at the beginning of Dec., instructions for the three having been given on Dec. 6.]

1649 having made the earl of Lothian Secretary of State in the place
of the earl of Lanricke, and the other two being (however
solicitous for the due observation of the Covenant, as he himself likewise pretended to be) known to be most averse from
Jan. 9. the Hambletonian party. Their private instructions were, that
they should not, in their enlargements and aggravations upon
the subject of their message, seem to take notice or to imply
that any violence had been used against the Parliament or any
member of it: that they should be so short in their amplifi-
cations, that they gave no occasion of offence: that nothing
should proceed from them justifying the King's proceedings,
nor in approbation of the late Engagement, or which might
import a breach, or give or be a ground of a new war: '[they
should urge,] that the Parliament would delay to meddle with
the King's person, according to their several promises and
declarations at Newcastle and at Holmby: that if they should
proceed to sentence against the King, then to enter their
dissent and protest, that this kingdom may be free from the
miseries which will inevitably follow, without offering in their
reasons that princes are exempted from trial and justice: that
none in the Parliament of Scotland hath or had any hand in
the proceedings against the King and members of Parliament
[in England]. If they proceed, then to shew the calamities
that will follow, and how grievous it must be to the kingdom of
Scotland, considering his delivering up at Newcastle: that if
the papers which were entitled *The Agreement of the People*,
appeared to be countenanced, and should import any thing
concerning the processing of the prince, or changing the fundamental government of the kingdom, that they should enter
their dissent: that they should alter those their instructions, or
manage their trust therein, according to the advice they should
receive from their friends there: that they should prosecute
their instructions concerning the Covenant and against any
toleration: that they should shew that the King's last concessions were unsatisfactory to those propositions which they
had made in point of religion.

9. These were their private instructions; and who those

friends at London were by whose advice they were to alter 1649
their instructions, or manage their trust therein, can be understood of no other men but Cromwell and young sir Harry
Vane, with whom Arguyle held close correspondence. The
commissioners observed their instructions very faithfully, and,
after the King had been twice brought before the High Court
of Justice, they gave in their very calm protestation; in which Jan. 22.
they put them in mind that they had near three weeks before Jan. 6[1].
represented to them what endeavours had been used for the
taking away the King's life, and for the change of the fundamental government of the kingdom, and introducing a sinful
and ungodly toleration in matters of religion; and that
therein they had expressed their thoughts and fears of the
dangerous consequences that might follow thereupon; and that
they had farther earnestly pressed that there might be no
farther proceeding against his majesty's person, which would
certainly continue the great distractions of the kingdom, and
involve them in many evils, troubles, and confusions, but that
by the free counsels of both Houses of Parliament of England,
and with the advice and consent of the Parliament of Scotland,
such course might be taken in relation to the King as might be
for the good and happiness of both kingdoms, both having an
unquestionable and undeniable right in his person, as king of
both; which duly considered, they had reason to hope that it
would have given a stop to all farther proceedings against his
majesty's person. But now understanding that, after the imprisonment and exclusion of divers members of the House of
Commons, and without and against the consent of the House of
Peers, by a single act of their own, and theirs alone, power was
given to certain persons of their own members, of the army,
and of some others, to proceed against his majesty's person, in
order whereunto he had been brought before that extraordinary
new court; they did therefore, in the name of the Parliament
of Scotland, for their vindications from false aspersions and
calumnies, declare, that though they were not satisfied with his
majesty's late concessions in the treaty at Newport in the Isle

[1] [*Acts of the Parl. of Scotland*, VI. ii. 694–5.]

1649 of Wight, especially in the matters of religion, and were resolved not to crave his restoration to his government before satisfaction should be given by him to that kingdom [1], yet they did all unanimously with one voice, not one member excepted, disclaim the least knowledge of, or accession to, the late proceedings of the army here against the King; and did sincerely profess that it would be a great grief to their hearts, and lie heavy upon their spirits, if they should see the trusting his majesty's person to the two Houses of the Parliament of England to be made use of to his ruin, contrary to the declared intentions of the kingdom of Scotland and solemn professions of the kingdom of England: and to the end that it might be manifest to the world how much they did abominate and detest so horrid a design against his majesty's person, they did, in the name of the Parliament and kingdom of Scotland, declare their dissent from the said proceedings, and the taking away of his majesty's life; protesting that, as they were altogether free from the same, so they might be free from all the miseries, evil confusions, and calamities, that might follow thereupon to the distracted kingdoms.

10. Whoever considers the wariness in the wording and timing this protestation, the best end whereof could be no other than the keeping the King always in prison, and so governing without him in both kingdoms, (which was thought to have been the purpose and agreement of Cromwell and Arguyle when they parted,) must conclude that both the commissioners and they who sent them laboured and considered more what they were to say in the future, than what they were to do to prevent the present mischieve they seemed to apprehend. And the Parliament best knew their temper; when they deferred taking any notice of their protestation till after they had Feb. 17. executed their execrable villainy; and then they sent them an answer that might suit with all their palates. They said, they had heretofore told them what power this nation had in the fundamentals of government: that if Scotland had not the same power or liberty, [as] they went not about to confine them so they

[1] ['his kingdoms;' the letter as printed at the time.]

would not be limited by them, but leaving them to act in theirs as they should see cause, they resolved to maintain their own liberties as God should enable them. And as they were far from any thought of imposing upon them, so they should not willingly suffer impositions from them, whilst God gave them strength or lives to oppose them. They said, the answer they made to their first and second letter was, that after a long and serious deliberation of their own intrinsical power and trust (derived to them by the providence of God through the delegation of the people,) and upon the like considerations of what themselves and the whole nation had suffered from the misgovernment and tyranny of that King, both in peace and by the wars, and considering how fruitless and full of danger and prejudice the many addresses to him for peace had been, and being conscious how much they had provoked and tempted God by the neglect of the impartial execution of justice, in relation to the innocent blood spilt and mischieve done in the late wars, they had proceeded in such a course of justice against that man of blood as they doubted not the just God (who is no respecter of persons) did approve, and would countenance with his blessings upon the nation; and though perhaps they might meet with many difficulties before their liberties and peace were settled, yet they hoped they should be preserved from confusion by the good-will of him who dwelt in the bush which burned and was not consumed; and that the course they had taken with the late King, and meant to follow towards others the capital enemies of their peace, was, they hoped, that which would be for the good and happiness of both nations; of which if that of Scotland would think to make use, and vindicate their own liberty and freedom, (which lay before them, if they gave them not away,) they would be ready to give them all neighbourly and friendly assistance in the establishing thereof; and desired them to take it into their most serious consideration, before they espoused that quarrel, which could bring them no other advantage than the entailing upon them and their posterities a lasting war, with all the miseries which attend it, and slavery under a tyrant and his issue.

1649   11. It cannot be denied but that Scotland had by this a fair invitation to have made themselves a poor republic, under the shelter and protection of the other, that was already become terrible. But the commissioners, who well knew how unsuitable such a change would be to the constitution of their government, and that they might be welcome to their own Feb. 24. country whither they were now to repair, made a reply to this answer with more courage than they had yet expressed; for Feb. 26, 28. which, notwithstanding their qualification, they were imprisoned by the Parliament, and, upon new instance from Scotland, set at liberty afterwards.

12. Matters being reduced to this state, the marquis of Arguyle could not hinder the new King's being acknowledged and proclaimed King, nor from being invited home; which since he could not obstruct, it would be his masterpiece to clog the proclamation itself with such conditions as might terrify the new King from accepting the invitation ; and therefore he caused this clause to be inserted in the body of the proclamation itself ; ' Because his majesty is bound, by the law of God and the fundamental laws of this kingdom, to rule in righteousness and equity, to the honour of God, the good of religion, and the wealth of his people, it is hereby declared that before he be admitted to the exercise of his royal power, he shall give satisfaction to this kingdom in those things which concern the security of religion, the unity betwixt the kingdoms, and the good and peace of this kingdom, according to the national Covenant and Solemn League and Covenant ; for which end they were resolved, with all possible expedition, to make their humble and earnest addresses to his majesty.'

13. This was the proclamation that sir Joseph Douglasse brought to the Hague, and the subject upon which the commissioners were to invite his majesty to go for Scotland, whose instructions were very suitable to the proclamation : and at the same time when the commissioners came from thence, Middleton and some other officers who had been in their last army, hearing that the Prince was proclaimed King, thought it was seasonable to put themselves into a posture to. serve

him upon his arrival, and so assembled some of those troops 1649
which had formerly served under them in the north of Scotland [1]; whereupon David Lashly was appointed forthwith, with Feb. 27.
a party of horse and foot, against those royalists, whom they
knew to be real assertors of his cause, without any other
interest or design than of their performing their duties as loyal
subjects ought to do: and the Kirk at the same time declared,
that before the King should be received, albeit they had
declared his right by succession, he should first sign the
Covenant, submit to the Kirk's censure, renounce the sins of
his father's house and the iniquity of his mother, with other
things of the like nature. All which information arrived at
the same time with the commissioners, that they who were about
the King might not be too much exalted with their master's
being declared King of one of his three kingdoms. And it was
very manifest, by all that passed then and afterwards, that the
marquis of Arguyle meant only to satisfy the people in declaring
that they had a King, without which they could not be satisfied,
but that such conditions should be put upon him as he knew
he would not submit to; and so he should be able with the
concurrence of the Kirk to govern the kingdom, till by Cromwell's assistance and advice [able] to reverse that little approach
he had made towards monarchy by the proclaiming a king.

14 [2]. It was a great misfortune to the King, and [one]
which always attends courts which labour under great wants
and necessities, that whilst the greatest union imaginable
amongst the few friends he had was necesssary, and of too little
power to buoy [3] him up from the distresses which overwhelmed
him, there was yet so great a faction and animosity amongst
them, that destroyed any the most probable design that could
offer itself; as it now fell out with reference to Scotland, which
if united might yet be able to give reputation at least, if not
a vigorous assistance, to the King's interest.

15. The marquis of Mountrose, who hath been mentioned
before, and had been obliged by the King, after he had performed such wonderful actions in Scotland, to lay down his

---

[1] [at Inverness.]   [2] [*Life*, p. 390.]   [3] [' bw'y,' MS.]

1649 arms, and left that kingdom upon his majesty's first coming in the Scots' army to Newcastle, had first arrived in France, and had not such a reception from the Queen of England and those who were in credit with her as he thought the notable services he had performed for the King had merited. The truth is, he was elated with the great actions he had done, which upon his first coming to Paris he caused to be published in a full relation in Latin, which was dedicated to the Prince of Wales [1]; and in which, as his own person and courage and conduct was well extolled, so the reputation of all the rest of that nation (upon whose affections the Queen at that time depended) was exceedingly undervalued and suppressed; which obliged the Queen and the Prince to look less graciously upon him; which he could not bear without expressing much disturbance at it. He was then a man of *éclat,* had many servants, and more officers, who had served under him and came away with him, all whom he expected the Queen should enable him to maintain with some lustre by a liberal assignation of moneys. On the other hand, the Queen was in straits enough, and never openhanded, and used to pay the best services with receiving [them [2]] graciously and looking kindly upon those who did them. And her graces were still more towards those who were like to do services than to those who had done them. So that after a long attendance, and some overtures made by him to cardinal Mazaryne to raise an army for the service of that King, which he did not think were received with that regard which his great name deserved, the marquis left France, and made a journey in Germany, to the Emperor's Court, desiring to see armies, till he could come to command them; and was returned to Bruxells about the time that the Prince came back into Holland with the fleet, and lay there very privately, and as *incognito,* for some time, till he heard of the murder of the King. And then he sent a servant over to the King with the tender of his service, and to know if his majesty thought his attendance upon him might bring any prejudice to his majesty;

---

[1] [By Wishart. This edition was apparently suppressed, upon a letter from the Prince, a copy of which is in Bodley MS. 895.]   [2] ['it,' MS.]

and if so, that he would send over the Chancellor of the 1649
Exchequer to Sevenbergh, a town in Flanders upon the river, ^{Jan. 28.}
where he was at present to expect him, and had matters to
communicate unto him of much importance to his majesty's
service. Whether he did this out of modesty, and that he might
first know his majesty's pleasure, or out of vanity that was pre-
dominant in him, that he might seem to come to the King, after
the coldness he had met with at Paris, by a kind of treaty, the
King commanded the Chancellor presently to go to him, and if he
could without exasperating him, (which he had no mind to do,)
wished he might be persuaded rather for some time to suspend
his coming to the Hague than presently to appear there; which
was an injunction very unagreeable to the Chancellor, who in his
judgment believed his majesty should bid him very welcome, and
prefer him before any other of that [nature[1]] in his esteem.

16. The sudden violent frost, which shut up all the rivers in
less than four and twenty hours, kept them at that time from
meeting; but within a short time after, and upon another
message from him, they met at a village three or four miles off
the Hague, whither the marquis had transported himself. The
Chancellor had never seen him from the time he had left
Oxford, when he seemed to have very much modesty, and
deference to the opinion and judgment of other men. But he
had since that time done so many signal actions, won so many
battles, and in truth made so great a noise in the world, that
there appeared no less alteration to be in his humour and discourse than there had been in his fortune. He seemed rather
to have desired that interview that he might the better know
what advice to give the King, and how to make a party that
would be fast to him, than out of any doubt that his presence
would not be acceptable to his majesty. There was yet no
news from Scotland since the murder of the King, and he
seemed to think of nothing but that the King would presently
send him thither with some forces, to prepare the way for
himself to follow after. They spent that night together in
conference, and the next morning the Chancellor prevailed with

[1] [' nature,' MS.]

him with great difficulty that he would stay in that place, which did not abound with all things desirable, or somewhere else, until he might give him notice what the King's sense should be of the matters discoursed between them; insisting, principally, that if his going into Scotland should be thought presently to be necessary, it would then be as necessary that he should not be taken notice of publicly to have been with the King; with which reason he seemed satisfied, and promised not to come to the Hague till he should first receive advice from the Chancellor. But when he heard of the commissioners being come from Scotland, and of the other lords' arrival there, he would no longer defer his journey thither, but came to the Hague well attended by servants and officers, and presented himself to the King, who received him with a very good countenance.

17. There were at this time in the Hague the commissioners who came from the Council and the Kirk to invite the King into Scotland, or rather to let him know upon what terms he might come thither, the duke Hambleton, [the] earl of Latherdale, and others of the nobility of that faction, who were now as odious and as much persecuted by that party which then governed Scotland, and which in that manner invited the King, as any men were who had served the King from the beginning. And then there was the marquis of Mountrose, with more of the nobility, as the earls of Seaforte and Kynoole and others, who adhered to Mountrose, and believed his clear spirit to be most like to advance the King's service. Of these three parties, it might reasonably have been hoped that the two last, being equally persecuted by the power that governed, should have been easily united to have suppressed the other. But it was a business too hard for the King to bring to pass; and he could as easily have persuaded the Parliament to reject Cromwell, as the lords of the Engagement, those who had joined with duke Hambleton, to be reconciled to Mountrose. So that when the King hoped to have drawn all the Scottish nobility together, to have consulted what answer he should give to the messages he had received from the Council and the Kirk, with which they themselves were enough offended, those lords of the En-

gagement did not only refuse to meet with the lord Mountrose, **1649** but as soon as he came into the room where they were, though his majesty himself was present, they immediately withdrew, and left the room, and had the confidence to desire the King that the marquis of Mountrose (whom they called James Gryme) might be forbidden to come into his majesty's presence or Court, because he stood excommunicated by the Kirk of Scotland, and degraded and forfeited by the judicatory of that kingdom. And this proposition and demand they made confidently in writing under their hands[1], and abounded so much in this sense, that a learned and worthy Scotch divine, Dr. Wisharte, who was then chaplain to a Scotch regiment in the service of the States, being appointed to preach before the King on the Sunday following, they formally besought the King that he would not suffer him to preach before him, nor to come into his presence, because he stood excommunicated by the Kirk of Scotland for having refused to take the Covenant, though it was known that the true cause of the displeasure they had against that divine was because they knew that he was the author of the excellent relation of the lord Mountrose's actions in Scotland. This carriage and behaviour of those lords appeared ridiculous to all sober men, that any men should have the presumption to accuse those who had served the King with that fidelity, and were only branded by those rebellious judicatories for having performed their duty of allegiance, and to demand that the King himself should condemn them for having served his father: which made those of his majesty's Council full of indignation at their insolence, and his majesty himself declared his being offended, by using the marquis of Mountrose with the more countenance, and hearing the doctor preach with the more attention. But from this very absurd behaviour, besides his majesty's desire being frustrated of receiving the joint advice of the nobility of that kingdom in an affair that so much concerned himself and them, and besides the displeasure and distance that it caused between them and the King's Council, (who thought they might as reasonably move the

April 8, 9,
N. S.

[1] [*Calend. Clar. S. P.* II. 5.]

1649 King that they might be removed, who lay under the same
brands and reproaches in England for adhering to the Crown
as the other did in Scotland,) the King had reason to be
troubled with another apprehension, which was, that the marquis of Mountrose (who could not be ignorant of any thing
which the other persons said or did) would out of just indignation take revenge upon those persons, whom he contemned
too much; and so that the peace of the country, where his
majesty was but a guest, would be violated by his subjects, as
it were in his own sight; which would make his absence from
thence the more desired.

18. He, to whom this unreasonable animosity was most
imputed, and who indeed was the great fomenter and prosecutor
of it, was the earl of Latherdale, whose fiery spirit was not
capable of any moderation. One of the Council [1] conferring
one day with him upon a subject that could not put him into
passion, and so being in a fair conversation, desired him to
inform him what foul offence the marquis of Mountrose had
ever committed that should hinder those to make a conjunction
with him, who in respect of the rebels were in as desperate a
condition as himself, and who could not more desire the King's
restitution than he did. The earl told him, calmly enough,
that he could not imagine or conceive the barbarities and
inhumanities that he was guilty of in the time he made a war
in Scotland; that he never gave quarter to any man, but pursued all the advantages he ever got with the utmost outrage
and cruelty; that he had in one battle killed fifteen hundred of
one family, of the Cambells, of the blood and name of Arguyle [2],
and that he had utterly rooted out several names and entire
noble families. The other told him, that it was the nature and
condition of that war that quarter was given on neither side;
that those prisoners which were taken by the Scots, as once
they did take some persons of honour of his party, were afterwards in cold blood hanged reproachfully, which was much
worse than if they had been killed in the field; and asked him

---

[1] [substituted for 'The Chancellor.']
[2] [at Inverlochy, Feb. 2, 1645.]

if Mountrose had ever caused any man to die in cold blood, or **1649** after the battle was ended; since what was done in it *flagrante* was more to be imputed to the fierceness of his soldiers than to his want of humanity. He confessed he did not know that he was guilty of any thing but what was done in the field; but concluded with more passion, that his behaviour there was so savage that Scotland would never forgive him. And in other company, where the same subject was debated, he swore with great passion, that though he wished nothing more in this world than to see the King restored, he had much rather that he should never be restored than that James Graham should be permitted to come into the Court: of which declaration of his the King was informed by William Legg and sir William Armorer, who were both present at the Hague, and in the company when he said it.

19. There was at that time in the Hague the lord New-burgh, who after the murder of the King was compelled, to-gether with his wife, the lady Aubigny, to fly out of England, Cromwell every day making discoveries of correspondences which had been between the King and them. And thereupon they made an escape from thence, and came to the Hague[1]; that lord having been too young to have had a part in the former war, but had been then sent by his majesty's direction to be bred in France, from whence he returned not till his majesty was in the hands of the Scots' army; and from that time he performed all the offices of fidelity and duty to the King that a generous and worthy person could find any oppor-tunity to perform, and with which his majesty was abundantly satisfied and pleased: and now transported himself and his wife into Holland, that he might leave her there, and himself attend the King in any expedition.

20. This lady was a woman of a very great wit, and most trusted and conversant in those intrigues which at that time

[1] [The following lines are here struck out in the MS.: ' The lady had in the life of her former husband the lord Aubigny, and during the time of her widowhood, held much friendship with the Chancellor, and was very willing it should continue with her new husband, whom he had not seen before.']

1649 could be best managed and carried on by ladies, who with less
jealousy could be seen in all companies; and so she had not
been a stranger to the most secret transactions with the Scots,
and had much conversation with the lord Lanricke during the
time the King was at Hampton Court, and whilst he stayed
afterwards in London when the King was imprisoned in the
Isle of Wight; and being now both in the Hague, they had
much conversation together. She had likewise had long acquaintance and friendship with one of the Council, who she
knew had been as much trusted as any by his father, and was
believed to have credit with the present King[1]. She lamented
those divisions amongst the Scots which every body spake of,
and every body knew the disorder they produced in the King's
councils, and said she desired nothing more than that there
were a good understanding between duke Hambleton and him[2];
which she said she was sure would easily be if they two had
but once a frank conference together. The other, who indeed
had an esteem for the duke, seemed very desirous of it; and she
thereupon told him that the duke had expressed to her that he
would be willing to embrace the occasion; and thereupon it
was so concerted that within a day or two they met as by
chance at her lodgings. And she so dexterously introduced
them to a civility towards each other, and to express their
inclinations to a mutual freedom, that after an hour's general
conversation there, to which she left them and went herself
abroad, they parted with fair professions of future good will;
and the other[2] promised to visit him the next morning early,
that they might have the more time without being interrupted;
and he was with him accordingly, and found him in his bed.
They continued together near two hours, the duke having commanded his servant to tell any who came to visit him that he
was asleep. The other[2] spake of the proclamation, and manner
of inviting the King into Scotland, and of the strange spirit
that possessed those who governed there and persuaded them

---

[1] [This sentence is substituted for the words, 'The Chancellor being one
day with this lady.']
[2] [' the Chancellor.']

to imagine it possible that the King could ever be persuaded **1649**
to take the Covenant, or that it could be profitable for him to
do so; since it could not but much alienate the affections of all
that party in England that had served his father, and upon
whom he ought chiefly to depend for his restoration to the
government of that kingdom. Then he spake of the differences
and jealousies which were between those of that nation who
had an equal desire to serve the King, and seemed to be
equally persecuted by the party that now prevailed and had
excluded both : and wished that some expedient might be found
out to unite all those, and particularly that his grace and the
marquis of Mountrose might be reconciled; towards which, he
said, he was sure that the marquis had great inclination, and
had always esteemed him a man of honour; which appeared by
the book which was published, where he was always worthily
mentioned, though it had not dealt well with many others.

21. When the duke had heard him with very civil attention,
he told him, as to the first part, concerning the proclamation
and the manner of inviting the King to come to them, he was
not to make any other judgment by it than only of the person
of the marquis of Arguyle, who, with the assistance of some
few ministers, and others who were his creatures, did at present
govern; that [Arguyle [1]] well knew that there was an absolute
necessity, in respect of the whole people, to proclaim the King
after the murder of his father, and therefore he could find no
other way to keep him from coming thither but by clogging
the proclamation and message with those unworthy expressions,
which might deter him from putting himself into their hands;
which Arguyle did not wish he should do, because in his
absence he was sure he should govern all, being well agreed
with Cromwell how the government should be carried;
and, so the King might be kept out, Cromwell would support him against all other parties ; but that they both knew
well enough that if his majesty were once there the whole
nation would stick to him and obey him. He confessed
that there was generally so great a superstition for the

[1] ['he,' MS.]

1649 Covenant that whosoever should speak against it for the present
would lose all credit, though he did acknowledge it had done
much mischieve, and would do more whilst it should be
insisted on; but he said that must be a work of time, and
an effect of the King's government, which would find it
necessary in many other respects to lessen the power of the
ministers; which being lessened, the reverence for the Covenant
would quickly fall too; and till then he and all men must
have patience. For the second, he said, he wished heartily
that there could be a union of all parties which desired the
King's restoration, and that the animosity against the marquis
of Mountrose might be extinguished. For his own part, that
he had only one quarrel against him, which was, that by his
unjust calumnies and prosecution he had driven him into rebellion, which nothing else could have done, and for which he
always asked God forgiveness from his heart, and desired
nothing more than to repair his fault by losing his life for the
King; and would with all his heart join to-morrow with the
marquis of Mountrose in carrying on the King's service, though
he did believe, in that conjuncture, the animosity against [the
marquis[1]] was so great, that if he should declare such an
inclination all his own friends would fall from him and abhor
him. He said his own condition was very hard; for that
having been always bred up in the Church of England, for
which he had a great reverence, he was forced to comply with
the Covenant, which he perfectly detested, and looked upon
it as the ruin of his nation, and would be as glad as any man of
a good opportunity to declare against it. 'But,' said he, 'I
dare not say this; and if I did, I should have no power or
credit to serve the King. There is,' said he, 'a very worthy
gentleman, who lodges in this house, the earl of Latherdale, my
friend and my kinsman, who upon my conscience loves me
heartily; and yet I dare say nothing of this to him, either against
the Covenant or for the marquis of Mountrose; and if I should,
I believe he would rather choose to kill me than to join with
me; so much he is transported with prejudice in both these

1 ['him,' MS.]

particulars, and so incapable to hear reason upon either of 1649
those arguments, though in all other things few men have a
better understanding or can discourse more reasonably.'

22. Whilst they continued in all possible freedom in this
conference, the earl of Latherdale, who it seems was informed of
the other's[1] being there, came in his night-gown into the
chamber, and so brake off the discourse. And the other[2],
after sitting some time in general conversation, departed.
And there continued afterwards all civility between the duke
and him ; but (as himself told the lady Aubigny, who shortly
after died there,) he could not, without giving jealousy to his
friend Latherdale, which he had no mind to do, spend so much
time with the other[2] in private as he could have been willing
to have done : and the death of that lady lessened the opportunities.

23. In this unsteady and irresolute condition of the King's
councils, it was very manifest that, how long soever his majesty
should defer the resolution to what place he would remove,
he should not be able to stay long in the place where he was.
The States, especially those of Holland, let fall somewhat every
day in their councils and consultations, that the King's residing
in the Hague would be very inconvenient to them ; and it was
the great interest of the prince of Aurange, not without much
dexterity, that kept the States from sending a message directly
to his majesty, to desire him that he would depart from that
country as soon as he could. And there happened an accident
at this time that made the resolution necessary, or that
would inevitably draw on that message, which had yet been
kept back.

24. It was touched before, that there was a purpose at § 3.
London to send over an envoy from thence into Holland, to
prepare the way for a farther good intelligence and negotiation,
which might end in a firm peace and reciprocal alliance between
the two republics. And to that purpose one Dorislaus, a doctor
in the civil law, was named ; who, being born in Delph in
Holland, had been bred at Leyden, and afterwards live   long

---

[1] ['the Chancellor's.']   [2] ['the Chancellor.']

1649 in London, having been received into Gresham[1] college as a
professor in one of those chairs which are endowed for public
lectures in that society[2], and had been from the beginning of
the troubles in the exercise of the judge advocate's office in the
earl of Essex his army. In this conjuncture this man arrived
at the Hague, and took his lodging in a house where strangers
used to repair, and were accommodated till they provided
otherwise for their better accommodation. Whilst he was at
May 2. supper, the same evening that he came to the town, in company
of many others who used to eat there, half a dozen gentlemen
entered the room with their swords drawn, and required those
who were at the table not to stir, for that there was no harm
intended to any but the agent who came from the rebels in
England, who had newly murdered their King. And one of
them, who knew Dorislaus, pulled him from the table, and with
a dagger killed him at his feet : and thereupon they all put up
their swords, and walked leisurely out of the house, leaving
those who were in the room in much amazement and consternation. Though all who were agreed in the enterprise went
quietly away, and so out of the town, insomuch as no one of
them was ever apprehended or called in question, yet they kept
not their own counsel so well, (believing they had done a
very heroic act,) but that it was generally known that they were
all Scotsmen, and most of them servants or dependants upon the
marquis of Mountrose.

25. The King was exceedingly troubled and perplexed with
this accident, which he could not foresee, and easily discerned
that it would be applied to his prejudice, and that the States
could not but highly resent it in many respects ; that the man
who was killed was in truth their own subject, and employed
to them as a public minister by those with whom they had no
mind to have any quarrel. Upon all which his majesty concluded that his presence there would quickly appear more unacceptable than ever : besides that there had been the same

[1] ['Gressum,' MS.]
[2] [Not at Gresham College, according to Ward's *Lives of the Gresham
Professors,* but for a short time at Cambridge.]

night some quarrels and fighting in the streets between some **1649** servants of the King and some gentlemen of the town, in which a son of one of the States was dangerously hurt, though he recovered afterwards.

26. It cannot be denied but that the States proceeded upon these disorders, to which they had not been accustomed, with great gravity, and more than ordinary respect to the King. They were highly offended with what was past, and sensible what expostulations and clamour for justice they must expect and sustain from England, and what reproaches they must undergo for suffering all those who had been guilty of such a crime to escape the ministers of justice, which could not but be imputed to them as a great scandal to their government: yet they proceeded very slowly in their inquisition, and with such formalities as were usual, and which could bring no prejudice to the offenders, who were either gone out of their dominions, or concealed themselves in other towns, where the same formalities were to be used if they were discovered; and without so much reflection upon the King as if they believed the guilty persons to have any relation to his service ; yet they took notice of the multitude of strangers which were in the town, and how impossible it would be for them to preserve the peace and good government thereof if such resort were not restrained. They aggravated exceedingly the indignity that had been offered to the State itself in the attempt that had been made upon a person under their protection, and for whose safety the public faith was upon the matter engaged, with insinuations enough that it would be fit for the King to remove from thence. Of all which his majesty receiving advertisement, he thought it better himself to give them notice of his purpose to leave them than to expect a plain injunction from them to do so. He found this the more necessary to be done, since from the time the Scots' commissioners were come thither they had taken great pains to infuse into the opinions of that people that they were sent from the kingdom of Scotland, that was entirely and unanimously at his majesty's disposal, to invite him to repair thither, and to take possession of his government

1649 there, where there was already an army preparing to assist
him towards the recovery of his other dominions ; but that
there was a party of evil councillors about his majesty, who
dissuaded him from acccepting that their invitation, except they
would be content to change the government of their Church,
and to establish episcopacy there again.   And by these insinuations they persuadèd many of the States to believe that
the defence of bishops, (for whom they had no regard) was
the sole difference between the King and them, and which kept
the King from going to Scotland : so that the King was not
without some apprehension that, by that mistake and false
information, the States might give him advice to accept their
invitation.   And therefore he sent to the States of Holland
that he had a desire to say somewhat to them, if they would
assign him an audience the next day ; which they readily did.

May 29,
N. S.

27. The King was received in the same manner he had been
formerly, and being conducted into their room of council, after
a short compliment, he delivered a paper to them, which he
desired might be read, and that he might receive their advice
thereupon as soon as they pleased.   The memorial contained, in
the first place, his majesty's acknowledgment of the civilities
he had received there, and his desire that by them the States
General (who were not at that time assembled) might be
informed of such his majesty's sense of their favours ; especially
in the full and high detestation they had expressed of the
impious and unparalleled murder of his royal father of blessed
memory, their fast and unshaken ally, by which the form and
rule of all kind of government were no less violated and dissolved than that of monarchy : that he came to inform them
that he did intend in a short time so to dispose of his person as
might, with God's blessing, most probably advance his affairs ;
and that for the better doing thereof, and that he might in
so important an affair receive their particular advice, he should
impart to them the true state and condition of his several
dominions.   That he needed not inform them of the deplorable
condition of his kingdom of England, where the hearts and
affections of his loyal subjects were so depressed and kept under

by the power and cruelty of those who had murdered their late 1649 sovereign, and who every day gave fresh and bloody instances of their tyranny, to fright men from their allegiance, that for the present no man could believe that miserable kingdom could be fit for his majesty to trust his person in. That in Scotland, it is very true that his majesty is proclaimed King, but with such limitations and restrictions against his exercise of his regal power, that in truth they had only given him the name and denied him the authority: that above five parts of six of the nobility and chief gentry of that kingdom were likewise excluded from their just right, and from any part in the administration of the public affairs; so that that kingdom seemed not sufficiently prepared for his majesty's reception; but that he hoped, and doubted not, that there would be in a short time a perfect union and right understanding between all his subjects of that his kingdom, and a due submission and obedience from them all to his majesty, for that he was resolved (and had never had the least purpose to the contrary) to preserve and maintain the government of Church and State in that kingdom as it is established by the laws thereof, without any violation or alteration on his part: so that there could be no difference between him and his subjects of that kingdom, except they should endeavour and press his majesty to alter the laws and government of his other kingdoms; which as it would be very unreasonable to desire, so it is not in his power to do, if he should consent and join with his subjects of Scotland to that purpose: which made him confident, that, when they had throughly weighed and considered what was good for themselves as well as for him, they would acquiesce with the enjoying the laws and privileges of that kingdom, without desiring to infringe or impose upon those of his brethren and neighbours. And his majesty desired the States, that, if any persons had endeavoured to make any impressions upon them, that he hath, or ever had, any other intentions or desires with reference to his subjects of Scotland than what himself now expressed to them to have, they[1]

---

[1] ['that they,' MS.]

1649 would give no credit to them; and assured them that they
should always find him constant to those resolutions, and
especially, that all ways and means which might tend to the
advancement and propagation of the Protestant religion should
be so heartily embraced by him, that the world should have
cause to believe him to be worthy of his title of *Defender of the
Faith*, which he valued as his greatest attribute.

28. This being the true present condition of his two kingdoms of England and Scotland, and it being necessary for
his majesty to give life to the afflicted state of his affairs by
his own personal activity and vigour, he told them, there
remained only that he should impart to them the like state
of his other kingdom of Ireland; which had likewise sent to
him, and desired him to repair thither, with great importunity:
that the marquis of Ormonde, his Lieutenant there, had concluded a peace there with the Roman Catholics, and that
thereby his majesty was entirely possessed of three parts of
four of that his large and fruitful kingdom, and of the command
of good armies, and of many good ships to be joined to his
own fleet; and that he had reason to hope and to believe
that Dublin itself, and the few other places which had submitted to the rebellious power in England, either already were,
upon the knowledge of that odious parricide, returned to their
allegiance, or would speedily be reduced; of which he expected
every day to receive advertisement; which if it should fall
out, yet he foresaw many objections might be made against
his going thither, not only in regard of the difficulty and
danger of his passage, but of the jealousies which would arise
upon the large concessions which were made unto the Roman
Catholics of that kingdom, and which could not be avoided.
And having thus given them a clear information of the state
of his three kingdoms, his majesty concluded with his desire,
that the States would give him their advice as freely as to
which of them he should repair, and that they would give
him all necessary assistance that he might prosecute their
counsel.

29. Many men had great fear that the King would have

brought great prejudice to himself by this communication, and, **1649** upon the matter, obliging himself to follow their advice ; which they apprehended would be contrary to his own judgment. For nothing was more commonly discoursed amongst the Dutch, and by many of the States themselves, than that the King ought without delay to throw himself into the arms of Scotland, and to gratify them in all they desired ; that bishops were not worth the contending for, and that the supporting them had been the ruin of his father, and would be his, if he continued in the same obstinacy. But the King knew well that they would not so much concern themselves in his broken affairs as to give him advice what to do ; and it was necessary for him to get a little more time, upon some occurrences which would every day happen, before he took a positive resolution which way to steer : for though in his own opinion Ireland was the place to which he was to repair, yet he knew that, notwithstanding the peace that was made there, there were several parties still in arms there, besides those who adhered to the Parliament, who refused to submit to that peace. Though the general Council at Kilkenny (which had been always looked upon as the representative of the confederate Catholics of that kingdom, and to which they had always submitted) had fully consented to the treaty of peace with the Lord Lieutenant, yet Owen O'Neale, who had the command of all the Irish in Ulster, and who was looked upon as the best general they had, totally refused to submit to it, and positively protested against [it,] as not having provided for their interest ; and the Council was not sorry for his separation, there being little less animosity between those of Ulster and the other Irish than was between them both and the English : and they knew that O'Neale more insisted on recompense in lands and preferments than upon any provision that concerned religion itself. Then the Scots in Ulster, who were very numerous, and under good discipline, and well provided with arms and ammunition, would not submit to the commands of the Lord Lieutenant, but were resolved to follow the example of their countrymen, and to see the King admitted and received, as well as pro-

1649 claimed, before they would submit to his authority: which made the marquis of Ormonde the less troubled at the obstinacy of O'Neale, (though he had used all the means he had to draw him in,) since he presumed the Scots and he would mortify each other during the time that he should spend in making himself strong enough to suppress them both : for the Scots who would not join with the marquis were very vigorous in prosecuting the war against O'Neale and the Irish of Ulster. These divisions, factions, and confusions in Ireland, made the King the more solicitous that his Council should be unanimous for his going thither, at least that the Scots, (how virulent soever against each other,) should all concur in their advice that it was not yet seasonable for him to go for Scotland; which made him labour so much to bring the Hambletonians and those who followed Mountrose, who[m] he believed both to be of that opinion, to meet together, and to own it jointly

§ 17. to the King in Council : but it is said before how impossible it was to obtain that conjunction.

30. When the King found that it was not possible to bring the lords of the Scots' nation together to confer upon the affairs of that kingdom, he thought to have drawn them severally, that is, those of the Engagement by themselves, and the marquis of Mountrose with his friends by themselves, to have given him their advice in the presence of his Council, that so, upon debate thereof between them, his majesty might the more maturely have determined what he was to do. And the marquis of Mountrose expressed a great willingness to give his majesty satisfaction this or any other way, being willing to deliver his opinion concerning things or persons before any body and in any place. But the lords of the Engagement positively refused to deliver their opinion but to the King himself, and not in the presence of his Council ; which, they said, would be to confess a kind of subordination of the kingdom of Scotland, which was independent on the Council of England ; and duke Hambleton told the councillor with whom he had before so freely conversed [1], and who expostulated with

---

[1] ['councillor ... conversed' substituted for the word 'Chancellor.']

him upon it, that it was the only ground of the heavy judg- **1649**
ment in Parliament against the earl of Trequare, that, having
been the King's commissioner in Scotland, he gave account to
the King of his transactions, and of the affairs of that kingdom,
at the Council table in England, whereof he was likewise a
member; so jealous that kingdom was and still is of their native
privileges; and therefore desired that he might not be pressed
to do what had been so penal to another in his own sight.

31. The King satisfied himself with having all their opinions
delivered to himself, subscribed under all their hands, which
every one consented to[1]. Though most of them would have **May 21,**
been glad that the King would have gone in[to] Scotland, upon **N. S.**
what condescensions soever, because they all believed his presence would quickly turn all, and that they should quickly be
restored to their estates, which they cared most for, yet nobody
presumed to give that advice, or seemed to think it seasonable.
So that the King resumed the former debate of going directly
for Ireland; and direction was given for providing ships, and
all other things necessary for that voyage. There remained
only one doubt, whether his majesty should take France in his
way, that he might see his mother, who by letters and messages
pressed him very earnestly so to do; or whether he should
embark in Holland directly for Ireland; which would be less
loss of time, and might be done so early in the spring, before
the Parliament fleet should put to sea.

32. They who did not wish that the Queen should exercise
any power over the King, or have too much credit with him,
were against his going into France, as an occasion of spending
more time than his affairs would permit, and an obligation to
make a greater expense than he had, or knew where to have,
means to defray: and they thought it an argument of moment,
that from the time of the murder of his father the King had
neither received letter of condolement from France nor the
least invitation to go thither. On the other side, they who
wished and hoped that the Queen would have such an influence
upon the King that his Council should have less credit with

[1] [See *Calend. Cl. S. P.* II. 12; *Nicholas Papers*, 1886, I. 126.]

1649 him, desired very much that his majesty would make France his way. The Scots desired it very much, believing they should find her majesty very propitious to their counsels, and inclined to trust their undertakings; and they were very sure that Mountrose would never go to Paris, or have credit with the Queen.

33. The Prince of Aurange and the princess royal his wife had a great desire to gratify the Queen, and that the King should see her in the way; and proposed that his majesty might appoint a place where the Queen and he might meet without going to Paris, and that after three or four days' stay together his majesty might hasten his journey to some convenient port, from whence he might embark for Ireland, and by a shorter passage than from Holland; and the Prince of Aurange would appoint two ships of war to attend his majesty in that French port, before he should get thither. His majesty inclined this way, without positively resolving upon it; yet directed that his own goods of bulk, and his inferior servants, should presently be embarked to take the quickest passage for Ireland, and directed that the rest, who were to wait upon his person, should likewise send their goods and baggage, and such servants who were not absolutely necessary for their present service, upon the same ships for Ireland; declaring that if he made France his way he would make all possible haste, and go with as light a train as he could. And hereupon two ships were shortly after provided; and many persons, and great store of baggage, embarked for Ireland, and arrived there in safety; but most of the persons and all the goods miscarried in their return, when they knew that the King was not to come thither, upon the accidents that afterwards fell out there.

34. This resolution being taken, the lord Cottington, who had a just excuse from his age, being then seventy-five years old, to wish to be in some repose, considered with himself how to become disentangled from the fatigue of those voyages and journeys which he saw the King would be obliged to make. In Holland he had no mind to stay, having never loved that people, nor been loved by them; and the climate itself was

very pernicious to his health, by reason of the gout, which **1649** frequently visited him. France was as ingrateful to him, where he had not been kindly treated, and was looked upon as one who had been always addicted to Spain, and no friend to that Crown. So that he was willing to find a good occasion to spend the remainder of his age where he had spent so much of his youth, in Spain, and where he believed that he might be able to do the King more service than in any other way. And there was newly come to the Hague an English gentleman, who had been an officer in the King's army, and who was in Madrid when the news came thither of the murder of the King: and he related many particulars of the passion and indignation of that Court upon that occasion against the rebels; that the King and all the Court put themselves into solemn mourning; and some expressions which the King and don Lewis de Haro had made of tenderness and compassion for the King; and that the King of Spain spake of sending an ambassador to his majesty.

35. These relations, and any thing of that kind, how weakly soever founded, were very willingly heard. And from hence the lord Cottington took occasion to confer with the Chancellor [of the Exchequer] (with whom he held a strict friendship, living and keeping house together) of the ill condition the King was in, and that he ought to think what prince's kindness was like to be of most use and benefit to him, and from whom he might hope to receive a sum of money, if not as much as might serve for a martial expedition, yet such an annual exhibition as might serve for his support: that he had already experience of France, and knew well the intelligence that the cardinal had at that very time with Cromwell: but he did verily believe that if the King of Spain were dexterously treated with, and not more asked of him than could consist with his affairs to spare, a good yearly support might be procured there, and the expectation of it might be worth the King's sending an ambassador thither. He said he was more of that opinion since the King had taken the resolution of going for Ireland, where the King of Spain's credit might be of great benefit to him: that Owen O'Neale with the old Irish of Ulster were still in

1649 arms against the King, and would not submit to the conditions which the general council of the confederate Catholics had consented to with the marquis of Ormonde: that O'Neale had been bred in Spain, and had a regiment in Flanders, and so must have an absolute dependence upon his Catholic majesty, for whom all the old Irish had ever had a particular devotion; if it were only to dispose him and that people to the King's obedience, and to accept those conditions which might conveniently be given to them, it were well worth such a journey; and the King of Spain would never refuse to gratify the King to the utmost [that] could be desired in that particular. The Chancellor thought the discourse not unreasonable, and asked him who would be fit to be sent thither, not imagining that he had any thought of going thither himself. He answered, that if the King would be advised by him he should send them two thither, and he did believe they should do him very good service; at which the Chancellor smiled, thinking he had only spoke in jest, and so the discourse ended.

36. The next day the lord Cottington resumed it again, and told him that he was not only in very good earnest in his former discourse, but that it was not sudden, nor without very serious deliberation. He said he might be thought principally to consider himself, that he might have the comfort of a friend whom he loved so well; but he assured him that did not prevail with him, but purely the consideration of the King's service, with a due regard to the person of the Chancellor, who he thought ought to be pleased with the employment. That himself was old, and not fit to be relied upon alone, in an affair of that weight; he might probably die upon the way, or shortly after his coming thither, and then the whole affair, how hopeful soever, must miscarry; whereas if he were with him the business would proceed upon all events, and he would have no reason to repent the experience of such a negotiation and the knowledge of such a Court, when he could not spend his time more pleasantly or more profitably: that he would take no great pleasure in France, nor find much grace with the Queen; and if the King delayed his journey for Ireland so long as he was like to do

if he would be advised by his mother, they might make their journey **1649** into Spain, and with so good success that the Chancellor might embark in a convenient port from Spain, and arrive in Ireland as soon as the King, with those advantages of arms, ammunition, and other supplies, as would make him very welcome. These conferences continued for some days between themselves, when they were alone, and when they came tired from other consultations.

37. The Chancellor was weary of the company he was in, and the business, which, having no prospect but towards despair, was yet rendered more grievous by the continual contentions and animosity between persons. He knew he was not in the Queen's favour at all, and should find no respect in that Court. However, he was very scrupulous that the King might not suspect that he was weary of his attendance, or that any body else might believe that he withdrew himself from waiting longer upon so desperate a fortune. In the end, he told the lord Cottington that he would only be passive in the point, and refer it entirely to him, if he thought fit to dispose the King to like it by all the arguments he could use; and if the King approved it so much as to take notice of it to the Chancellor, and commend it as a thing he thought for his service, he would submit to his command, and very cheerfully accompany him through the employment; with which Cottington was very well pleased, taking upon him what concerned the King.

38. The lord Cottington's heart was much set upon this employment, and [he] knew well that if it took air before the King was well prepared and resolved, it would be much opposed as to the Chancellor's part; because many who did not love him yet thought his presence about the King to be of some use, and therefore would do all they could to divert his going : and therefore he managed it so warily with the King, and presented the whole scheme to him so dexterously, that his majesty was much pleased with it, and approved it, and spake of it to the Chancellor [1] as a business he liked, and promised himself much good from it, and therefore persuaded him to undertake it cheerfully. Whereupon the Chancellor desired him to think

[1] [On April 3 or 4; *Nicholas Papers*, 1886, I. 124.]

1649 well of it, for he was confident many would dissuade his majesty
from employing him that way; therefore he only besought him,
that, when he was so far resolved upon it as to publish it, he
would not be afterwards prevailed with to change his purpose;
which the King said he would not do; and shortly after declared his resolution publicly to send the lord Cottington and
the Chancellor of the Exchequer his ambassadors extraordinary
into Spain, and commanded them to prepare their own commission and instructions[1], and to begin their journey as soon
as was possible. This was no sooner known but all kind of
people, who agreed in nothing else, murmured and complained
of this counsel, and the more, because it had never been mentioned or debated in Council. Only the Scots were very glad
of it, (Mountrose excepted,) believing that when the Chancellor
was gone, their beloved Covenant would not be so irreverently
mentioned, and that the King would be wrought upon to withdraw all countenance and favour from the marquis of Mountrose: and the marquis himself looked upon it as a deserting
him, and complying with the other party; and from that time,
though they lived with civility towards each other, he withdrew
very much of his confidence which he had formerly reposed in
him. They who loved him were sorry for him and themselves;
they thought he deserted a path he had long trod, and was
well acquainted with, and was henceforward to move *extra
sphæram activitatis*, in an office he had not been acquainted
with, and then they should want his credit to support and
confirm them in the King's favour and grace. And there were
many who were very sorry when they heard it out of particular
duty to the King, who being young they thought might be
without that counsel and advertisements which they knew well
he would still administer to him. No man was more angry
and offended with the counsel than the lord Culpeper, who
would have been very glad to have gone himself in the employment if he could have persuaded the lord Cottington to have
accepted his company, which he would by no means do; and

[1] [The commission was dated May 10 and the instructions May 24.
Cal. Clar. S. P. II. 9; *Cl. S. P.* II. 481.]

though he and the Chancellor were not thought to have the greatest kindness for each other, yet he knew he could agree with no other man so well in business, and was very unwilling he should be from the person of the King. But the Chancellor himself, from the time that the King had signified his own pleasure to him, was exceedingly pleased with the commission, and did believe that he should in some degree improve his understanding, and very much refresh his spirits, by what he should learn by the one, and by his absence from being continually conversant with those wants which could never be severed from that Court, and that company which would be always corrupted by those wants. And so he sent for his wife and children to meet him at Antwerp, where he intended they should reside whilst he continued in Spain, and where they were like to find some civilities in respect of his employment.

39. Before the King could begin his own journey for France, and so to Ireland, and before his ambassadors for Spain could begin theirs, his majesty thought it necessary, upon the whole prospect of his affairs with reference to all places, to put his business into as good a method as he could, and to dispose of that number of officers and soldiers, and other persons, who had presented themselves to be applied to his service, or to leave them to take the best course they could for their own subsistence. Of these, many were sent into Ireland with the ships which carried the King's goods, and with recommendation to the marquis of Ormonde to put them into his army till the King came thither. Since the Scots were no better disposed to serve or receive the King for the present, his majesty was resolved to give the marquis of Mountrose all the encouragement he desired to visit them, and to incline them to a better temper.

40. There was then at the Hague Cornificius Wolfelte, ambassador extraordinary from the King of Denmark to the States General, who came with a great train and great state, and was himself a man of vanity and ostentation, and took pains to be thought so great a man, in his own interest, that he did not enough extol the power of his master; which proved his ruin after his return. He had left Denmark before

the news came thither of the murder of the King, and so he had no credentials for his majesty, by reason whereof he could not receive any public formal audience; but desired the King's leave that he might, as by accident, be admitted to speak to him at the Queen of Bohemia's Court, where his majesty used to be every day, and where the ambassador often spake to him. The marquis of Mountrose had found means to endear himself much to this ambassador, who gave him encouragement to hope for a very good reception in Denmark, if the King would send him thither, and that he might obtain arms and ammunition there for Scotland. And the ambassador told him that if the King would write a letter to him to that purpose, he would presently supply him with some money and arms, in assurance that his master would very well approve of what he should do. The marquis of Mountrose well knew that the King was not able to supply him with the least proportion of money to begin his journey, and therefore he had only proposed that the King would give him several letters, in the form he prescribed, to several princes in Germany, whose affections he pretended to know; which letters he sent by several officers, who were to bring the soldiers or arms they should obtain, to a rendezvous he appointed near Hamborough; and resolved himself to go into Sweden and Denmark, in hope to get supplies in both those places, both from the Crowns and by the contribution of many Scots' officers who had command and estates in those countries; and so to have credentials, by virtue of which he might appear ambassador extraordinary from the King, if he should find it expedient; though he did intend rather to negotiate his business in private, and without any *fausto* [1]. And all this was resolved before his confidence, at least his familiarity, with the ambassador was grown less. But, upon the encouragement he had from him, he moved the King for his letter to the ambassador, to assist the marquis of Mountrose with his advice, and with his interest in Denmark and in any other Court, to the end

---

[1] [For this Spanish word, meaning *ostentation* or *display*, have been substituted in former editions the bracketed words 'public character.']

that he might obtain the loan of moneys, arms, and am- **1649**
munition, and whatever else was necessary to enable the
marquis to prosecute his intended descent into Scotland. The
King, who was exceedingly tired with his importunities, glad
that he did not press for ready money, which he was not
able to supply him with, gave him such letters as he desired
to all persons, and particularly to the ambassador himself, June 28,
who, having order from his master to present the King with N. S.
a sum of money for his present occasions, never informed the
King thereof, but advised Mountrose to procure such a letter
from his majesty to him ; which being done, the marquis
received that money from him, and likewise some arms ; with June 30.
which he began his unfortunate enterprise, and prosecuted
his journey to Hamborough, where he expected to meet his
German troops, which he believed the officers he had sent
thither with the King's letters would be well able to raise,
with the assistance of those princes to whom they had been
sent. But he was carried on by a stronger assurance he had
received from some prophecies and predictions, to which he
was naturally given, that he should by his valour recover
Scotland for the King, and from thence conduct an army
that should settle his majesty in all his other dominions.

41. There had been yet nothing done with reference to
England since the murder of the King, nor did there appear
any thing of any kind to be attempted there : there was so
terrible a consternation that still possessed the spirits of that
people, that though the affections were greater and more general
towards the King, out of the horror and detestation they had
of the late parricide, yet the owning it was too penal for their
broken courage, nor was it believed possible by any man for
them to contribute any thing at present for their deliverance.
However, most men were of opinion that it was necessary for
the King to publish some declaration, that he might not seem
utterly to give over his claim there, and to keep up the spirits
of his friends. And many from England, who in the midst
of their despair would give some counsel, advised that there
might be somewhat published by the King that might give

1649 some check to the general submitting to the Engagement, which was so universally pressed there. The King being every day advertised how much this was desired and expected, and the Scots' lords being of the same opinion, hoping that somewhat might be inserted in it that might favour the Presbyterians, his majesty proposed at the Council that there might be some draught prepared of a proclamation, or declaration, only with reference to the kingdom of England ; and the Chancellor [of the Exchequer,] who had been most conversant in instruments of that nature, was appointed to make one ready ; though he had declared that he did not know what such a declaration could contain, and therefore that he thought it not seasonable to publish any. The Prince of Aurange was present at that Council, and, whether from his own opinion or from the suggestion of the Scots' lords, who were much favoured by him, he wished that, in regard of the great differences which were in England about matters of religion, the King would offer in this declaration to refer all matters in controversy concerning religion to a national synod, in the which there should be admitted some foreign divines from the Protestant churches ; which he thought would be a popular clause, and might be acceptable abroad as well as at home : and the King believed no objection could be made against it, and so thought fit such a clause should be inserted.

42. Within a short time after the Council was parted, the Prince of Aurange sent for the lord Cottington, and told him he was not enough acquainted with the Chancellor but desired him to entreat him not to be too sharp in this declaration, the end whereof was to unite and reconcile different humours, and that he found many had a great apprehension that the sharpness of his style would irritate them much more. [The Chancellor] knew well enough that this came from the lord Latherdale, and he wished heartily that the charge might be committed to any body else, protesting that he was never less disposed in his own conceptions and reflections to undertake any such task in his life, and that he could not imagine how it was possible for the King to publish a declaration at this

time, (his first declaration,) without much sharpness against the 1649
murderers of his father ; which nobody could speak against, nor
could he be excused from the work imposed upon him ; and
the Prince of Aurange assured him it was not that kind of
sharpness which he wished should be declined : and though
he seemed not willing farther to explain himself, it was evident
that he wished that there might not be any sharpness against
the Presbyterians, for which there was at that time no occasion.

43. There was one particular, which, without a full and
particular instruction, he could not presume to express. The
great end of this declaration was to confirm the affection of
as many as was possible for the King, and consequently as
few were to be made desperate as might consist with the King's
honour and necessary justice ; so that how far that clause
which was essential to a declaration upon this subject, concerning the indemnity of persons, should extend, was the question.
And in this there was a difference of opinion. The most
prevalent was, that no persons should be excepted from pardon
but only such who had an immediate hand in the execrable
murder of the King, by being his judges and pronouncing
that sentence, and they who performed the execution. Others
knew that some were in the list of the judges, and named by
the Parliament, who found some excuses to be absent ; and
others, who were not named, more contrived and contributed
to that odious proceeding than many who were actors in it.
But the resolution was, that the former should be only com-
prehended.

44. When the declaration was prepared, and read at the
Board, there was a deep silence, no man speaking to any part
of it. But another day was appointed for a second reading
it, against which time every man might be better prepared to
speak to it : and in the mean time the Prince of Aurange, in
regard he was not perfect master of the English tongue, desired
he might have a copy of it, that he might the better understand
it. The Chancellor desired that not only the Prince of Aurange might have a copy but that his majesty would likewise

1649 have one, and, after he should have perused it himself, he would shew it to any other who he thought was fit to advise with; there being many lords and other persons of quality about him who were not of the Council: and he moved that he might have liberty himself to communicate it to some who were like to make a judgment how far any thing of that nature was like to be acceptable, and agreeable to the minds of the people, and named Harbert the Attorney General, and Dr. Steward, who was dean of the chapel to the King, and whose opinion in all things relating to the Church the King had been advised by his father to submit to. All which was approved by the King; and for that reason a farther day was appointed for the second reading. The issue was, that, except two or three of the Council who were of one and the same opinion of the whole, there were not two persons who were admitted to the perusal of it who did not take some exception to it, though scarce two made the same exception.

45. Dr. Steward (though a man of a very good understanding) was so exceedingly grieved at the clause of admitting foreign divines into a synod that was to consult upon the Church of England, that he could not be satisfied by any arguments that could be given, of the impossibility of any effect, or that the Parliament would accept the overture, and that there could be no danger if it did, because the number of those foreign divines must be still limited by the King; but came one morning to the Chancellor, (with whom he had a friendship,) and protested he had not slept that night out of the agony and trouble that he, who he knew loved the Church so well, should consent to a clause that was so much against the honour of it, and went from him to the King to beseech him never to approve it. Some were of opinion that there were too few excepted from pardon, by which the King would not have confiscations enough to satisfy and reward his party: and others thought that there were too many excepted, and that it was not prudent to make so many men desperate, but that it would be sufficient to except Cromwell and Bradshaw, and three or four more of those whose malice was most

notorious; the whole number not to exceed six. The Scots did not value the clause for foreign divines, who they knew could persuade little in an English synod; but they were implacably offended that the King mentioned the government of the Church of England and the Book of Common Prayer with so much reverence and devotion, which was the sharpness they most feared of the Chancellor's style, when they thought now the Covenant to be necessary to be insisted upon more than ever.

46. So that when the declaration was read at the Board the second time, most men being moved with the discourses and fears which were expressed abroad of some ill effects it might produce, it was more faintly debated, and men seemed not to think that the publishing any at this time was of so much importance as they formerly had conceived it to be. By all which, men may judge how hard a thing it was for the King to resolve and act with that steadiness and resolution which the most unprosperous condition doth more require than that state that is less perplexed and entangled. The declaration slept without farther proposition to emit any.

47. All things being now as much provided for as they were like to be, the two ambassadors for Spain were very solicitous to begin their journey, the King being at last resolved not to give his mother the trouble of making a journey to meet him, but to go himself directly to St. German's, where her majesty was. The Prince of Aurange, to advance that resolution, had promised to supply the King with twenty thousand pounds; which was too great a loan for him to make, who had already great debts upon him, though it was very little for the enabling the King to discharge the debts he and his family had contracted at the Hague, and to make his journey. Out of this sum the lord Cottington and the Chancellor were to receive so much as was designed to defray their journey to Paris: what was necessary for the discharge of their embassy, or for making their journey from Paris, was not yet provided. The King had some hope that the duke of Lorraine would lend him some money, which he designed for this service: which made it

1649 necessary that they should immediately resort to Bruxells to
finish that negotiation, and from thence to prosecute their
journey.

48. In the soliciting their first despatch at the Hague, they
made a discovery that seemed very strange to them, though
afterwards it was a truth that was very notorious. Their
journey having been put off some days, only for the receipt
of that small sum which was to be paid out of the money to be
lent by the Prince of Aurange, and Henflet, the Prince his
chief officer in such affairs of money, had been some days at
Amsterdam to negotiate that loan, and no money was returned,
they believed that there was some affected delay; and so went
to the Prince of Aurange, who had advised, and was well
pleased with, that embassy, to know when that money would
be ready for the King, that he might likewise resolve upon the
time for his own journey. The Prince told them that he
believed that they who knew London so well, and had heard
so much discourse of the wealth of Holland, would wonder very
much that he should have been endeavouring above ten days to
borrow twenty thousand pounds, and that the richest men in
Amsterdam had promised him to supply him with it, and that
one half of it was not yet provided. He said, it was not that
there was any question of his credit, which was very good;
and that the security he gave was as good as any body desired,
and upon which he could have double the sum in less time if he
would receive it in paper, which was the course of that country;
and where, bargains being made for one hundred thousand
pounds to be paid within ten days, it was never known that
twenty thousand pounds was paid together in one town, but by
bills from Rotterdam, Harlem, the Hague, and Antwerp, and
other places, which was as convenient, or more, to all parties;
and he did verily believe that though Amsterdam could pay a
million within a month upon any good occasion, that yet they
would be troubled to bring twenty thousand pounds together
into any one room; and that was the true reason that the
money was not yet brought to the Hague, which it should
be within few days; as it was accordingly.

49. They took their leave of the King at the Hague before **1649**
the middle of May, and had a yacht[1] from the Prince of
Aurange, that expected them at Rotterdam, and transported June 1,
them with great convenience to Antwerp, where the Chan- N. S.
cellor's wife and his family were arrived ten days before, and
were settled in a good and convenient house, where the lord
Cottington and he both lodged whilst they stayed in that city.
And there they met the lord Jermin in his way towards the
King, and to hasten the King's journey into France, upon the
Queen's great importunity. He was very glad they were both
come away from the King, and believed he should more easily
prevail with the King in all things, as indeed he did. After
two or three days stay at Antwerp, they went to Bruxells, to June 5,
deliver their credentials both to the archduke and the duke of N. S.
Lorraine, and to visit the Spanish ministers, and, upon their
landing at Bruxells, they took it for a very good omen that
they were assured that Le Brune, who had been one of the
plenipotentiaries at the treaty of Munster, on the behalf of the
King of Spain, was then in that town, with credentials to visit
the King and to condole with him. They had an audience the
next day with the archduke : they performed the compliments
from the King, and informed him of their embassy into Spain,
and desired his recommendation and good offices in that Court ;
which he, according to his slow and formal way of speaking,
consented to : and they had no more to do with him, but received the visits from his officers, in his name, according to the
style of that Court. Their main business was with the duke
of Lorraine, and to procure money for their journey into Spain.

50. The duke was a prince that lived in a different manner
from all other sovereign princes in the world. From the time
that he had been driven out of his country by France, he had
retired to Bruxells with his army, which he kept up very strong,
and served the King of Spain with it against the French, upon
such terms and conditions as were made and renewed every
year between them ; by which he received great sums of money
yearly from the Spaniard, and was, sure, very rich in money.

[1] ['yuaght,' MS.]

1649 He always commanded a part in the field; and his officers
received no orders but from himself: and he always agreed
at the council of war what he should do, and his army was
in truth the best part of the Spanish forces. In the town
of Bruxells he lived without any order, method, or state of
a prince, except towards the Spaniards in his treaties, and
being present in their councils, where he always kept his full
dignity: otherwise he lived in a jolly familiarity with the
bourgeo[i]s and their wives, and feasted with them, but scarce
kept a coach, and no number of servants or retinue. And the
house wherein he lived was a very ordinary one, and worse
furnished; nor was he often there, or easy to be found; so that
the ambassadors could not easily send to him for an audience.
He received them in a lower room with great courtesy and
familiarity, and visited them at their own lodging. He was a
man of great wit and presentness of mind, and, if he had not
affected extravagancies, no man knew better how to act the
prince. He loved his money very much; yet the lord Cottington's dexterity and address prevailed with him to lend the
King two thousand pistoles; which was all that was in their
view for the defraying their embassy. But they hoped they
should procure some supply in Spain, out of which their own
necessary expenses must be provided for.

51. There were two Spaniards by whom all the councils there
were governed and conducted, and which the archduke himself
could not control; the conde of Pignoranda (who was newly
come from Munster, being the other plenipotentiary there, and
stayed only at Bruxells in expectation of renewing the treaty
again with France, but whilst he stayed there was in the
highest trust in all the affairs) and the conde of Fuensaldagñã,
who was the governor of the arms, and commanded the army
next under the archduke; which was a subordination very
little inferior to the being general. They were both very able
and expert men in business; and if they were not very wise
men, the nation had none. The former was a man of the robe,
of a great wit and much experience, proud, and, if he had not
been a little too pedantic, might very well be looked upon as

a very extraordinary man, and was much improved by the 1649
excellent temper of Le Brune, (the other plenipotentiary,) who
was indeed a wise man, and by seeming to defer in all things
to Pignoranda governed him. The conde of Fuensaldagñã was
of a much better temper, more industry and more insinuation,
than Spaniards use to have: his greatest talent lay to business;
yet he was the best general of that time to all other offices and
purposes than what were necessary in the hour of battle, when
he was not so present and composed as at all other seasons.

52. Both these received the ambassadors with the usual
civility, and returned their visits at their own lodging, but
seemed not pleased with their journey to Madrid, and spake
much of the necessities that Crown was in, and disability to
assist the King; which they imputed to the influence don
Alonso de Cardinas had upon them both, who remained still
under the same character in England he had done for many
years before. The same civilities were performed between Le
Brune and them; who treated them with much more freedom,
and encouraged them to hope well from their negotiation in
Spain; acquainted them with his own instructions, to give the
King all assurance of the affection of his Catholic majesty, and
of his readiness to do any thing for him that was in his power.
He said he only deferred his journey because he heard that the
King intended to spend some time at Breda; and he had rather
attend him there than at the Hague.

53. When they had despatched all their business at Bruxells,
and received the money from the duke of Lorraine, they returned to Antwerp, where they were to negotiate for the return
of their monies to Madrid; which required very much wariness,
the bills from thence using to find more difficulties at Madrid
than they had done in former times.

54. What was imagined fell out. By the letters the lord
Jermin brought, and the importunity he used, the King resolved to begin his journey sooner than he thought to have June 10.
done, that is, sooner than he thought he should have been able, N. S.
all provisions being to begin to be made, both for his journey
into France and from thence into Ireland, after the money was

1649 received that should pay for them. But the Queen's impatience was so great to see his majesty, that the Prince of Aurange and the Princess royal his wife were as impatient to give her satisfaction. Though her majesty could not dislike any resolution the King had taken, nor could imagine whither he should go but into Ireland, she was exceedingly displeased that any resolution had been taken before she was consulted. She was angry that the councillors were chosen without her directions, and looked upon all that had been done as done in order to exclude her from meddling in the affairs; all which she imputed principally to the Chancellor. And yet she was not pleased with the design of his negotiation in Spain; for though she had no confidence of his affection to her, or rather of his complying with all her commands, yet she had all confidence in his duty and integrity to the King, and therefore wished he should be still about his person, and trusted in his business; which she thought him much fitter for than such a negotiation, which she believed (out of her natural prejudice to Spain) would produce no advantage to the King.

55. That the Queen might receive some content in knowing that the King had begun his journey, the Prince of Aurange desired him, whilst his servants prepared what was necessary at the Hague, that himself and that part of his train that was ready would go to Breda, and stay there till the rest were ready to come up to him; that being his best way to Flanders, through which he must pass to France. Breda was a town of the Prince's own, where he had a handsome palace and castle, and a place where the King might have many divertisements. Hither the Spanish ambassador Le Brune came to attend his majesty, and deliver his master's compliments to his majesty, and offered his own services to him whilst he should remain in those provinces; he being at that time designed to remain ambassador to the United Provinces, as he did, and died shortly after at the Hague, to the general regret. He was born a subject to the King of Spain, in that part of Burgundy that was under his dominion; and having been from his cradle always bred in business, and being a man of great parts

June 15. N.S. (margin)

1654 Jan. 2. (margin)

and temper, he might very well be looked upon as one of the 1649 best statesmen in Christendom, and who best understood the true interest of all the princes of Europe.

56. As soon as the lord Cottington and the Chancellor heard of the King's being at Breda, and that he intended to hasten his journey for France, they resolved, having in truth not yet negotiated all things necessary for their journey, to stay till the King passed by, and not to go to St. German's till the first interview and *éclaircissements* were passed between the King and Queen, that they might then be the better able to judge what weather was like to be.

57. The King was received at Antwerp with great magnifi- June 21, cence: he entered in a very rich coach with six horses, which N. S. the archduke sent for a present to him when he came into the Spanish dominions: he was treated there at the charge of the city very splendidly for two days, and went then to Bruxells, where he was lodged in the palace, and royally entertained. But the French army, under the command of the count Harcourt, was two days before sat down before Cambray; with the news whereof the Spanish council was surprised, and in so much disorder that the archduke was gone to the army to Mons and Valenciennes whilst the King was in Antwerp[1]; so that the King was received only by his officers, who performed their parts very well.

58. Here the conde of Pignoranda waited upon the King in the quality of an ambassador, and covered. And his majesty stayed here three or four days, not being able suddenly to resolve which way he should pass into France. But he was not troubled long with that doubt; for the French thought to have surprised the town, and to have cast up their line of circumvallation before any supplies could be put in; but the count of Fuensaldagnia found a way to put seven or eight hundred foot into the town; upon which the French raised the siege; and so the King made his journey by the usual way, and about Valenciennes had an interview with the archduke; and after some short ceremonies continued on his journey, and

---

[1] [On June 18, while the King was at Breda, *Cal. Cl. S. P.* II. 15.]

1649 lodged at Cambray, where he was likewise treated by the count
of Garcies, who was governor there, and a very civil gentleman.

59. About a week after the King left Bruxells, the two
ambassadors[1] prosecuted their journey for Paris; where they
stayed only one day, and then went to St. German's; where the
King and the Queen his mother, with both their families and
the duke of York's, then were; by whom they were received
graciously. They had no reason to repent their providence in
staying so long behind the King, for they found the Court so
full of jealousy and disorder that every body was glad that they
were come. After the first two or three days that the King
and Queen had been together, which were spent in tears and
lamentations for the great alteration that was happened since
their last parting, the Queen began to confer with the King
of his business, and what course he meant to take; in which
she found him so reserved as if he had no mind she should be
conversant in it. He made no apologies to her; which she
expected; nor any professions of resigning himself up to her
advice. On the contrary, upon some expostulations, he had
told her plainly, that he would always perform his duty towards
her with great affection and exactness, but that in his business
he would obey his own reason and judgment, and did as good
as desire her not to trouble herself in his affairs: and finding
her passions strong, he frequently retired with some abruptness,
and seemed not to desire to be so much in her company as she
expected, and prescribed some rules to be observed in his own
retirement, which he had not been accustomed to. This kind
of unexpected behaviour gave the Queen much trouble. And
she began to think that this distance which the King seemed
to affect was more than the Chancellor could wish, and that
there was somebody else who did her more disservice: insomuch as to the ladies who were about her, whereof some were

---

[1] [The words 'the two ambassadors' are substituted for the following:
'The Chancellor took leave of his family, which he had not been conversant with before near the space of four years, and the lord Cottington
and he having coaches and all other things necessary for their journey,
which expected them at Bruxells, they went again thither, and so '—]

very much his friends, she seemed to wish that the Chancellor were come.

60. There was a gentleman who was newly come from England, and who came to the Hague after the Chancellor had taken his leave of the King, and had been ever since very close about him, being one of the grooms of his bedchamber, one Mr. Thomas Ellyott, a person spoken of before; whom the King's father had sent into France at the same time that he resolved that the Prince should go for the west, and for no other reason but that he should not attend upon his son. And he had given order that if he should return out of France and come into the west, the Council should not suffer him to be about the Prince, with whom he thought he had too much credit, and would use it ill; and he had never seen the Prince from the time he left Oxford till now. He was a bold man, and spake all things confidently, and had not that reverence for the late King which he ought to have, and less for the Queen, though he had great obligations to both; yet being not so great as he had a mind to, he looked upon them as none. This gentleman came to the King just as he left the Hague, and both as he was a new comer, and as one for whom he had formerly much kindness, was very well received; and he, being one who would receive no injury from his modesty, made the favour the King shewed him as bright, and to shine as much in the eyes of all men, as was possible. He was never from the person of the King, and always whispering in his ear, taking upon him to understand all the sense and opinion of all the loyal party in England: and when he had a mind that the King should think well or ill of any man, he told him that he was much beloved by, or very odious to, all his party in England. By these infusions he had prevailed with him to look with less grace upon the earl of Bristol, who came from Caen, where he had hitherto resided, to kiss his hands, than his own good nature would have inclined him to; and more to discountenance the lord Digby, and to tell him plainly that he should not serve him in the place of Secretary of State, in which he had served his father, and from which men have

1649 seldom been removed upon the descent of the Crown; and not
to admit either father or son to be of his Council, which was
more extraordinary. He told the King that it would be the
most unpopular thing he could do, and which would lose him
more hearts in England, if he were thought to be governed by
his mother. And in a month's time that he had been about
the King, he began already to be looked upon as very like to
become the favourite. He had used the Queen with wonderful
neglect when she spake to him, and had got so much interest
with the King that he had procured a promise from his majesty
to make colonel Windham, whose daughter Mr. Ellyott had
married, Secretary of State; an honest gentleman, but marvel-
lously unequal to that province, and towards which he could
not pretend a better qualification than that his wife had been
nurse to the Prince who was now King.

61. In these kinds of humour and indisposition they found
the Court when they came to St. German's. And they had,
during their stay at Paris in their way, conferred with the earl
of Bristol and his son the lord Digby, who had breathed out
their griefs to them ; and the lord Digby was the more troubled
to find that Mr. Ellyott, who was a known and declared enemy of
his, had gotten so much credit with the King as to be able to
satisfy his own malice upon him by the countenance of his
majesty, in whom he knew his father desired that he should of
all men have the least interest. After they had been a day or
two there, the Chancellor thinking it his duty to say something
to the Queen in particular, and knowing that she expected he
should do so, and the King having told him at large all that
had passed with his mother, and the ill humour she was in, (all
which he related in a more exalted dialect than he had been
accustomed to,) and his majesty being very willing that he
should clearly understand what the Queen thought upon the
whole, he [the Chancellor] asked a private audience, which her
majesty readily granted. And after she had easily expostulated
upon the old passages at Jarsy, she concluded with the mention
of the great confidence the King her husband had always reposed in him, and thereupon renewed her own gracious pro-

fessions of good-will towards him. Then she complained (not 1649 without tears) of the King's unkindness towards her, and of his way of living with her, of some expressions he had used in discourse in her own presence, and of what he had said in other places, of the great credit Mr. Ellyott had with him, and of his rude behaviour towards her majesty, and lastly of the incredible design of making Windham Secretary, who, besides his other unfitnesses, she said, would be sure to join with the other to lessen the King's kindness to her all they could. The Chancellor, after he had made all the professions of duty to her majesty which became him, and said what he really believed of the King's kindness and respect for her, asked her whether she would give him leave to take notice of any thing she had said to him, or in general that he found her majesty unsatisfied with his kindness. The Queen replied that she was well contented that he should take notice of every thing she had said, and above all of his purpose to make Windham Secretary: of which the King had not made the least mention, though he had taken notice to him of most other things the Queen had said to him.

62. The Chancellor shortly after found an opportunity to inform the King of all that had passed from the Queen, in such a method as might give him occasion to enlarge upon all the particulars. The King heard him very greedily, and protested that he desired nothing more than to live very well with the Queen; towards whom he would never fail in his duty, as far as was consistent with his honour and the good of his affairs, which at present, it may be, required more reservation towards the Queen, and to have it believed that he communicated less with her than he did, or than he intended to do; if he did not seem to be desirous of her company, it was only when she grieved him by some importunities in which he could not satisfy her; and that her exception against Ellyott was very unjust, and that he knew well the man to be very honest, and that he loved him well; and that the prejudice the King his father had against him was only by the malice of the lord Digby, who hated him without a cause, and that he had likewise informed the Queen of some falsehoods, which had incensed her majesty

1649 against him ; and seemed throughout much concerned to justify Ellyott, against whom the Chancellor himself had no exceptions, but received more respects from him than he paid to most other men.

63. When he [the Chancellor] spake of making Windham Secretary, the King did not own the having promised to do it but that he intended to do it. The Chancellor said, he was glad he had not promised it, and that he hoped he would never do it ; that he was an honest gentleman, but in no degree qualified for that office. He put him in mind of Secretary Nicholas, who was then there to present his duty to him ; that he was a person of such known affection and honesty, that he could not do a more ungracious thing than to displace him. The King said, he thought Secretary Nicholas to be a very honest man, but he had no title to that office more than another man: that Mr. Windham had not any experience, but that it depended so much upon forms that he would quickly be instructed in it: that he was a very honest man, for whom he had never done any thing, and had now nothing else to give him but this place ; for which he doubted not but in a short time he would make himself very fit. All that the Chancellor could prevail with him was, to suspend the doing it for some time, and that he would hear him again upon the subject before he took a final resolution. For the rest, he promised to speak upon some particulars with the Queen, and to live with her with all kindness and freedom, that she might be in good humour. But he heard her and all others very unwillingly who spake against Mr. Windham's parts for being Secretary of State.

64. One day the lord Cottington, when the Chancellor and some others were present, told the King very gravely, (according to his custom, who never smiled when he made others merry,) that he had an humble suit to him on the behalf of an old servant of his father's, and whom he assured him upon his knowledge his father loved as well as he did any man of that condition in England ; and that he had been for many years one of his falconers, and he did really believe him to be one of the best falconers in England ; and thereupon enlarged himself

(as he could do excellently in all the terms of that science) to **1649**
shew how very skilful he was in that art. The King asked
him what he would have him do for him. Cottington told
him, it was very true that his majesty kept no falconers, and
the poor man was grown old, and could not ride as he had used
to do; but that he was a very honest man, and could read very
well, and had as audible a voice as any man need to have; and
therefore he besought his majesty that he would make him his
chaplain; which speaking with so composed a countenance, and
somewhat of earnestness, the King looked upon him with a
smile to know what he meant; when he with the same gravity
assured him the falconer was in all respects as fit to be his
chaplain as colonel Windham was to be Secretary of State;
which so surprised the King, who had never spoken to him
of the matter, all that were present being not able to abstain
from laughing, that he was somewhat out of countenance: and
this being merrily told by some of the standers by, it grew to
be a story in all companies, and did really divert the King
from the purpose, and made the other so much ashamed of
pretending to it that there was no more discourse of it.

65. Whilst all endeavours were used to compose all ill
humours here, and that the King might prosecute his intended
voyage for Ireland, and the two ambassadors might proceed in
their journey towards Spain, there came very ill news from
Ireland[1]. As soon as the marquis of Ormonde was arrived, as
hath been said before, the confederate Catholics, who held their
assembly, as they had always done, at Kilkenny, sent commissioners to him to congratulate his arrival, and to enter upon
a treaty of peace, that they might all return to their obedience

---

[1] [The following passage is here struck out:—'The marquis of Ormonde,
after all the promises of assistance made by the cardinal, had been compelled to transport himself without any supply of men or arms or money;
which he would never have done, if the importunity from the lord Inchiquin and the confederate Catholics, who could not agree without him, had
not obliged him to it. They had agreed upon a cessation, which had
driven the nuncio from thence; but they could not agree upon a peace,
(without which they could not join together against the Parliament,) until
the Lord Lieutenant came thither, who had the only power to make it.
Whereupon, with all the presages of ill fortune within himself, and about

1649 [to [1]] the King. But the inconstancy of that nation was such, that notwithstanding their experience of the ruin they had brought upon · themselves by their falling from their former peace, and notwithstanding that themselves had sent to Paris to importune the Queen and the Prince to send the marquis of Ormonde back to them, with all promises and protestations that they would not insist upon any unreasonable concessions; now he was come upon their invitation to them, they made new demands in point of religion, and insisted upon other things, which if he should consent to would have irreconciled all the English who were under the lord Inchiquin, and upon whom his principal confidence was placed. By this means so much time was spent, that the winter passed without any agreement whereby they might have advanced against the Parliament forces, which were weak, and in want of all manner [of] supplies, whilst the distractions continued in England between the Parliament and the army, the divisions in the army, and the prosecution of the King; during which the governors had work enough to look to themselves, and left Ireland to provide for itself: and if that unfortunate people would have made use of the advantages that were offered, it might indeed have been entirely reduced to the King's obedience.

66. That the Lord Lieutenant might even compel them to preserve themselves, he went himself to Kilkenny, where their council sat, about Christmas, after three months had been spent from his arrival, that no more time might be lost in their commissioners' coming and going, and that the spring might not **Jan. 17.** be lost as well as the winter. And at last a peace was made and concluded; by which, against such a day, the confederate

the time that the Scots army under duke Hambleton was defeated, he embarked himself, only with his own servants and some officers, at Havre de Grace, and arrived safely at Cork in the province of Munster, where the lord Inchiquin delivered up the government to him, and was by him made lieutenant-general of the army, which were all his own men who had long served under him in the province of Munster, of which he was president, and with which he had reduced the Irish into those straits that they were willing to unite with him on the King's behalf against the Parliament forces, which possessed Dublin and the parts thereabout.']

[1] ['of,' MS.]

Catholics obliged themselves to bring into the field such a body **1649**
of horse and foot, with all provisions for the field, which should
be at the disposal of the Lord Lieutenant, and to march as
he should appoint. The treaty had been drawn out into the
more length, in hope to have reduced the whole nation under
the same agreement. And the general assembly, to which they
all pretended to submit, and from which all had received their
commissions, as hath been said, sent to Owen O'Neale, who
remained in Ulster with his army, and came not himself to
Kilkenny as he ought to have done, upon pretence of his indisposition of health. He professed to submit to whatsoever the
general assembly should determine : but when they sent the
articles to which they had agreed to be signed by him, he took
several exceptions, especially in matters of religion, which he
thought was not enough provided for ; and in the end positively
declared that he would not submit [to] or be bound by them :
and at the same time he sent to the marquis of Ormonde that
he would treat with him apart, and not concern himself in what
the assembly resolved upon.

67. The truth is, there was nothing of religion in this contention ; which proceeded from the animosity between the two
generals, O'Neale and Preston, and the bitter faction between
the old Irish and the other, who were as much hated by the
old as the English were, and, lastly, [from[1]] the ambition of
Owen O'Neale ; who expected some concessions to be made
to him in his own particular, which would very much have
offended and incensed the other party if they had been granted
to him : so that the assembly was well pleased to leave him
out, and concluded the peace without him.

68. Hereupon the Lord Lieutenant used all possible endeavours that the army might be formed, and ready to march in
the beginning of the spring. And though there was not an
appearance answerable to their promise, yet their troops seemed
so good, and were so numerous, that he thought fit to march
towards Dublin, and in the way to take all the castles and **June 14.**
garrisons which were possessed by the Parliament, in which

[1] ['by,' MS.]

1649 they had very good success. For many of the Parliament soldiers having served the King, they took the first opportunity, upon the marquis of Ormonde's approach within any distance, to come to him; and by that means many small places surrendered likewise to him. Colonel Munke, who had formerly served the King, and remained for the space of three or four years prisoner in the Tower, had been at last prevailed with by the lord Lisle to serve the Parliament against the Irish, pleasing himself with an opinion that he did not therein serve against the King. He was at this time governor of Dundalk, a garrison within ten[1] miles of Dublin; which was no sooner

June 28. summoned (Tredaugh and those at a [nearer[2]] distance being taken) but he was compelled by his own soldiers to deliver it

July 17. up; and if the officer who commanded the party that summoned him had not been his friend, and thereby hoped to have reduced him to the King's service, his soldiers would have thrown him over the walls, and made their own conditions afterwards; [and] most of that garrison betook themselves to the King's service.

69. And upon all these encouragements, before the troops were come up to make the army numerous enough, the marquis

July 25. was persuaded to block up Dublin at a very little distance, having good reason to hope, from the smallness of the garrison and a party of well affected people within the town, that it would in a short time have been given up to him. In the mean time he used all the means he could to hasten the Irish troops, some whereof were upon their march and others not yet raised, to come up to the army. [By] all their letters from London (with which, by the way of Dublin and the ports of Munster, there was good intelligence) they understood that there were 1500 or 2000 men shipped for Ireland: and the wind having been for some time against their coming for Dublin, there was an apprehension that they might be gone for Munster: whereupon the lord Inchiquin, who was not confident of all his garrisons

July 27. there, very unhappily departed with some troops of horse to

---

[1] [about fifty.]

[2] ['greater,' MS. Drogheda, or Tredagh, is twenty-eight miles from Dublin.]

look after his province, there being then no cause to apprehend **1649**
any sally out of Dublin, where they were not in a condition
to look out of their own walls. But he was not gone above
two days when, the wind coming fair, the ships expected came
into the port of Dublin, and landed a greater number of July 25.
soldiers, especially of horse, than was reported, and brought
the news that Cromwell himself was made Lieutenant of Ireland, June 22.
and intended to be shortly there with a very great supply of
horse and foot. This fleet that was already come had brought
arms and clothes and money and victuals; which much exalted
the garrison and the city; which presently turned out of the
town some of those who were suspected to wish well to the
marquis of Ormonde, and imprisoned others. And the second
day after the arrival of the succours[1], Jones, who had been a
lawyer, and was then governor of Dublin, at noonday marched Aug. 2.
out of the city, with a body of three thousand foot and three
or four troops of horses, and fell upon that quarter which was
next the town ; where they found so little resistance that they
adventured upon the next, and in short so disordered the whole
army, one half whereof was on the other side the river, that
the Lord Lieutenant, after he had, in the head of some officers
whom he drew together, charged the enemy with the loss of
many of those who followed him, was at last compelled to draw
off the whole army; which, though the loss was not great, was
so discomfited, that he did not think fit to return again to their
posts till both the troops which he had were refreshed and
composed, and their numbers increased by the levies which
ought to have been made before, and which were now in a good
forwardness.

70[2]. It may be remembered, that the general insurrections
in the last year, the revolt of the navy, and the invasion of
the Scots, encouraged and drawn in by the Presbyterian party,
had so disturbed and obstructed the counsels both in Parliament and in the army, that nothing had been done in all

---

[1] [a week after.]
[2] [Sections 70–74 are from the *Hist.*, pp. 5–7, and are in the handwriting
of an amanuensis.]

1649 that year towards the relief of Ireland, except the sending over
the lord Lisle as Lieutenant, with a commission that was
determined at the end of so many months, and which had given
so little relief to the English that it only discovered more their
weakness, and animosity towards each other, than obstructed
the Irish in making progress in all the parts of the kingdom ;
and the more confirmed the lord Inchiquin to pursue his
resolutions of serving the King, and of receiving the marquis
of Ormonde, how meanly soever attended, and to unite with
the Irish ; the perfecting of which conjunction with so general
a success brought so great reproach upon the Parliament, with
reference to the loss of Ireland, that the reproach and noise
thereof was very great: so that Cromwell thought it high
time in his own person to appear upon a stage of so great
action. There had been always men enough to be spared out
of the army to have been sent upon that expedition, when
the other difficulties were at highest; but the conducting it
then was of that importance, that it was, upon the matter, to
determine which power should be superior, the Presbyterian
or the Independent. And therefore the one had set up and
designed Waller for that command ; and Cromwell, against
him and that party, insisted that it should be given to
Lambert, the second man of the army, and who was known to
have as great a detestation of the Presbyterian power as he
had of the prerogative of the Crown : and the contests between
the two factions, which of these should be sent, had spent a
great part of the last year and of their winter councils. And
now, when all the domestic differences were so composed
by their successes in the field and the bloody prosecution of
their civil counsels, so that there could be little done to the
disturbance of the peace of England [1], Cromwell began to think
that the committing the whole government of Ireland, with

---

[1] [Here in previous editions are inserted the words, sometimes within
brackets, ' and when Waller's friends were so suppressed that he was no
more thought of.' The words are found in the transcript from which the
first edition was printed, but are not in the original MS., and were wrongly
inserted, Waller being one of the ' two persons ' mentioned below.]

such an army as was necessary to be sent thither, was too 1649
great a trust even for his beloved Lambert himself, and was
to lessen his own power and authority, both in the army which
was commanded by Fayrefax and in the other, that, being in
Ireland, would upon any occasion have great influence upon
the affairs of England. And therefore, whilst there appeared
no other obstruction in the relief of Ireland (which was every
day loudly called for) than the determining which of the
two persons named for the command of it should take that
charge, some of his friends, who were always ready upon such
occasions, on a sudden proposed, as a good expedient to put
an end to that debate, wherein two persons of great merit were
concerned, and who might possibly thin that it would be some
prejudice for either of them to be preferred before the other,
to nominate a third person who might reasonably be preferred
before them both, and thereupon named Cromwell the lieutenant March 30
general to conduct that expedition.

71. Cromwell himself was always absent when such overtures
were to be made, and whoever had proposed Lambert had
proposed it as a thing most agreeable to Cromwell's desire;
and therefore, when they heard Cromwell himself proposed
for the service, and by those who they were sure intended
him no affront, they immediately acquiesced in the proposition,
and looked upon the change as a good expedient. On the other
side the Presbyterian party was no less affected, and concluded
that this was only a trick to defer the service, and that he
never did intend to go thither in person; or that if he did,
his absence from England would give them all the advantages
they could wish, and that they should then recover entirely
their general Fayrefax to their party; who was already much
broken in spirit upon the concurrence he had been drawn
to, and declared some bitterness against the persons who had
led him to it. And so in a moment both parties were agreed,
and Oliver Cromwell elected and declared to be Lord Lieu- June 22.
tenant of Ireland, with as ample and independent a commission
as could be prepared.

72. Cromwell, how surprised soever with this designation,

1649 appeared the next day in the House full of confusion and irresolution, which the natural temper and composure of his understanding could hardly avoid when he least desired it, and therefore, when it was now to his purpose, could act it to the life. And after much hesitation, and many expressions of his own unworthiness, and disability to support so great a charge, and of the entire resignation of himself to their commands, and absolute dependence upon God's providence and blessing, from whom he had received many instances of his favour, he submitted to their good will and pleasure; and desired them that no more time might be lost in the preparations which were to be made for so great a work; for he did confess that kingdom to be reduced into so great straits, that he was willing to engage his own person in this expedition for the difficulties which appeared in it; and more out of hope with the loss of his life to give some obstruction to the successes which the rebels were at present exalted with, (for so he called the marquis of Ormonde, and all who joined with him,) that so the Commonwealth might retain still some footing in that kingdom till they might be able to send fresh supplies, than out of any expectation that, with the strength he carried, he should be able in any signal degree to prevail over them.

73. It is an incredible expedition that he used from this minute, after his assuming that charge, in the raising of money, providing of shipping, and drawing of forces together, for this enterprise. And before he could be ready himself to march, he sent three thousand foot and horse to Milford Haven, to be transported as soon as they arrived to Dublin, there being all things ready there for their transportation; which troops, by the contrary and adverse winds, were constrained to remain there for many days. And that caused the report in Ireland, by their intelligence from London, that Cromwell intended to make a descent in Munster; which unhappily divided the lord Inchiquin and a good body of his men from the Lord Lieutenant, when he marched towards Dublin. Nor did the marquis of Ormonde, in truth at that time intend to have marched thither with that expedition, until his army

should be grown more numerous and more accustomed to 1649 discipline; but the wonderful successes of those troops, which were sent before, in the taking of Trim, Dundalk, and all the out-garrisons, and the invitation and intelligence he had from within Dublin, made him unwilling to lose any more time, since he was sure that the crossness of the wind only hindered the arrival of those supplies which were designed thither out of England : and the arrival of which supplies, the very day before [1] his coming before Dublin, enabled the governor thereof to make that sally which is mentioned before, and which had that success which is mentioned.

74. The marquis of Ormonde at that time drew off his whole army from Dublin to Tredaugh, where he meant to remain till he could put his army into such a posture that he might prosecute his farther design. And a full account of all these particulars met Cromwell at his arrival at Milford Haven, when he rather expected to hear of the loss of Dublin, and was in great perplexity to resolve what he was then to do. But all those clouds being dispersed upon the news of the great success his party had that he had sent before, he deferred not to embark his whole army, and, with a very prosperous wind, arrived at Dublin within two or three days after the marquis of Ormonde had retired from thence [2] ; where he was received with wonderful acclamation ; which did not retard him from pursuing his active resolutions to prosecute those advantages which had already befallen him. And the marquis of Ormonde was no sooner advertised of his arrival, than he concluded to change his former resolution, and to draw his army to a greater distance, till those parties which were marching towards him from the several quarters of the kingdom might come up to him, and in the mean while to put Tredaugh into so good a posture as might entertain the enemy until he might be able to relieve them. And so he put into that place, which was looked upon, besides the strength of the situation, to be in a good degree fortified, the flower of his army, both of soldiers

[1] [the same day.]
[2] ['On or about Aug. 15 ;' Carte's *Ormonde,* ii. 83.]

1649 and officers, most of them English, to the number of three thousand foot, and two or three good troops of horse, provided with all things; and committed the charge and command thereof to sir Arthur Aston, who hath been often mentioned before, and was an officer of great name and experience, and who at that time made little doubt of defending it against all the power of Cromwell, for at least a month's time. And the marquis of Ormonde made less doubt in much less time to relieve and succour it with his army, and so retired to those parts where he had appointed a rendezvous for his new levies.

75 [1]. This news coming to St. German's broke all their measures, at least as to the expedition: the resolution continued for Ireland, but it was thought fit that they should expect another account from thence before the King began his journey; nor did it seem counsellable that his majesty should venture to sea whilst the Parliament fleet covered the ocean, and were then about the coast of Ireland, but that he should expect the autumn, [when [2]] the season of the year would call home or disperse the ships. But where to stay so long was the question; for it was now the month of August; and as the King had received no kind of civility from France since his last coming, so it was notorious enough that his absence was impatiently desired by that Court; and the Queen, who found herself disappointed of that dominion which she had expected, resolved to merit from the cardinal by freeing him of a guest that was so unwelcome to them, though he had not been in any degree chargeable to them; and so was not at all solicitous for his longer stay. And so his majesty considered how he should make his departure; and, upon looking round, he resolved that he would make his journey through Normandy, and embark himself for his island of Jarsy, which still continued under his obedience, and under the government of sir George Carteret; who had in truth the power over the place, though he was but the lieutenant of the lord Jermin, who, in those straits the King was in, and the great plenty which he enjoyed, was wonderfully jealous that the King's being there would lessen

some of the profit which he challenged from thence ; and there- **1649**
fore, when it was found, in order to the King's support whilst
he should stay there, necessary to sell some of the King's
demesnes in that island, the yearly rent whereof used to be
received by him towards the discharge of the garrisons there,
he insisted, with all possible importunity, that some of the
money which should be raised upon that sale should be paid to
him, because his receipt for the time to come would not remain
so great as it had been formerly. And though this demand
appeared so unjust and unreasonable that the Council would
not admit it, yet he did prevail with the King in private to
give him such a note under his hand as enabled him to receive
a good sum of money, after the return of his majesty into
England, upon that consideration. This resolution being taken
for Jarsy, the King sent to the prince of Aurange, that he
would cause two ships of war to ride in the road before St.
Maloes, (which they might do without notice,) and that he
might have a warrant remain in his hands, by which the ships
might attend his majesty when he should require, which they
might do in very few hours ; and in these he meant to transport himself, as soon as it should be seasonable, into Ireland.
And these ships did wait his pleasure there accordingly.

76. France had too good an excuse at this time for not
giving the King any assistance in money, which he might expect, and did abundantly want, by the ill condition their own
affairs were in. Though the sedition that had been raised in
Paris the last winter was at present so much appeased by the
courage and conduct of the prince of Condé, (who brought the
army which he commanded in Flanders with so great expedition before Paris, that the city yielded to reason,) so that his
majesty [the French King], the Queen his mother, and the
whole Court, were at this present there, yet the wound was far
from being closed up. The town continued still in ill humour ;
more of the great men adhered to them than had done before ;
the animosities against the cardinal increased, and, which made
those animosities the more terrible, the prince of Condé, who
surely had merited very much, either unsatisfied or not to be

1649 satisfied, brake his friendship with the cardinal, and spake
with much bitterness against him: so that the Court was far
from being in that tranquillity as to concern itself much for
the King [of England,] if it had been otherwise well inclined
to it.

77. All things standing thus, about the middle of September
the King left St. German's, and began his journey towards
Jarsy; and the Queen the next day removed from thence to
Paris, to the Louvre. And the two ambassadors for Spain
waited upon her majesty thither, having nothing now to do
but to prepare themselves for their journey to Spain, where
they longed to be, and whither they had sent for a pass to meet
them at St. Sebastian's, and that they might have a house provided for them at Madrid against the time they should come
thither: both which they recommended to an English gentleman who lived there to solicit, and to advertise them in their
journey of the temper of that Court[1].

[1] [The following passage is here struck out in the MS.: 'During the
time of their short stay at Paris, the Queen used the Chancellor very
graciously, but still expressed trouble that he was sent in that embassy,
which she said would be fruitless as to any advantage the King would receive from it ; and she said she must confess, that though she was not confident of his affection and kindness towards her, yet she believed that
he did wish that the King's carriage towards her should be always fair
and respectful ; and that she did desire that he might be always about his
majesty's person, not only because she thought he understood the business
of England better than any body else, but because she knew that he loved
the king, and would always give him good counsel towards his living
virtuously ; and that she thought he had more credit with him than any
other who would deal plainly and honestly with him.   There was a passage
at that time, of which he used to speak often, and looked upon as a great
honour to him.   The Queen one day, amongst some of her ladies in whom
she had most confidence, expressed some sharpness towards a lord of the
King's Council, whom she named not, who she said always gave her the
fairest words and promised her every thing she desired, and had persuaded
her to affect somewhat that she had before no mind to, and yet she was
well assured that, when the same was proposed to the King on her behalf,
he was the only man who dissuaded the King from granting it.   Some of
the ladies seemed to have the curiosity to know who it was, which the
Queen would not tell.   One of them, who was known to have a friendship
for him, said, she hoped it was not the Chancellor.   To which her majesty
replied with some quickness, that she might be sure it was not he, who was
so far from making promises, or giving fair words and flattering her, that

78. They thought it convenient, since they were to desire **1649** a pass to go from Paris into Spain, that they should wait upon the Queen [of France] and the cardinal; and likewise upon the duke of Orleance and the prince of Condé, who were then in a cabal against the Court. And the prince of Condé spake so publicly and so warmly against the cardinal, that most people thought the cardinal undone; and he himself apprehended some attempt upon his person, and therefore had not in many days gone out of his house, and admitted few to come to him, and had a strong guard in every room; so that his fear was not dissembled.

79. In this so general disorder they declined any formal audiences, for which their equipage was not suitable. So the lord Cottington went privately to the Queen regent, who received him graciously, and desired him to recommend her very kindly to her brother the King of Spain, without enlarging upon any thing else. From her he went to the duke of Orleance, whom he found in more disorder; and when the ambassador told him he came to know whether he had any service to command him into Spain, the duke, who scarce stood still whilst he was speaking, answered aloud, that he had nothing to do with Spain, and so went hastily into another room; and the lord Cottington then withdrew. They intended both to have gone together to the prince of Condé and to the cardinal. But when they sent to the prince, he wisely, but with great civility, sent them word, that they could not be ignorant of the disorder that Court was in, and of the jealousies which were of him; and therefore desired them to excuse him that he did not see them.

80. The cardinal appointed them an hour, and met them in an outward room, and conducted them into his inward room, where they sat down and conferred above half an hour, the lord Cottington speaking Spanish, and the cardinal and he conferring wholly in the same language. The cardinal acknowledged the apprehension he was in, in his looks; and took

she did verily believe that if he thought her to be a whore he would tell her of it; which when that lady told him, he was not displeased with the testimony.']

1649 occasion in his discourse to mention the unjust displeasure which monsieur le prince had conceived against him. He seemed earnestly to desire a peace between the two Crowns, and said that he would give a pound of his blood to obtain it; and desired the ambassadors to tell don Lewis de Haro from him, that he would with all his heart meet him upon the frontiers, and that he was confident if they two were together but three hours they should compose all differences: which message he afterwards disavowed, when don Lewis accepted the motion, and was willing to have met him. When they took their leave of him, he brought them to the top of the stairs, in disorder enough, and his guards being very circumspect, and suffering no stranger to approach any of the rooms.

81. When they had provided all things for their journey, and contracted [with Blavett, the sole person who could furnish coaches,[1]] for the transportation of themselves, their baggage, and family, which consisted of twenty persons and no more, to the *rayo* of Spain within twenty days, [for which they paid him in hand before they left Paris four hundred pistoles, their whole charge of their journey to that place being to be defrayed, as it was very handsomely [1],] they began their journey

Sept. 29. from Paris upon Michaelmas day, and continued it, without resting one day, till they came to Bourdeaux, which was then in rebellion against the King. The city and parliament had not only sent several complaints and bitter invectives against the duke of Espernon, their governor, for his acts of tyranny in his government, but had presumed, in order to make his person the more ungracious, to asperse his life and manners with those reproaches which they believed would most reflect upon the Court. And the truth is, their greatest quarrel against him was, that he was a fast friend to the cardinal, and would not be divided from his interest [2]. They had driven the

---

[1] [The words within brackets are struck out in the MS.]

[2] [The words, 'had presumed . . . his interest,' are substituted in the MS. for the following: 'but for his vicious life in keeping women in his house, to the more public scandal because his wife was much respected in those parts, and was subjected to the insolence of those women in her own house,

duke out of the town, and did not only desire the King that he 1649
might no more be their governor but that his majesty would
give the government to the prince of Condé; which made their
complaints the less considered as just. And it was then one
of the most avowed exceptions that prince had against the
cardinal, that he had not that government upon the petition of
Bourdeaux, since he offered to resign his of Burgundy, which
was held to be of as much value, to accommodate and repair
the duke of Espernon. At Blay, the ambassadors were visited
by the marshal of Plessy Praslin, who was sent by the Court
to treat with the parliament of Bourdeaux, but could bring
them to no reason, they positively insisting upon the remove
of their old governor, and conferring the command upon the
prince [1]. When they came to Bourdeaux they found the Chateau
Trompett, which still held for the King, shooting at the town,
the town having invested it very close, that no succour could
be put into them, the duke of Espernon being at his house
at Cadilliacke, from whence his horse every day infested the
citizens when they stirred out of town. Here they were compelled to stay one whole day, the disorders upon the river and
in the town not suffering their coaches and baggage to follow
them so soon as they should have done. They were here visited
by some counsellors and presidents of the parliament, who professed duty to the King, but irreconcilable hatred to the duke
of Espernon, against whom they had published several remonstrances in print, and dedicated them to the prince of Condé.
After a day's rest there, which was not unwelcome to them,
they continued their journey to Bayon[ne]; and were delivered,
after they had broken their fast at St. Jean de Luce, upon the
twentieth day from their leaving Paris, at the *rayo*; where
they took boat, and in an hour or two they arrived at Jeron [2] Oct. 19

and was shortly after turned out of it, for being displeased with her rude
treatment.']
   [1] [The following lines are here struck out: ' The marshal, who had then
no old look, told them, it was full forty years since he was first made
captain of a foot company in Italy; and he was alive above twenty years
after this discourse.']
   [2] [Irun: altered to *Girona* in previous editions.]

1649 where they lay that night, and sent away to the governor of
St. Sebastian's that they would be there the next day.   In
their passage upon the river they had the view of Fuentarabia,
1638 which had been so lately besieged by the prince of Condé, and
the duke de la Valet[te], who was now duke of Espernon; and
they saw the ruins the French army had made in all the
places adjacent, the greatest part of Jeron itself having been
burned, and still remaining unrepaired; and it was very manifest to them, by the discourses of all the people of that country,
that so great a consternation had seized upon the hearts of all
that people upon the approach of the French army, that if it
had advanced to St. Sebastian's, that important place was so ill
provided to make resistance that it would have been presently
quitted to them, after which Fuentarabia had not been worth
the contending for[1].   The next day they went by the river to
Passage, and when they came out of their boats, which were
rowed by women, according to their privilege there, they found
mules which were sent from St. Sebastian's to carry them
thither; and about half a mile from the town they were met
by the governor of Guipusc[o]a, don Anthonio de Cardinas, an
old soldier and a knight of the order, the corregidor, and all
the magistrates of St. Sebastian's, and the English merchants
which inhabited there; and were conducted by the governor
Oct. 20. to one of the best houses in the town, which was provided for
their reception; where they were no sooner, than the governor
and the rest of the magistrates took their leave of them, and
left them to their repose.

   [1] [The lines 'and it was very manifest . . . contending for' are substituted in the MS. for the following: 'Here they found an old priest, who
governed the town, and was master of the posts, which office he had held
when the lord Cottington had been last there, which was when the Prince
was in Spain, who was a jolly talking man, and glad to remember old
stories.   They were no sooner in their lodging, but the inquisitors came to
examine what books they brought into their country; [and[2]] at first with
some rudeness, the chief of them being a priest of a large size and a very
barbarous aspect and behaviour, they urged to have the view of all the
books they had, but afterwards were contented with a catalogue of the
names of them subscribed by one of their secretaries, and received a piece
of eight very thankfully.']

   [2] ['which,' MS.]

82. They had not been half an hour in their lodging, conferring with the English merchants about conveniences to prosecute their journey, when the corregidor came to them, and
desired to speak with them in private, and after some compliment and apology, he shewed them a letter which he had
received from the Secretary of State, the contents whereof were,
that when the ambassadors of the Prince of Wales should arrive
there, they should be received with all respect, but that he
should find some means to persuade them to stay and remain
there till he should give the King notice of it, and receive his
farther pleasure. And at the same time an English merchant
of the town, who had told them before that he had letters from
Madrid for them, and had gone home to fetch them, brought
them a packet from sir Benjamin Wright, who was intrusted
by them at Madrid to solicit for their pass, and for a house
to be prepared for them. And in his letter their pass was enclosed, under the same style, as ambassadors from the Prince of
Wales; which he had observed, and desired to have it mended,
but could procure no alteration, nor could he obtain any order
for the providing a house for them, but was told that it should
be done time enough. This was an unexpected mortification
to them; but they seemed not to be troubled at it, and as if
they had intended to stay there a month, to refresh themselves
after their long journey, and in expectation of other letters
from the King their master. The corregidor had offered to send
away an express the same night, if they would write by him,
or that he should stay a day or two for their letters, if they
were not yet ready to write; but they desired that the messenger might be despatched away with all diligence, and they
writ their letters presently. They writ to don Lewis de Haro,
that the King their master had sent them his ambassadors to
his Catholic majesty upon affairs of the highest importance;
that they were come so far on their way, but had, to their great
wonder, met there with a signification of the King's pleasure
that they should stay and remain there until they should receive his majesty's pleasure; which troubled them not so much,
as to find themselves styled the ambassadors of the Prince of

1649 Wales, which they thought very strange, after his Catholic majesty had sent an ambassador to the King their master before they left him: they desired therefore to know whether their persons were unacceptable to his Catholic majesty, and if that were the case, they would immediately return to their master; otherwise, if his majesty was content to receive them, they desired they might be treated in that manner as was due to the honour and dignity of the King their master. And they writ to sir Benjamin Wright to attend don Lewis, and if he found that they were expected at Madrid, and that they reformed the errors they had committed, he should then[1] use those importunities which were necessary for the providing a house for them against they should come.

83. Though the Court was then full of business, being in daily expectation of their new Queen, who was landed, and at that time within few days journey of Madrid, yet the very next day after the letter was delivered to don Lewis de Haro he returned an answer full of civility, and imputed the error that was committed to the negligence or ignorance of the Secretary, and sent them new passes in the proper style, and assured them that they should find a very good welcome from his majesty. And sir Benjamin Wright sent them word that he had received the warrant for the providing the house, and the officer to whom it was directed had called upon him to view two or three houses; and that don Lewis told him, that as soon as he had found a house that pleased him orders should be given to the King's officers of the wardrobe to furnish it, and that, when the ambassadors came, there should be one of the King's coaches to attend them whilst they stayed. And hereupon they made haste in their journey, with some satisfaction and confidence that they should find a Court not so hard to treat with[2], that could begin to receive them with so barefaced

---

[1] [The following words are here struck out in the MS.: 'send two letters to meet them at Victoria, and']

[2] [The words 'And hereupon . . . to treat with' are substituted in the MS. for the following: 'As soon as they received these advertisements they made haste to begin their journey, choosing rather to make use of mules till they came to Victoria, where they were sure to meet their litters, than

and formed an affront, and then so easily recede from it with **1649**
weak apologies. And it was plain enough that they heartily
wished that they had not come, and imagined that this might
put them to return again, and then were ashamed of their own
expedient, and, being pressed, chose rather to decline than avow
it : so unnatural a thing it is for that nation to stoop to any
ugly action without doing it so ungraciously as to confess it in
their own countenance, and quickly receding from it[1].

84. It was about the middle of November when they left Nov. 8.
St. Sebastian's, the weather yet continuing fair ; and a gentleman of quality of the country was appointed to accompany
them out of the jurisdiction of Guipusc[o]a, which was to
the city of Victoria, where they found their litters ; and from
thence they entered into Castile[2].

85. When they came to Alcavendas, a little town belonging
to the conde de Poino en Rostro, within three leagues of
Madrid, they discharged all their mules and litters, resolving
to stay there till they sent notice to the Court of their arrival,
and to sir Benjamin Wright, to know what house was provided
for them. He came to them, and told them all things were
in the same state they were when he writ to them to St.
Sebastian's : that though don Lewis gave him very good words
when he came to him, and seemed much troubled and angry
with the officers that the house was not ready, and the officers
excused themselves upon the jollities the town was in [during]
the *fiestas* which were held every day for the Queen's arrival,

to stay their coming to St. Sebastian's, of which they were heartily weary
either because they had been compelled to stay there near twenty days
against their will, or that it be indeed a most unpleasant place to live in,
and where there are no kind of divertisements, and they were in great
doubt that they should find a Court very hard to treat with,' &c.]

[1] [The words 'so unnatural ... from it' are a subsequent addition in
the MS.]

[2] [The following lines are here struck out: ' When they came to Burgos Nov. 14.
the magistrates invited them to see the *toros*, which was performed the
next day to celebrate the arrival of the Queen, who was now come to
Madrid ; and all the country making their *fiestas*, they stayed that day to
see that sight, which was new to all but the lord Cottington. The rains
began to fall, which made their journey forward less pleasant, yet not with
any great violence, as they seldom do in that country in the beginning.']

1649 [so] that nobody could attend any particular affair, yet it was evident there was not that care taken from the Court that there ought to have been, and that don Alonso de Cardinas from England had done the ambassadors all the ill offices possible, as if their good reception in Spain would incense the Parliament, and make them more propitious to France, which valued itself upon having driven all the royal family from thence.

86. Upon this new mortification, they writ again from thence to don Lewis, to desire that they might not be put to stay there for want of a house, and so be exposed to contempt ; nor were they accommodated in that place in any degree. He always answered their letters with great punctuality, and with courtesy enough, as if all things should be ready by the next day. The English merchants who resided at Madrid came every day to visit them, but still brought them word that there was no appearance of any provision made to receive them ; so that after a week's stay in that little town [1], and ill accommodation, they accepted the civil offer and invitation which sir Benjamin Wright made them, of reposing themselves *incognito* in his house ; which could only receive their persons with a valet de chambre for each, and the rest of their family was quartered in the next adjacent houses for the reception of strangers ; and so they went privately in the

Nov. 26. evening into Madrid in sir Benjamin Wright's coach, having sent all their servants before, and came to his house, where they were very conveniently lodged, and where there were good rooms, handsomely furnished for the reception of visitants ; and if by his generosity they had not been thus accommodated, they must have been exposed to reproach and infamy by the very little respect they received from the Court. Sir Benjamin was a gentleman of a good family in Essex ; and, being a younger brother, had been bred a merchant in Madrid, where as a merchant he had great business and great reputation, but was of a nature and spirit above that employment, and affected another and a higher, after he had lived there above twenty years, and was become a perfect Spaniard, not only in

[1] [They left on Nov. 21. See MS. narrative of the journey ; *Calend. Clar. S. P.* ii. 33.]

the language but in the generous part of their nature and customs, affected horsemanship and the use of his weapon, and excelled in both, and gave several testimonies of his courage upon particular encounters, most with his countrymen, who, in respect of his being a merchant, exercised some insolencies towards him. So that he accustomed himself to the outward *fausto* of the Spaniard abroad, and kept the custom and manner of his own country at home, by living plentifully and splendidly in his house, very contrary to the custom of that nation. He resolved to give over that profession of a merchant; and having got a very plentiful estate by it, he entered into treaties with the ministers of state to supply the King's affairs upon such *assientos* as were usually made, with providing ships, and supplying moneys in those parts of Italy and Flanders where the public affairs required it; an adventure that the merchants of Genoa were most conversant in, and wherein many had gotten very great estates whilst the Crown prospered and made good its contracts; and in his first entrance into that kind of commerce he [had[1]] performed some very acceptable services to that King, and got very well himself, according to which he always increased the expense and port of his living. He married into the family of Toledo, a young lady, who brought little more than her noble blood into his house; and he willingly took care that she should live in an expense equal to her birth. He had always performed great duty to his own King, and made himself still grateful to the English ambassador, by his paying all respects to him, and behaving himself always for the honour of his nation; and by the ambassador's interposition his own King made him a baronet; the patent whereof no sooner came to his hands than he entered it with the *Conseio de los ordines,* and with much difficulty and contest he procured ·it to be registered; and then was treated with the style of *Don* in all places, which wiped out the memory of the merchant; but in these contests and the *rodomontados* which accompanied them, in the presents he made, and in the whole course and

[1] ['did,' MS.]

1649 expense of his living, he stirred up the envy of the Spaniard
and lost the affection of his own countrymen, that is, of the
merchants, for of all others he was well beloved.

87. About the year of 1640, when the Crown was very
much declined in credit, and its necessities increased by the
anticipation of all their revenue, they had no more security
to give for any money they borrowed but such as brought
in nothing till the present lease which had been granted should
be expired; so that to make such a security to be accepted,
they were obliged to grant great interest, and other too
advantageous conditions; and by this temptation many were
drawn in to venture their estates. The affairs of Flanders were
in great distress, for supplying whereof sir Benjamin Wright,
upon assurance from his friends in England and in Flanders
that they would join with him and assist him, made an *assiento*
with the ministers, that he would presently pay so much money
by the month in Flanders, upon such a branch of the revenue
being assigned by the King to him for so many years, to begin
three years after, when the lease that was on foot would be
expired; so that he was to be out of his money near three
years before he should receive any thing towards his reimburse-
ment, but then he should enter upon a revenue which would
abundantly satisfy him with principal and interest. He performed his part very punctually, expecting to enter at his time
upon his assignation; and by this means, and by the same
kinds of security, the necessities of that time had been provided
for. When the expiration of the term drew near, by which the
new *assentistaes* were to enter upon their several bargains, the
necessities of the State appeared to be greater than before, by
the unprosperousness of their affairs in all places; and there was
now no possible way in view to provide for the future proportionable supplies. Hereupon the King did make a junto of
divines, whereof his confessor and other eminent prelates were
some, who were to consider and certify the King, whether
he might with a good conscience break his contract with those
men whose money he had received already, and make them
satisfaction some other way, according as should be judged

reasonable; whereby he might, by taking those farms into his 1649 own hands upon which others ought to enter, be able to borrow and provide money to supply the crying necessities of the Crown. This consultation was held without calling any of the parties concerned before them; but upon the information of the ministers of estate of the public necessity, and the computation of the immoderate gains the *assentistaes* would receive if they enjoyed their bargain and had the benefit of all their covenants, the divines (not without great deliberation and contests between themselves) gave it under their names, That the King might with a good conscience resume those parts of his revenue which he had granted to others into his own hands, if he first gave other satisfaction to those to whom such grants had been made. And when the King's conscience was thus satisfied, a decree was made, that all those persons (who were all named) to whom the King had granted such parts of his revenue, (which were likewise named,) and upon which they were to enter upon a day to come, should receive full satisfaction and repayments of the moneys they had advanced, with interest, upon the *juros* of the Crown, which should be assigned and made over to them by a good form in the law; and that all other persons who would advance money for the King's service, upon those parts of his revenue which he now took into his hands, should immediately enter into the receipt. The *juros* are of the nature of our tenures, or of our fee-farm rents, for they are not all of one kind nor of one value, so that men knew not how to treat for them; nor could be morally sure that the same might not be suddenly taken from them again, at least by a new king. However, many, who only looked for a competent revenue for their money, made tolerable bargains, and rested contented; but they who had laid out more money than their own, or who knew how to employ their money better, were undone by the overture, and utterly refused to accept them in satisfaction; but the decree left them no election, but determined both points positively, that they should not enjoy the benefit of their contracts, and that they should accept satisfaction by the *juros*.

1649 By these means poor sir Benjamin was reduced into great
straits, when the King owed him very near two hundred
thousand pounds sterling, according to the account then stated ;
and some friends of his both in England and Flanders were
exceedingly damnified, and others utterly ruined by this decree.
He himself, though fallen from his usual splendour, and his
wife being likewise very seasonably dead, still enjoyed a good
house, into which he received the ambassadors, kept good
horses, and a coach with six mules, and retained so much of his
natural generosity that there appeared no want in the condition
of his living ; and he hoped and expected, by the interposition
of the ambassadors, to receive some justice from the King in
some extraordinary way [1].

88. The Court well knew of their arrival, but took no notice
of it. The lord Cottington therefore sent to don Lewis, to
desire that he might have a private audience of him *incognito ;*
which he presently consented to, and appointed the next
morning to meet in the King's garden ; which was at such
a distance from the Court that it was not in the view of it ;
and there they met at the hour. Don Lewis was a man of
little ceremony, and used no flourishes in his discourses, which
made most men believe that he said all things from his heart ;
and he seemed to speak so cordially, that the lord Cottington,
who was not easy to be imposed upon, did think that they
should have a house very speedily, and that he had a good
inclination to favour them in what they came about. He
spake with more commotion than was natural to him in the
business of the murder of the King ; excused all the omissions
towards the ambassadors, which should be all repaired out
of hand, after the few days which yet remained to be spent in
fiestas for the Queen ; during which time, he said, no officers
would obey any orders which diverted them from the sight

---

[1] [The words 'that there appeared ... extraordinary way' are substituted for the following : 'that he defrayed their own diet whilst they stayed
in his house ; which made them much the more impatient to be in a house
of their own, and to have their family about them, which was dispersed,
and at a much greater expense than if they had been under their own
roof.']

of the triumphs; and wished that the ambassadors would see **1649**
the masquerade that afternoon, and the *toros* the day following.

89. The lord Cottington returned home very well satisfied;
and he had not been half an hour in the house, when a gentleman came from don Lewis to invite the ambassadors to see
those exercises which are mentioned before, and sent them
word that there should be places provided for them. The
Chancellor went that afternoon to the place assigned, where he
saw the masquerade and the running the course. That of the
masquerade is an exercise they learned from the Moors, performed by squadrons of horse seeming to charge each other
with great fierceness, with bucklers in their left hands, and
a kind of cane in their right, which, when they come within
little more than a horse-length, they throw with all the strength
they can, and against them they defend themselves with very
broad bucklers; and as soon as they have thrown their darts,
they wheel about in a full gallop, till they can turn to receive
the like assault from those whom they had charged; and so
several squadrons of twenty or five and twenty horse run
round and charge each other. It hath at first the appearance
of a martial exercise; the horses are very beautiful, and well
adorned; the men richly clad, and must be good horsemen,
otherwise they could not obey the quick motion and turns
of their horses; all the rest is too childish: the darts are
nothing else but plain bulrushes of the biggest growth. After
this they run the course; which is like our running at the
ring, save that two run still together, and the swifter hath the
prize, a post dividing them at the end. From the start they
run their horses full speed about fifty paces, and the judges are
at that post to determine who is first at the end. There the
King and don Lewis ran several courses, in all which don
Lewis was too good a courtier to win any prize, though he
always lost it by very little. The appearance of the people
was very great, and the ladies in all the windows made a
very rich show; otherwise the show itself had nothing wonderful. Here there happened to be some sudden sharp words
between the admirante of Castile, a haughty young man, and

1649 the marquis de Leche, the eldest son of don Lewis de Haro;
the which being taken notice of, they were both dismissed the
squadrons wherein they were, and committed to their chambers.

90. The next day, and so for two or three days together,
both the ambassadors had a box prepared for them to see the
toros; which is a spectacle very wonderful [1]. Here the place
was very noble, being the market-place, a very large square,
built with handsome brick houses, which had all balconies,
which were adorned with tapestry and very beautiful ladies.
Scaffolds were built round the first story, the lower rooms
being shops, and for ordinary use; and in the division of
those scaffolds all the magistrates and officers of the town
knew their places. The pavement of the place was all covered
with gravel, which in summer time was upon those occasions
watered by carts charged with hogsheads of water. As soon as
the King comes, some officers clear the whole ground from
the common people, so that there is no man seen upon the
plain but two or three *alguazils*, magistrates, with their
small white wands. Then one of the four gates which lead
into the streets is opened, at which the *torreadors* enter, all
persons of quality richly clad, and upon the best horses in
Spain, every one attended by eight or ten more lackeys, all
clinkant with gold and silver lace, who carry the spears which
their masters are to use against the bulls; and with this entry
many of the common people break in, for which sometimes they
pay very dear. The persons on horseback have all cloaks
folded up upon their left shoulder, the least disorder of which,
much more the letting it fall, is a very great disgrace; and in
that grave order they march to the place where the King
sits, and after they have made the reverences, they place
themselves at a good distance from one another, and expect the
bull. The bulls are brought in the night before from the
mountains by people used to that work, who drive them into
the town when nobody is in the streets, into a pen made for

---

[1] [The following lines are here struck out: 'different from what they
had seen at Burgos, where the bulls were much tamer, and where they
were not charged by men on horseback, and little harm done.']

them, which hath a door that opens into that large space ; **1649** the key whereof is sent to the King, which the King, when he sees everything ready, throws to an alguazil, who carries it to the officer that keeps the door, and he causes it to be opened, when a single bull is ready to come out. When the bull enters, the common people, who sit over the door or near it, strike him, or throw short darts with sharp points of steel, to provoke him to rage. He commonly runs with all his fury against the first man he sees on horseback, who watches him so carefully, and avoids him so dexterously, that when the spectators believe him to be even between the horns of the bull, he avoids by the quick turn of his horse, and with his lance strikes the bull upon a vein that runs through his poll, with which in a moment he falls down dead. But this fatal stroke can never be struck but when the bull comes so near upon the turn of the horse that his horn even touches the rider's leg, and so is at such a distance that he can shorten his lance, and use the full strength of his arm in the blow. And they who are the most skilful in the exercise do frequently kill the beast with such an exact stroke, insomuch as in a day two or three fall in that manner : but if they miss the vein, it only gives a wound that the more enrages him. Sometimes the bull runs with so much fierceness, (for if he scapes the first man, he runs upon the rest as they are in his way,) that he gores the horse with his horns that his guts come out, and he falls before the rider can get from his back. Sometimes by the strength of his neck he raises horse and man from the ground, and throws both down, and then the greatest danger is another gore upon the ground. In any of these disgraces, or any other by which the rider comes to be dismounted, he is obliged in honour to take his revenge upon the bull by his sword, and upon his head, towards which the standers by assist him by running after the bull and hocking him, by which he falls upon his hinder legs ; but before that execution can be done, a good bull hath his revenge upon many poor fellows. Sometimes he is so unruly that nobody dares to attack him, and then the King calls for the mastives, whereof two are let out at a time, and if

1649 they cannot master him, but are themselves killed, as frequently they are, the King then, as the last refuge, calls for the English mastives; of which they seldom turn out above one at a time ; and he rarely misses taking the bull and holding him by the nose till the men run in; and after they have hocked him, they quickly kill him. In one of those days there were no fewer than sixteen horses, as good as any in Spain, the worst of which would that very morning have yielded three hundred pistoles, killed, and four or five men, besides many more of both hurt: and some men remained perpetually maimed : for after the horsemen have done as much as they can, they withdraw themselves, and then some accustomed nimble fellows, to whom money is thrown when they perform their feats with skill, stand to receive the bull, whereof the worst are reserved till the last : and it is a wonderful thing to see with what steadiness those fellows will stand a full career of the bull, and by a little quick motion upon one foot avoid him, and lay a hand upon his horn, as if he guided him from him ; but then the next standers by, who have not the same activity, commonly pay for it ; and there is no day without much mischieve. It is a very barbarous exercise and triumph, in which so many men's lives are lost, and always ventured ; but so rooted in the affections of that nation, that it is not in the King's power, they say, to suppress it, though, if he disliked it enough, he might forbear to be present at it. There are three festival days in the year, whereof midsummer is one, on which the people hold it to be their right to be treated with these spectacles, not only in great cities, where they are never disappointed, but in very ordinary towns, where there are places provided for it. Besides those ordinary annual days, upon any extraordinary accidents of joy, as at this time for the arrival of the Queen, upon the birth of the King's children, or any signal victory, these triumphs are repeated, which no ecclesiastical censures or authority can suppress or discountenance. For Pope Pius the Fifth, in the time of Philip the Second, and very probably with his approbation, if not

1567 Nov. 1. upon his desire, published a bull against the *toros* in Spain,

which is still in force, in which he declared, that nobody should 1649
be capable of Christian burial who lost his life at those
spectacles, and that every clergyman who should be present at
them stood excommunicated *ipso facto ;* and yet there is
always one of the largest galleries assigned to the office of the
Inquisition and the chief of the clergy, which is always filled.
besides that many religious men in their habits get other
places ; only the Jesuits, out of their submission to the supreme
authority of the Pope, are never present there, but on those
days do always appoint some such solemn exercise to be performed that obliges their whole body to be together.

91. There was another accident upon one of these days,
the mention whereof is not unfit, to shew the discipline and
severity of that nation in the observation of order. It was
remembered that at the last masquerade the admirante and
the marquis of Leche were sent to their chambers ; and afterwards, the matter being examined, they were both commanded
to leave the town, and to retire each to a house of his own,
that was within three or four leagues of the town. The
marquis of Leche was known to have gone the next day, and
nobody doubted the same of the admirante, those orders being
never disputed or disobeyed. The King going to the *toros,* Dec. 23.
either himself discerned at another balcony, or somebody else
advertised him of it, that the duchess, who was wife to the
admirante, was there, and said, he knew that lady was a
woman of more honour than to come out of her house and be
present at that *fiesta* whilst her husband was under restraint
and in the King's displeasure, and therefore concluded that her
husband was likewise there ; and thereupon sent an alguazil to
that room, with command to examine carefully with his eye
whether the admirante was there ; for there appeared none
but women. The admirante being a young rash man, much in
the King's favour, and a gentleman of his bedchamber, thought
he might undiscerned see the triumph of that day ; and therefore caused himself to be dressed in the habit of a lady,
which his age would well bear, and forced his wife to go with
him ; who exceedingly resisted his command, well knowing to

1649 what reproach she exposed her own honour, though she had no
fear of his being discovered.   The alguazil brought the King
word that he was very sure the admirante was there in the
habit of a woman, and sat next his wife, amongst many other
ladies.   Whereupon the King sent the officer to apprehend him
in the habit he was in, and to carry him to his, the officer's,
own house.   And as soon as the King returned to the palace,
there was an order that the alguazil should the next morning
carry the admirante to Valliodalid, four days journey from
Madrid, where he had a house of his own, where he was confined not to go out of the limits of that city ; and under this
restraint he remained for the space of full three years : so
penal a thing it is amongst that people for any man, of how
great a quality soever, (there was not in Spain a man of a
greater than the admirante of Castile,) to disobey or elude the
judgment of the King.

92 [1]. It may not be thought unnatural, or impertinent to
the work in hand, to make this digression upon this embassy,
and to enlarge upon many circumstances which occurred in it,
and to make a short description of their reception in that
Court, of the formality and constitution of it, and of the
nature and humour of that people ; which seem foreign to the
affairs of England.   But since the King, after his leaving
Paris, remained in Jarsy for many months, waiting such a
revolution as might administer an opportunity and occasion to
him to quit that retirement, in all which time there was no
action or counsel to be mentioned at present, and this being
the first and only embassy in which his majesty's person was
represented until his blessed return into England, (for though
some other persons were afterwards sent to other princes with
commissions to perform that function, if they found encouragement so to do, yet none assumed that character, nor were
treated as such in any other court in Christendom, Spain only
excepted,) it may therefore be reasonably thought a material

---

[1] [This and the next section are inserted as §§ 98, 99, in previous
editions, but their place is clearly marked in the MS. for insertion here.
They are found at pp. 7, 8 of the *Hist.*]

part of this history even to give such a relation of this negoti- **1649**
ation, that it may appear what sense other kings and princes
had of those revolutions in England, and of the miserable
condition to which this young innocent prince was reduced,
when it was fully pressed to them in the most efficacious terms
in which it was to be represented, and to which it was very
hard to avoid giving some categorical [1] answer ; and every
circumstance of their reception and treatment serves to illus-
trate those particulars ; and therefore we shall proceed farther
in the relation thereof.

93. Before their audience [2], (which they importuned for before
they could procure any house to be assigned for their habitation, as that which would, as it did, accelerate the other,) don
Lewis de Haro sent them word of the imprisonment of the **1650**
prince of Condé, the prince of Conty, and the duke of Longue- **Jan. 18.**
ville, and that marshal Turyn [Turenne] had made his escape
into Flanders ; the news whereof gave that Court much trouble ;
for they had promised themselves a better harvest from that
seed which they had carefully and industriously sown, and that
the cardinal, whom they perfectly hated, would be totally suppressed, and all his power entirely taken from him ; which
they concluded would forthwith produce a peace, which was no
less desired in France than in Spain ; or that those princes and
all their dependants would appear in arms in that kingdom, by
which they should be able to recover much of what they had
lost in Flanders ; the hopes of either of which appeared
now blasted, by this unexpected and unfeared power of the
cardinal.

94. [3] Though it is not the course for ambassadors to make
their visits to those who come last before they receive their
first audience from the King, yet the very night they came to
the town, the Venetian ambassador sent to congratulate their
arrival, and to know what hour they would assign of the next
day to receive a visit from him ; to which they returned their
acknowledgments, and that when they had obtained their
audience of the King they would be ready to receive that

---

[1] ['catectorigall,' MS.]　　[2] [some weeks after.]　　[3] [*Life*, p. 413.]

1649 honour from him. However, the very next day he came to visit them; and he was no sooner gone, but the German ambassador, not sending notice till he was at the bottom of the stairs, likewise came to them; and then the other ambassadors and public ministers took their times to make their visits, without attending the audience. There was one thing very notable, that all the foreign ministers residing then in Madrid (the English ambassadors and the resident of Denmark only excepted) were Italian, and all but the Venetian subjects of the Great Duke. Julio Rospiglioso, nuncio for the Pope, was of Pistoja, and so subject to the Duke of Florence, a grave man, and at that time, save that his health was not good, like to come to what he was afterwards, to be Pope, as he was Clement the IXth. The Emperor's ambassador, the marquis of Grana, was likewise an Italian, and a subject of Florence: he had been general of one of the Emperor's armies, and was sent afterwards ambassador to Madrid. He was a man of great parts, and the removing the conde duke Olivarez from Court was imputed to his artifice. He made the match between the King and the present Queen, for which he expected to have the cap of a cardinal, and had received it if he had not died before the
1652 following creation, the cardinal of Hesse being nominated by the Emperor upon his death. He was a man of an imperious and insolent nature, and capable of any temptation, and nobody more glad of his death than his own servants, over whom he was a great tyrant. The ambassador of Venice [Pietro Basadonna[1]] a noble Venetian, was a man, as all that nation is, of great civility and much profession. He was the first who told the ambassadors that the King their master had a resident at Venice, which was Mr. Killigrew; which they did not at first believe, having before they left St. Germ[ain's] dissuaded the King from that purpose; but afterwards his majesty was prevailed upon, only to gratify him, that in that capacity he might borrow money of English merchants for his own subsistence, which he did, and nothing to the honour of his master, but was at last compelled to leave the republic for his

[1] [blank in the MS.]

vicious behaviour, of which the Venetian ambassador complained **1649** to the King when he came afterwards to Paris.

95. The ambassador of the King of Poland[1] was likewise a Florentine, who was much in favour with the King Vladislaus, from whom he was sent, and continued by King Casimir. He had lived in great splendour, but by his vicious course of life and some miscarriages he fell very low, and was revoked with some circumstances of dishonour. He was a man of a great wit, if it had not served him to very ill purposes.

96. The ambassador of Florence[2] was a subject of his master, and an abbot, a grave man; and though he was frequently called ambassador, he was in truth but resident; which was discovered by a contest he had with the Denmark resident for place, who alleged that the other was no more than resident; which was true, and made the discovery that the Florentine sent no ambassadors to Madrid, because they are not suffered to cover, which they used to do in many other courts.

97. The archduke of Inspruck's minister[3] was likewise a Florentine, and had been bred in Spain, and was a knight of the Order, and supported that character upon a small assignation from his master, for some benefit and advantage it gave him in negotiations and pretences he had in that Court.

98. The resident of Denmark was don Henrique Williamson[4], (he was afterwards called Rosewell[4],) who came secretary to Hannibal Zested[5] who had been the year before ambassador in that Court, and lived in extraordinary splendour, as all the northern ministers do, who have not their allowance from the King but from a revenue that is purposely set aside for that kind of service. When he went away, he left this gentleman to remain there as resident. He was a grave and a sober man, wiser than most of his nation, and lived with much more plenty, and with a better retinue, than any other minister of that rank in that Court.

99. They had not been many days in Madrid, when don Lewis sent them the news of the imprisonment of the prince of Condé, the prince of Conty and the duke of Longueville, and

[1] [Franc. Biboni.]   [2] [Jac. Incontri.]   [3] [Geron. Biffi.]
[4] [Willemsen Rosenvinge.]   [5] [Schestedt.]

1649 that marshal Turyn was fled into Flanders: so much the cardinal had improved his condition from the time that they had left Paris. There was yet no house provided for them, which they took very heavily, and believed that it might advance that business, if they had once a public reception as ambassadors, and therefore they resolved to demand an audience. Don Lewis came to be advertised that the ambassadors had prepared mourning for themselves and all their train against their audience, which was true, for they thought it the most proper dress for them to appear in, and to demand assistance to revenge the murder of their master, it being yet within the year; but don Lewis sent to them, that he hoped that when the whole Court was *in gala* upon the joy of the marriage of the King, and to give the Queen a cheerful reception, they would not dishonour the festival by appearing *in luto*, which the King could not but take unkindly; which, he said, he thought fit to advertise them of, out of friendship, and without any authority. Whereupon, as well to comply in an affair which seemed to have somewhat of reason in it, as out of apprehension that from hence they might take occasion to defer their audience, they changed their purpose, and caused new clothes to be made, and then sent to demand their audience; upon the subject whereof, and what followed of the negotiation, the relation shall be continued[1].

Dec. 10.   100. Upon the day assigned for their audience, it being resolved that, when they had ended with the King, they should likewise have their audience with the Queen, don Lewis de Haro sent horses to their lodging, for the accommodation of the ambassadors and their servants; it being the fashion of that Court that all ambassadors ride to their first audience. And so they rode, being attended by all their own servants, and all the English merchants who lived in the town, together with many

---

[1] [Here, in the MS. of the *Life* (p. 411), is added this note: 'All that passed at the Hague both with the States and the Scots is more particularly contained in papers and memorials which will be found in the hair cabinet, out of which any thing that is material may be added or altered; as also the names of all the ministers at that time in Madrid are in a paper book that stands in the shop.']

Irish officers who were in the service of his Catholic majesty, **1649** all on horseback; so that their cavalcade appeared very fair, all the coaches of the ambassadors likewise following them.

101. And in this manner they came to the Court about ten of the clock in the morning, and being conducted by [*blank in MS.*], who had been sent to their lodging and rode with them to the Court, through several rooms, where there was only one officer, who attended to open and shut the doors, they came to the next room where his majesty was; where, after a little stay, whilst their conductor went in and out, they found the King standing upright, with his back against the wall, and all the grandees at a distance, in the same posture, against the wall. When they had made their several respects, and came to the King, he lightly moved his hat, and bade them cover. The lord Cottington spake only general things, of the confidence the King had in his majesty's kindness, and believed his condition such as that all the kings of the world were concerned to vindicate the wrong he sustained; and that this was the first embassy he had sent, relying more upon the honour of his majesty's nature and generosity than upon any other prince; with discourses of the same nature; and then presented their credentials.

102. The King expressed a very tender sense of the King's condition, and acknowledged that it concerned all kings to join together for the punishment of such an impious rebellion and parricide; and if his own affairs would permit it, he would be the first that would undertake it; but that they could not but know how full his hands were; and whilst he had so powerful an adversary to contend with, he could hardly defend himself; but that when there should be a peace with France, (which he desired,) the King, his *sobrino*, (for so he still called the King his nephew,) should find all he could expect from him; in the mean time he would be ready to do all that was in his power towards his assistance and relief[1]. After the formal part was

---

[1] [The following lines are here struck out: 'They then said somewhat of themselves, of their respect to him, and of their desire to render themselves as acceptable to his Catholic majesty as they could. The King was ob-

1649 over, the King asked many questions, most with reference to his sister the Queen of France; and discoursed very intelligently of every thing; so that his defects proceeded only from the laziness of his mind, not from any want of understanding; and he seemed then, when he was about eight and forty years of age, to have great vigour of body, having a clear ruddy complexion [1].

103. From the King they were conducted to the Queen, who used very few words, and spake so low that she could scarce be heard. She stood, in the same manner the King did, against a wall, and her ladies on both sides, as the grandees did; the Infanta at a little distance from her, to whom likewise they passed a compliment from their master. The Queen was then about eighteen years of age, not tall, round-faced, and inclined to be fat. The Infanta was much lower, as she ought to be by her age, but of a very lovely complexion, without any help of art, which every one else in the room, the Queen herself, was beholding to; and she was then the fullest of spirit and wit of any lady in Spain, which she had not improved afterwards when she had more years upon her. Their audience ended, they returned, and in few days after made all their visits, as well to don Lewis and to the other councillors as to the ambassadors; and at last they had a house provided for them in the Calle de Alcala, belonging to the marquis of Villa Magna, to whom the King paid four hundred pounds sterling by the year; a good house, wherein three grandees had lived; and yet, after it was put into their hands, they were compelled to defer their remove for at least a week, to devise a place where to make a kitchen, there being no chimney in the house but in the garrets, and of those not one big enough to roast a joint of

served to speak with much more grace upon that occasion to the Chancellor than to the other; told him he had heard much of him, of his parts, and of his zeal for his master's service, for which he should be sure to have his favour always; saying very little of grace to the lord Cottington.']

[1] [The following line is here struck out: 'yet he had been accustomed to fevers from his deboshes with women, by which he was much wasted.']

meat; but rather hearths, upon which several pipkins might **1649** be set together, according to the custom and manner of living there in the greatest families. So that there being a stable adjoining to the house, they were compelled to build a chimney and ovens there, which accommodated them well. All the rooms of reception and entertainment were well furnished out of the King's wardrobe, with tapestry-hangings and chairs, which were changed upon the change of the season, with a cloth of state, and two very good beds for the ambassadors themselves; but they were put to hire all beds and other necessaries for the accommodation of their retinue and servants. The King's coach always waited upon them at their door [1].

104. It will not be unseasonable in this place to take a view of the state of that Court at this time, and of the kingdom, that it may be the less wondered at that an embassy which had

---

[1] [The following passage, hitherto (like many others) included in the printed text, is here struck out in the MS.: 'So that they began to be at more ease, and looked more like ambassadors than they had done, and began to think of their negotiation; and in regard that they had no servant who understood any thing of the Court, to be sent up and down to demand audiences, and who understood what form and method was to be observed at home upon the reception of visits, and to advise the servants how they were to behave themselves on those occasions, they entertained Christopher Winnibanke, a younger son of secretary Winnibanke, to serve them. He had been bred at Magdalene college in Oxford, and sent from thence, when he was a young man, by his father into Spain to understand that Court, under the countenance of the lord ambassador Hopton, who received him into his house as a friend for his father's sake; where he lived much made of, till, according to the custom of his family, he fell in love with a woman, who deprived him of the conveniency he had of living in the ambassador's house, and brought him no other way of subsistence; so that his father's misfortune falling out about the same time, he was reduced to poverty, having only by change of his religion made himself the more capable of receiving obligations from the Court, which, in regard of former good offices they had received from his father, promised him some pension, which they did not pay; so that this relation to the ambassadors was very welcome and convenient to him; and his service was useful to them, being a perfect Spaniard, and an honest man. Sir Benjamin's kindness was still very necessary to them; for as they had intrusted him to receive their money which was returned from Antwerp, so he issued it out to their *mayor domo* as there was occasion, and contracted with the dispensers, and did many other good offices for them: which good intelligence continued between them during the time of their stay there.']

1649 no other end than to procure relief and support for a distressed prince had no better effect.

105. The Council of State consisted of don Lewis de Haro, duke de Medina de las Torres, duke de Monterey, marquis de Castle Rodrigo, marquis de Vall Periso [Valparaiso], the conde of Castrilio, and don Francisco de Melo. There were no more residing in that Court then; the duke de Medina Celi residing constantly at his government of St. Lucar; the marquis of Liganesse being general against Portugal, and so remained at Badajoz, and came seldom to Madrid; and the duke of Arcos stood confined to his own house, since the defection of Naples when it was under his government; and the conde de Pi[g]noranda [was] not yet come out of Flanders.

106. Don Lewis was as absolute a favourite in the eyes of his master, had as entire a disposal of all his affections and faculties, as any favourite of that age: nor was any thing transacted at home or abroad but by his direction and determination: and yet, of all the favourites of that or any other time, no man ever did so little alone, or seemed less to enjoy the delight and empire of a favourite. In the most ordinary occurrences, which for the difficulty required little deliberation, and in the nature of them required expedition, he would give no order without formal consultation with the rest of the Council; which hindered despatch, and made his parts the more suspected, and his power the more grumbled and murmured at. He was son of the marquis of Carpio, who had married the sister of Olivarez, and had been before his favour put about the person of the King, being about the same age with his majesty, and so had grown up in his affection, and was not thought to have been displeased at the disgrace of his uncle, but rather to have contributed to it, though he did not succeed in that in many years, nor seemed to be concerned in any business till **1644** after the death of the [then] Queen, and was rather drawn into **Oct. 6.** it by the violence of the King's affection, who had a great kindness for his person, than by the ambition of his own nature, or any delight in business. His education had not fitted him for it, and his parts of nature were not sharp; yet

his industry was great, and the more commendable because his 1649 nature had some repugnancy to it, and his experience had so fitted him to it that he never spake impertinently, and discoursed reasonably and weightily upon all subjects. He was of a melancholic complexion, seldom smiled, and was very hypochondriac; which, it may be, was the reason that he did not trust himself in himself, which was his defect. He seemed to be a very honest and well-natured man, and did very rarely manifest his power in acts of oppression or hard-heartedness; which made him grateful enough to most particular men, when he was hated enough by the generality. His port and grandeur was very much inferior to that of either of the French cardinals who were successively favourites during his administration; nor did he affect wealth as they did, not leaving a fortune behind him much improved by his industry: yet it cannot be denied that the affairs of Spain declined more in the time they were under his government than at any time before, and that less was done with the consumption of so much money than might have been expected. But it must be likewise considered, that he entered upon that administration in a very unhappy conjuncture, after the loss of Portugal and the defection in Catalonia, which made such a rent in that diadem as would have required more than an ordinary statesman to have soldered it again, and made it flourish as before.

107. The duke of Medina de las Torres was a cadet of the house of Gusman, whom for that reason the duke of Olivarez, (who was of the same family,) had made choice [of] to continue his house, by giving him his only daughter in marriage, and raised him to be a duke and grandee, made him *somelier de corps,* (which is groom of the stole with us, and the second, if not the first, place in the Court,) and then sent him viceroy into Naples; where burying his wife without child, he married again the princess of Aviliana, an inheritrix of that kingdom of a great fortune, by whom he had children, and so the alliance and friendship with the condé duke expired. He was of a free and lively humour, unlike the Spaniards, and addicted to all kinds of deboshry alike, whereas they are usually in-

1649 dulgent but to one. He neither depended upon [n]or loved don Lewis, being as unlike him in his nature and humour as in his complexion, and had power enough with the King to do his own business, which was only to provide for his vast expenses,. and being indeed the King's greatest confident in his walks of liberty, and so never crossed don Lewis in the general managery, and seldom came to Council except he was sent for, there being likewise great suits between don Lewis and him about some estate of the duke of Olivarez, which kept them from any intimate correspondence. He was a man of parts, and wanted nothing to be a very good statesman but application, and he was industriously without that. The duke of Monterey had married another of the sisters of the condé duke, and had been ambassador in Rome and viceroy of Naples, and was now *Presidente de consejo de Italia*, which is one of the greatest offices. He was esteemed a good man. He was slow, both by his nature and by his infirmities, being in a consumption, and spake not to be heard at any distance. He was of great courtesy, and believed to be of great judgment, and [on][1] which don Lewis depended more than any other man's. The marquis of Castle [Rode]rigo was the son of that Juan de Mora, the Portuguese, who was secretary to Philip the Second, and was owner to a very great estate in Portugal, of which he was dispossessed entirely from the time of the general defection of that kingdom, and was now *major-domo* in that Court, which is the greatest office. He had been ambassador in Rome, and afterwards governor of the Low Countries. He was a man of long experience, (his son being then ambassador in the Emperor's court, and had treated the marriage of the King,) and much esteemed by the King and don Lewis, but a man of mean natural parts, and by his age peevish. He had been corrupted, during the time of his government in Flanders, by his correspondence with don Alonso de Cardinas, in his affection towards the King, and in his understanding the affairs of England; so that he was looked upon as the author of those disrespects which the ambassadors had undergone. However, he made

---

[1] ['of,' MS.]

great professions to them of a desire to serve his majesty; but **1649** he died during the time of their stay at Madrid. The marquis of Vall Periso was an old man, who was for the most part kept in his bed or in his chamber by the gout, so that he was seldom at the Council, but his judgment [was] much esteemed. He had formerly had a command of horse in Flanders: and there was a marvellous difference between those men who had ever employment out of Spain, and those whose education and business had been only in Spain. He was a grave man, very civil, and esteemed for his wisdom and integrity, and thought to have good affection for the King, and a great detestation of the rebels, in England; but his age and infirmity kept him too much within doors to have a notable influence upon their counsels. The conde de Castrilio was the younger brother of the marquis de Carpio, the father of don Lewis, otherwise of no kind of kin to his nephew. He had been bred up in the study of the law in Salamanca, where he had been eminent; and upon his stock in that knowledge came early into the Court, and was so much trusted by the late Queen, after the disgrace of the conde duke, to which he was thought to [have contributed] very much, that if she had lived and held that power which she had newly got he was very like to be the first minister; which did him no good when he missed it. He was *Presidente de las Indias*, which is one of the greatest offices, and, without comparison, of the greatest benefit. He was a man of great parts, and a very wise man, grave and eloquent in his discourse, and understood the state of Spain better than any man. He lived within himself, as if he had a mind to be rich; and by the prejudice don Lewis had towards him, he had not that authority with the King that he deserved to have. Don Francisco de Melo was a cadet of that family in Portugal, and coming young from thence into the Court, and being of sharp and quick parts, and having seen other countries, grew into great reputation there, which was not much clouded by the rebellion of the other kingdom, where he had a small estate, and in Spain a great one. He had been viceroy in several **1643** kingdoms, and governor in Flanders, where he lost the battle **May 19.**

1649 of Rocroy to the prince of Condé. He was a wise man, and much trusted by don Lewis; yet he had no reputation of integrity, and was thought to affect being rich by what means soever.

108. The ambassadors had not been there long, when the conde of Pi[g]noranda returned thither from his negotiation in the treaty of Munster; and as he had been declared to be of the *Consejo de stado* after he had made that peace with Holland, so he was admitted to it as soon as he returned. He was only conde in the right of his wife; and before, being of a good family, don Diego de Brachamonte, and bred in the study of the law, was looked upon as a good man of business, and so employed in matters of greatest trust. And he was indeed a man of great parts, and understood the affairs of the world better than any man in that Court, but was proud to the height of his nation, and retained too much of the pedantry which he had brought with him from Salamanca. And as soon as he returned, according to the method of that Court upon great and successful employments, the Presidentship *de los ordines,* an office of great reputation, becoming void, it was the very next day conferred upon him. The ambassadors found no benefit by his arrival, coming from Bruxells, which was throughly infected by don Alonso. The truth is, don Alonso, who had no affection for the King upon the memory of some disobligations when he first came over, and liked well his employment and residence in England, used all the endeavours imaginable to have the King's condition thought to be irrecoverable and desperate, and therefore that all civilities extended towards him were cast away, and would yield no fruit, and that the Commonwealth was so established that it could never be shaken. So that Spain thought only of how to make a firm friendship there, and to forget that there ever had been a King, in the confidence that there would be no more. And therefore when the ambassadors, after all ceremonies were over,

Dec. 24. had a private audience with the King, and desired that he
Friday. would appoint commissioners, with whom they might treat about the renewing the alliance between the two Crowns, which

had been provided for by the last treaty to be renewed within 1649 so many months after the death of either King, and with whom they might likewise confer upon such relief in arms and money as his Catholic majesty would think to send to their master into Ireland, whither one of the ambassadors desired to hasten his journey as soon as might be ; (and in that memorial, which they then delivered to his Catholic majesty, they desired like-wise that he would write to Owen O'Neale to dispose him to submit to the King, since his standing out did only weaken the Catholic party, and would make them less united to oppose the Parliament, whereby their own destruction would inevitably follow, as well as an irreparable damage to the King their master ;) they received shortly after an answer, sent to them by don Francisco de Melo, who told them that the King had sent him to them, to confer with them upon the substance of their last memorial. He said, the King did not think it necessary to appoint any committee to renew the last treaty of peace ; which was still in force, and might well be observed between the two nations ; and that the renewing might be deferred till the times should mend; implying very little less than that when the King should be in England, it would be a fit time to renew the alliance. He said, he was ready to receive any propositions from them, wherein they might more particularly set down their desires, if they were ready to depart ; and for writing to Owen O'Neale, (whom he called don Eugenio,) he had so misbehaved himself towards his Catholic majesty, by leaving his service in Flanders and transporting himself into Ireland without his license, that his majesty could not in honour write to him ; but that he would take such care, that he should know that it would be agreeable to his majesty's good liking that he betook himself to the service of the King of Great Britain without reserve ; which he did believe would dispose him to it : which method they did conceive was proposed because they should believe that the Spaniard had no hand in sending him into that kingdom or in fomenting the rebellion ; whereas at the same time don Diego de la Torre was with the Irish as resident or envoy from Spain.

1649   109. This answer was evidence enough to them how little they were to expect from any avowed friendship of that Crown, though they still thought they might be able to obtain some little favour in private, as arms and ammunition, and a small supply of money for the King's subsistence, that could hardly be taken notice of.   And therefore the Chancellor of the Exchequer, who was designed by the King to attend him in Ireland, expected [1] only to hear that he was arrived there, till when he could not present his memorial so particularly as was demanded, nor prepare himself for his voyage thither : and so they rested for some time, without giving the Court any farther trouble by audiences [2].

110. Whilst they were in this impatient expectation to hear from the King, who yet remained at Jarsy, by which they might take their own resolutions, prince Rupert came upon the

Nov. coast of Spain with the fleet under his command, which he had brought from Ireland, and had sent a letter on shore to be sent to the Chancellor of the Exchequer, one of the ambassadors, and which the officer upon the place sent presently to don Lewis de Haro, who in the same moment sent it to him with a very civil salutation.   The prince writ him word that he had brought away all the fleet from Ireland, and that he had received an assurance from Portugal that he should be very welcome thither ; upon which he was resolved, after he had attended some days to meet with any English ships which might be prize, to go for Lisbon ; and desired him to procure orders from the Court that he might find a good reception in all the ports of Spain, if his occasions brought him thither. The ambassadors sent immediately for an audience to don

---

[1] [The words ' who was . . . expected' are substituted for ' was so weary of his embassy that he expected.']

[2] [The following lines are here struck out :—' and enjoyed themselves in no unpleasant retreat from business, if they could have put off the thought of the miserable condition of their master and their own particular concernments in their own country. The Chancellor betook himself to the learning the language by reading their books, of which he made a good collection, and informing himself the best he could of their government and the administration of their justice : and there began his devotion upon the Psalms, which he finished in another banishment.']

Lewis, who received them with open arms, and another kind of **1649**
countenance than he had ever done before.   A fleet of the King
of England, under the command of a prince of the blood, upon
the coast of Spain, at a season of the year when they expected
the return of their galleons from the Indies, made a great
consternation amongst the people, and the Court received the
news of it with disorder enough.   All that the ambassadors
asked was granted without hesitation ; and letters were despatched away that very night (copies whereof were sent to the
ambassadors) by several expresses, to all the governors of the
ports and other officers, for the good reception of prince Rupert
or any ships under his command, if they came into any of the
ports[1], and for the furnishing them with any provisions they
should stand in need of, with as many friendly clauses as could
have been inserted if the King had been in possession of his
whole empire : so great an influence a little appearance of
power had upon their spirits ; and the ambassadors found they
lived in another kind of air than they had done, and received
every day visits and caresses from the Court and from those in
authority.

111.   But the government of these benign stars was very
short.   Within few days after, they received news that the
prince with the gross of his fleet was gone into the river of **Dec.**
Lisbon, and that a squadron of four or five ships, under the
command of captain Allen, being severed from the prince by a **1650**
storm, was driven upon the rocks at Cartagena ; where the **Nov. 14.**
people of the country had treated them very rudely, and seized
both upon the ships and persons of the men, and the storm
continuing had wrecked two or three of their vessels in the
road, though the guns and all things in the ships were saved.
When the ambassadors demanded justice, and that restitution
might be made of all those goods and ordnance and rigging of
the ships, which not only the people but the governors and
officers themselves had seized upon, they were received with
much more cloudy looks than before, nor was there the same
expedition in granting what they could not deny.   Orders were

---

[1] [See *Calend. Clar. S. P.* ii. 39.]

1650 at last given for the setting all the men at liberty, and re-delivery of the goods, that thereby they might be enabled to mend their vessels and transport their men.

112. But as these orders were but faintly given, so they were more slowly executed; and colonel Popham then appeared upon the coast in the head of a stronger fleet sent out by the Parliament, which came into the road of St. Andera's; from

Nov. whence he writ [1] a very insolent letter in English to the King of Spain, wherein he required that none of those ships under the command of prince Rupert, and which had revolted from the Parliament, and were in rebellion against it, might be received into any of the ports of Spain, and that those ships which were in the ports of Cartagena might be delivered to him, and the ordnance and tackling of the other which were wrecked might be carefully kept and delivered to such person as should be authorized to receive the same by the Common-wealth of England, to whom they belonged: and concluded, that as the Commonwealth of England was willing to live in amity and good intelligence with his Catholic majesty, so they knew very well how to do themselves right for any injury or discourtesy which they should be put to sustain.

113. This imperious style made such an impression upon the Court, that all the importunity the ambassadors could use could get nothing done at Cartagena in pursuance of the orders they had sent from the Court; but the poor men were, after long attendance, forced to transport themselves as they were able; and two or three hundred of them marched over land, and were compelled to list themselves in the Spanish service at land, where they for the most part perished; care being in the mean time taken that Popham should be received in all places with all possible demonstration of respect and kindness, and the King sent him a ring of the value of fifteen hundred pounds. And in this triumph he sailed from thence into Portugal, and dropped his anchors in the river of Lisbon, at a very small distance from the fleet of prince Rupert; and suffered not any ship to enter into that river, but denounced war against that

[1] [Not Popham, but Blake; *Calend. Clar. S. R.* ii. 87.]

kingdom if that fleet were not presently delivered up into his 1650
hands.

114. The Portuguese had received prince Rupert very civilly,
bought all the prizes he had brought thither, gave him the free
use of all their ports, and furnished him with all things which
[he] [1] stood in need of. The Queen, and the prince of Portugal
then living, who was a young man of great hope and courage,
made great professions of friendship to the King, and of a
desire to assist him by all the ways and means which could be
proposed to them. But when their river was blocked up, their
ships taken, and the whole kingdom upon the matter blocked
up and besieged by Popham, of which they knew the Spaniard
would quickly make use, the Council were astonished, and
knew not what to do: their free trade with England was not
only their profit but their reputation; and if they should be
deprived of that, they should not be able to preserve it any
where else, which would put the whole kingdom into a flame;
and therefore they besought the King that prince Rupert might
be desired to leave the river; and to carry his fleet from thence;
which was not possible for him to do without fighting with the
enemy, to whom he was much inferior in strength of shipping
and number of men by the loss he had sustained at Cartagena.

115. The prince of Portugal had so great indignation at this
overture made by the Council, that he declared he would have
all the ships in the port made ready, and would himself go on
board, and join with prince Rupert, and so fight the English
and drive them from thence; and he manifested a great desire
to do so; but the Council prevailed with the Queen not to
consent to that. So that in the end, after many months' stay
there, and the fleet being fully supplied with whatsoever it
stood in need of, prince Rupert found it necessary, upon the
assurance the Portuguese gave him that Popham should not
follow him till after two tides, to set sail and leave that kingdom; which he did with so full a gale, that Popham, after so Oct. 22.
long a stay, found it to no purpose to follow him [2], but took

---

[1] ['they,' MS.]

[2] [A different account, which says that the parliamentary fleet had first

1650 full vengeance upon Portugal for rescuing his prey from him, until they were compelled, after great sufferings, to purchase their peace from Cromwell upon very hard conditions.

1649   116. It seemed no good sign to the ambassadors that prince Rupert had left Ireland, where there were so many good ports, and where the fleet had been so necessary for the carrying on his majesty's service. But in a short time after, they received advertisement that the King had laid aside his purpose of going thither, and had taken new resolutions. Before the marquis of

Sept. 3. Ormonde could draw his army together, Cromwell had besieged Tredagh: and though the garrison was so strong in point of number, and that number of so choice men, that they could wish for nothing more than that the enemy would attempt to

Sept. 9. take them by storm, the very next day after he came before the town he gave a general assault, and was beaten off with considerable loss. But after a day more he assaulted it again in

Sept. 11. two places with so much courage that he entered in both; and though the governor and some of the chief officers retired in disorder into a fort where they hoped to have made conditions, a panic fear so possessed the soldiers that they threw down their arms upon a general offer of quarter : so that the enemy entered the work without resistance, and put every man, governor, officer, and soldier, to the sword; and the whole army being entered the town, they executed all manner of cruelty, and put every man that related to the garrison, and all the citizens who were Irish, man, woman, and child, to the sword; and there being three or four officers of name, and of good families, who had found some way, by the humanity of some soldiers of the enemy, to conceal them[selves] for four or five days, being afterwards discovered, [they] were butchered in cold blood.

117. This insupportable loss took away all hopes from the marquis of Ormonde of drawing an army strong enough, and resolute enough, together, to meet Cromwell in the field during

withdrawn from the coast, is given by Dr. Rich. Hart, in a letter to Hyde, dated from Messina, 24 Dec., 1650, which is among the Clarendon MSS. See *Calend. Clar. S. P.* ii. 92.]

the summer, which was drawing to an end; and obliged him to **1649**
retire into those quarters where, in respect of the necessary
passes, he might be secure, and from whence he might attempt
upon the enemy. Cromwell in the mean time took no rest,
but, having made himself terrible by that excess of rigour and
cruelty, marched into Munster against the lord Inchiquin and
that body of English which was under his command. And here
he defied fortune again; and marched so far out of the places
devoted to him, and from whence he had any reasonable hope
to receive supplies, that he must necessarily have been starved,
and could not have retired, all the bridges over which he had
passed being broken down, if the city of Cork, which he could
not have forced, had not been by the garrison basely delivered **Oct. 16[1].**
up to him; those officers who had been most obliged to the
lord Inchiquin, and in whom he had most confidence, unworthily betraying him, and every day forsaking him: so that
by the example of Cork, and by the terror of Tredagh, the
whole province of Munster in a very short time fell into
his hands, except some few towns and sea-ports, which, being
garrisoned by the Irish, would neither, officers nor soldiers,
receive or obey any orders which were sent from the lord of
Ormonde. The King receiving information of this at Jarsy
gave over the thought very reasonably of adventuring himself
into Ireland, and dismissed the two ships which by the direction of the prince of Aurange had attended so long at St. Malo's
to have wafted him thither.

118. Though duke Hambleton and the earl of Latherdale,
and the other Scots' lords who remained in Holland when the
King came into France, durst not return into their own country,
yet they held intelligence with their party there. And though
the marquis of Arguyle had the sole power, yet he could not
extinguish the impatient desire of the whole nation to have
their King come to them, and every day produced instances
enough which informed him [2] how the affections of the people

---

[1] [*Report on Carte MSS. to the Master of the Rolls*, 1871, p. 143.]
[2] [The words 'and every day ... informed him' are substituted for the
following lines :—'and the too great precipitation which the marquis of

1649 were generally disposed, and upon how slippery ground himself stood if he were not supported by the King; and that the
government he was then possessed of could not be lasting,
except he had another force to defend him than that of his own
nation. And he durst not receive any from Cromwell, who
would willingly have assisted him, for fear of being entirely
deserted by all his friends, who had been still firm to him.
Hereupon he thought of drawing the King into Scotland, and
keeping the Hambletonian faction from entering with him by
the sentence that was already against them, and to oblige the
King to submit to the Covenant and all those other obligations
which were at that time established; and if his majesty would
put himself into his hands upon those conditions, he would be
sure to keep the power in himself, under the King's name, and
might reasonably hope that Cromwell, who made no pretence
to Scotland, might be well enough pleased that his majesty
might remain there under his government, and assurance that
he should not give England nor Ireland any disturbance.

119. And upon this presumption he wished the Council of
Scotland, and that committee of the Parliament in whom the
authority was vested, to send again to the King, (who they
thought by this time might be weary of Jarsy,) to invite him
to come to them upon the old conditions; and by gratifying
them in this particular, which all the people did so passionately
desire, he renewed all the solemn obligations they had been
before bound in, never to admit the King to come amongst
them but upon his first submitting to and performing all those
conditions. And all things being thus settled and agreed, they
Dec. sent a gentleman [1] with letters into Jarsy to invite his majesty
again to come into his kingdom of Scotland, not without a rude
insinuation that it was the last invitation he would receive.

Mountrose had used in making a desperate descent into the Highlands, with
about one hundred and twenty officers, presuming he should have lain concealed till he could have drawn a strength to him, and his being betrayed,
and so surprised the next day after he was landed, and the barbarous
murdering in that solemn manner, how fatal soever it was to him, had
enough informed Arguyle—']

[1] [George Wynram, or Windram, of Liberton.]

The lords who are mentioned before to be then in Holland **1649** were glad of this advance; and believed that if the King were there they should easily find the way home again. And therefore they prevailed with the prince of Aurange to write very earnestly to the King, and to recommend it to the Queen; and themselves made great instance to the Queen, with whom they had much credit, that the King would not lose this opportunity to improve his condition. Nobody presumed to advise him to submit to all that was proposed; and yet it was evident that if he did not submit to all he could have the benefit of none; but that he should make such an answer as might engage the Scots into a treaty, for the King's better information and satisfaction in some particulars: which being done, he should imply a purpose to transport his person thither.

120. The spring was now coming on, and though Jarsy was **1650** a convenient place to retire to in order to consider what was next to be done, yet it was not a place to reside in, nor would be longer safe than whilst the Parliament had so much else to do that it could not spare wherewithal to reduce it. The design for Ireland was at an end, and the despair of being welcome in any other place compelled the King to think better of Scotland; and so, according to the advice he had received, **Jan. 11.** he returned an answer to the message he had received, ' That there were many particulars contained in the propositions which he did not understand, and which it was necessary for him to be advised in; and in order thereunto, and that he might be well informed and instructed in what so nearly concerned him, here solved by such a time, (which was set down,) to find himself in Holland; where he desired to meet such persons as his kingdom of Scotland would send to him, and to confer and treat and agree with those upon all things which might give his subjects of that kingdom satisfaction; which his majesty did very much desire to do.'

121[1]. The Queen had so good an opinion of many of the Scottish lords, and so ill a one of many of the English who

---

[1] [This section, as far as the words ' where both their majesties met,' is from the *Hist.*, p. 8.]

1650 were about the King, in truth she had so entire a despair of all other ways, that she was very desirous that the overtures from Scotland should be hearkened unto and embraced: besides that she found that her authority was not so great with the King as she expected, she saw no possibility that they might be together : she knew well that France, that grew every day into a closer correspondence with Cromwell, would not endure that the King should make his residence in any part of that kingdom, and so shortened the assignations which they had made for her own support that she was at no ease, and began to think of dissolving her own family, and of her own retiring into a monastery; which from that time she practised by degrees. And no doubt that consideration which made most impression upon the King, as it had done upon his father, and terrified him most from complying with the Scots' demands, which was the alteration it would make in religion and the government of the Church, seemed not to her of moment enough to reject the other conveniences; nor did she prefer the glory of the Church of England before the sordidness of the Kirk of Scotland, but thought it the best expedient to advance her own religion that the latter should triumph over the former. And therefore she writ earnestly to the King her son that he would entertain this motion from Scotland, as his only refuge; and that he would invite commissioners to meet him in Holland, in such a place as the prince of Aurange should advise; and desired that in his passage thither he would appoint some place where her majesty would meet him, that they might spend some days together in consultation upon what might concern them jointly. In all which his majesty complying, the city of

Feb. 21. Beauv[a]ise in Picardy was appointed for the interview; where
O. S.[1]
both their majesties met, and conversed together three or four
March 6. days; and then the Queen returned to Paris, and the King
O. S.[1]
passed through Flanders to Breda; which the prince of Aurange thought to be the fittest place for the treaty, the States having no mind that the King should come any more to the Hague.

[1] [Intelligence from John Trethewy, among the Clarendon MSS. *Calend. Clar. S. P.* ii. 45.]

122. The Scots' commissioners came to Breda with the very 1650 same propositions which had been formerly sent, and without Mar. 15,19. the least mitigation, and as positive an exception to persons: O. S.[1] so that if the King should incline to go thither, he must go without any one chaplain of his own : there were ministers sent to attend and to instruct him. He must not carry with him any one councillor, nor any person who had ever served his father in the war against the Parliament. And, that nobody might have cause to complain if they did go thither that they were worse treated than they had reason to expect, the King himself and all who should attend upon him were first to sign the Covenant before they should be admitted to enter into the kingdom. Very fair warning indeed ; nor could any man justly except against any thing that was afterwards done to him.

123. Here was no great argument for consultation : no man had so ill an understanding as not to discern the violence that was offered to honour, justice, and conscience ; yet whoever objected against what was proposed, upon either of those considerations, was looked upon as a party, because he himself could not be suffered to attend the King. It was thought to be of great weight, that they who dissuaded the King from going into Scotland upon those rude and barbarous terms could not propose any thing else for him to do, nor any place where he might securely repose himself with any hope of subsistence : a very sad state for a prince to be reduced to, and [which] made it manifest enough that the kings of the earth are not such a body as is sensible of the indignity and outrage that is offered to any limb of it. The Scotch lords were thought to be the most competent counsellors, since they by going were to be exposed to great rigour, and to undergo the severest part of all censures. They could not sit in the Parliament nor in the Council, and knew well that they should not be suffered to be about the person of the King : yet all these resolved to wait upon him, and persuaded him to believe that his majesty's presence would dissipate those clouds, and that a little time would produce many alterations which could not be presently

[1] [Carte's *Original Letters,* i. 339, 373.]

1650 effected. For his majesty's signing the Covenant, he should tell the commissioners that he would defer it till he came thither, that he might think better of it; and that if then the Kirk should press it upon him, he would give them satisfaction. And they were confident that after he should be there, he should be no more importuned in it, but that even the churchmen, themselves would contend to make themselves gracious to him.

124. This kind of argumentation wrought much with the prince of Aurange, but more with the duke of Buckingham, who had waited upon the King from the time of his adventure with the earl of Holland, (and against whose person there was no exception,) and [with] Wilmott and Wentworth, (who resolved to go with his majesty, and would submit to any conditions which could be required of them); and with others about the King who could not digest[1] the Covenant, the hope that it would not be required from them, and the many promises those Scotch lords made to them who were like to grow into authority again when they should be once in their native air and upon their own soil, prevailed with them to use all their credit with the King to embark himself, and try how propitious fortune would be to him in Scotland. And in the end, a faint hope in that, and a strong despair of any other, expedient, prevailed so far with his majesty, that he resolved, upon what terms soever, to embark himself in Holland upon a fleet which the prince of Aurange provided for him; and so with all the Scotch, and very few English servants, June 1. he set sail for Scotland.

125[2]. There were two very strong arguments which made deep impression [on][3] those lords who very vehemently dissuaded, and even protested against, his majesty's going for Scotland, and which, as it often falls out in matters of the highest importance, they could not make use of to convert others, especially in the place and company in which they were to urge them. The first, that the expedition of duke Hambleton the year before, with an army as numerous, and much

---

[1] ['disgest,' MS.]
[2] [This section is from the *Hist.*, pp. 8, 9.]
[3] ['in,' MS.]

better furnished and provided than Scotland could in many **1650**
years be again enabled to send out, made it manifest enough
how little that nation, how united soever, could prevail against
the forces of England : the other, that the whole and absolute
power of Scotland being at that time confessedly vested in the
marquis of Arguyle, it might reasonably be feared and expected
that the King should no sooner arrive there, and the least
appearance be discovered of such revolutions or alterations in
the affections of the people, upon which the Hambletonian
faction wholly and solely depended, but Arguyle would immediately deliver up the person of the King into the hands of
Cromwell, and, with the assistance he would willingly give,
make that kingdom tributary or subservient to him, whilst the
King remained his prisoner, and Arguyle continued his vice-
gerent in Scotland. And no doubt these objections had too
much weight in them not to be thought worthy of apprehension
by many men who were not blinded with passion or amazed
with despair : and though they were not able to give any other
counsel what course the King might steer with reasonable
hope and security, they might yet warrantably dissuade his
exposing himself to so many visible dangers as that voyage was
subject to both at sea and land, and might prudently believe,
that the enjoying the empty title of king, in what obscurity
soever, in any part of the world, was to be preferred before the
empty name of king in any of his own dominions ; which was
the best that could reasonably be expected from the conditions
which were imposed upon him, and to which he was compelled
to submit.

126. When the ambassadors who were in Spain expected
every day to hear of his majesty's being arrived in Ireland,
and had thereupon importuned for a despatch, the King gave
them notice of this his resolution, and directed them to remain
where they were till he could better judge of his own fortune.
They were extremely troubled, both of them having always had
a strong aversion that the King should ever venture himself in
the hands of that nation which had treated his father so per-
fidiously. And they were now necessitated to stay there where

1650 they had received so little encouragement, and had no reason
to expect more ; yet they knew not whither else to go. They
therefore resolved to set the best face they could upon it,
and desired an audience from the King: in which they told his
Catholic majesty that they had received letters from the King
their master, who commanded them to inform his majesty, who
he knew well would be glad to hear of any good fortune that
befell him, that it had now pleased God to work so far upon
the hearts and affections of his subjects of Scotland, that they
had given over all those factions and animosities which had
heretofore divided them, and made them rather instruments of
mischieve than benefit to his blessed father and to himself :
that they were now sensible of all those miscarriages, and had
sent unanimously to entreat his majesty to come into that
kingdom, and to take them all into his protection : with which
his majesty was so well satisfied, that he had laid aside the
thought of transporting himself into Ireland, which he had
intended to do, and was gone into Scotland ; where the kingdom was entirely at his devotion, and from whence he could
visit England or Ireland, as he found it most convenient: and
that he had reason to believe that his friends in either of the
kingdoms would quickly appear in arms, when they were sure
to be so powerfully assisted and seconded.   And they said they
would from time to time inform his majesty of the good success
that should fall out.   The King professed to be very glad of
this good news ; and that they should assure the King their
master that he would be always ready to make all the demonstration of a brotherly affection that the ill condition of his own
affairs would permit ; and that if it pleased God to give a
peace to the two Crowns, the world should see how forward he
would be to revenge the wrong and indignity the King of Great
Britain had undergone.

127. Though the ambassadors themselves were afflicted with
the news of his majesty's being gone for Scotland, upon the too
much knowledge they had of the treachery of that people, yet
they found he was much the more esteemed in this Court by it.
He was before looked upon as being dispossessed and dis-

inherited of all his dominions, and as if he had no more subjects **1650** than those few who were banished with him, and that there was an entire defection in all the rest. But now, that he was possessed of one whole kingdom, in which no man appeared in arms against him, a kingdom which had been famous for many warlike actions, and which always bred very warlike people which had borne good parts in all the wars of Europe in this age, and had been more celebrated in them than the English had been, was a happy advance, and administered reasonable hope that he might be established in the other two kingdoms, in one of which he was thought to have a good, and was known to have a numerous, army on foot at that very time. So that the ambassadors were much better looked upon than they had been; and when they made any complaints of injuries done to any of the English merchants who lived in the ports of Spain, as they had sometimes occasion to do, upon taxes and impositions laid upon them, contrary to the treaties which had been made, and which they said were still in force, they were heard with respect, and the merchants were relieved, and many favours were done to particular persons upon their desires and interposition : so that they were not so much out of countenance as they had been, and all men spake with more freedom and detestation against the rebellion in England, and the barbarity thereof, than they had used to do.

128 [1]. There fell out at this time, and before the King left **1649** Holland, an accident of such a prodigious nature, that, if Providence had not for the reproach of Scotland determined that the King should once more make experiment of the courage and fidelity of that nation, could not but have diverted his majesty from that northern expedition; which, how unsecure soever it appeared to be for the King, was predestinated for a greater chastisement and mortification to that people, as it shortly after proved to be. When the King had left Holland the summer before, and intended only to make France his way to Ireland, he had given his commission to the marquis of Mountrose to

---

[1] [The text from hence to the end of book xii is from the *Hist.*, pp. 9-16.]

1649   gather such a force together as by the help of the northern princes
he might be enabled to do.   Upon which the marquis, who was
naturally full of great thoughts and confident of success, sent
several officers, who had served in Germany and promised very
much, to draw such troops together as they should be enabled
to do, and himself with a great train of officers and servants
went for Hamborough; which he appointed for the rendezvous
for all his troops, and from whence he could in the mean time
visit those Courts of the neighbour princes and states as he
should be encouraged to, and keep such intelligence with his
friends in Scotland as should provide for his reception.

129. Besides the hopes and encouragement which he had
received from the ambassador Wolfelte to expect good supplies
in Denmark, there were many officers of good name and
account in Sweden of the Scots' nation, who were grown rich,
and lived in plenty in that kingdom.   And with the principal
of them the marquis had held correspondence; who undertook,
as well for others as for themselves, that if the marquis engaged himself in the King's service in the kingdom of Scotland,
they would give him notable assistance in money, arms, and
men.   In a word, he sent or went in person to both those
kingdoms, where he found the performance very disproportion-
able to their promises.   Queen Christina had received an ambassador[1] from England with wonderful civility and grace, and
expressed a great esteem of the person of Cromwell, as a man
of glorious achievements; and before she resigned that crown,
1654. which she shortly after did, she engaged it in a fast alliance
June 16. with the new Commonwealth, and disposed her successor to
look upon it as a necessary support to his crown.   In Denmark
the marquis found good wishes enough, a hearty detestation of
all the villainies which had been acted in England, and as
hearty wishes for the advancement and prosperity of the King's
affairs; but the kingdom itself was very poor, and full of discontents, the King not so much esteemed, because not so much
feared, as his father had been, and had been compelled to make
many unreasonable concessions to Holland, that he might have

[1] [Col. Christ. Potley. See Thurloe's *S. P.* i. 130.]

assistance from them to protect him from those assaults and **1649** invasions which were threatened from Sweden. So that the marquis was obliged to return to Hamborough with very small supplies from either or both those kingdoms: and there he received no better account from those officers who had been sent into Germany. His design had always been to land in the Highlands of Scotland before the winter season should be over, both for the safety of his embarkation, and that he might have time to draw those people together who he knew would be willing to repair to him, before it should be known at Edenborough that he was landed in the kingdom. He had by frequent messages kept a constant correspondence with those principal heads of the clans who were most powerful in the Highlands, and were of known or unsuspected affection to the King, and advertised them of all his motions and designs, and by them advertised those of the Lowlands of all his resolutions; who had promised, upon the first notice of his arrival, to resort with all their friends and followers to him.

130. Whether these men did really believe that their own strength would be sufficient to subdue their enemies, who were grown generally odious, [or [1]] thought the bringing over troops of foreigners would lessen the numbers and affections of the natives, they did write very earnestly to the marquis, to hasten his coming over with officers, arms, and ammunition, for which he should find hands enough; and gave him notice that the Committee of Estates at Edenborough had sent again to the King to come over to them, and that the people were so impatient for his presence that Arguyle was compelled to consent to the invitation. It is very probable that this made the greatest impression upon him. He knew very well how few persons there were about the King who were like to continue firm in those principles which could only confirm the King in his former resolutions, against the persuasions and importunities of many others, who knew well how to present the desperateness of his condition any other way than by repairing into Scotland upon any conditions. He knew that

[1] ['and,' MS.]

1649 of the two factions there, which were not like to be reconciled, they were both equally his implacable enemies; so that which soever prevailed he should be still in the same state, the whole Kirk, of what temper soever, being alike malicious to him; and hearing likewise of the successive misfortunes in Ireland, he concluded the King would not trust himself there. Therefore, upon the whole, and concluding that all his hopes from Germany and those northern princes would not increase the strength he had already, he caused, in the depth of the winter, those soldiers he had drawn together, which did not amount to above five hundred, to be embarked, and sent officers with them who knew the country, with directions that they should land in such a place in the Highlands, and remain there, as they might well do, till he came to them, or sent them orders. And then in another vessel, manned by people well known to him, and commanded by a captain very faithful to the King, **1650** and who was well acquainted with all that coast, he embarked Jan. 10[1]. himself, and near one hundred officers, and landed in another creek[2], not far from the other place whither his soldiers were directed. And both the one and the other party were set safely on shore in the places they designed; from whence the marquis himself, with some servants and officers, repaired presently to the house of a gentleman of quality, with whom he had corresponded, and who expected him, by whom he was well received, and thought himself to be in security till he might put his affairs in some method: and therefore ordered his other small troops to contain themselves in those uncouth quarters in which they were, and where they were not like to be disturbed by the visitation of any enemy.

131. After he had stayed there a short time, being in March about the end of the year 1649[3], [O. S.] he quickly possessed himself of an old castle; which, in respect of the situation, in a country so impossible for an army to march in, he thought

---

[1] [Intelligence from J. Trethewy, *Cal. Cl. S. P.* ii. 45.]

[2] [In Orkney.]

[3] [In a letter written on March 26, from Kirkwall, to lord Seaforth, he said he was about to leave Orkney for the mainland.]

strong enough for his purpose : and thither he brought the 1650 arms and ammunition and troops which he had brought with him. And then he published his Declaration; That he came with the King's commission, to assist those of his good subjects, and to preserve them from oppression : that he did not intend to give any interruption to the treaty that he heard was entered into with his majesty, but, on the contrary, hoped that his being in the head of an army, how small soever, that was faithful to him, [the King,] might advance the same : however, he had given sufficient proof in his former actions, that if any agreement were made with the King, upon the first order from his majesty he should lay down his arms, and dispose himself according to his majesty's good pleasure. These declarations he sent to his friends to be scattered by them, and dispersed amongst the people, as they could be able. And he writ likewise to those of the nobility, and the heads of the several clans, to draw such forces together as they thought necessary to join with him; and he received answers from many of them, by which they desired him to advance more into the land, (for he was yet in the remotest parts of Catness,) and assured him that they would meet him with good numbers : and they did prepare so to do, some really, and others with a purpose to betray him.

132. And in this state stood that affair in the end of the year 1649 : but because the unfortunate tragedy of that noble person succeeded so soon after, without the intervention of any notable circumstances to interrupt it, we will rather continue the relation of it in this place, than defer it to be resumed in the proper season; which quickly ensued in the beginning of the next year. The marquis of Arguyle was vigilant enough to observe the motion of an enemy that was so formidable to him, and had present information of his arrival in the Highlands, and of the small forces which he had brought with him. The Parliament was then sitting at Edenborough, their messenger being returned to them from Jarsy, with an account that the King would treat with their commissioners at Breda; for whom they were preparing their instructions.

133. The alarum of Mountrose's being landed startled them

1650 all, and gave them leisure to think of nothing else than of
sending forces to hinder the recourse of others to join with
him. They immediately sent colonel Straghan, a diligent and
active officer, with a choice party of the best horse they had,
to make all possible haste towards him, and to prevent the
insurrection which they feared would be in several parts of the
Highlands; and within few days after David Lashly followed
with a stronger party of horse and foot. The encouragement
the marquis of Mountrose received from his friends, and the
unpleasantness of the quarters in which he was, prevailed with
him to march with his few troops more into the land; and the
Highlanders flocking to him from all quarters, though ill armed
and worse disciplined, made him undervalue any enemy who he
thought was yet like to encounter [him.] Straghan made such
haste, that the earl of Southerland, who at least pretended to
have gathered together a body of fifteen hundred men to meet
Mountrose, chose rather to join with him; and others did the
like who had made the same promises, or stayed at home to
expect the event of the first encounter. The marquis was without any body of horse to discover the motion of any enemy, but
depended upon all necessary intelligence from the affection of
the people, which he believed to be the same it was when he
left them. But they were much degenerated; the tyranny of
Arguyle, and his having caused very many to be barbarously
murdered, without any form of law or justice, who had been in
arms with Mountrose, notwithstanding all Acts of pardon and
indemnity, had so broken all their hearts, that they were ready
to do all offices which might gratify and oblige him.

April 27.   134. And so Straghan was within a small distance of him
before he heard of his approach; and those Highlanders who
had seemed to come with much zeal to him, whether terrified
or corrupted, left him on a sudden, or threw down their arms;
so that he had none left but a company of good officers, and
five or six hundred foreigners, Dutch and Germans, who had
been acquainted with their officers. With these, he betook
himself to a place of some advantage by the inequality of the
ground, and the bushes and small shrubs which filled it, and

there they made a defence for some time with notable courage ; **1650**
but the enemy being so much superior in number, the common
soldiers, being all foreigners, and after about a hundred of them
were killed upon the place, threw down their arms. And the
marquis, seeing all lost, found means to throw away his ribbon
and George, (for he was a knight of the Garter,) and to change
his clothes with a fellow of the country, and so, after having
gone on foot two or three miles, he got into a house of a gentleman, where he remained concealed about two days. Most of
the other officers were likewise shortly after taken prisoners,
all the country desiring to merit from Arguyle by betraying
all those into his hands who they believed to be his enemies.
And so, whether by the owner of the house or any other way,
the marquis himself became their prisoner. The strangers who
were taken prisoners were set at liberty to transport themselves
into their own country; and the castle, in which there was a
little garrison, presently rendered itself; so that there was no
more fear of an enemy in those parts.

135. The marquis of Mountrose and the rest of the prisoners
[were [1]] the next day, or soon after, delivered to David Lashly, April 29.
who was come up with his forces, and had now nothing left to
do but to carry him in triumph to Edenborough, whither notice
was quickly sent of their great victory, and was received there
with wonderful joy and acclamation. David Lashly treated
him with great insolence, and for some days carried him in the
same clothes and habit in which he was taken, but at last
permitted him to buy better clothes. His behaviour was, in
the whole time, such as became a great man ; his countenance
serene and cheerful, as one that was superior to all those reproaches which they had prepared the people to pour out upon
him in all the places through which he was to pass.

136. When he came to one of the gates of Edenborough he May 18.
was met by some of the magistrates of Edenborough, to whom
he was delivered, and by them presently put into a new cart
purposely made, in which there was a high chair or bench upon
which he sat, that the people might have a full view of him,

[1] ['was,' MS.]

1650 being bound with a cord drawn over his breast and shoulders,
and so through holes made in the cart. When he was in this
posture, the hangman took off his hat, and rode himself before
the cart in his livery and with his bonnet on; the other officers
who were taken prisoners with him walking two and two before the cart; the streets and windows being full of people to
behold the triumph over a person whose name had made them
tremble two or three years before, and into whose hands the
1645 magistrates of that place had upon their knees delivered the
Aug. 23. keys of that city. In this manner he was carried to the
common gaol, where he was received and treated as the most
May 20. common malefactor. Within two days after, he was brought
before the Parliament, where the earl of Lowden, the Chancellor, made a very bitter and virulent declamation against
him : told him he had broken all the Covenants by which that
whole nation stood obliged, and had impiously rebelled against
God, the King, and the kingdom; that he had committed many
horrible murders, treasons, and impieties, for all which he was
now brought to suffer condign punishment; with all those insolent reproaches upon his person and his actions which the
liberty of that place gave him leave to use.

137. Permission was then given to him to speak; and without the least trouble in his countenance, or disorder, upon all
the indignities he had suffered, he told them, since the King
had owned them so far as to treat with them, he had appeared
before them with reverence, and bareheaded, which otherwise
he would not have done : that he had done nothing of which
he was ashamed, or had cause to repent; that the first Covenant he had taken, and complied with it, and with them who
took it, as long as the ends for which it was ordained were
observed; but when he discovered, which was now evident to
all the world, that private and particular men designed to
satisfy their own ambition and interest, instead of considering
the public benefit, and that under the pretence of reforming
some errors in religion they resolved to abridge and take away
the King's just power and lawful authority, he had withdrawn
himself from that engagement : that for the League and Cove-

nant, he had never taken it, and therefore could not break it; 1650 and it was now too apparent to the whole Christian world what monstrous mischieves it had produced: that when, under colour of it, an army from Scotland had invaded England in assistance of the rebellion that was then against their lawful King, he had, by his majesty's command, received a commission from him to raise forces in Scotland, that he might thereby divert them from the other odious prosecution: that he had executed that commission with the obedience and duty that he owed to the King, and in all the circumstances of it had proceeded like a gentleman, and had never suffered any blood to be shed but in the heat of the battle; and that he saw many persons there whose lives he had saved: when the King commanded him, he laid down his arms, and withdrew out of the kingdom, which they could not have compelled him to have done. He said he was now again entered into the kingdom by his majesty's command and with his authority; and what success soever it might have pleased God to have given him, he would always have obeyed any command he should have received from him. He advised them to consider well of the consequence before they proceeded against him, and that all his actions might be examined and judged by the laws of the land, or those of nations.

138. As soon as he had ended his discourse he was ordered to withdraw, and after a short space was again brought in, and told by the Chancellor that he was on the morrow, being the one and twentieth of May 1650, to be carried to Edenborough cross, and there to be hanged upon a gallows thirty foot high, for the space of three hours, and then to be taken down, and his head to be cut off upon a scaffold, and hanged on Edenborough tollbooth, and his legs and arms to be hanged up in other public towns of the kingdom, and his body to be buried at the place where he was to be executed, except the Kirk should take off his excommunication, and then his body might be buried in the common place of burial. He desired that he might say somewhat to them, but was not suffered, and so was carried back to the prison.

139. That he might not enjoy any ease or quiet during the

1650 short remainder of his life, their ministers came presently to
insult over him with all the reproaches imaginable, pronounced
his damnation, and assured him that the judgment he was the
next day to undergo was but an easy prologue to that which
he was to undergo afterward. And after many such barbarities, they offered to intercede for him to the Kirk upon his
repentance, and to pray with him; but he too well understood
the form of their common prayers in those cases to be only the
most virulent and insolent imprecations against the persons of
those they prayed against, (' Lord, vouchsafe yet to touch the
obdurate heart of this proud incorrigible sinner, this wicked,
perjured, traitorous, and profane person, who refuses to hearken
to the voice of thy Kirk,' and the like charitable expressions,)
and therefore he desired them to spare their pains, and to leave
him to his own devotions. He told them that they were a
miserable, deluded, and deluding people; and would shortly
bring that poor nation under the most insupportable servitude
ever people had submitted to. He told them he was prouder
to have his head set upon the place it was appointed to be,
than he could have been to have had his picture hung in the
King's bedchamber: that he was so far from being troubled
that his four limbs were to be hanged in four cities of the
kingdom, that he heartily wished that he had flesh enough to
be sent to every city in Christendom, as a testimony of the
cause for which he suffered.

May 21.   140. The next day they executed every part and circumstance
of that barbarous sentence with all the inhumanity imaginable;
and he bore it with all the courage and magnanimity, and
the greatest piety, that a good Christian could manifest. He
magnified the virtue, courage, and religion of the last King,
exceedingly commended the justice and goodness and understanding of the present King, and prayed that they might not
betray him as they had done his father. When he had ended
all he meant to say, and was expecting to expire, they had yet
one scene more to act of their tyranny. The hangman brought
the book that had been published of his truly heroic actions
whilst he had commanded in that kingdom, which book was

tied in a small cord that was put about his neck. The marquis **1650** smiled at this new instance of their malice, and thanked them for it; and said he was pleased that it should be there, and was prouder of wearing it than ever he had been of the Garter; and so renewing some devout ejaculations, he patiently endured the last act of the executioner.

141. Soon after, the officers who had been taken with him, sir William Hurry, sir Francis Hay, and many others of as good families as any in the kingdom, were executed, to the number of thirty or forty, in several quarters of the kingdom[1]; many of them being suffered to be beheaded. There was one whom they thought fit to save, one colonel Whitford; who, when he was brought to die, said, he knew the reason why he was put to death, which was only because he had killed Dorislaus at the Hague, who was one of those who had murdered the last King. One of the magistrates, who were present to see the execution, caused it to be suspended, till he presently informed the council what the man had said; and they thought fit to avoid the reproach, and so preserved the gentleman[2], who was not before known to have had a hand in that action.

142. Thus died the gallant marquis of Mountrose, after he had given as great a testimony of loyalty and courage as a subject can do, and performed as wonderful actions in several battles, upon as great inequality of numbers and as great disadvantages in respect of arms and other preparations for war, as hath been performed in this age. He was a gentleman of a very ancient extraction, many of whose ancestors had exercised the highest charges under the King in that kingdom, and had been allied to the Crown itself. He was of very good parts, which were improved by a good education: he had always a great emulation, or rather a great contempt, of the marquis of

---

[1] [Urry was executed at Edinburgh, with capt. John Spottiswood, on May 29, sir William Hay, laird of Dalgetty, and col. Sibbald, also at Edinburgh on June 7, and capt. Alex. Charteris at Edinburgh on June 22 (Balfour's *Annals of Scotland*, iv. 32, 37, 44, 56). The rest of the prisoners are said in Wishart's Life of Montrose to have been released.]

[2] [A pass to leave the country was granted to him on June 25. Balfour's *Annals*, iv. 60.]

1650 Arguyle, (as he was too apt to contemn those he did not love,)
who wanted nothing but honesty and courage to be a very
extraordinary man, having all other good talents in a great
degree. He was in his nature fearless of danger, and never
declined any enterprise for the difficulty of going through with
it, but exceedingly affected those which seemed desperate to
other men and did believe somewhat to be in him[self] which
other men were not acquainted with, which made him live
more easily towards those who were, or were willing to be,
inferior to him, and towards whom he exercised wonderful
civility and generosity, than with his superiors or equals. He
was naturally jealous, and suspected those who did not concur
with him in the way not to mean so well as he. He was not
without vanity, but his virtues were much superior, and he
well deserved to have his memory preserved and celebrated
amongst the most illustrious persons of the age in which he
lived.

143. The King received an account and information of all
these particulars before he embarked from Holland, without
any other apology for the affront and indignity to himself than
that they assured him that the proceeding against the late
marquis of Mountrose had been for his service. They who
were most displeased with Arguyle and his faction were not
sorry for this inhuman and monstrous prosecution; which at
the same time must render him the more odious, and had rid
them of an enemy that they thought would have been more
dangerous to them; and they persuaded the King, who was
enough afflicted with the news and all the circumstances of it,
that he might sooner take revenge upon that people by a
temporary complying with them and going to them, than by
staying away and absenting himself, which would invest them
in an absolute dominion in that kingdom, and give them power
to corrupt or destroy all those who yet remained faithful to
him, and were ready to spend their lives in his service: and so
he pursued his former resolution and embarked for Scotland.

1649   144. In Ireland, after the massacre of that body of English
in Tredagh, and the treacherous giving up the towns in

Munster by the officers of the lord Inchiquin [1], there broke out **1649** so implacable a jealousy against all the English amongst the Irish, that no orders of the marquis of Ormonde found any obedience, nor could he draw any army together. At the making of the peace he had consented that the Confederate Catholics should name a number of commissioners, by whose orders and ministry all levies of men and all collections of money were to be made, according to the directions of the Lord Lieutenant. And such persons were named, in whose affections for the most part the Lieutenant was well satisfied, and the rest were such as were not like to be able to give any inter- ruption. A certain number of these were appointed to be always in the army, and near the person of the Lord Lieu- tenant, and the rest in their several stations, where they were most like to advance the service. Many of these commissioners were of the Catholic nobility, persons of honour, and very sensible of the weakness, wilfulness, and wickedness of that rebellion, and did manifest all possible zeal and affection to the King's service, engaging their persons in all enterprises of danger, and using all possible industry to raise men and money whereby the Lord Lieutenant might be enabled to carry on the war in the spring. But many of the other, after those mis- fortunes had fallen out which are mentioned before, either totally desponded, and rather thought of providing for them- selves than for the preservation of the public, or fomented the jealousies which were amongst the Irish, and incensed them against those English who were still with the Lord Lieutenant; so that his orders were not obeyed at all, or not in time, which was as bad; and the clergy and friars publicly incensed the people against the articles of the peace, and desired to have an army raised apart under a general of their own.

145. The Lord Lieutenant now discovered the reason why Owen O'Neale had refused to consent to the peace which the Confederate Catholics had made with the King, and kept his army in Ulster from submitting thereunto, and pretended to desire to treat apart with the Lord Lieutenant for himself;

[1] [' in Munster,' repeated in the MS.]

1649 which was then thought to proceed from the jealousy that was between him and Preston, and the animosity between those old Irish of Ulster and the other of the other provinces. But the truth was, from the time of the marquis of Ormonde's transporting himself out of France, and that the correspondence was discovered to be between him and the lord Inchiquin, and the treaty begun with the Confederate Catholics, the close committee at Westminster sent secret instructions to general Munke, who commanded their forces in Ireland, that he should endeavour to treat with Owen O'Neale, and so divide him from the rest of the Irish; which Munke found opportunity to do: and it was no sooner proposed than hearkened unto by O'Neale, who presently sent a trusty messenger with such propositions to Munke as he desired to have granted to him. He offered, with his army, which should always consist of such a number of horse and foot and artillery as should be agreed between them, to serve the Parliament, and not to separate from their interest; and proposed that he, and all his party that should adhere to him, should enjoy the exercise of their religion without any prejudice or disadvantage: that himself might be restored to those lands which his ancestors had been possessed of in Tyrone, Londonderry, or any other parts of Ireland, and that all those who had or would adhere to him should be likewise restored to their estates; and that an Act of oblivion might be granted. Munke received these propositions; and after he had perused them, he sent him word that there were some particulars which, he doubted, would shock and offend the Parliament, and therefore [desired] they might be altered; and proposed the alterations he advised; which principally concerned the public exercise of their religion, which he so qualified that might well enough satisfy; and proposed that if O'Neale would consent to those alterations he[1] would return the treaty signed by him, which he would immediately send over to the Parliament for their confirmation; and·that in the mean time, that there might be a cessation of arms between them for three months, in which time, and much less, he

[1] ['that he,' MS.]

presumed he should receive a ratification of the treaty from the 1649 Parliament.

146. Owen O'Neale consented to the alterations, set his May 8. hand and seal to the treaty, and returned it to Munke, with his consent likewise to the cessation for three months. And at this time he refused to agree with the Confederate council at Kilkenny in the peace with the King. Munke sent it presently to the committee, which had given him authority to do what he had done. But their affairs were now better composed at home, and some preparations were made towards sending relief for Ireland ; besides, they had not authority to make any such ratification, but presented it to the Parliament, which could only give it. It was no sooner reported there but the House Aug. 10. was on fire; all men inveighed against the presumption of Munke, who deserved to be displaced, and to have his command taken from him, and to have exemplary punishment inflicted on him. They remembered how criminal they had declared it to be in the King himself to have treated and made a peace with the Irish rebels: and what would the people think and say, if any countenance should be given to the same transgression by the Parliament, if they should ratify a treaty made by the most notorious of the rebels, and with that people under his command, who were the most notorious contrivers of that rebellion and the most bloody executioners of it ? for the most merciless massacres had been committed in Ulster by that very people who now constituted that army of which Owen O'Neale was now general. After all the passion and choler which they thought necessary to express upon this subject, they declared that they had given no authority to Munke to enter into that treaty, and therefore that it was void, and should never be confirmed by them; but that since he had proceeded out of the sincerity of his heart, and as he thought (how erroneously soever) for the good and benefit of the Commonwealth, he should be excused, and no farther questioned thereupon; for they knew well that he could produce such a warrant from those in authority as would well justify his proceeding. And so the treaty with Owen O'Neale was become void, though they

1649 received a very considerable benefit by it; for though the Scots in Ulster had not yet submitted to the peace, and had not received directions from Edinburgh [1] to acknowledge the authority of the Lord Lieutenant, which they ought to have had before that time, yet after the murder of the late King they had used all acts of hostility against the Parliament forces, and had besieged Londonderry, the only considerable place that yielded obedience to [the Parliament [2],] which was defended by sir Charles Coote, and when it was brought to some extremity, by the cessation made with Owen O'Neale,

Aug. 8. and by his connivance and assistance, Londonderry was relieved; and O'Neale, finding himself deluded by the Parliament, sent to offer his service and conjunction to the Lord Lieutenant, with abundant professions of fidelity and revenge.

147. Cromwell made notable use of this animosity between the Irish amongst themselves, and of the jealousy they all appeared to have of the marquis of Ormonde and of those who adhered to him; and used all the endeavours he could, by some prisoners who were taken, and by others who were in the towns which were betrayed to him, and were well known to have affection for [the marquis [3]] to procure a conference with him. He used to ask in such company, what the marquis of Ormonde had to do with Charles Steward, and what obligations he had ever received from him; and then would mention the hard measure his grandfather had received from King James, and the many years imprisonment he had sustained by him for not submitting to an extrajudicial and private determination of his, which yet he was at last compelled to do [4]. He said he was confident if the marquis and he could meet together, upon conference they should part very good friends. And many of those with whom he held these discourses, by his permission and license, informed the marquis of all he said; who en-

---

[1] [Thus spelt in this instance by Clarendon himself.]

[2] ['it,' MS.]   [3] ['him,' MS.]

[4] [Walter, eleventh earl of Ormonde, was committed to the Fleet in June, 1619, for not submitting to an order made by James I respecting the division of his estates, and was not liberated until after the King's death.]

deavoured nothing but to put himself into such a posture as to **1650**
be able to meet him as he desired to do.

148. When Cromwell saw that he should be able to do
nothing that way, and knew well enough that, besides the
army that yet remained under Owen O'Neale, so much disobliged and provoked, there were still vast bodies of the Irish
which might be drawn together into several armies, much
greater and superior in number to all his forces, and that they
had several great towns and strong holds in their power, he
declared a full liberty and authority to all the officers with the
Irish, and to all other persons whatsoever, to raise what men
they would, and to transport them for the service of any
foreign princes with whom they could make the best conditions;
and gave notice to the Spanish and French ministers and
agents at London of the liberty he had granted. Upon which
many officers who had served the King, and remained in
London in great poverty and want, made conditions with don
Alonso de Cardinas, to raise regiments and transport them
into Spain; and many officers who were already in Spain, as
well English as Irish, contracted with the ministers in that
Court to raise and transport several regiments into that kingdom from Ireland; for which they received very great sums of
money in hand; many merchants joining with them in the
contract, and undertaking the transportation upon very good
conditions, there being no other danger but of the sea in the
undertaking; insomuch that in very few months above a year
there were embarked in the ports of Ireland about five and
twenty thousand men for the kingdom of Spain; whereof not
half were ever drawn into the field, and very few ever lived to
return. For the officers and masters of ships who contracted,
and were bound to deliver their men at such ports as were
assigned to them, and where care was taken for their reception
and conduct to the quarters which were appointed, according
to the service to which they were designed, either for Catalonia
or Portugal, (after they had been long at sea, by which the
soldiers, who were crowded more together into one ship than
was fit for so long voyages, had contracted many diseases, and

1650 many were dead and thrown overboard,) as soon as they came upon the coast made all haste to land, how far soever from the place at which they stood bound to deliver their men; by which, in those places which could make resistance they were not suffered to land, and in others no provision was made for their reception or march, but very great numbers were starved or knocked in the head by the country people, and few ever came up to the armies, except officers, who flocked to Madrid for the remainder of their moneys; where the ministers received them with reproaches for not observing their conditions, and refused to pay either them or the masters of the ships what remained to be paid by them. This was the case of too many: though the truth is, where the articles were punctually observed, and the ships arrived in the very ports assigned, by the defect in the orders sent from the Court, or the negligent execution of them, the poor men were often kept from disembarking till some officers went to Madrid and returned with more positive orders, and afterwards so ill provision [was] made for their refreshing and march, that rarely half of those who were shipped in Ireland ever lived to do any service in Spain: and nothing could be more wonderful, than that the ministers there should issue out such vast sums in money for the raising soldiers, and bringing them into the kingdom, at very liberal and bountiful rates to the officers, and take so very little care to cherish and nourish them when they came thither; which manifested how loose the government was.

149. It is very true, that there was at that time a much greater inclination in the Irish for the service of Spain than of France; yet the cardinal employed more active and dexterous instruments to make use of the liberty that was granted, and shipping was more easily procured, and the passage shorter; insomuch that there were not fewer than twenty thousand men at the same time transported out of Ireland into the kingdom of France; of whose behaviour in the one kingdom and the other there will be abundant argument hereafter to discourse at large. In the mean time, it is enough to observe that when the King's Lieutenant, notwithstanding all the promises, obli-

gations, and contracts, which the Confederate Catholics had 1650 made to and with him, could not draw together a body of five thousand men, (by which he might have been able to have given some stop to the current of Cromwell's successes,) Cromwell himself found a way to send above forty thousand men out of that kingdom for the service of foreign princes; which were enough to have driven him from thence, and to have restored it to the King's entire obedience.

150. In England, the spirit of all the loyal party was so broken and subdued, that they could scarce breathe under the insupportable burdens which were laid upon them by imprisonments, compositions, and sequestrations. Whatever articles they had made in the war, and whatever promises had been made of pardon and indemnity, they were now called upon to finish their compositions for their delinquency, and paid dear for the credit they had given to the professions and declarations of the army, when they seemed to pity, and complain of, the severe and rigorous proceeding against the King's party, and extorting unreasonable penalties from them, which they desired might be moderated. But now the mask was off; they sequestered all their estates, and left them nothing to live upon till they should compound; which they were forced to do at so unreasonable rates, that many were compelled to sell half that they might enjoy the other towards the support of their families; which remainder was still liable to whatever impositions they at any time thought fit to inflict upon them, as their persons were to imprisonment, when any unreasonable and groundless report was raised of some plot and conspiracy against the State.

151. The Parliament, which consisted only of those members who had sat in judgment and solemnly murdered the King, and of those who as solemnly under their hands had approved and commended what the others had done, met with no opposition or contradiction from any, but an entire submission from all to all they did, except only from that part of their own army which had contributed most to the grandeur and empire of which they were possessed, the Levellers. That people had

1650 been countenanced by Cromwell to enter into cabals and confederacies to corrupt and dissolve the discipline of the army, and by his artifices had been applied to bring all his crooked designs to pass. By them he brake the strict union between the Parliament and the Scots, and then took the King out of the hands of the Parliament and kept him in the army, with so many fair professions of intending better to his majesty and his party than the other did; by them the Presbyterians had been affronted and trodden under foot, and the city of London exposed to disgrace and infamy; and by them he had broken the treaty of the Isle of Wight, driven out of the Parliament by force of arms all those who desired peace, and at last executed his barbarous malice upon the sacred person of the King: and when he had applied them to all those uses, for which he thought them to be most fit, he hoped and endeavoured to have reduced them again by a severe hand into that order and obedience from whence he had seduced them, and which was now as necessary to his future purpose of government. But they had tasted too much of the pleasure of having their part and share in it to be willing to be stripped and deprived of it, and made an unskilful computation of what they should be able to do for the future by the great things they had done before in those changes and revolutions which are mentioned; not considering [that] the officers of the army were now united with the Parliament, and concurred entirely in the same designs. And therefore when they renewed their former expostulations and demands from the Parliament, they were cashiered, imprisoned, and some of them put to death. Yet after Cromwell, who had persecuted them with great fury, was gone for Ireland, they recovered their courage, and resolved to obtain those concessions by force which would not be granted upon their request; and so they mutinied in several parts, upon presumption that those of the army who would not join with them in public would yet never be prevailed with to oppose and reduce them by force. But this confidence deceived them; for the Parliament no sooner commanded their general Fayrefax to suppress them, than he drew troops together, and fell upon them

at Banbury and in other places [1]; and by killing some upon 1650
the place, and executing others to terrify the rest, he totally
suppressed that faction; and the orders of those at Westminster
met with no more opposition.

152. This was the state and condition of the three kingdoms
when the King embarked himself in Holland for Scotland, and
at the end of the year 1649 [O. S.].   Since the next year afforded
great variety of unfortunate action, we will end this discourse,
according to the method we have used, with this year; though
hereafter we shall not continue the same method, but compre-
hend the occurrences of many years, whilst the King rested in
a patient expectation of God's blessing and deliverance, in less
room.

[1] [At Banbury on May 10 ; Burford, Oxfordshire, on May 14 ; and Wel-
lingborough, Northamptonshire, on May 19.]

THE END OF THE TWELFTH BOOK.

BOOK XIII.

And in very deed for this cause have I raised thee up, for to shew in thee
my power, and that my name may be declared throughout all the earth.
As yet exaltest thou thyself against my people ?—EXODUS ix, 16, 17.[1]

1650   1 [2]. THE marquis of Arguyle, who did not believe that the
King would ever have ventured thither [into Scotland] upon
[the] conditions [he had sent [3],] was surprised with the account
the commissioners had given him, that his majesty resolved to
embark the next day, that he would leave all his chaplains and
his other servants behind him, and only deferred to take the
Covenant himself till he came thither, with a resolution to
satisfy the Kirk if they pressed it; and thereupon he immediately despatched away another vessel with new propositions,
which the commissioners were to insist upon, and not to consent
to the King's coming into that kingdom without he likewise
consented to those. But that vessel met not with the King's fleet,
which, that it might avoid that of the Parliament which attended
to intercept the King, had held its course more northward, where
there is plenty of good harbours; and so had put into a harbour
June 23. near Sterlin[g] [4], that is, within a day's journey of it, but where
there was no town nearer for his majesty's reception, or where
there was any accommodation for very ordinary passengers.

2. From thence notice was sent to the Council of the King's
arrival. The first welcome he received was a new demand that
he would sign the Covenant himself before he set his foot on
shore, which all about him pressed him to do: and he now
found that he had made haste thither upon very unskilful
June 23. imaginations and presumptions: yet he consented unto what
they so imperiously required, that he might have leave to put

---

[1] [*Hist.*, p. 16.]   [2] [*Life*, p. 423.]
[3] [' those conditions,' MS.]
[4] [Garmouth, in Cromarty Frith, at the mouth of the Spey. (Walker's
Hist. Disc., pp. 158, 9.) Clarendon probably mistook this for Grange-
mouth in the Frith of Forth.]

himself into the hands of those who resolved nothing less than 1650
to serve him. The lords of the other party, who had prevailed
with him to submit to all that he had done, quickly found
that they had deceived both him and themselves, and that
nobody had any authority but those men who were their mortal
enemies ; so that they would not expose themselves to be
imprisoned or to be removed from the King, but, with his
majesty's leave, and having given him the best advice they
could what he should do for himself and what he should do for
them, they put themselves on shore before the King disem- June 26.
barked[1], and found means to go to those places where they might
be some time concealed, and which were like to be at distance
enough from the King. And shortly after, duke Hambleton
retired to the island of Arran, which belonged to himself, where
he had a little house well enough accommodated, the island
being for the most part inhabited with wild beasts: Latherdale concealed himself amongst his friends ; both taking care to
be well informed of all that should pass about the King, and
that he might receive their advice upon any occasions.

3. The King was received by the marquis of Arguyle with
all the outward respect imaginable ; but within two days after
his landing, all the English servants he had of any quality July 10.[2]
were removed from his person, the duke of Buckingham only
excepted. The rest for the most part were received into the
houses of some persons of honour who lived at a distance from
the Court, and were themselves under a cloud for their known
affections, and durst only attend the King to kiss his hand, and
then retired to their houses, that they might give no occasion
of jealousy. Others of his servants were not suffered to remain
in the kingdom, but were forced presently to re-embark themselves for Holland ; amongst which was Daniel O'Neale, who
hath been often mentioned before, and who came from the marquis of Ormonde into Holland just when his majesty was ready
to embark, and so waited upon him, and was no sooner known
to be with his majesty, (as he was a person very generally
known,) but he was apprehended by order from the Council, for

[1] [Two days after. Walker's *Hist. Disc.*, p. 159.]   [2] [*Cal. Cl. S. P.* ii. 69.]

1650 being an Irishman, and having been in arms on the late King's behalf in the late war; for which they were not without some discourse of putting him to death; but they did immediately
Aug. 15. banish him the kingdom, and obliged him to sign a paper by which he consented to be put to death if he were ever after found in the kingdom.

4. And they sent away likewise Mr. Robert Longe, who was his principal, if not only, Secretary of State, and had very much persuaded his going thither, and sir Edward Walker, who was clerk of the Council, and had been secretary at war during the late war, and some others, upon the like exceptions. They placed other servants of all conditions about the King, but principally relied upon their clergy, who were in such a continual attendance about him that he was never free from their importunities, under pretence of instructing him in religion: and so they obliged him to their constant hours of their long prayers, and made him observe the Sundays with more rigour than the Jews accustomed to do; and reprehended him very sharply if he smiled on those days, and if his looks and gestures did not please them, whilst all their prayers and sermons, at which he was compelled to be present, were libels and bitter invectives against all the actions of his father, the idolatry of his mother, and his own malignity.

5. He was not present in their councils, nor were the results thereof communicated to him, nor was [he] in the least degree communicated with in any part of the government: yet they made great show of outward reverence to him, and even the chaplains, when they used rudeness and barbarity in their reprehensions and reproaches, approached him still with bended knees and in the humblest postures. There was never a better courtier than Arguyle, who made all the possible address to make himself gracious to the King, entertained him with very pleasant discourses, with such insinuations that the King did not only very well like his conversation but often believed that he had a mind to please and gratify him; but then, when [the King[1]] made any attempt to get some of his servants about

---

[1] ['he,' MS.]

him, or to reconcile the two factions, that the kingdom might **1650**
be united, he gathered up his countenance, and retired from
his address, without ever yielding to any one proposition that
was made to him by his majesty. In a word, the King's table
was well served, and there he sat in majesty, waited upon with
decency: he had good horses to ride abroad to take the air, and
was then well attended, and in all public appearances seemed
to want nothing that was due to a great king. In all other
respects, with reference to power to oblige or gratify any man,
to dispose or order any thing, or himself to go to any other
place than was assigned to him, he had nothing of a prince, but
might very well be looked upon as a prisoner.

6[1]. But that which was of state and lustre made most noise,
and was industriously transmitted into all nations and states;
the other, of disrespect or restraint, was not communicated,
and if it could not be entirely concealed it was considered only
as a faction between particular great men, who contended to
get the power into their hands, that they might the more notoriously and eminently serve that prince whom they all equally
acknowledged. The King's condition seemed wonderfully advanced, and his being possessed of a kingdom without a rival,
in which there was no appearance of an enemy, looked like an
earnest for the recovery of the other two, and, for the present,
as a great addition of power to him in his kingdom of Ireland, by
a conjunction and absolute submission of all the Scots in Ulster
to the marquis of Ormonde, the King's Lieutenant there.

7. All men who had dissuaded his majesty's repair into Scotland were looked upon as very weak politicians, or as men who
opposed the public good because they were excluded, and might
not be suffered to act any part in the adventure; and they who
had advanced the design valued themselves exceedingly upon
their activity in that service. The States of Holland thought
they had ·merited much in suffering their ships to transport
him, and so being ministerial to his greatness, which they hoped
would be remembered; and they gave all countenance to the
Scottish merchants and factors who lived in their dominions,

[1] [*Hist.*, p. 16.]

1650 and some secret credit, that they might send arms and ammunition and whatsoever else was necessary for the King's service into that kingdom. France itself looked very cheerful upon the change; congratulated the Queen with much ceremony and many professions; and took pains to have it thought and believed that they had had a share in the counsel, and contributed very much to the reception the King found in Scotland by their influence upon Arguyle and his party. And it hath been mentioned before [1] how great a reputation this little dawning of power, how clouded soever, gave to the ambassadors in Spain, and had raised them from such a degree of disrespect as was nearest to contempt to their full dignity, and estimation in that Court that was due to the station in which they were.

8 [2]. There fell out an accident at this time which was a great manifestation of the affection of that Court, and indeed of the nation. As don Alonso de Cardinas had used all the credit he had to dispose that Court to a good correspondence with the Parliament, so he had employed as much care to incline those in England to have a confidence in the affection of his master, and assured them that if they would send an ambassador or other minister into Spain he should find a very good reception. The Parliament, in the infancy of their Commonwealth, had more inclination to make a friendship with Spain than with France, having at that time a very great prejudice to the cardinal; and therefore upon this encouragement from don Alonso they re-

Feb. 2 solved to send an envoy to Madrid, and made choice of one Ascham, a scholar who had written a book [3] to determine in what time, and after how many years, the allegiance which is due from subjects to their sovereign comes to be determined after a conquest; and that from that term it ought to be paid to those who had subdued them, or to the conqueror: a speculation they thought fit to cherish.

9. This man, unacquainted with business, and unskilled in language, attended by three others, the one a renegado Franciscan friar, who had been bred in Spain and was well versed in

---

[1] [Book xii. § 127.]   [2] [*Life*, p. 420.]
[3] [*Of the Confusions and Revolutions of Governments*, 1649.]

the language, another who was to serve in the condition of a **1650**
secretary, and the third an inferior fellow for any service,
arrived all at Siville or Calice in an English merchant's ship: **March 24.**
of which don Alonso gave such timely notice, that he was
received and entertained there by the chief magistrate, until
they gave notice of it to the Court. The town was quickly full
of the rumour that an ambassador was landed from England, and
would be received there; which nobody seemed to be well
pleased with. And the ambassadors expostulated with don
Lewis de Haro with some warmth, that his Catholic majesty
should be the first Christian prince that would receive an
ambassador from the odious and infamous murderers of a
Christian king, his brother and ally; which no other prince had
yet done, out of the detestation of that horrible parricide; and
therefore they desired him that Spain would not give so horrid
an example to the other parts of the world. Don Lewis assured them that there was no such thing as an ambassador
coming from England, nor had the King any purpose to receive
any; that it was true, they were informed that there was an
English gentleman landed at Calice, and come to Siville, who
said he was sent from the Parliament with letters for the
King; which was testified by a letter from don Alonso de
Cardinas to the duke of Medina Celi, who thereupon had
given order for his entertainment at Siville till the King should
give farther order: that it was not possible for the King to
refuse to receive the letter, or to see the man who brought it,
who pretended no kind of character: that having an ambassador residing in England to preserve the trade and commerce
between the two nations, they did believe that this messenger
might be sent with some propositions from the English merchants for the advancement of that trade; and if they should
refuse to hear what he said, it might give a just offence, and destroy
all the commerce, which would be a great damage to both nations.

10. That the man might come securely to Madrid, an old
officer of the army was sent from Siville to accompany this new
agent to Madrid; who came with him in the coach, and gave
notice every night to don Lewis of their advance. There were

1650 at that time, over and above the English merchants, many
officers and soldiers in Madrid who had served in the Spanish
armies both in Catalonia and in Portugal; and these men had
consulted amongst themselves how they might kill this fellow,
who came as an ambassador or agent from the new republic of
England; and half a dozen of them, having notice of the day he
was to come into the town, which was generally discoursed of,
rode out of the town to meet him; but missing him, they
returned again to the town, and found that he had entered into
it by another way; and having taken a view of his lodging,
they met again the next morning, and finding accidentally one
of the ambassadors' servants in the streets, they persuaded him
to go with them, and so went to the house where Ascham
lodged; and without asking any questions walked directly up
the stairs into his chamber, leaving a couple of their number at
the door of the street, lest upon any noise in the house that
door might be shut upon them. They who went up drew their
swords, and, besides their intentions, in disorder, killed the
June 5. friar as well as the agent; and so returned to their companions
with their swords naked and bloody, and some foolish expressions of triumph, as if they had performed a very gallant
and a justifiable service. Notwithstanding all which, they
might have dispersed themselves, and been secure, the people
were so little concerned to inquire what they had done. But
they being in confusion, and retaining no composed thoughts
about them, finding the door of a little chapel open, went in
thither for sanctuary: only he who served the ambassadors
separated himself from the rest, and went into the house of the
Venetian ambassador. By this time the people of the house
where the man lay had gone up into the chamber; where
they found two dead, and the other two crept, in a terrible
fright, under the bed; and the magistrates and people [were]
about the church, and talking with and examining the persons
who were there; and the rumour was presently divulged about
the town that one of the English ambassadors was killed.

11. They were at that time entering into their coach to
take the air, according to an appointment which they had made

the day before, when they were informed of what had passed, **1650** and that Harry Progers, a servant of theirs, had been in the action, and was retired to the house of the Venetian ambassador. They were both in extraordinary trouble and perplexity, dismissed their coach, and returned to their lodging. Though they abhorred the action that was committed, they foresaw the presence of one of their own servants in it, and even some passionate words they had used in their expostulation with don Lewis against the reception of such a messenger, as if the King their master had too many subjects in that place for such a fellow to appear there with any security, would make it be believed by many that the attempt had not been made without their consent or privity. In this trouble of mind they immediately writ a letter to don Lewis de Haro, to express the sense they had of this unfortunate rash action, of which they hoped he did believe, if they had had any notice or suspicion, they would have prevented it by the exposing their own persons. Don Lewis returned them a very dry answer; that he could not June 7. imagine that they could have a hand in so foul an assassination in the Court, (for all Madrid is called and looked upon as the Court,) of a person under the immediate protection of the King: however, that it was an action so unheard of, and so dishonourable to the King, that his majesty was resolved to have it examined to the bottom, and that exemplary justice should be done upon the offenders; that his own ambassador in England might be in great danger upon this murder, and that they would send an express presently thither, to satisfy the Parliament how much his Catholic majesty detested and was offended with it, and resolved to do justice upon it; and if his ambassador underwent any inconvenience there, they were not to wonder if his majesty was severe here; and so left it to them to imagine that their own persons might not·be safe.

12. But they knew the temper of the Court too well to have the least apprehension of that: yet they were a little surprised when they first saw the multitude of people gathered together about their house, upon the first news of the action, insomuch as the street before their house, which was the broadest in

1650 Madrid, (the Calle de Alcala,) was so thronged that men could hardly pass. But they were quickly out of that apprehension, being assured that the jealousy that one of the English ambassadors had suffered violence had brought that multitude together; which they found to be true; for they no sooner shewed themselves in a balcony to the people, but they saluted them with great kindness, prayed for the King their master, cursed and reviled the murderers of his father, and so departed. They who had betaken themselves to the chapel were the next June 6. day, or the second, taken from thence by a principal officer after examination, and sent to the prison[1]; the other was not inquired after, but, having concealed himself for ten or twelve days, he went out of the town in the night, and without any interruption or trouble went into France.

13. Of all the Courts in Christendom Madrid is that where ambassadors and public ministers receive the greatest respect, which, besides the honour and punctuality of that people, which is bred up in the observation of distances and order, proceeds from the excellent method they have of living with mutual respect towards each other, and in mutual concernment for each other's honour and privileges : so that if any ambassador, in himself or his servants, receive any affront or disrespect, all the other ambassadors repair to him, and offer their service and interposition; by which means they are not only preserved from any invasion from any private and particular insolence, but even from some acts of power which the Court itself hath sometimes thought fit to exercise, upon an extraordinary occasion, towards a minister of whom they had no regard. All are united on the behalf of the character, and will not suffer that to be done towards one which, by the consequence, may reflect upon all.

14. It cannot be imagined with what a general compassion all the ambassadors looked upon these unhappy gentlemen, who had involved themselves by their rashness in so much peril. They came to the [English] ambassadors to advise and consult what might be done to preserve them, every one

[1] [*Calend. Clar. S. P.* ii. 63.]

offering his assistance. The action could in no degree be 1650
justified; all that could be urged and insisted upon in their
behalf was the privilege of sanctuary; they had betaken themselves to the church, and the taking them from thence, by what
authority soever, was a violation of the rights and immunities
of the Church, which by the law of the kingdom was ever
defended with all tenderness. So that before the guilt of the
blood could be examined, the prisoners desired that their
privilege might be examined, and that they might have counsel
assigned them to that purpose; which was granted; and
several arguments were made upon the matter of law before the
judges, who were favourable enough to the prisoners. The
King's counsel urged, that in case of assassination the privilege of sanctuary was never allowed, (which is true,) and
cited many precedents of late years in Madrid itself, where
for less crimes than of blood men had been taken out of the
sanctuary, and tried and executed. The ambassadors thought
not fit to appear on their behalfs, and yet were not willing that
the new republic should receive so much countenance from that
Court as would have resulted from the putting those gentlemen
to death, as if they had killed a public minister. The Pope's
nuncio, Julio Rospiglioso, (who was afterwards Clement IX,)
could not, according to the style of the Roman Court, either
give or receive visits from the English ambassadors, but they
performed civilities to each other by messages, and passed
mutual salutations, with all respect to each other, as they met
abroad. And the Venetian ambassador brought them frequent
assurances that the nuncio had spoken very effectually to the
King and to don Lewis for the re-delivery of [the prisoners[1]]
to the church, and pressed it so hard upon the conscience of
the King, that he had some promise that they should not
suffer.

15. In the mean time thundering letters came from the
Parliament, with great menaces what they would do, if exemplary justice was not inflicted upon those who had murdered
their envoy ; and don Alonso urged it as if he thought himself

---

[1] ['them,' MS.]

1650 in danger till full satisfaction should be given in that particular; all which for the present made deep impression, so that
they knew not what to do; the King often declaring that he
would not infringe the privilege of the church, and so undergo
the censure of the Pope, for any advantage he could receive
with reference to any of his dominions. In the end, (that the
discourse of this affair may not be resumed again hereafter,)
after a long imprisonment, (for during the ambassadors' stay
they would not bring them to any trial, lest they might seem
to do any thing upon their solicitation,) they were proceeded
against as soon, or shortly after [the ambassadors [1]] had left
Madrid, and were all condemned to die; and as soon as the
sentence was declared, all the prisoners were again delivered
into the same church; where they remained many days, having
provisions of victual sent to them by many persons of quality,
until they had all opportunity to make their escape, which was
very successfully done by all but one [2]; who, being the only
Protestant amongst them, was more maliciously looked after
and watched, and was followed and apprehended after he had
made three days' journey from Madrid, and carried back
1654 thither, and put to death: which was all the satisfaction the
Jan. Parliament could obtain in that affair; which is an instance
how far that people was from any affection to those of England
in their hearts, how much soever they complied with them out
of the necessity of their fortune.

16. When some weeks were passed after that unlucky accident, the ambassadors went to confer with don Lewis upon
some other occurrence, with no purpose of mentioning any
thing of the prisoners. Don Lewis spake of it in a manner
they did not expect; one expression was, *Yo tengo invidia de
estos cavaleros, &c.;* 'I envy those gentlemen for having done
so noble an action, how penal soever it may prove to them, to
revenge the blood of their King.' Whereas, he said, the King
his master wanted such resolute subjects; otherwise he would
never have lost a kingdom, as he had done Portugal, for want
of one brave man, who, by taking away the life of the usurper,

---

[1] ['they,' MS.]   [2] [Will. Sparke.]

might at any time during the first two years [have] put an end **1650**
to that rebellion.

17. Though the privileges of ambassadors were much
greater in that Court than in any other, and that they lived
much better towards each other than ambassadors used to do in
any other Court, yet they used to communicate those privileges
more easily, and to admit men to usurp that title who had no
pretence to it ; not that the King permitted them to cover,
which they never affected, nor he would ever have endured ;
but in all other respects they were treated as such, and the
ambassadors were obliged to do so, except they were under
ome obligation to the contrary.   There were at that time two
instances of that kind, though upon different negotiations.   The
one was in the count of Swaffenburgh [1], who came, as they said,
ambassador from the archduke Leopold, who was only a prince
by appellation, without any territory, and was then actually in
the service of the King of Spain, as governor of the Low
Countries, though under such a restrained commission that the
count of Fuensaldagna, with two or three other Spanish councillors, had authority in many cases to control his determinations.
The count of Swaffenburgh was his chief servant and confident ;
and, being a man of good parts and spirit, used to enter into
sharp contests and disputes with those ministers in the right
and behalf of his master ; whereupon he was become suspected and disliked in the Court of Madrid, and was now sent
by the archduke, not only to insist upon the rights of his place
and to complain of the infringement of them, but to justify
himself and to wipe off those aspersions which had been cast
upon him ; and yet he was received under the title and style of
ambassador, treated with *Excellenza*, and waited upon by
one of the King's coaches, and upon the day of his audience
rode to the Court attended by all the other ambassadors'
coaches.   And because they neither liked his person or his
business, and resolved not to gratify him in any thing he came
about or desired, they used him with the more ceremony and
respect ;   and there being a sudden accident one day, which

[1] [Schwarzenburgh.]

1650 looked like an affront to him, when in a crowd of coaches, upon one of those solemn days when the King and all the Court and all ambassadors use to take the air, in a little field that can hardly receive all the company, the count's coach stood where the duke of Alberquerque had a mind to pass; and the other coachman refusing to yield the way, the duke alighted out of his coach, and with his sword in the scabbard struck him over the head, the count being himself in the coach, which the duke protested not to have known till after he had struck his coachman; when the count bade his coachman drive out of the field; and as soon as he was retired out of the company, he sent a gentleman to the duke, to let him know that he expected to see him with his sword in his hand. But the business was taken notice of before, and the King had commanded the duke of Alberquerque to his house; and it being so unusual a thing, and unsuitable to the Spanish gravity, for a grandee to go out of his coach to strike a coachman, it was looked upon as a purposed and designed injury. All the ambassadors met the next morning at the count's lodging, to offer their service, and to consult what was to be done to repair their character, but found the conde most inclined and resolved to do justice to himself; but the punctuality of the Court prevented any further pursuit, by obliging the duke of Alberquerque first to write to the count, and to protest that he did not know that he was in the coach, nor had the least thought to affront him, and then to go to him to his lodging and ask his pardon; both which he performed: which was an imposition and condescension that the grandees looked upon as very extraordinary.

18. The other who was received and countenanced as an ambassador was the marquis of Lusignon, who was sent by the prince of Condé, and was commonly called the prince of Condé's ambassador, who was likewise attended by one of the King's coaches. It is true, he had not so formal an audience as the count of Swaffenburgh had, but intimation was given to all the ambassadors that the King expected that they should visit him; which all did but the English ambassadors, who did not think

fit, both in respect of their master or themselves, to give such **1650** umbrage to France, and so forbore to shew any respect or civility towards him. This unhappy gentleman, after a journey or two in that negotiation to Madrid, was taken in his return, and after some months of imprisonment had his process made, and lost his head.

19. By this time the ill news from Scotland brought a new mortification upon the ambassadors, which the King himself had undergone there in a more severe degree. Whether, when the marquis of Arguyle first knew that the King would venture himself into Scotland, he suspected his own strength, and so sent for his friend Cromwell to assist him ; or whether it seemed more reasonable to the Parliament, when it was assured of the King's being there, to visit him in that kingdom than to expect a visitation from him, is not enough clear at this time. But as soon as the King was in Scotland, Cromwell, being sent for by the Parliament, left what remained to be **1646** done in Ireland to Ireton, (who had married his daughter,) and ${}^{June 15.}_{1650}$ made him deputy, and transported himself into England; where **May 29.** the Parliament, not without great opposition from all the Presbyterian party, resolved to send an army into Scotland. Many opposed it, as they thought it an unjust and unprofitable war, and knew it must be a very expensive one; and others, because it would keep up and increase the power and authority of the army in England, which was already found to be very grievous.

20. This resolution produced another great alteration. Fayrefax, who had hitherto worn the name of general, declared positively that he would not command the army against Scotland. The Presbyterians said it was because he thought the war unlawful, in regard it was against those of the same religion ; but his friends would have it believed that he would not fight against the King. Hereupon Cromwell was chosen general; **June 26.** which made no alteration in the army, which he had modelled to his own mind before, and commanded as absolutely, but in all other places he grew more absolute and more imperious. He discountenanced and suppressed the Presbyterians in all places, who had been supported by Fayrefax. The Independents

1650 had all credit about him; and the churches and pulpits were
open to all kind of people who would shew their gifts there,
and a general distraction and confusion in religion covered the
whole kingdom; which raised as general a discontent in the
minds of the people, who, finding no ease from the burdens
they had so long sustained, but an increase of the taxes and
impositions every day, grew weary of their new government,
and heartily prayed that their general might never return from
Scotland, but that being destroyed there, the King might return
victorious into London. The bitterness and persecution against
their brethren in England, and the old animosity they had long
borne against the person of Cromwell, made those in authority
June 25. in that kingdom resolve to defend themselves against his invasion, and to draw together a very numerous body of men
well provided, and supplied with all things necessary but
courage and conduct. They were so careful in the modelling
this army, that they suffered neither officer or soldier who had
been in the Engagement of duke Hambleton, or who gave the
least occasion to be suspected to wish well to the King or to
the Hambletonian party, to be listed or received into their
service; so that they had only some old discredited officers,
who, being formerly thought unworthy of command, had stuck
close to Arguyle and to the party of the Kirk. The truth is,
the whole army was under the government of a committee of
the Kirk and the State, in which the ministers exercised the
sole authority, and prayed and preached against the vices of
the Court and the impiety and tyranny of Cromwell equally,
and promised their army victory over the enemy as positively
and in as confident terms as if God himself had directed them
to declare it. The King desired that he might command this
army, at least run the fortune of it. But they were hardly
prevailed with to give him leave once to see it; and after he
had been in it three or four hours, upon the observation that
the common soldiers seemed to be much pleased to see him,
they caused him to return, and the next day carried him to a
place at a greater distance from the army; declaring that they
found the soldiers too much inclined to put their confidence in

the arm of flesh, whereas their hope and dependence was to be 1650
only in God; and they were most assured of victory by the
prayers and piety of the Kirk.

21. In [July[1]] Cromwell entered Scotland, and marched July 22.
without any opposition till he came within less than a day's
journey of Edenborough; where he found the Scottish army
encamped upon a very advantageous ground; and he made his
quarters as near as he could conveniently, and yet with disadvantages enough, for the country was so destroyed behind
him, and the passes so guarded before, that he was compelled
to send for all his provision for horse and foot from England
by sea, (and Cromwell being seized upon by a fever, which held
him about six weeks, during which time the army lay still;)
insomuch as the army was reduced to great straits, and the
Scots really believed that they had them all at their mercy,
except such as would embark on board their ships. But as
soon as Cromwell had recovered a little strength, his army
began to remove, and seemed to provide for their march.
Whether that march was in order to retire out of so barren a
country for want of provisions, (which no doubt were very
scarce, and the season of the year would not permit them to
depend upon all necessary supplies by sea, for it was now the
month of September,) or whether that motion was only to draw
the Scots from the advantageous post of which they were possessed, is not yet understood; but it was confessed on all sides,
that if they had remained within their trenches, and sent parties of horse to have followed the English army closely, they
must have so disordered them, that they would have left their
cannon and all their heavy carriage behind them, beside the
danger the foot must have been in. But the Scots did not
intend to part with them so easily; they doubted not but to
have the spoil of the whole army. And therefore they no
sooner discerned that the whole army was upon their march,
but they discamped, and followed with their whole body all the
night following, and found them[selves] in the morning within
a small distance of the enemy: for Cromwell was quickly ad-

[1] ['August,' MS.]

1650 vertised that the Scots' army was dislodged and marched after him, and thereupon he made a stand, and put his men in good order. The Scots found they were not upon so clear a chase as they imagined, and placed themselves again upon such a side of a hill as they believed the English would not have the courage to attack them there.

Sept. 3.   22. But Cromwell knew them too well to fear them upon any ground, when there were no trenches or fortifications to keep him from them; and therefore he made haste to charge them on all sides, upon what advantage-ground soever they stood upon. Their horse did not sustain one charge, but fled, and were pursued with a great execution. The foot depended so much[1] upon their ministers, who preached and prayed, and assured them of the victory, till the English were upon them; and some of their preachers were knocked in the head whilst they were promising the victory. Though there was so little resistance made that Cromwell did not want twenty men by that day's service[2], yet the execution was very terrible upon the enemy, the whole body of the foot being, upon the matter, cut in pieces; no quarter was given till they were weary of killing, so that there were between five and six thousand dead upon the place; and very few, but they who escaped by the heels of their horse, were without terrible wounds, of which very many died shortly after; especially such of their ministers who were not killed upon the place, as very many were, had very notable marks about the head and the face, that any body might know that they were not hurt by chance or in the crowd but by very good will. All the cannon, ammunition, carriages, and baggage, were entirely taken, and Cromwell with his victorious army marched directly to Edenborough; where he found plenty of all things which he wanted, and good accommodation for the refreshing his army, which stood in need of it.

23. Never victory was attended with less lamentation: for as

[1] [*Read*, too much?]

[2] [' I do not believe we have lost twenty men ' are Cromwell's own words in his letter to the Speaker on the day following. Another account written on that day says, ' We lost not forty men.' The Scottish loss was estimated at from 3000 by Cromwell to 4000 in the latter account.]

Cromwell had great argument of triumph in the total defeat **1650** and destruction of the only army that was in Scotland, which[1] had put a great part of that kingdom, and the chief city of it, under his obedience, [so][2] the King, who was then at St. John-ston's, was glad of it, as the greatest happiness that could befall him, in the loss of so strong a body of his enemies; and if they should have prevailed, his majesty did believe that they would have shut him up in a prison the next day; which had been only a more confinement than he suffered already, for the lord Lorne, eldest son to the marquis of Arguyle, being captain of his guard, had so strict a care of him both night and day that he could not go any whither without his leave. But after this defeat they all looked upon the King as one they might stand in need of; they permitted his servants, who had been seques-tered from him from his arrival in the kingdom, to attend and wait upon him, and began to talk of calling a Parliament, and of a time for the King's coronation, which had not hitherto been spoken of. Some ministers began to preach obedience to the King; the officers who had been cashiered for their malignity talked aloud of the miscarriages in the government, and that the kingdom was betrayed to the enemy for want of confidence in the King, who alone could preserve the nation. They of the Council seemed not to have so absolute a dependence upon the marquis of Arguyle, but spake more freely than they had used to do; and the marquis applied himself more to the King and to those about him; so that the King did in a good degree enjoy the fruit of this victory as well as Cromwell; but his was only in the observation of a few men, reduced into an obscure quarter of the kingdom, but the other made the éclat.

24. The destruction of the only army, and the possessing of Edenborough, was looked upon in all places as the entire con-quest of the whole kingdom; and don Alonso made haste to send the news into Spain of the total and irrecoverable defeat of the King; that he was driven into the Highlands, from whence he would be compelled to fly as soon as he could get means to escape; that the republic was now settled, and no more fear

[1] ['and which,' MS.] [2] ['and,' MS.]

1650 or hope of the King: the effect of all which the ambassadors quickly found at Madrid, by the carriage and countenance of the King and the Council; though it cannot be denied that the common people appeared to have a much more generous sense of the alteration than the others did. The ambassadors received shortly a full advertisement of the truth, and that the King thought his condition much improved by the defeat; and they used all the means they could, by several audiences, to inform the King and don Lewis of the truth, and that they were misinformed as if the army overthrown was the King's, whereas they were indeed as much his enemies as Cromwell was. But they could obtain no credit, and all ways were taken to make them perceive that it was heartily wished that they were gone; which they were resolved to take no notice of.

Dec. [1]. 25. In the end, one morning the Secretary of State came to them from the King, and told them that they had been now above a year in that Court, where they had been well treated, notwithstanding some miscarriages which might very justly have incensed his Catholic majesty, mentioning the death of Ascham; that they were extraordinary ambassadors, and so needed not any letters of revocation; that they had received answers to all that they had proposed, and were at liberty to depart; which his Catholic majesty desired they would do, since their presence in the Court would be very prejudicial to his affairs. This unexpected and unusual message, delivered ungracefully enough, by an old man, who, notwithstanding his office, was looked upon with little reverence to his parts, made them believe that he had mistaken his message, at least that he had delivered it with less courtly circumstances than he ought to have done. And therefore they returned no other answer, than that they would attend don Lewis de Haro, and understand from him the King's pleasure. And the next day they sent for an audience to don Lewis; whom they found with a less open countenance than he used to have, nor did he appear

---

[1] [The ambassadors wrote to the King on Dec. 9, acknowledging the message received through Geronymo de la Torre. This is the date in Hyde's own draft of his letter; in a copy by his secretary Edgeman it is given as Nov. 9. See *Calend. Clar. S. P.* ii. 85, 89.]

any thing more courtly than the Secretary had done, but told **1650** them that there were orders sent to such a person (whom he named) to prepare their present, which should be ready within very few days; and pressed them very plainly, and without any regard to the season of the year, it being then towards the end of January[1], to use all possible expedition for their departure, as a thing that even in that respect did exceedingly concern the service of the King. This made them imagine, which was likewise reported, that there was a formal ambassador upon his way from England, and they [the Court] would be no more liable to the like accidents. But they knew afterwards that the cause of all this haste was, that they might bring into the town as many pictures, and other choice and rich furniture, as did load eighteen mules, which don Alonso had bought of the King's goods, and then sent to the Groyne, and which they did not then think could be decently brought to the palace whilst the ambassadors should continue and remain in the town.

26. This injunction to leave Madrid in so unseasonable a time of the year was very severe to the ambassadors, who knew not whither to go. The lord Cottington was at this time seventy-six years of age, once or twice in a year troubled with the gout, in other respects of great vigour of body and mind, nor did there appear in his natural parts any kind of decay. He resolved when he first proposed this embassy to the King (and it may be it was the chief reason of proposing it), that if there should be no door open to let him return into England by the time that his embassy should expire, he[2] would remain and die in Spain. But he did then believe that he should have found another kind of entertainment there than he had done. He had without doubt deserved very well from that nation, having always performed those offices towards them which made him looked upon at home as too well affected to that people, which, together with his constant opposition of the French, had rendered him very ungracious to the Queen: yet there were some seasons in which his credit and authority was not great enough to obtain all things for them which they desired and

---

[1] [in December.]   [2] ['that he,' MS.]

1650 expected; as when their fleet, under the command of Oquendo, about the year 1635 or 36[1], had been assaulted in the Downs and defeated by the Dutch fleet, for want of that protection which they thought the King might have given to them. And it is probable their ambassadors who were then in England, whereof don Alonso was one, did not find that readiness and alacrity in him to appear in their service as they had formerly done; he very well knowing that being solicitous for them in that conjuncture might do himself harm and could do them no good. But these omissions were now remembered, and all his services forgotten: so that (as hath been touched before)[2] his reception, from the first hour of his coming last thither, was very cold both from the King and the Court. And though he was now willing to resume his former resolution of staying there, yet the treatment he had received, and this last farewell, made him doubt very reasonably whether he should be permitted to stay there or not.

27. There was another circumstance which was necessary to his residing in Spain, in which he met with some difficulties that he did not foresee, and which did exceedingly perplex him, and which he plainly enough discerned and knew to be the true cause of all the discountenance he had met with in that Court, (though he was willing the other ambassador, who knew nothing of it, should believe that it proceeded from what had passed in England,) and which were then remembered in the discourses of the Court, and [were[3]] the true cause of the general prejudice to him there. He had been formerly reconciled in that kingdom to the Church of Rome, and had constantly gone to the mass there; and declaring himself afterwards in England to be of the religion of that Church [of England], he was apostatized from the other, which in that country is looked upon as such a brand as the infamy of it can never be wiped out; and this indeed was the reason of that King's so notable aversion from him. The truth is, he had never made any inquiry into religion to inform himself, but had conformed to that which the province he held obliged him to;

---

[1] [Oct. 11, 1639.]   [2] [Book xii. § 102 *n.*]   [3] ['was,' MS.]

and though he could never get the reputation in England of **1650** being well affected to that Church, and was always looked upon as most inclined to the Roman, yet he convinced those who would have taken advantage of that guilt by being present at prayers and sermons, and sometimes receiving the sacrament, as he did the very last Sunday he stayed in the Hague before he began his journey towards Spain, and even after his arrival there was constant at the reading the common prayers both morning and evening by their own chaplain in their house, as long as he [the chaplain [1]] lived; and many who knew him very well did believe that if he had died in England he would have died in the communion of that Church. But there is no doubt he did resolve from the time that he meant to remain and die in Spain that he would become a Roman Catholic [again]; which he thought to be a much easier thing than it was, and that he might have been reconciled by any priest in as private a manner as he could desire. But when he consulted that affair with a Jesuit who frequently came to the house, he found that after an apostasy it was not in the power of any priest to reconcile him, but that it was reserved to the Pope himself, who rarely gives the faculty to any but to his own nuncios. This obliged him to resort thither; which he could not easily do without communicating it to the other ambassador, towards whom this was the only secret he ever reserved. And he found a way, as he thought, to elude him in this particular. He told him, several days, that the nuncio had sent him such and such messages by that Jesuit concerning those gentlemen who were in prison, the substance whereof did not differ from what the Venetian ambassador had formerly delivered from him; at last he told him, that he found the nuncio had somewhat to say in that affair which he would not communicate by message, but wished to speak with him in private, for publicly he must not be known to have any conference with him, and that hereupon he resolved to go *incognito* in sir Benjamin Wright's coach to him; which he did, and was then reconciled, and returned

[1] [William Beale, dean of Ely, who died 1 Oct. N. S. 1650. *Calend. Clar. S. P.* ii. 41.]

1650 home, making such a relation of their conference to his companion as he thought fit, and delivered the nuncio's salutations to him. But within two or three days he knew what the affair was; for, besides that the nuncio could not perform the office alone but was to have the assistance of two or three so qualified, there was really care taken that the other ambassador might know it. And before that time, when they both visited the *Presidente de la hazienda,* who carried them into his library, whilst the other was casting his eyes upon some books, (it being the best private library in Madrid,) the lord Cottington told the President that he was himself a Catholic but that his companion was an obstinate heretic: of which the President sent him information the next day. But since himself forbore ever to communicate this secret to him, out of an opinion, it is very probable, that he might give him some disturbance in his resolution, he likewise took no manner of notice of it to him, to the minute of their departure from each other.

28. This difficulty being over, there remained yet another; which was, his permission to stay in that country; for which he addressed himself to don Lewis, mentioned his age, his infirmity of the gout, which would infallibly seize upon him if in that season of the year he should provoke it by an extraordinary motion; in a word, that it was impossible for him to make the journey. Don Lewis told him he could answer him to part, without speaking with the King; that he must not think of staying with the character of an ambassador, nor of residing in Madrid in how private a condition soever: if he desired any thing with these two restraints, he would move the King in it. The other told him, that he submitted to both these conditions, and only desired license to reside in Valliodolid, where he had lived many years when the Court remained there in the time of King Philip the Third.

29. This place was not disliked; and within few days don Lewis sent him word that the King approved it, and that he should have a letter to the chief magistrate there to treat him with all respect, and that his majesty would take care that he should not undergo any distress, but would supply him as his

necessities required.   And shortly after a message was sent to **1651**
the ambassadors to let them know that the King had appointed
such a day for to give them an audience to take their leave.
Which new importunity was as extraordinary as the former;
which was not at all grievous to the lord Cottington, who,
having obtained all he desired, was willing to be in his new
habitation, which he had sent to be made ready for him; but
the other much desired that the winter might be a little more
over, which continued yet very sharp, and was resolved not to
obey their summons till the weather mended; and likewise, out
[of] indignation for their treatment, he very heartily resolved
to refuse their present for the smallness of it, it being less than
had been used to be given to any single ordinary ambassador.
But the lord Cottington, with great importunity, prevailed with
him to decline both those contests, lest it might prove prejudicial to him[1]; and so they performed their ceremonies, and
about the beginning of March, after they had been in that March 6 (?)
Court near fifteen months, they both left Madrid in the same
hour: the lord Cottington taking his course for Valliodolid,
where he had the same house provided and made ready for him
by the care of the English Jesuits there in which he had dwelt
at the time of his agency when the Court resided there, and 1652
where he died within one year after, in the 77th[2] year of his June 19.
age.

30. He was a very wise man, by the great and long experience he had in business of all kinds, and by his natural
temper, which was not liable to any transport of anger or any
other passion, but could bear contradiction, and even reproach,
without being moved or put out of his way: for he was very
steady in pursuing what he proposed to himself, and had a
courage not to be frighted or amazed with any opposition.   It
is true he was illiterate as to the grammar of any language, or
the principles of any science; but by his perfectly understand-

---

[1] [On Dec. 13 they wrote a joint letter to de Haro asking for immediate payment of the promised payment of 38,000 reals, but complaining
of its being so much less than the present to their predecessor, which was
60,000 reals.   *Calend. Clar. S. P.* ii. 90.]

[2] [74th in the inscription on his monument in Westminster Abbey.]

1651 ing the Spanish, (which he spake as a Spaniard,) French, and
Italian languages, and having read very much in all, he could
not be said [to be] ignorant in any part of learning, divinity
only excepted; and had a very fine and extraordinary understanding in the nature of beasts and birds, and, above all, in all
kind of plantations and arts of husbandry. He was born a
gentleman both by father and mother, his father having a pretty
entire seat near Bruton in Somersetshire, worth above two
hundred pounds a year, which had descended from father to
son for many hundred years, and is still in the possession of
his elder brother's children, the family having been always
Catholic. His mother was a Stafford, nearly allied to sir Edward Stafford, who was vice-chamberlain to Queen Elizabeth,
1583 and had been ambassador in France; by whom this gentleman
was brought up, and was gentleman of his horse, and left one
of his executors of his will, and by him recommended to sir
Robert Cicill, then principal Secretary of State; who preferred
him to sir Charles Cornewallis, when he went ambassador into
1605 Spain, in the beginning of the reign of King James; and he
March. remained there for the space of eleven or twelve years in the
condition of secretary or agent, without ever returning into
England in all that time. He raised by his own virtue and
industry a very fair estate, [of] which though the revenue did
not exceed above four thousand pounds by the year, yet he had
four very good houses and three parks, the value whereof was
not reckoned into that computation. He lived very nobly, well
served and attended in his house; had a better stable of horses,
better provision for sports, especially of hawks, in which he
took great delight, and lived always with great splendour; for
though he loved money very well, and did not warily enough
consider the circumstances of getting it, he spent it well all
ways but in giving, which he did not affect. He was of an
excellent humour, and very easy to live with; and under a
grave countenance covered the most of mirth, and caused more,
than any man of the most pleasant disposition. He never used
any body ill, but used many very well for whom he had no
regard: and his greatest fault was that he could dissemble, and

make men believe that he loved them very well when he cared 1651
not for them. He had not very tender affections, nor bowels
apt to yearn at all objects which deserved compassion. He
was heartily weary of the world, and no man was more willing
to die, which is an argument that he had peace of conscience;
and left behind him a greater esteem of his parts than love to
his person.

31[1]. The other ambassador was dismissed with much more
courtesy: for when they heard that his family remained at
Antwerp in Flanders, and that he intended to go thither, and
stay there till he received other orders from the King his
master, they gave him all despatches thither which might be
of use to him in those parts. The King himself used many
gracious expressions to him at his last audience, and sent afterwards to him a letter for the archduke Leopold, in which he
expressed the good opinion he had of the ambassador, and commanded that, whilst he should choose to reside in those parts
under his command, he should receive all respect, and enjoy all
privileges as an ambassador: and don Lewis de Haro writ likewise to the archduke and the count of Fuensaldagna, to look March 4.
upon him as his particular friend. All which ceremonies,
though they cost them nothing, were of real benefit and advantage to the ambassador: for besides the treatment he received
from the archduke himself in Bruxells, as ambassador, such
directions or recommendations were sent to the magistrates at
Antwerp that he enjoyed the privilege of his chapel, and all the
English, who were numerous then in that city, repaired thither
with all freedom for their devotion and the exercise of their
religion: which liberty had never been before granted to any
man there, and which the English and Irish priests, and the
Catholics of those nations, exceedingly murmured at, and used
all the endeavours they could to have taken away, though in
vain.

32. In his passage through France he waited upon the Queen
mother, who received him very graciously; and he found there
that the success which Cromwell had obtained in Scotland

[1] [*Hist.*, p. 16.]

1651 (though the King was still there, and in a better condition than he was before) had the same effect in the Court of France as it had in the Court of Spain; it gave over all thought of the King, as in a condition not only deplorable but as absolutely desperate.

1650   33. There had a little before fallen out an accident that troubled France very much, and no less pleased Spain ; which Nov. 6. was the death of the prince of Aurange ; a young prince of great hope and expectation, and of a spirit that desired to be in action.   He found that the peace between Spain and the Low Countries, which his father had been so solicitous to make, even at his expiration, was not like to preserve him in equal lustre to what the three former princes had enjoyed ; and therefore he wished nothing more than that an opportunity might be offered to enter upon the war.   He complained loudly that the Court of Spain had not observed and performed many of those conditions which it was obliged to do for the particular benefit of him and his family : whereby he continued involved in many debts, which were uneasy to him ; and so, upon all occasions, which often fell out, he adhered to that party in the States which were known most to favour the interest of France ; which good inclination the cardinal, and the other ministers of that Crown, used all possible care and endeavour to culti- vate ; and Spain was so much affected with the apprehension of the consequence of that alteration, and with the conscience of their own having promoted it by not having complied with their obligations, that they resolved to redeem their error, and to reconcile him again, if possible, to them.   To this purpose, a very great present was prepared at Madrid to be sent to him ; ten brave Spanish horses, the worst of which cost there three hundred pounds sterling, with many other rarities of great value, as likewise a present of plate, jewels, and perfumed leather, to the princess royal his wife ; and a full assurance that they would forthwith begin to perform all the articles which were to be done by them, and finish all within a short time.

     34. The express who was appointed to accompany the pre-

sent, and to perform the other function, was to begin his journey within two days, when the news arrived, by an express from Bruxells, who came in as short a time as could be imagined, that the prince of Aurange was dead of the small-pox, and had left the princess with child, and very near her time ; who was brought to bed of a son within few days after his decease. The Court at Madrid could not conceal its joy, nor dissemble their opinion that the enemy whose influence they most apprehended was fortunately taken out of the way. On the other hand, France owned a great sorrow and grief for the loss of a man whom they believed to be more than ordinarily affected to them, and who, by a conjunction with their friends in Holland, might in a short time be much superior to that party in the States which adhered to the Spanish interest.

35. But nobody received so insupportable prejudice and damage by this fatal blow as the King of Great Britain did, towards whom that brave prince gave all the testimony and manifestation of the most entire, fast, and unshaken affection and friendship that hath ever been performed towards any person under any signal misfortune. Besides the assisting him upon several immergent occasions with greater sums of money than were easy to his incumbered fortune, his reputation, and declared resolution that he would venture all he had in that quarrel, disposed many to be the more concerned for his majesty. Though he could not prevail over that faction in Holland which were known to favour Cromwell, (and the more out of their aversion to him, and to his power and greatness,) and induce them to serve the King, yet he kept the States General from consenting to that infamous alliance and conjunction which shortly after his death they entered into with the new republic, and which they would never have yielded to if he had lived. And no doubt the respect both France and Spain had for him, and his interposition, had prevailed with both to be less impudent than they afterwards appeared to be, in a total declining all consideration of the King, and rejecting all thoughts of his restoration. It contributed very

(marginal notes:) 1650   Nov. 6.   Nov. 14.

1650 much to the negligent farewell the ambassadors had received in
Spain ; for the news of that prince's death had arrived there
some months before their departure ; and it did not only
extinguish all imaginations in France of any possible hope
[for [1]] the King, but very much lessened the respect and civility
which [that Court [2]] had always shewed to the Queen herself, a
daughter of France, towards whom they expressed not that
regard [they [2]] had formerly done.

36. But there was another accident which at this time gave
the Queen more trouble than this, and of which her majesty
made great complaint to the Chancellor [of the Exchequer]
upon his return from Spain. Upon the interview which had
been between the King and the Queen at Beauvais, when the
King went for Holland, upon the foresight, if not the resolution, that it would be fit for him to adventure his own
person into Scotland, he had left his brother the duke of York
with the Queen, with direction that he should conform himself
entirely to the will and pleasure of the Queen his mother,
matters of religion only excepted. And there was the less
doubt of his conformity to her commands, because, besides his
piety and duty, which was very entire towards her, he was to
depend wholly upon her bounty for his support, the Court
of France not taking any notice of the change, nor paying her
own narrow assignation with any punctuality ; so that she was
not able, besides the reservedness in her nature, so to supply
him as to make his condition pleasant to him, but exercised the
same austere carriage towards him which she had done to the
prince his brother, and as unsuccessfully. The duke was very
young, not above thirteen years of age, with a numerous family
of his own, not well enough inclined to be contented, and
consisting of persons who loved not one another, nor their
master well enough to consider him before themselves : which
wrought that effect upon him, that none of them had that
credit with him that at such an age some good men ought to
have had : which proceeded from want of reasonable providence
and circumspection. For when he made his escape out of

<hr>

[1] ['of,' MS.]   [2] ['it,' MS.]

England, (as is mentioned before,) [1] he had only one person 1650
attending him, who had before no relation or pretence to his
service, and whose merit might have been otherwise requited
than by giving him a title and dependence upon him, and who
quickly appeared to be so unworthy of it that he was removed
from it. Then was the time that such persons should have
been placed about him as might have both discovered such
infirmities as his nature might incline him to, and infused those
principles of piety and honour as he was most capable of and
disposed to, and which had been as proper for his present
misfortune as for his highest dignity. But that province was
wholly committed to the Queen his mother by the [late] King,
who was then in prison; and her majesty being then at Paris
when the duke landed in Holland, she could not deliberate so
long upon it as such a subject required, and so was persuaded
by others to consider them more than her son; and made haste
to put such a family about him, with reference to the number
and to the offices which they were designed to serve in, as was
above the greatness to which the younger son of the Crown of
England could pretend to by the usage and custom of that
kingdom when it was in the greatest splendour; and all this,
when there was not in view the least revenue to support it, but
that the whole charge and burden of it must inevitably fall
upon her; of which her majesty was quickly sensible, and paid
the penalty, at least in the peace and quiet of her mind.

37. The duke was full of spirit and courage, and naturally
loved designs, and desired to engage himself in some action
that might improve and advance the low condition of the
King his brother, towards whom he had an inviolable affection
and fidelity, superior to any temptation. He was not pleased
with the treatment he received in France, nor had confidence
enough in any of his servants, to be advised by [them], towards
the contriving any expedient that he might reasonably dispose
himself to, or to the dissuading him from any enterprise which
his own passion might suggest to him; though too many had
too much credit with him in contributing to his discontents,

[1] [Book xi. § 20.]

1650 and in representing the uncomfortableness of his own condition
to him, the little regard the Queen appeared to have of him,
the lustre that some of her servants lived in and all who
depended upon them, whilst his royal highness wanted all that
was necessary, and his servants were exposed to the most
scandalous necessities and contempt; and so endeavoured to
abate that reverence in him to the Queen his mother to which
he was very dutifully inclined.

38. There were at that time two persons who, though without any relation to the Court, very much frequented the duke's
lodgings, and had frequent discourses with him, sir Edward
Harbert, the late King's Attorney General, (of whom much is
said before,) and sir George Ratcliffe, who had been designed
by the late King to attend upon the duke of York into Ireland,
when he once thought of sending him thither; but that design
being quickly laid aside, there was no more thought of any
relation for him there. The duke looked upon them both as wise
men, and fit to give him advice; and finding that they both
applied themselves to him with diligence and address, he communicated his thoughts more freely to them than to any other.
And they took pains to persuade him to dislike the condition
he was in, and that he might spend his time more to his
advantage in some other place than in France; spake often to
him of the duke of Lorraine, as a pattern and example for all
unfortunate princes to follow: that he, being by the power and
injustice of the King of France driven out of his own prin-
cipality and dominions, had by his own virtue and activity put
himself in the head of an army; by which he made himself
so considerable that he was courted by both the Crowns of
France and Spain, and might make his conditions with either,
according to his own election; and in the mean time lived with
great reputation and in great plenty, esteemed by all the world
for his courage and conduct. With these and the like discourses the duke was much pleased and amused, and wished in
himself that he could be put into such a condition, when in
truth there could not a more improper example have been
proposed to him, whose condition was more unlike his, or

whose fortune and manners he was less to wish to follow or less **1650** able to imitate. For the duke of Lorraine had for many years before his misfortunes had a great name in war, and was looked upon as one of the greatest captains in Christendom, and had drawn the arms and power of France upon him by his in-constancy, and adhering to Spain contrary to his treaty and obligation with the other Crown ; and when he was driven out of his own country, and not able to defend it, he was in the head of a very good army, and possessed of great wealth, which he carried with him, and could not but be very welcome (as he well knew), into Flanders, both as his misfortunes proceeded from his affection to that King, and as his forces were necessary for their defence. And so he made such conditions with them as were most beneficial to him, and yet in the consequence so unsuccessful, as might well terrify all other princes from tread-ing in the same footsteps.

39. With the report of the defeat of that army by Cromwell in Scotland, (which was the first good fortune to the King,) or shortly after, some letters from England brought intelligence, without any ground, that the King was very dangerously sick, and, shortly after, that he was dead; which was believed in England, and from thence transmitted into France. This gave a new alarum to those two gentlemen who are mentioned before, who received the information from such friends in England that they did really believe it to be true ; and there-upon concluded, that both the place and the company would not be fit for the new King to be found in, and therefore that it would be necessary for the duke to remove from thence before the report should be confirmed and believed.

40. Whether they imparted this nice consideration to the duke or not, his highness, without any preface of the motives, told the Queen that he was resolved to make a journey to Bruxells; who, being exceedingly surprised, asked him the reason, and how he could be able to make such a journey; which she in truth believed impossible for him, since she knew he had no money. His answer in short was, that he would visit the duke of Lorraine, who had been always a friend to his

1650 father, and continued his affection to the King his brother, and
he had some reason to believe that he would enable him to
appear in action that might be for his majesty's service, and
that he was resolved to begin his journey the next day; from
which neither the Queen's advice or authority could divert him.
Her majesty quickly discerned that neither the lord Byron or
sir John Berkely or Mr. Bennett, his secretary, knew any thing
of it; and therefore easily concluded who the counsellors were;
both who were very ungracious to her, and she had long done
all she could to lessen the duke's esteem of them.   They well
foresaw that the want of money would be of that force, that,
without any other difficulty, the journey would be rendered
impossible; and they had therefore, upon their own credit or
out of their own store, procured as much as would defray the
journey to Bruxells; which by the duke's direction was put
into the hands of sir George Ratcliffe, and to be managed by
Sept. his providence and discretion.   And then he publicly declared
his resolution to begin his journey the next day for Bruxells,
leaving his servants to make what shift they could to attend or
follow him.

41. Since there was no remedy, the Queen thought it necessary that his chief servants should wait on him, that she
might receive advertisement what progress he made, and what
this design could be: and so the lord Byron and Mr. Bennett
make themselves ready for the journey; sir John Berkely
choosing to stay behind, that he might not appear inferior
where he had exercised the supreme charge.   And so, with the
other two counsellors, and many of the inferior servants, the
duke according to his resolution left the Queen; and when he
came to Bruxells he lodged at the house of sir Henry De Vic,
the King's resident, without being taken notice of by any of
that Court.   There the two counsellors began to form his
family, and to confer offices upon those who were most acceptable
to them, presuming that they should shortly receive news from
England which would confirm all that they had done under
other titles.   In the mean time the government of the house
and ordering the expense was committed wholly to sir George

Ratcliffe, whilst the other contented himself with presiding in 1650 the councils and directing all the politic designs. The duke of Lorraine had visited the duke upon his first arrival, and, being informed of the straits in which his royal highness was in, presented him with one thousand pistoles. But now the secret ground of all their counsels was found to be without any reality: the King was not only alive, and in good health, but known to be in the head of an army that looked Cromwell in the face; which destroyed all the machine they had raised: yet, being too far embarked to retire with any grace, and being encouraged by the civility the duke of Lorraine had shewed towards the duke, they had the presumption to propose that there might be a marriage between the duke of York and the daughter of the duke of Lorraine by the countess of Canticroy, whom he had publicly married, but which marriage was de- 1637 clared at Rome to be void, by reason that his former wife was still alive.

42. When the duke of Lorraine saw how the affairs of this young prince were conducted, and that the lord Byron and Mr. Bennett, who were men well bred, and able to have dis- coursed any business to him, and that one was his governor and the other his secretary, who by their offices ought to be most trusted in an affair of that moment, [were not acquainted with it,] and that the other two persons, who were men of a very unusual mien, appeared in it, and that only sir George Ratcliffe undertook to speak to him in it, who could only make himself understood in Latin, which the duke cared not to speak in, he declined entertaining the motion till he might know that it was made with the King's approbation; which the other did not pretend it to be, but that he did not doubt it would be approved by his majesty[1]. They were now at the end of their projects: and there being no means to stay longer at Bruxells, they per- suaded the duke to visit his sister at the Hague, and there to 1651 consider and advise what was next to be done. Jan. 2.O.S.[2]

[1] [On March 16, 1652, the King wrote to the earl of Norwich, author- izing him to propose the marriage. *Calend. Clar. S. P.* ii. 126.]

[2] [*Nicholas Papers*, i. 214.]

43. Of all these particulars the Queen complained to the Chancellor [of the Exchequer], with great bitterness against the folly and presumption of those two gentlemen, whose infidelity to the King she did not suspect, nor could imagine the motive that had engaged them to such a bold undertaking; but she required him, that as soon as he should come into Flanders he would make a journey to the Hague, and prevail with the duke (to whom she writ to the same purpose [1]) to return again to Paris; which the Chancellor promised to endeavour heartily to do, being exceedingly troubled at the general discourse which that sally had administered, as if there were a schism in the royal family, in a season when so much unity was requisite.

44. There was another instance of the extreme lowness of the King's condition, and of the highest disrespect the Court of France could express towards him, and of which all the Protestant part of the Queen's family complained very vehemently. From the time of the Queen's being in France, the [late] King had appointed a chaplain of his own, (Dr. Cosins, who was afterwards bishop of Durham,) to attend upon her majesty for the constant service of that part of her household, the number of her Protestant servants being much superior to those who were Catholic. And the Queen had always punctually complied with the King's directions, and used the chaplain very graciously, and assigned him a competent support with the rest of her servants. An under room in the Louvre, out of any common passage, had been assigned for their morning and evening devotions, the key whereof was committed to the chaplain, who caused the room to be decently furnished and kept; being made use of to no other purpose. And here, when the prince first came thither, and afterwards whilst he stayed, [he] performed his devotions all the week, but went Sundays still to the resident's house to hear sermons. At this time an order was sent from the Queen Regent that that room should be no more applied to that purpose, and that the King would not permit the exercise of any other religion in any of his houses than the Catholic: and the Queen

---

[1] [He received the letter at the beginning of June, 1651. *Nicholas Papers*, i. 254.]

gave notice to the chaplain that she was no longer able to continue 1650
the payment of the exhibition she had formerly assigned to him.
The Protestants, whereof many were of the best quality, lamented
this alteration to the Chancellor [of the Exchequer], and desired
him to intercede with the Queen; which he had the more title
to do, because at his going into Spain she had vouchsafed to
promise him, (upon some rumours of which he took notice,) that
the same privilege which had been, should still be continued and
enjoyed by the Protestants of her house, and that she would
provide for the chaplain's subsistence. He presumed to speak
with her majesty upon it, and besought her to consider what ill
impression this new order would make upon all the Protestants
of his majesty's dominions, upon whom he was chiefly to depend
for his restoration, and how much prejudice it might be to
herself, to be looked upon as a greater enemy to Protestants
than she had been taken notice of to be; and likewise, whether
this order, which had been given since the departure of the
duke of York, might not be made use of as an excuse for his not
returning, or indeed for his remove, since the precise time when
it issued would not be generally understood. The Queen heard
him very graciously, and acknowledged that what he said had
reason in it, but protested that she knew not what remedy to
apply to it; that she had been herself surprised with that order,
and was troubled at it; but that the Queen Regent was positive
in it, and blamed her for want of zeal in her religion, and that
she cared not to advance it, or to convert any of her children.
She wished him to confer with Mr. Mountague upon it, and
implied that his bigotry in his new religion had contributed
much to the procuring that order. He had newly taken orders, 1651
and was become priest in that Church, and had great power March [1].
with the Queen Regent, as well for his animosity against that
religion he had professed as for his vehement zeal for the Church
of which he now was. And upon this occasion her majesty expressed a great sense of the loss she had sustained by the death 1647
of her old confessor, father Phillipps, who, she said, was a prudent Jan.
and discreet man, and would never suffer her to be pressed to

---

[1] [*Nicholas Papers*, i. 220.]

1650 any passionate undertakings under pretence of doing good for Catholics, and always told her that as she ought to continue firm and constant to her own religion, so she was to live well towards the Protestants, who deserved well from her, and to whom she was beholding. She said it would not be possible to have the same or any other room set aside, or allowed to be used, as a chapel, but that she would take such course that the family might meet for the exercise of their devotions in some private room that belonged to their own lodgings; and that though her own exhibition was so ill paid that she was indebted to all her servants, yet she would give order that Dr. Cosins (against whom she had some personal exception) should receive his salary in proportion with the rest of her servants. She bade him assure the duke of York that he should have as free exercise of his religion as he had before, though it must not be in the same place.

45. The Chancellor conferred with Mr. Mountague upon the subject, and offered the same reasons which he had done to the Queen; which he looked not upon as of moment; [but] said that the King of France was master in his own house, and he was resolved, though his majesty himself should come thither again, never to permit any solemn exercise of the Protestant religion in any house of his. The consideration of what the Protestants in England might think on this occasion was of least moment to him, and it was indeed the common discourse of all men that the Protestants could never do the King service, but that all his hope must be in the Roman Catholics and the Presbyterians; and that he ought to give all satisfaction to both those parties.

46. When the Chancellor came to Antwerp, with a purpose to make a journey speedily to the Hague, he was informed that the States were much offended that the duke of York remained there; and therefore that the princess royal (who now more depended upon their favour than ever, her own jointure, as well as the fortune of her son, being to be resolved in their judicatory) could no longer entertain him, but that he would be the next day at Breda [1]. Thither he immediately went; and found him

[1] [March $\frac{17}{27}$, 1651; *Nicholas Papers*, i. 230.]

[the duke] there with a family in all the confusion imaginable, **1651** in present want of every thing, and not knowing what was to be done next.   They all censured and reproached the counsel by which they had been guided, and the counsellors as bitterly inveighed against each other, for undertaking many things which prevailed upon either, which had no foundation in truth.   They who concurred in nothing else were equally severe against the Attorney, as a madman, and of that intolerable pride that it was not possible for any man to converse with him.   And he as frankly reproached them all with being men of no parts, of no understanding, no learning, no principles, and no resolution, and was so just to them all as to contemn every man of them alike.   And in truth he had rendered himself so grievous to them all, that there was no man who desired to be in his company; yet by the knack of his talk, which was the most like reason without being it, he retained still too much credit with the duke, who, being amused and confounded with his positive discourse, thought him to be wiser than those who were more easily understood; and was himself so young, that he was rather delighted with the journeys he had made than sensible that he had not entered upon them with reason enough; and he was fortified with a firm resolution never to acknowledge that he had committed an error.   He was very glad to receive the Queen's letter which the Chancellor delivered to him, and heard his advice very willingly, and resolved to begin his journey to Paris without any delay; and looked upon the occasion as a very seasonable redemption.   The next day he went to Antwerp, and from thence, with the same retinue he had carried with him, made haste to Paris, and was received by the Queen his mother **June.** without those expostulations and reprehensions which he might reasonably have expected, though her severity was the same towards all those who she thought had had the credit and power to seduce him; and they were not solicitous by any apologies or confession to recover her favour, for the true reason that had swayed them being not to be avowed, any other that they could devise and suggest would have rendered [them] more inexcusable.

1650

§ 23.

47[1]. During all this time the King underwent all kinds of mortifications. After the defeat of the Scots' army in September, with which the King and Cromwell were equally delighted, as hath been said before, the marquis of Arguyle's empire seemed not to be so absolute. A new army was appointed to be raised; the King himself interposed more than he had done, and the noblemen and officers came to him with more confidence; and his majesty took upon him to complain and expostulate when those things were done which he did not like: yet the power was still in Arguyle's hands, who, under all the professions of humility, exercised still the same tyranny; insomuch as the King grew weary of his own patience, and resolved to make some attempt in his own vindication. Dr. Frayzer, who was the King's physician many years before, and had constantly attended upon his person, and very much contributed to the King's journey into Scotland, was shortly after his coming thither disliked by Arguyle, who knew that he was a creature of the Hambletons, and found him to be of an unquiet and over-active spirit; and thereupon sequestered from his attendance. There were many officers who had served in duke Hambleton's Engagement, as Middleton and others, who had very entire affections for the King; and many of them had corresponded with Mountrose, and resolved to have joined with him; and finding themselves excluded, (as all of them were,) from any employment by the power of Arguyle, had retired into the Highlands, and remained there concealed in expectation of some good season in which they might avowedly appear. With some of these Dr. Frayzer had held correspondence whilst he was in the Court, and had often spoken to the King of their affection, and readiness to serve him, and of their power to do it, and had returned his majesty's gracious acceptation of their service, and his resolution to employ them. And now, being not himself suffered to come to the Court, he found means to meet and confer with many of them, and held intelligence with the lord Latherdale, who had always great confidence in him; and the

---

[1] [The commencement of this section, to the word 'vindication,' is from the *Life*, p. 433.]

officers undertaking to do more than they could, or the doctor 1650
understanding them to undertake more than they did, (for his
fidelity was never suspected,) he gave the King such an account
of their numbers, as well as resolutions, that his majesty appointed a day for their rendezvous, and promised to be present
with them, and then to ·publish a declaration (which was likewise prepared) of the ill treatment he had endured, and against
the person of Arguyle; [1]to whom the duke of Buckingham, notwithstanding all former professions, gave himself wholly up,
[and] imparted all this correspondence, having found some of
the letters which had passed, by the King's having left his
cabinet open; for he was not at all trusted.

48. But they did not think the time so near; so that the
King did prosecute this purpose so far, that he rode one day
with a dozen or twenty horse into the Highlands, and lodged Oct. 4.
there one night; the earl of Arguyle nor any body else
knowing what was become of him; which put them all into
great distraction. It was indeed a very empty and unprepared
design, contrived and conducted by Dr. Frayzer, without any
foundation to build upon, and might well have ruined the
King, and was afterwards called the Start; yet it proved,
contrary to the expectation of wise men, very much to his
majesty's advantage. For though he was compelled the next Oct. 5.
day to return, and with a circumstance that seemed to have
somewhat of force in it, for as the company he looked for failed
to appear, so there was a troop of horse, which he looked not
for, sent by Arguyle, who used very effectual instance with
him to return, notwithstanding [this][2], this declaration of
resentment, together with the observation of what the people
generally spake upon it, 'that the King was not treated as he
ought to be,' made the marquis of Arguyle change his counsels,
and to be more solicitous to satisfy the King. A summons
was sent out in the King's name to call a Parliament, and
great preparations were really made for the coronation:
and the season of the year, (for whilst Cromwell was securing

---

[1] [*Life*, pp. 433–448, for all that follows, to the middle of § 108.]
[2] ['which,' MS.]

1650 himself in Edenborough, and making provisions for his army, the winter came on,) and the strong passes, which were easy to be guarded, hindered the enemy's advance; so that the King resided sometimes at Sterling and sometimes at St. Johnstone's, Nov. 26. with commodity enough.   The Parliament met at Sterling[1], and shortly after brought all the lords of the other party thither, who appeared to have credit enough to wipe off all those stains with which the Engagement had defaced them, yet with submission to stand publicly in the stool of repentance, acknowledging their former transgression; as they all did.

49. Duke Hambleton and Latherdale were welcome to the King, and nearest his confidence; which [neither] the duke of Buckingham, who had cast off their friendships as unuseful, nor the marquis of Arguyle, were pleased with.   The King himself grew very popular, and, by his frequent conferences with the knights and burgesses, he got any thing passed in the Parliament which he desired.   He caused many infamous acts to be repealed, and provided for the raising an army, whereof himself was general; and no exceptions were taken to those officers who had formerly served the King [his father.]

1651 50. The coronation was passed with great solemnity and Jan. 1. magnificence, all men making show of joy, and of being united to serve his majesty : yet the marquis of Arguyle preserved his greatness and interest so well, and was still so considerable, that it was thought very expedient to raise an imagination in him that the King had a purpose to marry one of his daughters; which was carried so far, that the King could no otherwise defend himself from it than by sending an express into France for the Queen his mother's consent, (which seemed Feb. not to be doubted of,) and to that purpose captain Titus, a person grateful to Arguyle and to all the Presbyterian party, was sent, who finding the Queen less warm upon the proposition than was expected, made less haste back; so that the fate of Scotland was first determined.

51. The King's army was as well modelled, and in as good

[1] [At Perth. The meeting of Parliament at Stirling was on May 23, 1651.]

a condition, as it was like to be whilst he stayed in Scotland, **1651**
by that time that Cromwell was ready to take the field. He
was persuaded to make David Lashly lieutenant general of the
army, who had very long experience, and a very good name
in war; and Middleton commanded the horse. The artillery
was in very good order under the command of Wemmes,
who had not the worse reputation there for having been
ingrateful to the King's father. He was a confessed good
officer; and there were, or could be, very few officers of any
superior command but such who had drawn their swords
against his late majesty, all those who had served under the
marquis of Mountrose having been put to death. Many of the
greatest noblemen had raised regiments or troops; and all the
young gentlemen of the kingdom appeared very hearty and
cheerful in commands, or volunteers : and in all appearance
they seemed a body equal in any respect, and superior in
number, to the enemy; which advanced all they could, and
made it manifest that they desired nothing more than to come
to battle, which was not thought counsellable for the King's
army to engage in, except upon very notable advantages;
which they had reason every day to expect, for there was a
very broad and a deep river between them, and if they kept the
passes of which they were possessed, and could hardly choose
but keep, Cromwell must in a very few days want provisions,
and so be forced to retire; whilst the King had plenty of all
things which he stood in need of, and could by the advantage of
the passes be in his rear as soon as he thought fit.

52. And in this posture both armies stood in view of each
other near the two months of June and July, with some small
attempts upon each other, with equal success. About the end **July 20.**
of July, by the cowardice or treachery of general major Bayly[1],
who had a body of four thousand men to keep it, Cromwell
gained the pass, by which he was got behind the King; and though

---

[1] [Sir John Browne was the major-general, who was taken prisoner in
the engagement on July 20, and lieut.-gen. Holburne was in chief command, who ' was thought to have played the traitor.' Balfour's *Annals*,
iv. 313.]

1651 he could not compel his majesty to fight, for there was still the great river between them, he was possessed, or might quickly be, of the most fruitful part of the country; and so would not only have sufficient provision for his own army, but in a short time would cut off much of that which should supply the King's. This was a great surprise to the King, and put him into new counsels; and he did, almost with the unanimous advice of the principal officers and all those who were admitted to council, take a resolution worthy of his courage; and, how unfortunate soever it proved, [there] was evidence enough that the same misfortune would have fallen out if he had not taken it.

53. The King was now, by Cromwell's putting himself behind him, much nearer to England than he: nor was it possible for him to overtake his majesty, in regard of the ways he was unavoidably to pass, till after the King had been many days' march before him: his majesty's fate depended upon the success of one battle: for a possible escape into the Highlands, after a defeat there, was no kingly prospect: all the northern parts of England had given him cause to believe that they were very well affected to his service, and if he could reach those countries, he might presume to increase the number of his army, which was numerous enough, with an addition of such men as would make it much more considerable. Hereupon, with the concurrence aforesaid, it was resolved that the army should immediately march, with as much expedition as was possible, into England, by the nearest ways which led into Lancashire, whither the King sent expresses to give those of whom he expected much, by reason some of them had been in Scotland with him with large undertakings, notice of his purpose, that they might get their soldiers together to receive him. And he sent likewise an express to the Isle of Man, where the earl of Darby had securely reposed himself from the end of the former war, that he would meet his majesty in Lancashire. The marquis of Arguyle was the only man who dissuaded his majesty's march into England, with reasons which were not frivolous; but the contrary prevailed; and he stayed behind,

and when the King began his march he retired to his house in **1651**
the Highlands. Some were of opinion that he should then have
been made prisoner, and left so secured that he might not be
able to do mischieve when the King was gone, which most men
believed he would be inclined to. But his majesty would not
consent to it, because he was confident he would not attempt
any thing while the army was entire: if it prevailed, he neither
would nor could do any harm; and if it were defeated, it would
be no great matter what he did.

54. Though Cromwell was not frequently without good intelligence what was done in the King's army and councils, yet
this last resolution was consulted with so great secrecy, and
executed with that wonderful expedition, that the King had
marched a whole day without the people's comprehending what
the meaning was, and before he received the least advertisement
of it. It was not a small surprise to him, nor was it easy for
him to resolve what to do. If he should follow with his whole
army, all the advantages he had got in Scotland would be
presently lost, and the whole kingdom be again united in any
new mischieve. If he followed but with part, he might be
too weak when he overtook the King, whose army he knew
could bear the fatigue of a long march better than his could do.
There were two considerations which troubled him exceedingly;
the one, the terrible consternation he foresaw the Parliament
would be in, when they heard that the King with his army was
nearer to them than their own army was for their defence; and
he knew that he had enemies enough to improve their fear, and
to lessen his conduct: the other was, the apprehension that if
the King had time given to rest in any place, he would infinitely
increase and strengthen his army by the resort of the people, as
well as the gentry and nobility, from all parts. And though
he did so much undervalue the Scots' army that he would have
been glad to have found himself engaged with it upon any
inequality of number or disadvantage of ground, yet he did
believe that by a good mixture with English they might be
made very considerable. He took a very quick resolution to
provide for all the best he could: he despatched an express to

1651 the Parliament, to prevent their being surprised with the news before they received it from him, and to assure them that he would himself overtake the enemy before they should give them any trouble ; and gave such farther orders for drawing the auxiliary troops together in the several counties as he thought fit.

55. He gave Lambert order immediately to follow the King with seven or eight hundred horse, and to draw as many others as he could from the country militia, and to disturb his march the most he could, by being near and obliging them to march close, without engaging his party in any sharp action (without a very notorious advantage,) but to keep himself entire till he should come up to him.   And with this order Lambert marched away the same day the advertisement came.

56. He resolved then to leave major general Munke, upon whom he looked with most confidence as an excellent officer of foot, and as entirely devoted to him, with a strong party of foot and some troops of horse, strong enough to suppress any forces which should arise after his departure, to keep Edenborough and the harbour of Leith ; to surprise and apprehend as many of the nobility and considerable gentry as he should find, and keep them under custody; to use the highest severity against all who opposed him, and, above all, not to endure or permit the license of the preachers in their pulpits, and to make himself as formidable as was possible : in the last place, that as soon as there appeared no visible force in the field he[1] should besiege Sterling, whither most persons of condition were retired with their goods of value, as to a place of strength and capable of being defended ; where the records of the kingdom and many other things of most account were deposited, it being the place where the King had for the most part resided.   He charged him, if at [Sterling[2]] or any place, he found a stubborn resistance, and were forced to spend much time, or to take it by storm, that he should give no quarter, nor exempt it from

---

[1] ['that he,' MS.]

[2] ['St. Johnston's,' MS., but crossed out, as also above, where 'Sterling' is substituted ; and doubtless the same substitution was intended here.]

a general plunder. All which rules Munke observed with the **1651**
utmost rigour, and made himself as terrible as man could be.

57. When he had despatched all these orders and directions
with marvellous expedition, and seen most of them advanced in
some degree of expedition, he began his own march with the
remainder of his army, three days after the King was gone, with
a wonderful cheerfulness, and assurance to the officers and
soldiers that he should obtain a full victory in England over
those who fled from him out of Scotland.

58. The King had, from the time that he had recovered any
authority in Scotland, granted a commission to the duke of
Buckingham to raise a regiment of horse, which Mass[e]y was
to command under him, and to raise another regiment of foot;
and the English which should resort thither, of which they
expected great numbers, should list themselves in one of those
regiments. And there were some who had listed themselves in
either of them ; but the discipline they [the Scots] had used to
the King, and their adhering to their old principles, even after
they seemed united for his majesty, had kept those who were
in England from repairing thither. They who came from
Holland with the King had disposed themselves as is said
before, and there was little doubt but that as soon as the King
should enter England those two regiments would be immediately
full. The duke of Buckingham had lost much ground, and
the more because the King was not pleased with it, by his
having broken off all manner of friendship with the duke Hambleton and the earl of Latherdale, to whom he had professed so
much, and entered into so fast a conjunction with the marquis
of Arguyle, their declared irreconcilable[1] enemy, and by his
adhering so firmly to him, when he was less dutiful to the King
than he ought to have been. Mass[e]y had got a great name by
his defending Gloster against the late King, and was looked
upon as a martyr for the Presbyterian interest, and so very dear
to that party; and therefore as soon as they came within the
borders of England he was sent with some troops before, and
was always to march at least a day before the army, to the end

---

[1] ['irreconciliable,' MS.]

1651 that he might give notice of the King's coming, and draw the
gentry of the counties through which he passed to be ready to
attend upon his majesty. Besides, he had particular acquaintance with most of the Presbyterians of Lancashire, whom nobody
imagined to be of the Scotch temper, or unwilling to unite and
join with the royal party, nor indeed were they.

59. But it was fatal to all Scotch armies to have always
in them a committee of ministers who ruined all; and though
there had been now all the care taken that could be, to choose
such men for that service who had the reputation of being the
most sober and moderate of that whole body, and who had
shewed more affection, and advanced the King's service more,
than the rest, yet this moderate people no sooner heard that
Mass[e]y was sent before to call upon their friends, and observed
that from the entrance into England those about the King
seemed to have less regard for the Covenant than formerly, but
they sent an express to him, without communicating in the
least degree with the King, with letters and declarations,
wherein they required him to publish that declaration which
signified the King's and the whole army's zeal for the Covenant, and resolution to prosecute the true intent of it; and
forbad him to receive or entertain any soldiers into his troops
but those who would subscribe that obligation. The King had
shortly notice of this, and lost no time in sending to Mass[e]y
not to publish any such declaration, and to behave himself with
equal civility towards all men who were forward to serve his
majesty. But before this inhibition was received, the matter
had taken air in all places, and was spread over the kingdom;
all men fled from their houses, or concealed themselves, who
wished the King very well; and his motion was so quick that
none repaired to him.

60. In Lancashire the earl of Darby met him [the King], who
as soon as he received his summons left the Isle of Man. When
they came about Warrington in Cheshire [1], they found that there
was a body of the enemy drawn up in a fair field, which did not
appear considerable enough to stop their march. This was Lam-

[1] [Lancashire.]

bert; who had made so much haste that he had that day fallen **1651** upon some of their troops, and beaten them into the army; but when the army came up, they [Lambert's troops] according to their order and purpose, retired, and, being pursued by the King's horse with a greater party, made more disorderly haste than a well ordered retreat requires, but with no considerable loss. This success made a great noise, as if Lambert had been defeated.

61. At Warrington it was thought counsellable, very unfortunately, that the earl of Darby, with the lord Withrington and several other officers of good name, should return into Lancashire, in order to raise the well affected in those two counties of Lancashire and Cheshire, who could not come in upon so quick a march as the King had made; and yet, it being out of the road that Cromwell was to follow, who was entered into Yorkshire, the remaining of those persons there was thought a good expedient to gather a body of English, which the King extremely desired, and if they found any great difficulties they might follow the army. In order to which they had a body of near two hundred horse, consisting for the most part of officers and gentlemen; which deprived the army of a strength they wanted, and was afterwards acknowledged to be a counsel too suddenly entered into.

62. Upon the appearance of that body of Lambert's, the whole army was drawn up, and appeared very cheerful. And the King having observed David Lashly throughout the whole march sad and melancholic, and at that time, when the enemy retired, and plainly in a quicker pace than retreats used to be made, slow in giving orders, and riding by himself, his majesty rode up to him, and asked him with great alacrity how he could be sad when he was in the head of so brave an army, which he said looked well that day, and demanded of him how he liked them. To which David Lashly answered him in his ear, being at some distance from any other, that he was melancholic indeed, for he well knew that army, how well soever it looked, would not fight: which the King imputed to the chagrin[1] of his humour, and gave [it] no credit, nor told it to any man, till,

[1] ['shaggringe,' MS.]

1651   many years after, upon another occasion which will be remembered in its place, he told the Chancellor [of the Exchequer] of it [1].

63. It was not thought fit to pursue Lambert; who, being known to be a man of courage and conduct, and his troops to be of the best, was suspected by so disorderly a retreat to have only designed to have drawn the army another way, to disorder and disturb their march; which they resolved to continue with the same expedition which they had hitherto used, which was incredible, until they should come to such a post as they might securely rest themselves. And there was an imagination that they might have continued it even to London, which would have produced wonderful effects; but they quickly found it to be impossible, and that both horse and foot grew so weary that they must have rest. The weather was exceedingly hot, the march having been begun near the beginning of August, which is the warmest season of the year; so that if they had not rest some time, before an enemy approached them, how willing soever they might be, they could not be able to fight.

64. There was a small garrison in Shrewsbury commanded by a gentleman [2] who it was thought might be prevailed with to Aug. 20. give it up to the King; but his majesty sending to him, he returned a rude denial: so that his majesty's eye was upon Worcester, that was so little out of the way to London, that the going thither would not retard the march to the other, if they found the army able to continue it. Worcester had always been a place very well affected in itself, and most of the gentlemen of that county had been engaged for the King in the 1646 former war, and the city was the last that had surrendered to July 23. the Parliament of all those which had been garrisoned for his majesty; when all the works were thrown down, and no garrison from that time had been kept there, the shrief and justices and committees having had power enough to defend it against any malignity of the town or country; and at this time all the principal gentry of that county had been seized upon, and were now prisoners there. Thither the King marched with his army

[1 Book xiv. § 109.]   2 [col. Mackworth.]

even as soon as they had heard that he was in England : where- **1651** upon the committee, and all those who were employed by the Parliament, fled in all the confusion imaginable, leaving their prisoners behind them, lest they should become prisoners to them ; and the city opened their gates, and received the King Aug. 22. with all the demonstration of affection and duty that could be expressed ; and made such provision for the army that it wanted nothing that it could desire, the mayor taking care for the present provision of shoes and stockings, the want whereof in so long a march was very apparent and grievous. The principal persons of the country found themselves at liberty, and they, and the mayor and aldermen with all the solemnity they could prepare, attended the herald who proclaimed the King, as he had done, in more haste and with less formality, in all those considerable towns through which his majesty had passed.

65. The army liked their quarters here so well that neither officer nor soldier was in any degree willing to quit them till they should be throughly refreshed ; and it could not be denied that the fatigue had been even insupportable ; never so many hundred miles had been marched in so few days and with so little rest ; nor did it in truth appear reasonable to any that they should remove from thence, since it was not possible that they should•be able to reach London, though it had been better prepared for the King's reception than it appeared to [be[1]], before Cromwell would be there, who, having with great haste continued his march in a direct line, was now as near to it as the King's army was, and stood only at gaze to be informed what his majesty meant to do. Worcester was a very good post, seated almost in the middle of the kingdom, and in as fruitful a country as any part of it ; a good city, served by the noble river of Severn from all the adjacent counties ; Wales behind it, from whence levies might be made of great numbers of stout men : it was a place whither the King's friends might repair if they had the affections they pretended to have ; and it was a place where he might defend himself, if the enemy would attack him, with many advantages, and could not be compelled to engage his

[1] ['me,' MS.]

1651 army in a battle till Cromwell had gotten men enough to encompass him on all sides : and then he might choose on which side to fight, since the enemy must be on both sides the river, and could not come suddenly to relieve each other, and this pressure would require much time; in which [there might be] several insurrections in the kingdom, if they were so weary of the present tyranny, and so solicitous to be restored to the King's government, as they were conceived to be : for nobody could ever hope for a more secure season to manifest their loyalty, than when the King was in the heart of the kingdom with a formed army of near twenty thousand men, horse and foot, (for so they might be accounted to be,) with which he might relieve those who were in danger to be oppressed by a more powerful party. These considerations produced the resolution to provide in the best manner to expect Cromwell there, and a hope that he might be exercised by other diversions : and there was like to be time enough to cast up such works upon the hill before the town as might keep the enemy at a distance, and their own quarters from being suddenly straitened : all which were recommended to the general to take care of, and to take such a perfect view of the ground that no advantage might be lost when the time required it.

66. The first ill omen that happened was the news of the defeat of the earl of Darby, and the total destruction of those gallant persons who accompanied him. The earl of Darby, within two or three days after he had left the King with a body of near two hundred horse, all gallant men, employed his servants and tenants to give the country notice of his staying behind the King, to head and command those persons who should repair to his service; which the quick march his majesty made through the country would not permit them to do. And in expectation of a good appearance of the people he went to a little market-town called Wiggan, in the duchy of Lancaster, Aug. 25. where he stayed that night; when in the morning a regiment of the militia of the neighbour counties, commanded by a man of courage[1], whom Cromwell had sent to follow in the track of the

[1] [col. Lilburne.]

King's march, to gather up the stragglers and such as were not 1651
able to keep pace with the army, having received some advertisement that a troop of the King's horse were behind the army in
that town, fell very early into it, before the persons in the town
were out of their beds, having, upon all the inquiry they could
make, assurance that there was no enemy near them ; nor indeed was there any suspicion of this regiment, which consisted
of the several troops of the several counties, and passed that
way by accident. As many as could get their horses, presently
mounted ; they who could not, put themselves together on foot ;
and all endeavoured to keep the enemy from entering into the
town ; and the few who were got on horseback charged them
with great courage. But the number of the enemy was too
great, and the town too open, to put a stop to them in any one
place, when they could enter at so many and encompass those
who opposed them.

67. The earl of Darby, after his horse had been killed under
him, made a shift on foot to get into some enclosed grounds,
and to conceal himself all that day, but was soon betrayed and
apprehended, and committed to prison[1]. The lord Withrington,
after he had received many wounds, and given as many, and
merited his death by the vengeance he took upon those who
assaulted him, was killed upon the place; and so was sir Thomas
Til[de]sley, and many other gallant gentlemen, very few escap-
ing to carry news of the defeat. Sir William Throgmorton,
(who had been major general of the marquis of Newcastle's
army, and was left to command in the same function,) received
so many wounds, that he was looked upon as dead, and not fit
to be carried away with the prisoners; and so fell into such
charitable and generous hands in the town, that, being believed
to be dead, [he] was afterwards so well recovered, (though with
great maims and loss of limbs,) that he at last got himself
transported into Holland; where he was at first appearance
taken for a ghost, all men having believed him to be buried
long before. Most of those who were taken prisoners, of any

---

[1] [He was only taken in flight after the battle of Worcester, and was
not betrayed.]

1651 quality, were afterwards sacrificed as a spectacle to the people, and barbarously put to death in several places, some with the earl of Darby, and others, near the same time, in other places.

68 [1]. The earl of Darby was a man of unquestionable loyalty to the King, and gave clear testimony of it before he received any obligations from the Court, and when he thought himself 1650 disobliged by it. This King, in his first year, sent him the Jan. 12. Garter, which, in many respects, he had expected from the last; and the sense of that honour made him so readily comply with the King's command in attending him, when he had no confidence in the undertaking, nor any inclination to the Scots, who he thought had too much guilt upon them in depressing it, to- be made instruments to repair and restore the Crown. He was a man of great honour and clear courage; and all his defects and misfortunes proceeded from his having lived so little time amongst his equals, that he knew not how to treat his inferiors; which was the source of all the ill that befell him, having thereby drawn such a prejudice from the persons of inferior quality, who yet thought themselves too good to be contemned, against him, that they pursued him to death. And the King's army was no sooner defeated (as it shortly after was) but they renewed their old method of murdering in cold blood, July 1. and sent a commission to erect a high court of justice in Lancashire [2] to persons of ordinary quality, many not being gentlemen, and all notoriously his enemies, to try the earl of Darby for his treason and rebellion; which they easily found him guilty of, and put him to death in a town of his own [3], against which he had expressed a severe displeasure for their obstinate rebellion against the King, with all the circumstances of rudeness and barbarity they could invent. The same night, one of those who was amongst his judges sent a trumpet to the Isle of Man with a letter directed to the countess dowager of Darby, by which he required her to deliver up the castles and island to the Parliament: nor did their malice abate, till they had

---

[1] [This section follows in this place in the MS., but has been transposed in former editions to follow § 81.]

[2] [at Chester.]　　　　　　　　　　　[3] [at Bolton, on Oct. 15.]

reduced that lady, (a woman of very high and princely ex- **1651** traction, being the daughter of the duke de [Tremouille[1]] in France, and a lady of the most exemplar virtue and piety of her time,) and that whole illustrious family, to the lowest penury and want, by disposing, giving, and selling, all the fortune and estate that should support it.

69. The lord Withrington was one of the most goodly persons of that age, being near the head higher than most tall men, and a gentleman of the best and most ancient extraction, of the county of Northumberland, and of a very fair fortune, and one of the four which the last King made choice of to be about the person of his son the Prince as gentlemen of his privy chamber, when he first erected his family. His affection to the King was always notorious; and serving in the House of Commons as knight of the shire for the county of Northumberland, he quickly got the reputation of being amongst the most malignant. And as soon as the war broke out, he was of the first who raised both horse and foot at his own charge, and served eminently with them under the marquis of Newcastle, from whom he had a very particular and entire friendship, as he was very nearly allied to him; and by his testimony that he had performed many signal services, he was about the middle of the war made a peer of the kingdom. He **1643** was a man of great courage and choler, by the last of which he **Nov. 10.** incurred the ill will of many, who imputed it to an insolence of nature, which no man was farther from, nor of a nature more civil and candid towards all in business or conversation. But having sat long in the House of Commons, and observed the uningenuity of the proceeding there, and the gross cheats by which they deceived and cozened the people, he had contracted so hearty an indignation against them and all who were cozened by them, and against all who had not his zeal to oppose and destroy them, that he often said things to slow and phlegmatic men which offended them, and it may be injured them; which his good nature often obliged him to acknowledge, and ask pardon of those who would not question him for it. He

[1] ['Trumolio,' MS.]

1651 transported himself into the parts beyond the sea at the same
time with the marquis of Newcastle, and to accompany him,
and remained still with him till the King went into Scotland;
and then waited upon his majesty, and endured the same
affronts which others did during the time of his residence there.
And, it may be, the observation of their behaviour, the knowledge of their principles, and the disdain of their treatment,
produced that aversion from their conversation that prevailed
upon his impatience to part too soon from their company, in
hope that the earl of Darby, (under whom he was very willing
to serve,) and he might quickly draw together such a body of
the royal party that might give some limits to the unbounded
imaginations of that nation.   It was reported by the enemy,
that, in respect of his brave person and behaviour, they did
offer him quarter, which he refused, and that they were thereby
compelled, in their own defence, to kill him; which is probable
enough; for he knew well the animosity the Parliament had
against him; and it cannot be doubted but that if he had
fallen into their hands they would not have used him better
than they did the earl of Darby, who had not more enemies.

70. Sir Thomas Til[de]sley was a gentleman of a good family
and a good fortune, who had raised men at his own charge at
the beginning of the war, and had served in the command of
them till the very end of it with great courage; and refusing
to make any composition, after the murder of the King he
found means to transport himself into Ireland to the marquis
of Ormonde; with whom he stayed, till he was, with the rest
of the English officers, dismissed, to satisfy the barbarous jealousy of the Irish, and then got over into Scotland a little
before the King marched from thence, and was desired by the
earl of Darby to remain with him.   The names of the other
persons of quality who were killed in that encounter, and of
those who were taken prisoners and afterwards put to death,
ought to be discovered and mentioned honourably, by him who
proposes to himself to communicate those transactions to the
view of posterity.

71. When the news of this defeat came to Worcester, as it

did even almost as soon as the King came thither, it exceedingly 1651
afflicted his majesty, and abated much of the hope he had of a
general rising of the people on his behalf. His army was very
little increased by the access of any English; and though he
had passed near the habitation of many persons of honour and
quality, whose affections and loyalty had been notorious, not
a man of them repaired to him. The sense of their former
sufferings remained, and the smart was not over; nor did his
stay in Worcester for so many days add any resort to his
Court. The gentlemen of the country whom his coming thither
had redeemed from imprisonment remained still with him, and
were useful to him; they who were in their houses in the
country, though as well affected, remained there, and came not
to him; and though letters from London had given him cause
to believe that many prepared to come to him, which for some
days they might easily have done, none appeared, except only
some common men who had formerly served the last King, who
repaired again to Worcester.

72. There were some other accidents and observations which
administered matter of mortification to the King. The duke
of Buckingham had a mind very restless, and thought he had
not credit enough with the King if it were not made manifest
that he had more than any body else: and therefore, as soon as
the King had entered England, though he had reason to believe
that his majesty had not been abundantly satisfied with his
behaviour in Scotland, he came to him, and told him, the
business was now to reduce England to his obedience, and
therefore he ought to do all things gracious and popular in the
eyes of the nation; and nothing could be less [so] to it than that
the army should be under the command of a Scotch general:
that David Lashly was only lieutenant general, and it had been
unreasonable whilst he remained in Scotland to have put any
other to have commanded over him; but that it would be as
unreasonable, now[1] they were in England, and had hope to
increase the army by the access of the English, upon whom his
principal dependence must be, to expect that they would be

---

[1] ['that now,' MS.]

1651 willing to serve under him; that it would not consist with the
honour of any peer of England to receive his orders, and he
believed that very few of that rank would repair to his majesty
till they were secure from that apprehension; and used much
more discourse to that purpose.   The King was so much surprised with it that he could not imagine what he meant, and
what the end of it would be, and asked him who it was that he
thought fit his majesty should give that command to; when, to
his astonishment, the duke told him he hoped his majesty would
confer it upon him; at which he was so amazed, that he found
an occasion to break off the discourse by calling upon somebody
who was near to come to him, and, by asking many questions,
declined the former argument.   But the duke would not be so
put off, but the next day, in the march, renewed his importunity, and told the King that he was confident what he had
proposed to him was so evidently for his service that David
Lashly himself would willingly consent to it.   The King, angry
at his prosecuting it in that manner, told him he could hardly
believe that he was in earnest, or that he could in truth believe that he could be fit for such a charge; which he seemed
to wonder at, and asked wherein his unfitness lay.   To which
the King replied, that he was too young; and he as readily
alleged, that Harry the Fourth of France commanded an army
and won a battle when he was younger than he.   So that in
the end he [the King] was compelled to tell him that he would
have no generalissimo but himself; upon which the duke was
so discontented, that he came no more to the council, scarce
spoke to the King, neglected every body else and himself,
insomuch as for many days he never put on clean linen nor
conversed with any body; nor did he recover this ill humour
whilst the army stayed at Worcester.

73. There was another worse accident fell out soon after the
King's coming thither.   Major general Mass[e]y, who thought
himself now in his own territory, and that all between Worcester and Gloster would be quickly his own conquest, knowing
Aug. 29. every step both of the land and the river, went out with a party
to secure a pass which the enemy might make over the river;

which he did very well; but would then make a farther inroad **1651** into the country, and possess a house which was of small importance, and in which there were men to defend it; where he received a very dangerous wound with ray-shot, that tore his arm and hand in such manner that he was in great torment, and could not stir out of his bed in a time when his activity and industry was most wanted. And by this means the pass which he secured was either totally neglected or not enough taken care for.

74. There was no good understanding between the officers of the army. David Lashly appeared dispirited and confounded, and gave and revoked his orders, and sometimes contradicted them. He did not love Middleton, and was very jealous that all the officers loved him too well; who was indeed an excellent officer, and kept up the spirits of the rest, who had no esteem of Lashly. In this very unhappy distemper was the Court and the army in a season when they were ready to be swallowed by the malice and multitude of the enemy, and when nothing could preserve them but the most sincere unity in their prayers to God, in which they were miserably divided, and a joint concurrence in their counsels and endeavours.

75. The King had been about [twelve[1]] days in Worcester, when Cromwell was known to be within less than half a day's march, with an addition of very many regiments of horse and foot to those which he had brought with him from Scotland; and many other regiments were drawing towards him of the militia of the several counties, under the command of the principal gentlemen of the country: so that he was already very much superior, if not double in number, to the army the King had with him. However, if those rules had been observed, those works cast up, and that order in quartering their men, as were resolved upon when the King came thither, there must have been a good defence made, and the advantages of the ground, the river, and the city, would have preserved them from being presently overrun. But, alas! the army was in amazement and confusion. Cromwell, without troubling himself with the for-

[1] [blank in MS.]

1651 mality of a siege, marched directly on as to a prey, and possessed the hill and all other places of advantages with very
Sept. 3. little opposition. It was upon the third of September when
the King, having been upon his horse most part of the night
and taken a full view of the enemy, and every body being upon
the post they should be, and the enemy making such a stand
that it was concluded he meant to make no attempt that night,
and, if he should, he would be repelled with ease, his majesty,
a little before noon, retired to his lodging to eat and refresh
himself; where he had not been near an hour when the alarum
came that both armies were engaged, and though his majesty's
horse was ready at the door, and he presently mounted, before,
or as soon as, he came out of the city, he met the whole body
of his horse running in so great fear that he could not stop
them, though he used all the means he could, and called to
many officers by their names, and hardly preserved himself, by
letting them pass by, from being overthrown and overrun by
them.

76. Cromwell had used none of the delay nor circumspection
which was imagined, but directed the troops to fall on in all
places at once, and had caused a strong party to go over the
river at that pass which Mass[e]y had formerly secured, which
was a good distance from the town, and being not at all guarded,
they were never known to be on that side the river till they
were even ready to charge the King's troops. On that part
where Middleton was, and with whom duke Hambleton charged,
there was a very brave resistance; and they charged the enemy
so vigorously that they beat the body that charged them back;
but they were quickly overpowered, and many gentlemen being
killed, and Middleton hurt, and duke Hambleton's leg broke
short off with a shot, the rest were forced to retire and shift
for themselves. In no other part there was resistance made;
but such a general consternation possessed the whole army, that
the rest of the horse fled, and all the foot threw down their
arms before they were charged. When the King came back
into the town, he found a good body of horse which had been
persuaded to make a stand, though much the major part passed

through upon the spur without making any pause. The King 1651 desired those who stayed that they would follow him, that they might look upon the enemy, who, he believed, did not pursue them. But when his majesty had gone a little way, he found most of the horse were gone the other way, and that he had none but a few servants of his own about him. Then he sent to have the gates of the town shut, that none might get in one way nor out the other: but all was confusion; there were few to command, and none to obey: so that the King stayed till very many of the enemy's horse were entered the town, and then he was persuaded to withdraw himself.

77. Duke Hambleton fell into the enemy's hands, and the next day [1] died of his wounds, and thereby prevented the being Sept. 12. made a spectacle, as his brother had been; which the pride and animosity of his enemies would no doubt have done, having the same pretence, by his being a peer of England as the other was. He was in all respects to be much preferred before the other, a much wiser, though it may be a less cunning, man: for he did not affect dissimulation, which was the other's master-piece. He had unquestionable courage, in which the other did not abound. He was in truth a very accomplished person, of an excellent judgment, and clear and ready expressions: and though he had been driven into some unwarrantable actions, he made it very evident he had not been led by any inclinations of his own, and passionately and heartily ran to all opportunities of redeeming it: and in the article of his death he expressed a marvellous cheerfulness that he had the honour to lose his life in the King's service, and thereby to wipe out the memory of his former transgressions, which he always professed was odious to himself.

78. As the victory cost the enemy no blood, so after it there was not much cruelty used to the prisoners who were then taken. [But [2]] very many of those who ran away were every day knocked in the head by the country people, and used with their barbarity. Towards the King's menial servants, (whereof

---

[1] [nine days after.]   [2] 'For,' MS.]

1651 most were taken) there was nothing of severity; but within
few days they were all discharged and set at liberty.

79. Though the King could not get a body of horse to fight,
he could have too many to fly with him; and he had not been
two hours from Worcester, when he found about him near, if
not above, four thousand of his horse. There was David
Lashly with all his own equipage, as if he had not fled upon
the sudden; so that good order and regularity and obedience
might yet have made a hopeful retreat even into Scotland
itself. But there was paleness in every man's looks, and
jealousies and confusion in their faces, and nothing could worse
befall the King than a safe return into Scotland; which yet he
could not reasonably promise to himself in that company. But
when the night covered them, he found means to withdraw
himself with one or two of his own servants, [whom][1] he likewise discharged when it began to be light; and after he had
made them cut off his hair, he betook himself alone into an
adjacent wood[2], and relied only upon Him for deliverance who
alone could and did miraculously deliver him.

80. When it was morning, and the troops, which had
marched all night, and who knew that when it began to be
dark the King was with them, found now that he was not
there, they cared less for each other's company, and all who
were English separated themselves, and went into other roads;
and where twenty horse appeared of the country, which was now
awake and upon their guard to stop and arrest the runaways,
the whole body of the Scots' horse would fly, and run several
ways, and twenty would give themselves prisoners to two
country fellows. However, David Lashly reached Yorkshire
with above fifteen hundred horse in a body; but the jealousies
increased every day; and those of his own country were so
unsatisfied with his whole conduct and behaviour, that they
did, that is many of them did, believe that he was corrupted
by Cromwell; and the rest who did not think so believed him
not to understand his profession, in which he had been bred
from his cradle. When he was in his flight considering one

---

[1] [' which,' MS.]   [2] [Spring coppice, at Boscobel.]

morning with the principal persons which way they should **1651**
take, some proposed this and others that way; sir William
Armorer asked him which way he thought best, which when he
had named, the other said he would then go the other, for, he
swore, he had betrayed the King and the army all the time;
and so left him.

81. They were all soon after taken. And it is hard to be
believed how very few of that numerous body of horse (for
there can be no imagination that any of the foot escaped)
returned into Scotland. Upon all the inquiry that was made,
when a discovery was made of most of the false and treacherous
actions which had been committed by most men, there appeared
no case to suspect that David Lashly had been unfaithful in his
charge, though he never recovered any reputation with those
of his own country who wedded the King's interest. And yet
it was some vindication to him, that from the time of his
imprisonment he never received any favour from the Parliament, whom he had served so long, nor from Cromwell, in
whose company he had served, but underwent all the severities
and long imprisonment the rest of his countrymen underwent.
The King did not believe him false, and did always think him
an excellent officer of horse, to distribute and execute orders,
but in no degree capable of commanding in chief. And without doubt he was so amazed in that fatal day, that he performed not the office of a general or of any competent officer.

82. They who fled out of Worcester, and were not killed but
made prisoners, were treated best, and found great humanity;
but all the foot, and others who were taken in the town, except
some few officers and persons of quality, were driven like cattle
with a guard to London, and there treated with great rigour;
and many perished for want of food; and being enclosed in
little room, till they were sold to the plantations for slaves,
they died of all diseases. Cromwell returned in triumph, and
was received with a universal joy and acclamation, as if he had
destroyed the enemy of the nation, and for ever secured the
liberty and happiness of the people: a price was set upon the
King's head, whose escape was thought to be impossible; and

1651 order taken for trial of the earl of Darby, and such other notorious prisoners as they had voted to destruction.

83. They of the King's friends in Flanders, France, and Holland, who had not been permitted to attend upon his majesty in Scotland, were much exalted with the news of his being entered England with a powerful army, and being possessed of Worcester, which made all men prepare to make haste thither. But they were confounded with the assurance of that fatal day, and more confounded with the various reports of the person of the King; of his being found amongst the dead; of his being prisoner; and all those imaginations which naturally attend upon such unprosperous events. Many who had made escapes arrived every day in France, Flanders, and in Holland, but knew no more what was become of the King than they did who had not been in England. And the only comfort any of them brought, was, that he was amongst those who fled, and some of them had seen him that evening many miles out of Worcester. This unsteady degree of hope tormented them very long; sometimes they heard he was at the Hague with his sister, which was occasioned by the arrival of the duke of Buckingham in Holland; and it was thought good policy to publish that the King himself was landed, that the search after him in England might be discontinued. But it was quickly known that he was not there, nor in any place on that side the sea. And this anxiety of mind disquieted the hearts of all honest men during that whole month of September (for the action was upon the third of that month) and all November[1]. About the beginning of December[2] his majesty was known to be at Rouen; where he made himself known, and stayed some days to make clothes, and from thence gave notice to the Queen of his arrival.

84. It is great pity that there was never a journal made of that miraculous deliverance, in which there might be seen so many visible impressions of the immediate hand of God. When

Sept. 4. the darkness of the night was over, after the King had cast himself into that wood, he discerned another man, who had gotten upon an oak, who was in that wood, near the place

---

[1] [October.] [2] [end of October.]

where the King had rested himself, and had slept soundly. The 1651
man upon the tree had first seen the King, and knew him, and
came down from the tree to him, and was known to the King,
being a gentleman of the neighbour county of Staffordshire,
who had served his late majesty during the war, and had now
been one of the few who resorted to the King after his coming
to Worcester. His name was Carelesse, who had had a command of foot, above the degree of a captain, under the lord
Loughborough. He persuaded the King, since it could not be
safe for him to go out of the wood, and that as soon as it
should be fully light the wood itself would probably be visited
by those of the country, who would be searching to find those
whom they might make prisoners, that he would get up into
that tree where he had been, where the boughs were so thick
with leaves, that a man would not be discovered there without
a narrower inquiry than people usually make in places which
they do not suspect. The King thought it good counsel, and
with the other's help climbed into the tree, and then helped his
companion to ascend after him; where they sat all that day,
and securely saw many who came purposely into the wood to
look after them, and heard all their discourse, how they would
use the King himself if they could take him. This wood was
either in or upon the borders of Staffordshire; and though there
was a highway near one side of it, where the King had entered
into it, yet it was large, and all other sides of it opened amongst
enclosures, and it pleased God that Carelesse was not unacquainted
with the neighbour villages. And it was part of the King's good
fortune that this gentleman was a Roman Catholic, and thereby
was acquainted with those of that profession of all degrees: and
it must never be denied that those of that faith, that is, some
of them, had a very great share in his majesty's preservation.

85. The day being spent in the tree, it was not in the King's
power to forget that he had lived two days with eating very
little, and two nights with as little sleep; so that when the
night came he was willing to make some provision for both:
so that he resolved, with the advice and assistance of his
companion, to leave his blessed tree; and so when the night

1651 was dark they walked through the wood into those enclosures
which were farthest from any highway, and making a shift to
get over hedges and ditches, and after walking at least eight or
nine miles, which were the more grievous to the King by the
weight of his boots, (for he could not put them off, when he
cut off his hair, for want of shoes,) before morning they came
to a poor cottage, the owner whereof, being a Catholic, was
known to Carelesse[1]. He was called up, and as soon as he knew
one of them he easily concluded in what condition they both
Sept. 5. were, and presently carried them into a little barn full of hay,
which was a better lodging than he had for himself. But when
they were there, and had conferred with their host of the news
and temper of the country, it was resolved that the danger
would be the greater if they stayed together; and therefore
that Carelesse should presently be gone, and should within two
days send an honest man to the King to guide him to some
other place of security; and in the mean time his majesty
should stay upon the hay-mow. The poor man had nothing
for him to eat, but promised him good buttermilk the next
morning; and so he was once more left alone, his companion,
how weary soever, departing from him before day; the poor
man of the house knowing no more than that he was a friend
of the captain's, and one of those who had escaped from Worcester. The King slept very well in his lodging, till the time
that his host brought him a piece of bread and a great pot of
buttermilk, which he thought the best food he had ever eaten.
The poor man spoke very intelligently to him of the country,
and of the people who were well and ill affected to the King,
and of the great fear and terror that possessed the hearts of
those who were best affected. He told him that he himself
lived by his daily labour, and that what he had brought him
was the fare he and his wife had; and that he feared if he
should endeavour to procure better it might draw suspicion
upon him, and people might be apt to think he had somebody
with him that was not of his own family; however, if he would
have him get some meat he would do it, but if he could bear

[1] [Mr. Wolfe, at Madeley.]

this hard diet, he should have enough of the milk, and some 1651 of the butter that was made with it. The King was satisfied with his reason, and would not run the hazard for a change of diet; desired only the man that he might have his company as often and as much as he could give it him; there being the same reason against the poor man's discontinuing his labour as the alteration of his fare.

86. After he had rested upon this hay-mow and fed upon this diet two days and two nights[1], in the evening before the third night another fellow, a little above the condition of his Sept. 5. host, came to the house, sent from Carelesse, to conduct the King to another house[2], more out of any road near which any part of the army was like to march. It was above twelve miles that he was to go, and was to use the same caution he had done the first night, not to go in any common road; which his guide knew well how to avoid. Here he new dressed himself, changing clothes with his landlord, and putting on those which he usually wore : he had a great mind to have kept his own shirt, but he considered that men are not sooner discovered by any mark in disguises than by having fine linen in ill clothes; and so he parted with his shirt too, and took the same his poor host had then on. Though he had foreseen that he must leave his boots, and his landlord had taken the best care he could to provide an old pair of shoes, yet they were not easy to him when he first put them on, and in a short time after grew very grievous to him. In this equipage he set out from his first lodging in the beginning of the night, under the conduct of his comrade, who guided him the nearest way, crossing over hedges and ditches, that they might be in least danger of meeting passengers. This was so grievous a march, and he was so tired, that he was even ready to despair, and to prefer being taken, and suffered to rest, before purchasing his safety at that price. His shoes had after the walking a few miles hurt him so much that he had thrown them away, and

---

[1] [One night and one day. The inaccuracy of Clarendon's narrative of the escape, with respect both to times and persons, is well known.]

[2] [Boscobel, returning to the place he had quitted the day before.]

1651 walked the rest of the way in his ill stockings, which were quickly worn out; and his feet, with the thorns in getting over hedges, and with the stones in other places, were so hurt and wounded, that he many times cast himself upon the ground, with a desperate and obstinate resolution to rest there till the morning, that he might shift with less torment, what hazard soever he run. But his stout guide still prevailed with him to make a new attempt, sometimes promising that the way should be better, and sometimes assuring him that he had but little further to go: and, in this distress and perplexity, before

Sept. 6. the morning they arrived at the house designed, which though it was better than that which he had left, his lodging was still in the barn, upon straw instead of hay, a place being made as easy in it as the expectation of a guest could dispose it. Here he had such meat and porridge as such people use to have, with which, but especially with the butter and the cheese, he thought himself well feasted; and took the best care he could to be supplied with other, little better, shoes and stockings: and after his feet were enough recovered that he could go, he was conducted from thence to another poor house, within such a distance as put him not to much trouble: for having not yet in his thought which way, or by what means, to make his escape, all that was designed was only by shifting from one house to another to avoid discovery; and being now in that quarter which was more inhabited by the Roman Catholics than most other parts in England, he was led from one to another of that persuasion, and concealed with great fidelity. But he then observed that he was never carried to any gentleman's house, though that country was full of them, but only to poor houses of poor men, which only yielded him rest, with very unpleasant sustenance; whether there was more danger in those better houses, in regard of the resort and the many servants, or whether the owners of great estates were the owners likewise of more fears and apprehensions.

Sept. 7   87. Within few days, a very honest and discreet person, one Mr. Hurlestone [1] [Huddlestone] a Benedictine monk, who

---

[1] [Substituted for, apparently, ' Ralessone,' which has been erased.]

attended the service of the Catholics in those parts, came 1651
to him, sent by Carelesse, and was a very great assistance
and comfort to him.   And when the places to which he carried
him were at too great a distance to walk, he provided him a
horse, and more proper habit than the rags he wore.   This
man told him that the lord Wilmott lay concealed likewise
in a friend's house of his; which his majesty was very glad
of, and wished him to contrive some means how they might
speak together; which the other easily did, and within a night Sept. 7.
or two brought them into one place[1].   Wilmott told the King
that he had by very good fortune fallen into the house of an
honest gentleman, one Mr. Lane, a person of an excellent
reputation for his fidelity to the King, but of so universal and
general a good name, that, though he had a son who had been
a colonel in the King's service during the late war, and was
then upon his way with men to Worcester the very day of the
defeat, men of all affections in the country and of all opinions
paid the old man a very great respect : that he had been very
civilly treated there, and that the old gentleman had used some
diligence to find out where the King was, that he might get
him to his house, where he was sure he could conceal him till
he might contrive a full deliverance.   He told him he had
withdrawn from that house, and put himself amongst the
Catholics, in hope that he might discover where his majesty
was, and having now happily found him, advised him to repair
to that house, which stood not near any other house.

88. The King inquired of the monk of the reputation of this
gentleman, who told him that he was a gentleman of a fair
estate, exceedingly beloved, and the oldest justice of peace
of that county of Stafford; and though he was a very zealous
Protestant, yet he lived with so much civility and candour
towards the Catholics, that they would all trust him as much
as they would do any of their own profession, and that he
could not think of any place of so good repose and security
for his majesty to repair to.   The King, who by this time had
as good a mind to eat well as to sleep, liked the proposition,

[1] [Mr. Whitgreave's, at Moseley.]

1651
Sept. 8.
yet thought not fit to surprise the gentleman, but sent Wilmott thither again, to assure himself that he might be received there, and was willing that he should know what guest he received; which hitherto was so much concealed, that none of the houses where he had yet been knew, or seemed to suspect, more than that he was one of the King's party that fled from Worcester. The monk carried him to a house at a reasonable distance, where he was to expect an account from the lord Wilmott, who returned very punctually, with as much assurance of welcome as he could wish. And so they two went together

Sept. 9. to Mr. Lane's house [1], where the King found he was welcome, and conveniently accommodated in such places as in a large house had been provided to conceal the persons of malignants, or to preserve goods of value from being plundered ; where he lodged and eat very well, and began to hope that he was in present safety. Wilmott returned under the care of the monk, and expected summons when any farther motion should be thought to be necessary.

89. In this station the King remained in quiet and blessed security many days [2], receiving every day information of the general consternation the kingdom was in, out of the apprehension that his person might fall into the hands of his enemies, and of the great diligence they used in inquiry for him. He saw the proclamation that was issued out and printed, in which a thousand pounds were promised to any man who would deliver and discover the person of Charles Steward, and the penalty of high treason declared against those who presumed to harbour or conceal him : by which he saw how much he was beholding to all those who were faithful to him. It was now time to consider how he might find himself near the sea, from whence he might find some means to transport himself : and he was now near the middle of the kingdom, saving that it was a little more northward, where he was utterly unacquainted with all the ports and with that coast. In the west he was best acquainted, and that coast was most proper to transport him into France ; to which he

---

[1] [Bentley Hall.]   [2] [He left Bentley Hall the next day.]

was most inclined. Upon this matter he communicated with 1651 those of the family to whom he was known, that is, with the old gentleman the father, a very grave and venerable person, the colonel his eldest son, a very plain man in his discourse and behaviour, but of a fearless courage and an integrity superior to any temptation, and a daughter of the house, of a very good wit and discretion, and very fit to bear any part in such a trust. It was a benefit, as well as an inconvenience, in those unhappy times, that the affections of all men were almost as well known as their faces, by the discovery they had made of themselves, in those sad seasons, in many trials and persecutions : so that men knew not only the minds of their next neighbours, and those who inhabited near them, but, upon conference with their friends, could choose fit houses, at any distance, to repose themselves in securely, from one end of the kingdom to another, without trusting the hospitality of a common inn : and men were very rarely deceived in their confidence upon such occasions but [that] the persons with whom they were at any time could conduct them to another house of the same affection.

90. Mr. Lane had a niece, or very near kinswoman, who was married to a gentleman, one Mr. Norton, a person of eight or nine hundred pounds *per annum*, who lived within four or five miles of Bristol, which was at least four or five days' journey from the place where the King then was, but a place most to be wished for the King to be in, because he did not only know all that country very well, but knew many persons very well to whom in an extraordinary case he durst make himself known. It was hereupon resolved that Mrs. Lane should visit this cousin, who was known to be of good affections, and that she should ride behind the King, who was fitted with clothes and boots for such a service, and that a servant of her father's, in his livery, should wait upon her. A good house was easily pitched upon for the first night's lodging, where Wilmott had notice given him to meet. And in this equipage the King Sept. 10. begun his journey ; the colonel keeping him company at a distance, with a hawk upon his fist, and two or three spaniels ; which, where there were any fields at hand, warranted him to

1651   ride out of the way, keeping his company still in his eye, and
not seeming to be of it. And in this manner they came to
their first night's lodging [1]; and they need not now to contrive
to come to their journey's end about the close of the evening,
for it was now in the month of October [2] far advanced, that the
long journeys they made could not be despatched sooner.
Here the lord Wilmott found them; and their journeys being
then adjusted, he was instructed where he should be every
night [3]: and so they were seldom seen together in the journey,
and rarely lodged in the same house at night. And in this
manner the colonel hawked two or three days, till he had
brought them within less than a day's journey of Mr. Norton's
house, and then he gave his hawk to the lord Wilmott, who
continued the journey in the same exercise.

91. There was great care taken when they came to any house
that the King might presently be carried into some chamber,
Mrs. Lane declaring that he was a neighbour's son, whom his
father had lent her to ride before her in hope that he would the
sooner recover from a quartan ague, with which he had been
miserably afflicted, and [was] not yet free. And by this artifice
she caused a good bed to be still provided for him, and the best
meat to be sent; which she often carried herself, to hinder
others from doing it. There was no resting in any place till
they came to Mr. Norton's [4], nor any thing extraordinary that
happened in the way, save that they met many people every
day in the way who were very well known to the King; and
Sept. 12.   the day that they went to Mr. Norton's they were necessarily
to ride quite through the city of Bristol, a place and people the
King had been so well acquainted with, that he could not but
send his eyes abroad to view the great alterations which had
been made there after his departure from thence: and when he
rode near the place where the great fort had stood, he could
not forbear putting his horse out of the way, and rode, with his
mistress behind him, round about it.

[1] [at Long Marston, *alias* Marston Sicca, near Stratford-on-Avon.]
[2] [*sic.*]   [3] [only one night; at Cirencester, on Sept. 11.]
[4] [at Abbotsleigh, Somerset.]

92. They came to Mr. Norton's house sooner than usual, and 1651 it being on a holyday, they saw many people about a bowling-green that was before the door; and the first man the King saw was a chaplain of his own, who was allied to the gentle-man of the house, and was sitting upon the rails to see how the bowlers played. So that William, by which name the King went, walked with his horse into the stable, until his mistress could provide for his retreat. Mrs. Lane was very welcome to her cousin, and was presently conducted to her chamber, where she no sooner was than she lamented the condition of a good youth who came with her, and whom she had borrowed of his father to ride before her, who was very sick, being newly recovered of an ague; and desired her cousin that a chamber might be provided for him, and a good fire made: for that he would go early to bed, and was not fit to be below stairs. A pretty little chamber was presently made ready, and a fire prepared, and a boy sent into the stable to call William, and to shew him his chamber; who was very glad to be there, freed from so much company as was below. Mrs. Lane was put to find some excuse for making a visit at that time of the year, and so many days' journey from her father, and where she had never been before, though the mistress of the house and she had been bred together, and friends as well as kindred. So she pretended that she was, after a little rest, to go into Dorsetshire to another friend.

93. When it was supper-time, there being broth brought to the table, Mrs. Lane filled a little dish, and desired the butler, who waited at the table, to carry that dish of porridge to William, and to tell him that he should have some meat sent to him presently. The butler carried the porridge into the chamber, with a napkin and spoon and bread, and spake kindly to the young man, who was willing to be eating. And the butler looking narrowly upon him fell upon his knees, and with tears told him he was glad to see his majesty. The King was infinitely surprised, yet recollected himself enough to laugh at the man, and to ask him what he meant. The man had been falconer to Tom Jermin, and made it appear that he knew well

1651 enough to whom he spake, repeating some particulars which
the King had not forgot. Whereupon the King conjured him
not to speak of what he knew, so much as to his master,
though he believed him a very honest man. The fellow
promised, and faithfully kept his word; and the King was the
better waited upon during the time of his abode there.

94. Dr. Gorge[s], the King's chaplain, being a gentleman of
a good family near that place, and allied to Mr. Norton, supped
with them; and, being a man of a cheerful conversation, asked
Mrs. Lane many questions concerning William, of whom he saw
she was so careful by sending up meat to him; how long his
ague had been gone, and whether he had purged since it left
him, and the like: to which she gave such answers as occurred.
The doctor, from the final prevalence of the Parliament, had, as
many others of that function had done, declined his profession,
and pretended to study physic. As soon as supper was done,
out of good nature, and without telling any body, he went to
see William. The King saw him coming into the chamber, and
withdrew to the inside of the bed, that he might be farthest
from the candle; and the doctor came and sat down by him,
felt his pulse, and asked him many questions, which he answered in as few words as was possible, and expressing great
inclination to go to his bed; to which the doctor left him, and
went to Mrs. Lane, and told her that he had been with William,
and that he would do well; and advised her what she should
do if his ague returned. And the next morning the doctor
went away, so that the King saw him no more, of which he was
right glad. The next day the lord Wilmott came to the house
with his hawk to see Mrs. Lane, and so conferred with William;
who was to consider what he was to do. They thought it
necessary to rest some days, till they were informed what port
lay most convenient for them, and what person lived nearest to
it upon whose fidelity they might rely: and the King gave him
directions to inquire after some persons, and some other particulars, of which when he should be fully instructed he should
return again to him. In the mean time he lodged at a house
not far from Mr. Norton's, to which he had been recommended.

95. After some days' stay here, and communication between **1651** the King and the lord Wilmott by letters, the King came to know that colonel Francis Windham lived within little more than a day's journey of the place where he was [1], of which he was very glad ; for, besides the inclination he had to his elder brother, whose wife had been his nurse, this gentleman had behaved himself very well during the war, and had been gover-nor of Dunstar Castle, where the King had lodged when he was in the west. After the end of the war, and when all other places were surrendered in that county, he likewise surrendered **1646** that, upon fair conditions, and made his peace, and afterwards **April 22.** married a wife [2] with a competent fortune, and lived quietly with her, without any suspicion of having lessenèd his affection towards the King.

96. The King sent Wilmott to him, and acquainted him where he was, and that he would gladly speak with him. It was not hard for him to choose a good place where to meet, and there, upon the day appointed, after the King had taken his leave of Mrs. Lane, who remained with her cousin Norton, the **Sept. 16.** King and the lord Wilmott met the colonel, and in the way encountered in a town through which they passed Mr. Kirton, a servant of the King's, who well knew the lord Wilmott, who had no other disguise than the hawk, but took no notice of him, nor suspected the King to be there; yet that day made the King more wary of having him in his company upon the way. At the place of meeting they rested only one night [3], and then **Sept. 16.** the King went to the colonel's house, where he rested many **Sept 17.** days, whilst colonel Windham projected at what place the King might embark, and how they might procure a vessel to be ready there ; which was not easy to find, there being so great caution in all the ports, and so great a fear possessing those who were honest, that it was hard to procure any vessel that was outward bound to take in any passenger.

97. There was a gentleman, one Mr. Ellison [4], who lived near

---

[1] [at Trent, in Somerset.]
[2] [Anne, daughter of Thomas Gerard, of Trent.]
[3] [at Castle Cary.]
[4] [William Ellesdon. His narrative is printed in *Clar. S.P.* ii. 563–571.]

1651 Lyme in Dorsetshire, and who was well known to colonel
Windham, having been a captain in the King's army, and was
still looked upon as a very honest man. With him the colonel
consulted how they might get a vessel to be ready to take in a
couple of gentlemen, friends of his, who were in danger to be
arrested, and transport them into France. Though no man
would ask who the persons were, yet every man suspected who
they were; at least they concluded that it was some of
Worcester party. Lyme was generally as malicious and disaffected a town to the King's interest as any town in England
could be, yet there was in it a master of a bark of whose
honesty this captain was very confident. This man was lately
returned from France, and had unladen his vessel, when Ellison
asked him when he would make another voyage, and he answered
as soon as he could get loading for his ship. The other asked,
whether he would undertake to carry over a couple of gentlemen, and land them in France, if he might be as well paid for
his voyage as he used to be when he was freighted by the
merchants; in conclusion, he told him he should receive fifty
pounds for his fare. The large recompense had that effect that
the man undertook it, though he said he must make his provision very secretly; for that he might be well suspected for
going to sea again without being freighted after he was so
newly returned. Colonel Windham, being advertised of this,
came together with the lord Wilmott to the captain's house, from
whence the lord and the captain rode to a house near Lyme,
where the master of the bark met them; and the lord Wilmott
being satisfied with the discourse of the man, and his wariness
and foreseeing suspicions which would arise, it was resolved that
on such a night, which upon consideration of the tides was
agreed upon, the man should draw out his vessel from the pier,
and being at sea should come to such a point about a mile from
the town, where his ship should remain upon the beach when
the water was gone; which would take it off again about the
break of day the next morning. There was very near that
point, even in the view of it, a small inn, kept by a man who
was reputed honest, to which the cavaliers of the country often

resorted; and London road passed that way, so that it was seldom without resort. Into that inn the two gentlemen were to
come in the beginning of the night, that they might put themselves on board. And all things being thus concerted, and
good earnest given to the master, the lord Wilmott and the
colonel returned to the colonel's house, above a day's journey
from the place, the captain undertaking every day to look that
the master should provide, and if any thing fell out contrary to
expectation, to give the colonel notice at such a place, where
they intended the King should be the day before he was to
embark.

98. The King, being satisfied with these preparations, came
at the time appointed to that house [1] where he was to hear that
all went as it ought to do; of which he received assurance from
the captain, who found that the man had honestly put his provisions on board, and had his company ready, which were but
four men, and that the vessel should be drawn out that night:
so that it was fit for the two persons to come to the aforesaid
inn; and the captain conducted them within sight of it, and
then went to his own house, not distant a mile from it; the
colonel remaining still at the house where they had lodged the
night before, till he might hear the news of their being embarked.

99. They found many passengers in the inn; and so were to
be contented with an ordinary chamber, which they did not
intend to sleep long in, but as soon as there appeared any light,
Wilmott went out to discover the bark, of which there was no
appearance. In a word, the sun rose, and nothing like a ship
in view. They sent to the captain, who was as much amazed,
and he sent to the town; and his servant could not find the
master of the bark, which was still in the pier. They suspected
the captain, and the captain suspected the master. However, it
being past ten of the clock, they concluded it was not fit for
them to stay longer there, and so they mounted their horses
again to return to the house where they had left the colonel,
who they knew resolved to stay there till he were assured that
they were gone.

[1] [at Charmouth.]

100. The truth of the disappointment was this. The man meant honestly, and had made all things ready for his departure; and the night he was to go out with his vessel he had stayed in his own house, and slept two or three hours; and the time of the tide being come, that it was necessary to be on board, he took out of a cupboard some linen and other things which he used to carry with him to sea. His wife had observed that he had been for some days fuller of thoughts than he used to be, and that he had been speaking with seamen who used to go with him, and that some of them had carried provisions on board the bark; of which she had asked her husband the reason; who had told her that he was promised freight speedily, and therefore he would make all things ready. She was sure that there was yet no lading in the ship, and therefore, when she saw her husband take all those materials with him, which was a sure sign that he meant to go to sea, and it being late in night, she shut the door, and swore he should not go out of the house. He told her he must go, and was engaged to go to sea that night; for which he should be well paid. His wife told him she was sure he was doing somewhat that would undo him, and she was resolved he should not go out of his house; and if he should persist in it, she would call the neighbours, and carry him before the mayor to be examined, that the truth might be found out. The poor man, thus mastered by the passion and violence of his wife, was forced to yield to her, that there might be no farther noise; and so went into his bed.

101. And it was very happy that the King's jealousy hastened him from that inn. It was the solemn fast day, which was observed in those times principally to inflame the people against the King and all those who were loyal to him; and there was a chapel in that village and over against that inn, where a weaver, who had been a soldier, used to preach, and utter all the villainy imaginable against the order of government: and he was then in the chapel preaching to his congregation when the King went from thence, and telling the people that Charles Steward was lurking somewhere in that country, and that they would merit from God Almighty if they could find him out.

The passengers who had lodged in the inn that night had, as **1651**
soon as they were up, sent for a smith to visit their horses, it
being a hard frost. The smith, when he had done what he was
sent for, according to the custom of that people, examined the
feet of the other two horses, to find more work. When he had
observed them, he told the host of the house that one of those
horses had travelled far, and that he was sure that his four
shoes had been made in four several counties; which, whether
his skill was able to discover or no, was very true. The smith
going to the sermon told this story to some of his neighbours,
and so it came to the ears of the preacher when his sermon was
done. And immediately he sent for an officer, and searched the
inn, and inquired for those horses; and being informed that
they were gone, he caused horses to be sent to follow them,
and to make inquiry after the two men who rode those horses,
and positively declared that one of them was Charles Steward.

102. When they came again to the colonel, they presently
concluded that they were to make no longer stay in those parts,
nor any more to endeavour to find a ship upon that coast; and
so, without farther delay, they rode back to the colonel's house,
where they arrived in the night [1]. Then they resolved to make
their next attempt more southward, in Hampshire and Sussex,
where colonel Windham had no interest. And they must pass
through all Wiltshire before they came thither, which would
require many days' journey: and they were first to consider
what honest houses there were in or near the way, where they
might securely repose; and it was thought very dangerous for
the King to ride through any great town, as Salisbury or Win-
chester, which might probably lie in their way.

103. There was between that and Salisbury a very honest
gentleman, colonel Robert Phillipps, a younger brother of a very
good family, which had always been very loyal, and he had
served the King during the war. The King was resolved to
trust him; and so sent the lord Wilmott to a place from
whence he might send to Mr. Phillipps to come to him, and

---

[1] [They were that night at Broad Windsor, and the following night,
Sept. 24, again at Trent, where he remained nearly a fortnight.]

1651 when he had spoken with him, Mr. Phillipps should come to the
King, and Wilmott was to stay in such a place as they two
should agree.   Mr. Phillipps accordingly came to the colonel's
house, which he could do without suspicion, they being nearly
allied.   The ways were very full of soldiers, which were sent
now from the army to their quarters; and many regiments of
horse and foot were assigned for the west, of which Desborough
was major general.   These marches were like to last for many
days, and it would not be fit for the King to stay so long in
that place.   Thereupon he resorted to his old security of taking
a woman behind him, a kinswoman of colonel Windham, whom
he carried in that manner to a place not far from Salisbury, to
which colonel Phillipps conducted him.   And in this journey
he passed through the middle of a regiment of horse, and presently after met Desborough walking down a hill with three or
four men with him, who had lodged in Salisbury the night
before; all that road being full of soldiers.

104. The next day, upon the plains, Dr. Hinchman, one of
the prebends of Salisbury, met the King, the lord Wilmott and
colonel Phillipps then leaving him to go to the sea-coast to
Oct. 6. find a vessel, the doctor conducting the King to a place called
Heale, three miles from Salisbury, belonging then to sergeant
Hyde, who was afterwards Chief Justice of the King's Bench,
and then in the possession of the widow of his elder brother, a
house that stood alone, from neighbours and from any highway;
where coming in late in the evening, he supped with some gentlemen who accidentally were in the house, which could not
Oct. 7. well be avoided.   But the next morning he went early from
thence, as if he had continued his journey; and the widow,
being trusted with the knowledge of her guest, sent her servants out of the way, and at an hour appointed received him
again, and accommodated him in a little room, which had been
made since the beginning of the troubles (the seat always
belonging to a malignant family) for the concealment of delin-
quents.

105. And here he lay concealed, without the knowledge of
some gentlemen who lived in the house and of others who daily

resorted thither, for many days, the widow herself only attend- **1651**
ing him with such things as were necessary, and bringing him
such letters as the doctor received from the lord Wilmott and
colonel Phillipps. A vessel being at last provided upon the
coast of Sussex, and notice thereof sent to Dr. Hinchman, he
sent to the King to meet him at Stonedge, upon the plains,
three miles from Heale, whither the widow took care to direct
him; and being there met, he attended him to the place, where Oct. 13.
colonel Phillipps received him : who the next day [1] delivered him
to the lord Wilmott, who went with him to a house in Sussex [2],
recommended by colonel Gunter, a gentleman of that country,
who had served the King in the war; who met him there, and
had provided a little bark at Brightemsted [3], a small fisher- Oct. 14.
town, where [4] he went early on board, and by God's blessing Oct. 15.
arrived safely in Normandy [5].   Oct. 16.

106. The earl of Southampton, who was then at his house
at Titchfeild in Hampshire, [and] had been advertised of the
King's being in the west and of his missing his passage at
Lyme, sent a trusty gentleman to those faithful persons in the
country who he thought were most like to be employed for his
escape if he came into those parts, to let them know that he
had a ship ready, and if the King came to him he should be
safe; which advertisement came to the King the night before
he embarked, and when his vessel was ready. But his majesty
ever acknowledged the obligation with great kindness, he being
the only person of that condition who had the courage to solicit
such a danger, though all men heartily wished his deliverance.
It was about the end of November [6] that the King landed in Oct. 16.
Normandy, in a small creek; from whence he got to Rouen,
and then gave notice to the Queen of his arrival, and freed his Oct. 17.
subjects in all places from their dismal apprehensions.

[1] [The same day.]
[2] [The house of Mr. Symons, or Symonds, brother-in-law to Col. Gunter,
at Hambledon, Hampshire. Gunter's own narrative was printed in 1846.]
[3] [*sic*; Brighthelmstone.]   [4] [At Shoreham.]
[5] [At Fécamp. The captain of the vessel, named Tattersall, was one of
those who attended the King on his voyage from Holland at his restoration.
Sir W. Lower's *Relation of the voiage of Chcrls II*, Hague, 1660, p. 53.]
[6] [*sic*.]

1651   107. Though this wonderful deliverance and preservation of the person of the King was an argument of general joy and comfort to all his good subjects, and a new seed of hope for future blessings, yet his present condition was very deplorable. France was not at all pleased with his being come thither, nor did quickly take notice of his being there. The Queen his mother was very glad of his escape, but in no degree able to contribute towards his support, they who had interest with her finding that all she had, or could get, too little for their own unlimited expense. Besides, the distraction that Court had been lately in, and was not yet free from the effects of it, made her pension to be paid with less punctuality than it had used to be; so that she was forced to be in debt both to her servants and for the very provisions of her house; nor had the King one shilling towards the support of himself and his family.

Oct. 30.   108. As soon as his majesty came to Paris, and knew that the Chancellor [of the Exchequer] was at Antwerp, he commanded Seymour, who was of his bedchamber, to send to him to repair thither: which whilst he was providing to do, Mr. Longe, the King's secretary, who was at Amsterdam, and had been removed from his attendance in Scotland by the marquis of Arguyle, writ to him, that he had received a letter from the King, by which he was required to let all his majesty's servants who were in those parts know, that it was his pleasure that none of them should repair to him to Paris until they should receive farther order, since his majesty could not yet resolve how long he should stay there: of which, Mr. Longe said, he thought it his duty to give him notice, with this, that the lord Culpeper and himself, who had resolved to have made haste thither, had in obedience to this command laid aside that purpose. The Chancellor concluded that this inhibition concerned not him, since he had received a command from the King to wait upon him. Besides, he had still the character of ambassador upon him, which he could not lay down till he had kissed his majesty's hand. So he pursued his former purpose, and came to Paris in the Christmas, and found that the command to Mr. Longe had been procured by the Queen with an eye

principally upon the Chancellor, who some there[1] had no mind 1651
should be with the King; though, when there was no remedy,
the Queen received him graciously. But the King was very
well pleased with his being come, and for the first four or five
days he spent many hours with him in private, and informed
him of very many particulars of the barbarous treatment he had
received in Scotland, and the reason of his march into England,
the confusion at Worcester, and all the circumstances of his
happy escape and deliverance; many parts whereof are compre-
hended within this relation, and are exactly true[2]. For, besides all those particulars which the King himself was pleased
to communicate unto him, so soon after the transaction of them,
and when they had made so lively an impression in his memory,
and of which the Chancellor at that time kept a very punctual
memorial, he had at the same time the daily conversation of the
lord Wilmott, who informed him of all he could remember : and
sometimes the King and he recollected many particulars in their
discourse together, in which the King's memory was much
better than the other's. And after the King's blessed return
into England, he had frequent conferences with many of those
who had acted several parts towards the escape; whereof many
were of his nearest alliance, and others his most intimate friends;
towards whom his majesty always made many gracious expressions of his acknowledgment. So that there is nothing in this
short relation the verity whereof can justly be suspected, though,
as is said before, it is great pity that there could be no diary
made, indeed no exact account of every hour's adventures from
the coming out of Worcester, in that dismal confusion, to the
hour of his embarkation at Brighthemsted; in which there
was such a concurrence of good nature, charity, and generosity,
in persons of the meanest and lowest extraction and condition,
who did not know the value of the precious jewel that was in
their custody, yet all knew him to be escaped from such an
action as would make the discovery and delivery of him to those
who governed over and amongst them of great benefit and pre-

---

[1] [The words 'some there' are substituted for 'she.']
[2] [From this point to the end of § 119 is from the *Hist.*, pp. 21–24.]

1651 sent advantage to them; and in those who did know him, of courage, loyalty, and activity; that we may reasonably look upon the whole as the inspiration and conduct of God Almighty, as a manifestation of his power and glory, and for the conviction of that whole nation, which had sinned so grievously; and if it hath not wrought that effect in both, it hath rendered both the more unexcusable.

109. As the greatest brunt of the danger was diverted by those poor people in his night-marches on foot, with so much pain and torment that he often thought that he paid too dear a price for his life, before he fell into the hands of persons of better quality and places of more conveniency, so he owed very much to the diligence and fidelity of some ecclesiastical persons of the Romish persuasion, especially to those of the order of St. Bennet; which was the reason that he expressed more favours after his restoration to that order than to any other, and granted them some extraordinary privilege about the service of the Queen, not concealing the reason why he did so; and which ought to have satisfied all men that his majesty's indulgence towards all of that profession, by restraining the severity and rigour of the laws which had been formerly made against them, had its rise from a fountain of princely justice and gratitude, as of royal bounty and clemency.

110. Whilst the counsels and ·enterprises in Scotland and England had this woful issue, Ireland had no better success in its undertakings. Cromwell had made so great a progress in his conquests before be left that kingdom that he might visit Scotland, that he was become, upon the matter, entirely possessed of the two most valuable and best inhabited provinces, Leinster and Munster; and plainly discerned that what remained to be done, if dexterously conducted, would be with most ease brought to pass by the folly and perfidiousness of the Irish themselves, who would save their enemies a labour in contributing to and hastening their own destruction. He had made the bridge fair, easy, and safe for them to pass over into foreign countries, by levies and transportations; which liberty they embraced, as hath been said before, with all imaginable greedi-

ness: and he had entertained agents and spies, as well friars as 1650 others, amongst the Irish, who did not only give him timely advertisements of what was concluded to be done, but had interest and power enough to interrupt and disturb the consultations, and to obstruct the execution thereof: and having put all things in this hopeful method of proceeding, in which there was like to be more use of the halter than the sword, he committed the managing of the rest, and the government of the kingdom, to his son Ireton, whom he made deputy under him of Ireland; 1650 a man who knew the bottom of all his counsels and purposes, May 29. of the same, or a greater, pride and fierceness in his nature, and most inclined to pursue those rules in the forming whereof he had had the chief influence, and who without fighting a battle, (though he lived not many months after[1]), reduced most of the rest that Cromwell left unfinished.

111. The marquis of Ormonde knew and understood well the desperate condition and state he was in, when he had no other strength and power to depend upon than that of the Irish for the support of the King's authority; yet there were many of the nobility and principal gentry of the Irish upon whose loyalty towards the King, and affection and friendship towards his own person, he had justly all confidence; and there were even amongst the clergy some moderate men, who did detest the savage ignorance of the rest: so that he entertained still some hope that the wiser would by degrees convert the weaker, and that they would all understand how inseparable their own preservation and interest was from the support of the King's dignity and authority, and that the wonderful judgments of God, which were every day executed by Ireton upon the principal and most obstinate contrivers of their odious rebellion, and who perversely and peevishly opposed their return to their obedience to the King, as often as they fell into his power, would awaken them out of their sottish lethargy, and unite them in the defence of their nation. For there was scarce a man whose bloody and brutish behaviour in the beginning of the rebellion, or whose barbarous violation of the peace that had been consented to,

[1] [He died Nov. 26, 1651.]

1650 had exempted them from the King's mercy, and left them only for subjects of his justice as soon as they could be apprehended, who was not taken by Ireton, and hanged with all the circumstances of severity that was due to their wickedness; of which innumerable examples might be given.

112. There yet remained free from Cromwell's yoke the two large provinces of Connaught and of Ulster, in which are the two strong cities of Lymerick and of Galloway, both garrisoned with Irish, and excellently supplied with all things necessary for their defence, and many other good port towns, and other strong places; all which pretended and professed to be for the King, and to yield obedience to the marquis of Ormonde, his majesty's Lieutenant. And there were still many good regiments of horse and foot together under Preston, who seemed to be ready to perform any service the marquis should require: so that he did reasonably hope, that by complying with some of their humours, by sacrificing somewhat of his honour, and much of his authority, to their jealousy and peevishness, he should be able to draw such a strength together as would give a stop to Ireton's career. O'Neale at this time, after he had been so baffled and affronted by the Parliament, and after he had seen his bosom friend, and still counsellor, the bishop of Clougher, (who had managed the treaty with Munke, and was taken prisoner upon the defeat of a party of horse), carried before
1650 Ireton, and by his order[1] hanged, drawn, and quartered as a
June 21. traitor[2], sent to offer his service to the marquis of Ormonde with the army under his command, upon such conditions as the
1649 marquis thought fit to consent to; and it was reasonably
Oct. 12. believed that he did intend very sincerely, and would have done very good service; for he was the best soldier of the nation, and had the most command over his men, and was best obeyed
1649 by them. But as he was upon his march towards a conjunc-
Nov. 6. tion with the Lord Lieutenant, he fell sick, and in few days died;

---

[1] ['by the positive order of Sir Charles Coot[e],' Borlase's *Irish Rebellion*, 1680, p. 253.]

[2] [O'Neill died nearly eight months before the execution of Ewer Mac-Mahon, R. C. bishop of Clogher.]

so that that treaty produced no effect; for though many 1650 of his army prosecuted his resolution, and joined with the marquis of Ormonde, yet their officers had little power over their soldiers; who, being all of the old Irish septs of Ulster, were entirely governed by the friars, and were shortly prevailed upon either to transport themselves, or to retire to their bogs, and prey for themselves upon all they met without distinction of persons or interest.

113. The marquis's orders for the drawing the troops together to any rendezvous were totally neglected and disobeyed; and the commissioners' orders for the collection of money, and contribution in such proportions as had been settled and agreed unto, were as much contemned: so that such regiments as with great difficulty were brought together were as soon dissolved for want of pay, order, and accommodation, or else dispersed by the power of the friars: as in the city of Lymerick, when the 1650 marquis was there, and had appointed several companies to be June 13. drawn into the market-place, to be employed upon a present expedition, an officer of good affection, and thought to have much credit with his soldiers, brought with him two hundred very likely soldiers well armed and disciplined, and having received his orders from the marquis, who was upon the place, began to march; when a Franciscan friar, [Wolfe,] in his habit and with a crucifix in his hand, came to the head of the company, and commanded them all, upon pain of damnation, that they should not march: upon which they all threw down their arms, and did as the friar directed them; who put the whole city into a mutiny, insomuch as the Lord Lieutenant was compelled to go out of it, and not without some difficulty escaped; though most of the magistrates of the city did all that was in their power to suppress the disorder, and to reduce the people to obedience; and some of them were killed and many wounded in the attempt. And for an instance of those judgments from heaven which we mentioned generally but now, Patrick Fanninge, who with the friar had the principal part in that sedition, the very next night 1651 after Ireton was without a blow possessed of that strong city, Oct. 27. was apprehended, and the next day hanged, drawn, and quartered. Oct. 28.

1650 Such of the commissioners who adhered firmly to the Lord Lieutenant, in using all their power to advance the King's service, and to reduce their miserable countrymen from affecting and contriving their own destruction, were without any credit, and all their warrants and summons neglected; when the others, who declined the service, and desired to obstruct it, had all respect and submission paid to them.

114. They who appeared after the first misfortune before Dublin to corrupt and mislead and dishearten the people, were the friars, and some of the inferior clergy; but now the titular bishops, which had been all made at Rome since the beginning of the rebellion, appeared more active than the other. They called an assembly of the bishops (every one of which had signed the articles of the peace) and chosen clergy, as a repre- sentative of their Church, to meet with all formality at [James Town [1]]; where, under the pretence of providing for the security of religion, they examined the whole proceedings of the war, and how the monies which had been collected had issued out. They called the giving up the towns in Munster by the lord Inchiquin's officers, the conspiracy and treachery of all the English, out of their malice to Catholic religion, and thereupon pressed the Lord Lieutenant to dismiss all the English gentle- men who yet remained with him. They called every unpros- perous accident that had fallen out a foul miscarriage; and published a declaration full of libellous invectives against the English, without sparing the person of the Lord Lieutenant, who, they said, being of a contrary religion, and a known in- veterate enemy to the Catholic, was not fit to be intrusted with the conduct of a war that was raised for the support and pre- servation of it; and shortly after sent an address to the Lord Lieutenant himself, in which they told him the people were so far unsatisfied with his conduct, especially for his aversion from the Catholic religion and his favouring heretics, that they were unanimously resolved, as one man, not to submit any longer to his command, nor to raise any more money or men to be applied to the King's service under his authority. But, on the other

1650
Aug. 6.

Aug. 10.

----

[1] [Left blank in the MS.]

side, they assured him that their duty and zeal was so entire 1650 and real for the King, and their resolution so absolute never to withdraw themselves from his obedience, that if he would depart the kingdom, and commit the command thereof into the hands of any person of honour of the Catholic religion, he would thereby unite the whole nation to the King; and they would immediately raise an army that should drive Ireton quickly again into Dublin. And that the Lord Lieutenant might know that they would not depart from this determination, they Sept. 15. published soon after an excommunication against all persons who should obey any of the Lieutenant's orders, or raise money or men by virtue of his authority.

115. During all these agitations, many of the Catholic nobility, and other persons of the best quality, remained very faithful to the Lord Lieutenant, and cordially interposed with the bishops to prevent their violent proceedings, but had neither power to persuade or restrain them. The Lord Lieutenant had no reason to be delighted with his empty title to command a people who would not obey, and knew the daily danger he was in of being betrayed and delivered into the hands of Ireton, or to be assassinated in his own quarters. He did not believe that the Irish would behave themselves with more fidelity and courage for the King's interest when he should be gone, well knowing that the bishops and clergy designed nothing but to put themselves under the government of some Catholic prince, and had at that time sent agents into foreign parts for that purpose, yet he knew likewise that there were in truth men enough and arms and all provisions, for the carrying on the war, who, if they were united, and heartily resolved to preserve themselves, would be much superior in number to any power Ireton could bring against them. He knew likewise that he could safely deposit the King's authority in the hands of a person of unquestionable fidelity, and whom the King would without any scruple trust, and whom the Irish could not except against, being of their own nation, of the greatest fortune and interest amongst them, and of the most eminent constancy to the Catholic religion of any man in the three kingdoms; and

1651 that was the marquis of Clanrickarde. And therefore, since it
was to no purpose to stay longer there himself, and in his
power safely to make the experiment whether the Irish would in
truth perform what was in their power to perform, and which
they so solemnly promised too, he thought he should be unexcusable to the King if he should not consent to that expedient.
The great difficulty was to persuade the marquis of Clanrickarde
to accept the trust, who was a man, though of unquestionable
courage, yet of an infirm health, and who loved and enjoyed
great ease throughout his whole life, and of a constitution not
equal to the fatigue and distresses that the conducting such a
war must subject him to. He knew well, and monstrously
detested, the levity, inconstancy, and infidelity of his countrymen; nor did he in any degree like the presumption of the
bishops and clergy, and the exorbitant power which they had
assumed to themselves and usurped; and therefore he had no
mind to engage himself in such a command. But [by] the extraordinary importunity of the marquis of Ormonde, with whom
he had preserved a fast and unshaken friendship, and his
pressing him to preserve Ireland to the King, without which it
would throw itself into the arms of a foreigner; and then the
same importunity from all the Irish nobility, bishops, and clergy,
after the Lord Lieutenant had informed them of his purpose,
that he would preserve his nation, which without his accept-
ance of their protection would infallibly be extirpated, and their
joint promise, that they would absolutely submit to all his commands, and hold no assembly or meeting amongst themselves
without his permission and commission, together with his unquestionable desire to do anything (how contrary soever to his
own inclination and benefit,) that would be acceptable to the
King, and might possibly bring some advantage to his [majesty's]
service, he was in the end prevailed upon to receive a commis-
1650 sion from the Lord Lieutenant to be deputy of Ireland, and
Dec. 6. undertook that charge.

116. How well they complied afterwards with their promises
and protestations, and how much better subjects they proved to
be under their Catholic governor than they had been under their

Protestant, will be related at large hereafter. In the mean time 1650
the marquis of Ormonde, who would not receive a pass from
Ireton, who would willingly have granted it, as he did to all
the English officers who desired it, embarked himself, with some Dec. 11.
few gentlemen besides his own servants, in a small frigate, and
arrived safely in Normandy[1]; and so went to Caen, where his
wife and family had remained from the time of his departure
from thence. And this was shortly after the King's defeat at
Worcester; and as soon as his majesty arrived at Paris he forthwith attended upon him, to whom he was most welcome.

117. Scotland being thus subdued, and Ireland reduced to 1651
that obedience as they [the Parliament] could wish, nothing
could be expected to be done in England for the King's advantage. From the time that Cromwell was chosen general in the
place of Fayrefax, he took all occasions to discountenance the
Presbyterians, and to put them out of all trust and employment,
as well in the country as in the army. And whilst he was in
Scotland he intercepted some letter from one Love, a Presbyterian
minister in London, (a fellow who hath been mentioned before[2],
in the time the treaty was at Uxbridge, for preaching against
peace,) to a leading preacher in Scotland; and [sent] such an
information against him, with so many successive instances that
justice might be exemplarily done upon him, that, in spite of all
the opposition which the Presbyterians could make, who appeared publicly with their utmost power, the man was condemned
and executed upon Tower Hill. And to shew their impartiality, Aug. 22.
at the same time and place they executed Browne Bushell, who Apr. 25.
had formerly served the Parliament in the beginning of the
rebellion, and shortly after served the King to the end of the
war, and had lived some years in England after the war expired,
untaken notice of, but upon this occasion, and to accompany
this preacher, was enviously discovered, and put to death.

118. It is a wonderful thing what operation this Presbyterian
spirit had upon the minds of those who were possessed by it.
This poor man [Love,] who had been guilty of as much treason

---

[1] [In Basse Bretagne, after a tempestuous voyage of about three weeks.]
[2] [Book viii. § 219.]

1651 against the King from the beginning of the rebellion as the
pulpit could contain, was so much without remorse for any
wickedness of that kind that he had committed, that he was
jealous of nothing so much as of being suspected to repent, or
that he was brought to suffer for his affection to the King. And
therefore, when he was upon the scaffold, where he appeared
with a marvellous undauntedness, he seemed so much delighted
with the memory of all that he had done against the late King
and against the bishops, that he was even then transported to
speak with animosity and bitterness against both, and expressed
great satisfaction in mind for what he had done against them,
and was as much transported with the inward joy of mind that
he felt in being brought thither to die as a martyr, and to give
testimony for the Covenant; whatsoever he had done being in
the pursuit of the ends, he said, of that sanctified obligation,
and to which he was in and by his conscience engaged.   And
in this raving fit, without so much as praying for the King,
otherwise than that he might propagate the Covenant, he laid
his head upon the block with as much courage as the bravest
and honestest man could do in the most pious occasion.

119. When Cromwell returned to London he caused several
high courts of justice to be erected, by which many gentlemen
of quality were condemned and executed in many parts of the
kingdom as well as in London, who had been taken prisoners at
Worcester, or discovered to have been there.   And that the
terror might be universal, some were put to death for loose discourses in taverns what they would do towards restoring the
King, and other for having blank commissions found in their
hands signed by the King, though they had never attempted to
do any thing thereupon, nor, for ought appeared, intended to
do.   And under [these [1]] desolate apprehensions all the royal
and loyal party lay grovelling and prostrate after the defeat at
Worcester.

120 [2]. There was at this time with the King the marquis

---

[1] ['this,' MS.]

[2] [§§ 120–169 are from the *Life*, pp. 448–461. In the second line of § 120,
after the word, 'Ormonde,' the following passage is struck out as being only

of Ormonde, some days before the Chancellor [of the Exchequer] **1651** came thither; and though his majesty was now in unquestionable safety, the straits and necessities he was in were as unquestionable, which exposed him to all the trouble and uneasiness which the masters of very indigent families are subjected to; and the more, because all men considered only his quality, and not his fortune; so that men had the same emulation and ambition as if the King had all to give which was taken from him, and thought it a good argument for them to ask because he had nothing to give; and asked very improper reversions because he could not grant the possession, and were solicitous for honours which he had power to grant, because he had no fortunes which he could give to them.

121. There had been a great acquaintance between the marquis of Ormonde, when he was lord Thurles, in the life of his grandfather, and the Chancellor, which was renewed when they both came to have shares in the public business, the one in Ireland and the other in England, by a mutual correspondence: so that when they now met at Paris, they met as old friends, and quickly understood each other so well that there could not be a more entire confidence between men, the marquis consulting with him in his nearest concernments; and the Chancellor esteemed and cultivated the friendship with all possible industry and application. The King was abundantly satisfied in the friendship they had for each other, and trusted them both entirely; nor was it in the power of any, though it was often endeavoured by persons of no ordinary account, to break or interrupt that mutual confidence between them, during the whole time the King remained beyond the seas; whereby the King's perplexed affairs were carried on with the less trouble.

a summary of what has just been inserted from the MS. of the *Hist.* '—who had been lately forced to leave Ireland, as much by the falsehood and treachery of the Irish as the power of the Parliament, having left the marquis Clanrickarde deputy in his place, who, though a native of the land, of the greatest family and greatest estate of all the Irish, and a Roman Catholic of the most notorious constancy, within the compass of a year, after having undergone the most notorious affronts from the Irish, was likewise compelled to leave the kingdom.']

1651 And the Chancellor did always acknowledge that the benefit of
this friendship was so great to him, that without it he could
not have borne the weight of that part of the King's business
which was incumbent to him, nor the envy and reproach that
attended the trust [1].

122. Besides the wants and necessities which the King was
pressed with in respect of himself, who had nothing, but was
obliged to provide himself with clothes and all other necessaries

---

[1] [The following passage (printed in part vi. of the *Life*) is here struck
out in the MS. 'And the marquis conferred his friendship upon him with
much the more generosity in that he plainly discerned that he should enjoy
the loss of the Queen's favour by the conjunction he made with the Chancellor, who was yet looked upon with no ungracious eye by her majesty; only
the Lord Jermin knew well he would never resign himself to be disposed of,
which was the temper that would only endear any man to him. For, besides
former experience, an attempt had been lately made upon him by Sir John
Berkely, who told him that the Queen had a good opinion of him, and
knew well in how ill a condition he must be in respect of his subsistence,
and that she would assign him such a competent maintenance that he should
be able to draw his family to him out of Flanders to Paris, and to live
comfortably together, if she might be confident of his service, and that he
would always concur with her in his advice to the King. To which he
answered, that he should never fail in his duty to the Queen, whom he
acknowledged to be his most gracious mistress, with all possible integrity;
but as he was a servant and councillor to the King, so he should always
consider what was good for his service, and never decline that out of any
compliance whatsoever, and that he did not desire to be supported from any
bounty than the King's, nor more by his than in proportion with what his
majesty should be able to do for his other servants. And shortly after, the
Queen herself speaking with him, and complaining that she had no credit
with the King, the Chancellor desired her not to think so; he knew well
the King had great duty for her, which he would still preserve towards her;
but as it would not be fit for her to affect such an interest as to be thought
to govern, so nothing could be more disadvan[ta]geous to the King and to
his interest than that the world should believe that he was absolutely governed
by his mother. Which he found (though she seemed to consent to it) was no
acceptable speech to her; however, she did often employ him to the King
upon such particulars as troubled or offended her, as once for the removal of
a young lady out of the Lou[v]re, who had procured a lodging there without her majesty's consent, and with whom her majesty was justly offended
for the little respect she showed towards her majesty. And when the
Chancellor had prevailed so far with the King that he obliged the lady to
remove out of the Lou[v]re, to satisfy his mother, the Queen was well content that the lady herself and her friends should believe that she had
undergone that affront merely by the malice and credit of the Chancellor.']

for his person by credit, and of his family, which he saw reduced **1651** to all extremities, he was much disquieted by the necessities in his brother the duke of York's family[1], and by the disorder and faction that was in it.   The Queen complained heavily of sir George Ratcliffe and the Attorney; and more of the first, be-cause that he pretended to some rights of being of the duke's family by a grant of the [late] King, which his [present] majesty determined against him, and reprehended his activity in the last summer.   Sir John Berkely had most of the Queen's favour; and though he had at that time no interest in the duke's affection, he found a way to re-ingratiate himself with his royal highness, by insinuating into him two particulars, in both which he foresaw advantage to himself.   Though no man acted the governor's part more imperiously than he had done whilst the lord Byron was absent, finding that he himself was liable to be in some degree governed upon his return, he had used all the ways he could that the duke might be exempted from any subjection to a governor, presuming, that when that title should be extinguished he should be possessed of some such office and relation as should not be under the control of any but the duke himself.   But he had not yet been able to bring that to pass ; which was the reason that he stayed at Paris when his highness visited Flanders and Holland.   Now he took advan-tage of the activity of the duke's spirit, and infused into him that it would be for his honour to put himself into action, and not to be learning his exercises in Paris whilst the army was in the field ; a proposition first intimated by the cardinal, that the duke was now of years to learn his *métier*[2], and had now the opportunity to improve himself by being in the care of a general reputed equal to any captain in Christendom, with whom he might learn that experience, and make those observations, as might enable him to serve the King his brother, who must hope to recover his right only by the sword.   This the cardinal had said both to the Queen and to the lord Jermin whilst the

---

[1] [The following line is here struck out : 'which the Queen did not provide for in the least degree.']

[2] ['miteere,' MS.]

1651 King was in Scotland, when no man had the hardiness to advise it in that conjuncture. But after the King's return there wanted nothing but the approbation of his majesty; and no man more desired it than the lord Byron, who had had good command, and preferred that kind of life before that which he was obliged to live in Paris. And there need be no spurs applied to inflame the duke, who was most impatient to be in the army. And therefore sir John Berkely could not any other way make himself so grateful to him as by appearing to be of that mind, and by telling him that whosoever opposed it, and dissuaded the King from giving his consent, was an enemy to his glory, and desired that he should live always in pupilage; not omitting to put him in mind that his very entrance into the army set him at liberty, and put him into his own disposal, since no man went into the field as under the direction of a governor: still endeavouring to improve his prejudice against those who should either dissuade him from pursuing that resolution, or endeavour to persuade the King not to approve it, which, he told him, could proceed from nothing but want of affection to his person. And by this means he hoped to raise a notable dislike in him of the Chancellor, who he believed did not like the design, because he having spoken to him of it, he had not enlarged upon it as an argument that pleased him.

123. The duke pressed it with earnestness and passion, in which he dissembled not, and found the Queen as well as the King very reserved in the point; which proceeded from their tenderness towards him, and lest they might be thought to be less tender of his safety than they ought to be. His highness then conferred with those who he thought were most like to be consulted with by the King, amongst which he knew the Chancellor was one; and finding him to speak with less warmth than the rest, as if he thought it a matter worthy of great deliberation, he was confirmed in the jealousy which sir John Berkely had kindled in him, that he was the principal person who obstructed the King's condescension. There was at that time no man with [the King] who had been a councillor to his father, or was sworn to himself, but the Chancellor. The mar-

quis of Ormonde, though he had administered the affairs in **1651**
Ireland, was never sworn a councillor in England; yet his
majesty looked upon him in all respects most fit to advise him,
and thought it necessary to form such a body as should be
esteemed by all men as his Privy Council, without whose advice
he would take no resolutions. He knew the Queen would not
be well pleased if the lord Jermin were not one; who in all
other respects was necessary to that trust, in respect all addresses
to the Court of France were to be made by him : and the lord
Wilmott, who had cultivated the King's affection during the
time of their peregrination, and drawn many promises from him,
and was full of projects for his service, could not be left out.
The King therefore called the marquis of Ormonde, the lord
Jermin, and the lord Wilmott to the Council board, and declared that they three, together with the Chancellor, should be
consulted with in all his affairs. The Queen very earnestly
pressed the King that sir John Berkely might likewise be made
a councillor, which his majesty would not consent to, and thought
he could not refuse the same honour to the lord Wentworth, the
lord Byron, or any other person of honour who should wait upon
him, if he granted it to sir John Berkely, who had no manner
of pretence.

124. He [Berkely] took this refusal very heavily, and thought
his great parts, and the services he had performed, which were
known to very few, might well enough distinguish him from
other men. But because he would not be thought without
some just pretence which others had not, he very confidently
insisted upon a right he had, by a promise of the late King, to
be Master of the Wards ; and that officer had usually been of
the Privy Council. And the evidence he had of that promise
was an intercepted letter from the late King to the Queen,
which the Parliament had caused to be printed [1]. And in that
letter the King answered a letter he had received from her

[1] [A letter dated March 27, 1645, printed at p. 3 of *The King's Cabinet
opened*, 4to Lond., 1645. The King's words are :—'As for Jack Barclay, I
do not remember that I gave thee any hope of making of him Master of
the Wards. For Cottington had it long ago before thou went hence.']

1651 majesty, in which she put him in mind that he had promised her to make Jack Berkely (which was the style in the letter) Master of the Wards; which the King said he wondered at, since he could not remember that she had ever spoken to him to that purpose; implying likewise that he was not fit for it. He pressed the Chancellor to urge this matter of right to the King, (and said the Queen would declare the King had promised it to her,) and to prevail with his majesty to make him presently Master of the Wards, which would give him such a title to the board that others could not take his being called thither as a prejudice to them.

125. The Chancellor had at that time much kindness for him, and did really desire to oblige him, but he durst not urge that for a reason to the King which could be none, and what he knew, as well as a negative could be known, had no foundation of truth. For besides that he very well knew that the late King had not so good an opinion of sir John Berkely as he did at that time heartily wish and endeavour to infuse into him, the King had, after[1] that promise was pretended to be 1644 made, granted that office at Oxford to the lord Cottington;
Jan. 4. who executed it as long as offices were executed under the grant of the Crown, and was possessed of the title till his death. He [the Chancellor] did therefore very earnestly endeavour to dissuade him from making that pretence and demand to the King; and told him the King could not at this time do a more ungracious thing, and that would lose him more the hearts and affections of the nobility and gentry of England, than in making a Master of the Wards, in a time when it could not be the least advantage to his majesty or the officer to declare that he resolved to insist upon that part of his prerogative which his father had consented to part with; and the resuming whereof in the full rigour, which he might lawfully do, would ruin most of the estates of England, as well of his friends as enemies, in regard of the vast arrears incurred in so many years; and therefore whatever he [the King] might think

---

[1] [before: see preceding note.]

to resolve hereafter, when it should please God to restore him, 1651 for the present there must be no thought of such an officer.

126. He [Berkely] was not satisfied at all in the reason that was alleged, and very unsatisfied with the unkindness (as he called it) of the refusal to interpose in it; and said, since his friends would not, he would himself require justice of the King; and immediately, hearing that the King was in the next room, went to him, and in the warmth he had contracted by the Chancellor's contradiction he pressed his majesty to make good the promise his father had made, and magnified the services he had done; which he did really believe to have been very great, and, by the custom of making frequent relations of his actions, grew in very good earnest to think he had done many things which nobody else ever heard of. The King, who knew him very well, and believed little of his history, and less of his father's promise, was willing rather to reclaim him from his importunity than to give him a positive denial, (which in his nature he affected not,) lest it might indispose his mother or his brother: and so, to every part of his request concerning the being of the Council, and concerning the office, gave him such reasons against the gratifying him for the present, that he could not but plainly discern that his majesty was very averse from it. But that consideration prevailed not with him; he used so great importunity, notwithstanding all the reasons which had been alleged, that at last the King prevailed with himself, which he used not to do, and gave him a positive denial and reprehension at once, and left him.

127. All this he imputed to the Chancellor, and though he knew well he had not nor could have spoken with the King from the time they had spoken together before himself had that audience from his majesty, he declared that he knew all that indisposition had been infused by him, because many of the reasons which his majesty had given against his doing what he desired were the very same that the Chancellor had urged to him, and which could not but have occurred to any reasonable man who had been called to consult upon that subject. This passion prevailed so far upon him, that, notwithstanding

1651 the advice of some of his best friends to the contrary, he took
an opportunity to walk[1] with the Chancellor shortly after;
and in a very calm, though a very confused, discourse, told him,
that since he was resolved to break all friendship with him,
which had continued now near twenty years, he thought it but
just to give him notice of it, that from henceforward he might
not expect any friendship from him, but that they might live
towards each other with that civility only that strangers use
to do. The Chancellor told him, that the same justice that
disposed him to give this notice would likewise oblige him to
declare the reason of this resolution; and asked him whether
he had ever broken his word to him, or promised him to do
what he had not done. He answered, his exception was that
he could not be brought to make any promise, and that their
judgments were so different that he would no more depend
upon him. And so they parted, without ever after having
conversation with each other whilst they remained in France.

1652 128. The spring was now advanced, and the duke of York
continued his importunity with the King that he might have
his leave to repair to the army. And thereupon his majesty
called his Council together, the Queen his mother and his
brother being likewise present. And there his majesty declared
what his brother had long desired of him, to which he had
hitherto given no other answer than that he would think of
it, and before he would give any other he thought it necessary
to receive their advice; nor did in the least discover what he
was inclined to. The duke then repeated what he had desired
of the King, and said he thought he asked nothing but what
became him; and if he did, he hoped the King would not deny
it to him, and that nobody would advise he should. The Queen
spake not a word; and the King required the lords to deliver
their opinion; who all sat silent, expecting who would begin;
there being no fixed rule of the board, but sometimes, according to the nature of the business, he who was first in place
began, at other times he who was last in quality; and when it
required some debate before any opinion should be delivered,

---

[1] [The words ' into the long gallery of the Lou[v]re ' are here struck out.]

any man was at liberty to offer what he would. But after a **1652** long silence, the King commanded the Chancellor to speak first. He said, it could not be expected that he would deliver his opinion in a matter that was so much too hard for him till he heard what others thought, at least till the question was otherwise stated than it yet seemed to him to be. He said, he thought the Council would not be willing to take it upon them to advise that the duke of York, the heir apparent of the Crown, should go a volunteer into the French army, and that the exposing himself to so much danger should be the effect of their counsel, who ought to have all possible tenderness for the safety of every branch of the royal family; but if the duke of York, out of his own princely courage, and to attain experience in the art of war, of which there was like to be so great use, had taken a resolution to visit the army, and to spend that *campania* in it, and that the question only was, whether the King should restrain him from that expedition, he was ready to declare his opinion that he should not; there being great difference between the King's giving him leave to go, which implied an approbation of it, and suffering him to do what his own genius inclined him to, and advising and directing him so to do[1]. The King and Queen liked the stating of the question, as suiting best with the tenderness they ought to have; and the duke was as well pleased with it, since it left him at the liberty he desired; and the lords thought it safest for them: and so all were pleased; and much of the prejudice which the duke had entertained towards the Chancellor was abated: and his royal highness, with the good liking of the French Court, went to the army, **1653** where he was received by the marshal of Turinn[e] with all **July 4**[2]. possible demonstrations of respect, and where in a short time he got the reputation of a prince of very signal courage, and to be universally beloved of the whole army by his affable behaviour.

129. The insupportable necessities of the King were now grown so notorious that the French Court was compelled to take notice of it, and thereupon, with some dry compliments for the smallness of the assignation in respect of the ill con-

[1] [The last six words interlined.]
[2] [*Cal. Clar. S. P.* ii. 222. Thurloe's, *S. P.*, i. 319.]

dition of their affairs, which indeed were not in any good
posture, they settled an assignation of six thousand livres by
the month upon the King, payable out of such a gabell;
which, beginning six months after the King came thither, found
too great a debt contracted to be easily satisfied out of such a
monthly receipt, though it had been punctually complied with;
which it never was. The Queen at his majesty's first arrival
had declared that she was not able to bear the charge of the
King's diet, but that he must pay one half of the expense of
her table, where both their majesties eat, with the duke of
York and the princess Henrietta, which two were at the
Queen's charge till the King came thither, but from that time
the duke of York was upon the King's account; and the' very
first night's supper which the King eat with the Queen began
the account, and a moiety thereof [was] charged to the King:
so that the first money that was received for the King upon his
grant was entirely stopped by sir Harry Wood, the Queen's
treasurer, for the discharge of his majesty's part of the Queen's
table, (which expense was first satisfied, as often as money
could be procured,) and the rest for the payment of other debts
contracted at his first coming for clothes and other necessaries,
there being very great care taken that nothing should be left to
be distributed amongst his servants; the marquis of Ormonde
himself being compelled to put himself in pension, with the
Chancellor and some other gentlemen, with a poor English
woman, the wife of one of the King's servants, at a pistole
a week for his diet, and to walk the streets on foot, which was
no honourable custom in Paris; whilst the lord Jermin kept an
excellent table for those who courted him, and had a coach
of his own, and all other accommodations incident to the most
full fortunes. And if the King had the most urgent occasion
for the use but of twenty pistoles, as sometimes he had, he
could not find credit to borrow it; which he often had experiment of. But if there had not been as much care to take that
from him which was his own as to hinder him from receiving
the supply assigned by the King of France, his necessities
would not have been so extraordinary.

130. When the King went to Jarsy in order to his journey 1652
into Ireland, and at the same time that he sent the Chancellor
into Spain, he sent likewise the lord Culpeper into Mosco, to
borrow money of that duke [1]; and into Poland he sent Mr. 1649
Crofts upon the same errand. The former returned whilst the Sept. 20 [2].
King was in Scotland, and the latter about the time that the 1652
King made his escape from Worcester. And both of them Feb. 22 [2].
succeeded so well in their journey, that he who received least
for his majesty's service had above ten thousand pounds over
and above the expense of their journeys. But, as if the King
had been out of all possible danger to want money, the lord
Jermin had sent an express into Scotland, as soon as he
knew what success the lord Culpeper had at Mosco and found
there were no less hopes from Mr. Crofts, and procured from
the King (who could with more ease grant than deny) warrants under his hand to both his ambassadors, to pay the
monies they had received to several persons; whereof a considerable sum was made a present to the Queen, more to the
lord Jermin, upon pretence of debts due to him, which were not
diminished by that receipt, and all disposed of according to
the modesty of the askers; whereof Dr. Goffe had eight
hundred pounds for services he had performed, and within few
days after the receipt of it changed his religion, and became
one of the fathers of the Oratory. So that when the King
returned in all that distress to Paris, he never received five
hundred pistoles from the proceed of both those embassies; nor
did any one of those who were supplied by his bounty seem
sensible of the obligation, or the more disposed to do him any
service upon their own expense; of which the King was
sensible enough, but resolved to bear it, and more, rather than
by entering into any expostulation with those who were faulty
to give any trouble to the Queen.

131. The lord Jermin, who in his own judgment was very
indifferent in all matters relating to religion, was always of
some faction that regarded it, and had been much addicted to

---

[1] [Culpeper arrived at Moscow on May 5, 1650, and left it July 4, having
received a loan of 20,000 roubles. *Cal. Clar. S. P.* ii. 71.]   [2] [*Ib.* 124.]

1652 the Presbyterians from the time that there had been any treaties with the Scots, in which he had too much privity. And now, upon the King's return, he had a great design to persuade the King to go to the congregation at Charenton, to the end that he might keep up his interest in that party; which he had no reason to believe would ever be able to do him service, or willing, if they were able, without such odious conditions as they had hitherto insisted upon in all their overtures. The Queen did not in the least degree oppose this, but rather seemed to countenance it, as the best expedient which might incline him by degrees to prefer the religion of the church of Rome. For though the Queen had never to this time by herself, or by others with her advice, used the least means to persuade him to change his religion, as well out of observation of the injunction laid upon her by the deceased King, as out of the conformity of her own judgment, which could not but persuade her that the change of his religion would infallibly make all his hopes of recovering England desperate; [yet[1]] it is as true, that from the King's return from Worcester she did really despair of the King's being restored by the affections of his own subjects, and [believed] that it could never be brought to pass without a conjunction of Catholic princes on his behalf, and by a united force to restore him; and that such a conjunction would never be entered into except the King himself became Catholic Roman. And therefore from this time she was very well content that any attempts should be made upon him to that purpose, and in that regard wished that he would go to Charenton; which she well knew was not the religion he affected, but would be a little discountenance to the Church in which he had been bred, and from which as soon as he could be persuaded in any degree to swerve, he would be more exposed to any other temptation. And the King had not positively refused to gratify the ministers of that congregation, who with great professions of duty had besought him to do them that honour before the Chancellor came to him; in which it was believed that they

[1] ['but,' MS.]

were the more like to prevail by the death of Dr. Steward, to **1652**
whose judgment in matters of religion the King had reverence,
by the earnest recommendation of his father; and he died after 1651
the King's return within fourteen days, and with some trouble ^{Nov. 14.}
upon the importunity and artifice he saw used to prevail with
the King to go to Charenton, though he saw no disposition in
his majesty to yield to it.

132. The lord Jermin still pressed it, as a thing that ought
in policy and discretion to be done, to reconcile that people,
which was a great body in France, to the King's service, which
would draw to him all the foreign churches, and thereby he
might receive considerable assistance. He wondered, he said,
why it should be opposed by any man; since he did not wish
that his majesty would discontinue his own devotions, according to the course he had always observed; nor propose that he
should often repair thither, but only sometimes, at least once,
to shew that he did look upon them as of the same religion
with him; which the Church of England had always acknowledged; and that it had been an instruction to all the English
ambassadors that they should keep a good correspondence with
those of the religion, and frequently to resort to divine service
at Charenton, where they had always a pew kept for them.

133. The Chancellor dissuaded his majesty from going thither
with equal passion; told him, that whatever countenance or
favour the Crown or Church of England had heretofore shewed
to those congregations was in a time when they carried themselves with modesty and duty towards both, and when they
professed great duty to the King and much reverence to that
Church, lamenting themselves that it was not in their power,
by the opposition of the State, to make their reformation so
perfect as it was in England. And by this kind of behaviour
they had indeed received the protection and countenance from
England as if they were of the same religion, though, it may be,
the original of that countenance and protection proceeded from
another less warrantable foundation, which he was sure would
never find credit from his majesty. But whatever it was, that
people had undeserved it from the King; for as soon as the

1652 troubles began, the Huguenots of France had generally expressed great malice to the [late] King, and very many of their preachers and ministers had publicly and industriously justified the rebellion, and prayed for the good success of it ; and their synod itself had in such a manner inveighed against the Church of England, that they, upon the matter, professed themselves to be of another religion, and inveighed against episcopacy as if it were inconsistent with the Protestant religion. That their great professor at their university of [Saumur][1], monsieur Amirante, who was looked upon as a man of the most moderate spirit amongst their ministers, published an apology for the general inclination of that party to the proceedings of the Parliament in England, lest it might give some jealousy to their own King of their inclination to rebellion, and of their opinion that it was lawful for subjects to take up arms against their prince; which, he said, could not be done in France without manifest rebellion, and incurring the displeasure of God for the manifest breach of his commandments; because the King of France is an absolute king, independent upon any other authority; but that the constitution of the kingdom of England was of another nature; because the King there is subordinate to the Parliament, which hath authority to raise arms for the reformation of religion, or for the executing the public justice of the kingdom against all those who violate the laws of the nation : so that the war might be just there which in no case would be warrantable in France[2].

134. He [the Chancellor] told the King, that after such an indignity offered to him and to his Crown, and since they had now made such a distinction between the episcopal and the presbyterian government that the professors were not of the same religion, his going to Charenton could not be without this effect, that it would be concluded every where that his majesty had renounced the Church of England and betaken himself to that of Charenton, at least that he thought the one and the other to be indifferent; which would be the most deadly wound

---

[1] ['Somers,' MS.]

[2] [See Amyraut s *Apologie pour ceux de la Religion*, 1648, pp. 76-81.]

to the Church of England that it hath yet ever suffered.   These **1652** reasons prevailed so far, with the King's own natural aversion from what had been proposed, that he declared positively that he would never go to Charenton; which determination eased him from any farther application of that people.   And the reproach of this resolution was wholly charged upon the Chancellor as the implacable enemy of all Presbyterians, and as the only man who diverted the King from having a good opinion of them: whereas, in truth, the daily information he received from the King of their barbarous behaviour in Scotland towards him, and of their insupportable pride and pedantry in their manners, did confirm him in the judgment he had always made of their religion; and he was the more grievous to those of that profession, because they could not, as they used to do to all that opposed and crossed them in that manner, accuse him of being popishly affected and governed by the Papists, to whom they knew he was equally odious; and the Queen's knowing him to be most disaffected to her religion made her willing to appear most displeased for his hindering the King from going to Charenton.

135. There was another accident which fell out at this time, and which the Chancellor foresaw would exceedingly increase the Queen's prejudice to him; which he did very heartily desire to avoid, and to recover her majesty's favour by all the ways he could pursue with his duty, and did never in the least degree dispose his majesty to deny any thing to her which she owned the desire of.   Lieutenant general Middleton, who had been taken prisoner at Worcester, after he was recovered of his wounds was sent prisoner to the Tower of London; where were likewise many noble persons of that nation, as the earl of Craford, the earl of Latherdale, and many others.   But as they of the Parliament had a greater reverence for Middleton than for any other of that nation, knowing him to be a man of great honour and courage, and much the best officer they [the Scots] had, so they had a hatred of him proportionable; and they thought they had him at their mercy, and might proceed against him more warrantably than against their other prisoners

1652 for his life, because he had heretofore, in the beginning of the war, served them; and though he had quitted their service at the same time when they cashiered the earl of Essex and made their new model, and was at liberty to do what he thought best for himself, yet they resolved to free themselves from any farther apprehension and fear of him.

136. And to that purpose they erected a new high court of justice for the trial of some persons who had been troublesome to them, and especially Middleton, and Massy, who, after he had escaped from Worcester, and travelled two or three days, found himself so tormented and weakened by his wounds, that being near the seat of the earl of Stamford, whose lieutenant colonel he had been in the beginning of the war, and being well known to his lady, he chose to commit himself to her rather than to her husband, hoping that in honour she would have found some means to preserve him. But the lady had only charity to cure his wounds, not courage to conceal his person; but such advertisements were given of him, that, as soon as

1651
Nov. 27. he was fit to be removed, he was likewise sent to the Tower, and destined to be sacrificed by the high court of justice together with Middleton, for the future security of the commonwealth.

137. But now the presbyterian interest shewed itself, and doubtless in enterprises of this nature was very powerful, having in all places persons devoted to them who were ready to obey their orders, though they did not pretend to be of their party. And the time approaching that they were sure Middleton was to be tried, that is, to be executed, they gave him so good and particular advertisement that he took his

Jan. 14. leave of his friends in the Tower and made his escape; and having friends enough to shelter him in London, after he had concealed himself there a fortnight or three weeks, that the diligence of the first examination and inquiry was over, he

March. was safely transported into France. And, within few days

Aug. 30. after, Massy had the same good fortune; to the grief and vexation of the very soul of Cromwell, who thirsted for the blood of these two persons.

138. When Middleton came to the King to Paris, he brought

with him a little Scottish vicar, who was known to the King, 1652
one Mr. Knox, who brought letters of credit to his majesty,
and some propositions from his friends in Scotland, and other
despatches from the lords in the Tower, with whom he had
conferred after Middleton had escaped from thence. He brought
the relation of the terror that was struck into the hearts of
that whole nation by the severe proceeding of general Munke,
(to whose care Cromwell had committed the reduction of that
kingdom,) upon the taking of Dundee, where persons of all 1651
degrees and qualities were put to the sword for many hours Sept. 1.
after the town was entered, and all left to plunder ; upon
which all other places rendered. All men complained of the
marquis of Arguyle, who prosecuted all the King's friends with
the utmost malice, and protected and preserved the rest according to his desire. He gave the King assurance from the
most considerable persons who had retired into the Highlands
that they would never swerve from their duty, and that they
would be able during the winter to infest the enemy by
incursions into their quarters ; and that if Middleton might
be sent to them with some supply of arms, they would have an
army ready against the spring, strong enough to meet with
Munke. He said he was addressed from Scotland to the lords
in the Tower, who did not then know that Middleton had
arrived in safety with the King : and therefore they had commanded him, if neither Middleton [n]or the lord Newburgh
were about his majesty, that then he should repair to the
marquis of Ormonde, and desire him to present him to the
King ; but that having found both those lords there, he had
made no farther application than to them, who had brought
him to his majesty. He told him that both those in Scotland
and those in the Tower made it their humble request, or rather
a condition, to his majesty, that, except it were granted, they
would no more think of serving his majesty : the condition
was, that whatsoever should have relation to his service in
Scotland, and to their persons who were to venture their lives
in it, might not be communicated to the Queen, the duke of
Buckingham, the lord Jermin, or the lord Wilmott. They pro-

1652 fessed all duty to the Queen, but they knew she had too good an opinion of the marquis of Arguyle, who would infallibly come to know whatever was known to either of the other.

139. The King did not expect that any notable service could be performed by his friends in Scotland for his advantage or their own redemption, yet did not think it fit to seem to undervalue the professions and overtures of those who had during his being amongst them made all possible demonstration of affection and duty to him; and therefore resolved to grant any thing they desired; and so promised not to communicate any thing of what they proposed to the Queen or to the other [three [1]] lords; but since they proposed some present despatches to be made of commissions and letters, he wished them to consider whom they would be willing to trust in the performing that service. And the next day they attended his majesty again, and desired that all matters relating to Scotland might be consulted by his majesty with the marquis of Ormonde, the lord Newburgh, and the Chancellor of the Exchequer, and that all the despatches might be made by the Chancellor; which the King consented to; and bid the lord Newburgh go with them to him, and let him know his majesty's pleasure. And thereupon the lord Newburgh brought Middleton to the Chancellor, who had never seen his face before.

140. The marquis of Ormonde and the Chancellor believed that the King had nothing at this time to do but to be quiet, and that all his activity was to consist in carefully avoiding to do any thing that might do him hurt, and to expect some blessed conjuncture from the amity of Christian princes, or some such revolution of affairs in England by their own discontents and divisions amongst themselves, as might make it seasonable for his majesty again to shew himself. And therefore they proposed nothing to themselves but patiently to expect one of those conjunctures, and in the mean time so to behave themselves to the Queen that, without being received into her trust and confidence, (which they did not affect,) they might enjoy

---

[1] ['two,' MS., the name of the duke of Buckingham having been added in the preceding paragraph in an interlineation.]

her grace and good acceptation. But the designation of them 1652 to this Scotch intrigue crossed all this imagination, and shook that foundation of peace and tranquillity upon which they had raised their present hopes: besides that the Chancellor was not without some natural prejudice to the ingenuity and sincerity of that nation, and therefore he went presently to the King, and besought him with earnestness that he would not lay that burden upon him, or engage him in any part of the counsels of that people. He put his majesty in mind of the continued avowed jealousy and displeasure which that whole nation had ever had against him, and that his majesty very well knew that those noble persons who served him best when he was in Scotland, and in whose affection and fidelity he had all possible satisfaction, had all imaginable prejudice against him, and would be troubled when they should hear that all their secrets were committed to him. He told him this trust would for ever deprive him of all hope of the Queen's favour, who could not but discern it within three or four days, and by the frequent resort of the Scotch Levite to him, who had the vanity to desire long conferences with him, that there was some secret affair in hand which was kept from her; and she would as easily discover that the Chancellor was privy to [it[1],] by his reading papers to his majesty, and his signing them; and would from thence conclude that he had persuaded him to exclude her majesty from the trust, which she would never forgive. And upon the whole he renewed his importunity that he might be excused from this confidence.

141. The King heard him with patience and attention enough, and confessed that he had reason not to be solicitous for that employment; but he wished him to consider withal, that he must either undertake it, or that his majesty must in plain terms reject the correspondence, and by it declare that he would no further consider Scotland as his kingdom and the people as his subjects; which he said, he thought he would not advise him to do. If he entertained it, it could not be imagined that all those transactions could pass through his own

[1] [' them,' MS.]

1652 hand, or if they could, his being shut up so long alone would make the same discovery. Whom then should he trust? The lord Newburgh, it was very true, was a very honest man, and worthy of any trust; but he was not a councillor, and nothing could be so much wondered at as his frequent being shut up with him; and more, his bringing any papers to him to be signed. To the general prejudice which he conceived was against him by that nation, his majesty told him the nation was much altered since he had to do with them, and that no men were better loved by them now than they who had from the beginning been faithful to his father and himself. To which he added, that Middleton had the least in him of any infirmities most incident to the nation that he knew, and that he would find him a man of great honour and ingenuity, with whom he would be well pleased. His majesty said, that he would frankly declare that he had received some intelligence out of Scotland to his mother, and that he was obliged, and had given his word to those whose lives would be forfeited if known, that he would not communicate it with any but those who were chosen by themselves; and after this she could not be offended with his reservation: and concluded with a gracious conjuration and command to the Chancellor, that he would cheerfully submit and undergo that employment, which he assured him should never be attended with prejudice or inconvenience to him. And in this manner he submitted himself to the King's disposal, and was trusted throughout that affair, which had several stages in the years following, and which did produce the inconveniences he had foreseen, and rendered him so unacceptable to the Queen, that she easily entertained those prejudices towards him which those she most trusted were always ready to infuse into her, and under which he was compelled to bear many hardnesses.

142. This uncomfortable condition of the King was rendered yet more desperate by the straits and necessities into which the French Court was about this time plunged; so that they which hitherto had shewed no very good will to assist the King were now become really unable to do it. The Parliament of

Paris had behaved themselves so refractorily to all the King's 1652 commands, pressed so importunately for the liberty of the princes, and so impatiently for the remove of the cardinal, that the cardinal was at last compelled to persuade the Queen to consent $^{1651}_{Feb. 6.}$ to both: and so himself rode to Havre de Grace, and delivered the Queen's warrant to set them at liberty, and after a short conference with the prince of Condé he continued his own journey towards Germany, and passed in disguise, with two or three servants, till he came near Cullen, and there he remained at a house belonging to that Elector.

143. When the princes came to Paris, they had received Feb. 16. great welcome from the Parliament and the city; and instead of closing with the Court, which it was thought they would have done, the wound was widened without any hope of reconciliation: so that the King and Queen Regent withdrew from Sept. 27. thence; the town was in arms, and fire and sword denounced against the cardinal; his goods sold at an outcry, and a price set upon his head; and all persons who professed any duty for the King found themselves very unsafe in Paris. And during all this time the Queen of England and the King with their families remained in the Lou[v]re, not knowing whither to go, nor able to stay there, the assignments which had been made for their subsistence being paid to neither; and the loose people of the town began to talk of the duke of York's being in arms against them. But the duke of Orleance, under whose name all the disorders were committed, and the prince of Condé, visited the King and Queen with many professions of civility; but those were shortly abated likewise, when the [French] King's army came upon one side of the town, and the $^{1652,}_{June,}$ Spanish army, with the duke of Lorraine's, upon the other. The French army thought they had the enemy upon an advantage, and desired to have a battle with them, which the other declined; all which time the Court had an underhand treaty with the duke of Lorraine; and upon a day appointed the French King sent to the King of England, to desire him to confer with the duke of Lorraine, who lay then with his army within a mile of the town. There was no reason visible for

1652 that desire, nor could it be conceived that his majesty's interposition could be of moment; yet his majesty knew not how to refuse it, but immediately went to the place assigned, where he found both armies drawn up in battalia, within cannon shot of each other. Upon his majesty's coming to the duke of Lorraine, the treaty was again revived, and messages sent between the duke and marshal Turinn[e]. And in fine, the night approaching, both armies drew off from their ground, and his majesty returned to the Lou[v]re; but before the next morning the treaty was finished between the Court and the duke of Lorraine; and he marched away with his whole army towards Flanders, and left the Spaniards to support the Parliament against the power of the French army; which advanced upon them with that

July 1. resolution, that, though they defended themselves very bravely, and the prince of Condé did the office of a great general in the fauxburgh of St. Marsoe, and at the port of St. Antoyne, in which places many gallant persons of both sides were slain, they had been all cut off, if the city had not been prevailed with to suffer them to retire into it; which they had no mind to do. And thereupon the King's army retired to their old post, four leagues off, and attended future advantages: the King having a very great party in the Parliament and the city, which abhorred the receiving and entertaining the Spaniards into their bowels.

144. This retreat of the duke of Lorraine broke the neck of the prince of Condé's design. And he knew well he should not be long able to retain the duke of Orleance from treating with the Court, or keep the Parisians at his devotion; and that the duke of Beauford, whom they had made governor of Paris, would be weary of the contention. For the present, they were all incensed against the duke of Lorraine, and were well enough contented that the people should believe that this defection in the duke was wrought by the activity and interposition of the King of England; and they who did know that his interest could not have produced that effect could not tell how to interpret his majesty's journey to speak with the duke in so unseasonable a conjuncture: so that, as the people expressed

and used all the insolent reproaches against the English Court 1652
at the Lou[v]re, and loudly threatened to be revenged, so
neither the duke of Orleance nor the prince of Condé made any
visit there, or expressed the least civility towards it. So that
in truth the King and Queen did not think themselves out of
danger, nor stirred out of the Lou[v]re for many days, until
the French Court thought themselves obliged to provide for
their security by advising the King and Queen to remove, and
assigned St. Germ[a]in's to them for their retreat. And then
their majesties sent to the duke of Orleance and prince of
Condé, that their purpose was to leave the town : upon which
there was a guard that attended them out of the town at the July.
evening, which could not be got to be in readiness till then ;
and they were shortly after met by some troops of horse sent
by the [French] king, which conducted them by torch-light to
St. Germ[a]in's, where they arrived about midnight ; and remained there without any disturbance till Paris was reduced to
the King's obedience.

145. It is a very hard thing for people who have nothing to
do to forbear doing somewhat which they ought not to do ; and
the King might well hope that, since he had nothing else left to
enjoy, he might have enjoyed quiet and repose, and that a Court
which had nothing to give might have been free from faction
and ambition ; whilst every man had composed himself to bear
the ill fortune he was reduced to for conscience sake, which
every man pretended to be his case, with submission and content, till it should please God to buoy[1] up the King from the
lowness he was in, who in truth suffered much more than any-
body else. But whilst there are Courts in the world, emulation
and ambition will be inseparable from them ; and kings who
have nothing to give shall be pressed to promise ; which often-
times proves more inconvenient and mischievous than any
present gifts could be, because they always draw on more of
the same title and pretence ; and as they who receive the
favours are not the more satisfied, so they who are not paid in
the same kind, or who out of modesty and discretion forbear to

---

[1] ['bw'y,' MS.]

1652 make such suits, are grieved and offended to see the vanity and presumption of bold men so unseasonably gratified and encouraged.

146. The King found no benefit in being stripped of all his dominions and all his power. Men were as importunate, as hath been said before, for honours and offices and revenues, as if they could have taken possession of them as soon they had been granted, though but by promise: and men who would not have had the presumption to have asked the same thing if the King had been in England, thought it very justifiable to demand it because he was not there; since there were so many hazards that they should [n]ever live to enjoy what he promised. And the vexations he underwent of this kind cannot be expressed; and whosoever succeeded not in his unreasonable desires imputed it only to the ill nature of the Chancellor, and concluded that he alone obstructed it, because they always received very gracious answers from his majesty: so that though his wants were as visible and notorious as any man's, and it appeared he got nothing for himself, he paid very dear in his peace and quiet for the credit and interest he was thought to have with his master.

147. The lord Wilmott had, by the opportunity of his late conversation with the King in his escape, drawn many kind expressions from his majesty; and he thought he could not be too solicitous to procure such a testimony of his grace and favour as might distinguish him from other men, and publish the esteem the King had of him. Therefore he importuned him that he would make him an earl, referring the time of his creation to his majesty's own choice: and the modesty of this reference prevailed; the King well knowing that the same honour would be desired on the behalf of another by one whom he would be unwilling to deny; but since it was not asked for the present, he promised to do it in a time that should appear to be convenient to his service.

148. But there were projects of another nature, which were much more troublesome, and in which the projectors still considered themselves in the first place, and what their condition

might prove to be by the success. The duke of York was so well **1652**
pleased with the fatigue of the war, that he thought his condition very agreeable to him; but his servants did not like that
course of life so well, at least desired so far to improve it that
they might reap some advantages to themselves out of his over-
plus. Sir John Berkely was now, upon the death of the lord
Byron, (by which the duke was deprived of a very good servant,)
become the superior of his family, and called himself, without any
authority, *Intendant des affaires de son altesse royale;* had the
management of all his receipts and disbursements; and all the
rest depended upon him. He desired by all ways to get a better
revenue for his master than the small pension he received from
France, and thought no expedient so proper as a wife of a great
and noble fortune, which he presumed he should have the
managing of.

149. There was then a lady in the town, mademoiselle de
Longueville[1], the daughter of the duke of Longueville by his
first wife, by whom she was to inherit a very fair revenue, and
had title to a considerable sum of money, which her father was
obliged to account for: so that she was looked upon as one of
the greatest and richest marriages in France in respect of her
fortune; in respect of her person not at all attractive, being a
lady of a very low stature, and that stature in no degree straight.
Her sir John designed for the duke, and treated with those ladies
who were nearest to her, and had been trusted with the education of her, before he mentioned it to his royal highness. Then
he persuaded him that all hopes in England were desperate:
that the government was so settled there that it could never be
shaken; so that his highness must think of no other fortune
than what he should make by his sword: that he was now upon
the stage where he must act out his life, and that he should do
well to think of providing a civil fortune for himself as well as
a martial, which could only be by marriage: and then spake of
mademoiselle de Longueville, and made her fortune at least
equal to what it was; which, he said, when once he [his high-
ness] was possessed of, he might sell, and thereby raise money to

[1] ['Longaville,' MS.]

1652 pay an army to invade England, and so might become the restorer of the King his brother: this he thought very practicable, if his highness seriously and heartily would endeavour it. The duke was not so far broken with age as to have an aversion from marriage, and the consideration of the fortune, and the circumstances which might attend it, made it not the less acceptable; yet he made no other answer to it, than that he must first know the King's and the Queen's judgment of it before he could take any resolution what to do. Upon which sir John undertook, with his highness's approbation, to propose it to their majesties himself, and accordingly first spake with the Queen of it, enlarging all the benefits which probably might attend it.

150. It was generally believed that the first overture and attempt had not been made without her majesty's privity and approbation; for the lord Jermin had been no less active in the contrivance than sir John Berkely: yet her majesty refused to deliver any opinion in it till she knew the King's: and so at last, when and after the young lady herself had been spoken to, his majesty was informed of it, and his approbation desired; with which he was not well pleased, and yet was unwilling to use his authority to obstruct what was looked upon as so great a benefit and advantage to his brother; though he did not dissemble his opinion of their presumption who undertook to enter upon treaties of that nature with the same liberty as if it concerned only their own kindred and allies: however, he was very reserved in saying what he thought of it. Whilst it was in deliberation, all the ways were taken to discover what the Chancellor's judgment was; and the lord Jermin spake to him of it, as a matter that would not admit any doubt on the King's part, otherwise than from the difficulty of bringing it to pass in regard the lady's friends would not without great difficulty be induced to give their consent. But the Chancellor could not be drawn to make any other answer, than that it was a subject so much above his comprehension, and the consequences might be such, that he had not the ambition to desire to be consulted with upon it; and that less than the King's command should not induce him to enter upon the discourse of it.

151. It was not long before the Queen sent for him ; and, 1651-2
seeming to complain of the importunity that was used towards
her in that affair, and as if it were not grateful to her, asked
him what his opinion of it was. To which he answered, that he
did not understand the convenience of it so well as to judge
whether it were like to be of benefit to the duke of York; but
he thought that neither the King nor her majesty should be
willing that the heir apparent of the Crown should be married
before the King himself, or that it should be in any woman's
power to say, that if there were but one person dead, she
should be a Queen ; with which her majesty, who no doubt did
love the King with all possible tenderness, seemed to be moved,
as if it had been a consideration she had not thought of before,
and said, with some warmth, that she would never give her consent that it should be so. However, this argument was quickly
made known to the duke of York, and several glosses made
upon it, to the reproach of the Chancellor : yet it made such an
impression, that there were then as active endeavours to find a
convenient wife for the King himself, and mademoiselle, the
daughter of the duke of Orleance by his first wife, and who in
the right of her mother was already possessed of the fair inherit-
ance of the duchy of Mountpensier, was thought of. And to
this the Queen was much inclined, and the King himself not
averse ; both looking too much upon the relief it might give to
his present necessities, and the convenience of having a place to
repose in as long as the storm should continue. But the
Chancellor had no thought, by the conclusion he had made in
the other overture, to have drawn on this proposition ; and the
marquis of Ormonde and he were no less troubled with this than
with the former, which made them be looked upon as men of
contradiction.

152. They represented to the King, that as it could administer
only some competency towards his present subsistence, so it
might exceedingly prejudice his future hopes, and alienate the
affections of his friends in England ; that the lady was elder
than he by many years, which was an exception amongst
private persons, and had been observed not to be prosperous to

kings; that he must expect to be pressed to those things in point of religion which he could never consent to, and yet he should undergo the same disadvantage as if he had consented, by many men's believing he had done so. They besought him to set his heart entirely upon the recovery of England, and to indulge to nothing that might reasonably obstruct that, either by making him less intent upon it, or by creating new difficulties in the pursuing it. His majesty assured them that his heart was set upon nothing else; and if he had inclination to this marriage, it was because he believed it might much facilitate the other; that he looked not upon her fortune, which was very great, as an annual support to him, but as a stock that should be at his disposal, and by sale whereof he might raise money enough to raise a good army to attempt the recovery of his kingdoms, and that he would be well assured that it should be in his power to make that use of it before he would be engaged in the treaty; that he had no apprehension of the pressures which would be made in matter of religion, because if the lady did once consent to the marriage, she would affect nothing but what might advance the recovery of his dominions, which she would quickly understand any unreasonable concessions in religion could never do. In a word, his majesty discovered enough to let them see that he stood very well inclined to the overture itself; which gave them trouble, as a thing which in many respects was like to prove very inconvenient.

153. But they were quickly freed from those apprehension[s]. The lady carried herself in that manner, and on the behalf of the prince of Condé, and so offensively to the [French] Court, having given fire herself to the cannon in the Bastile upon the King at the port of St. Anthoyne, and done many reprooffull things against the King and Queen, that [1] they no sooner heard of this discourse but they quickly put an end to it, the cardinal having long resolved that [our [2]] King should never owe any part of his restitution to any part of the countenance or assistance he should receive from France; and from the same conclu-

---

[1] ['so that,' MS.]   [2] ['the,' MS.]

sion the like end was put to all overtures which had concerned 1652
the duke of York and the other lady.

154. There was, shortly after, an unexpected accident that
seemed to make some alteration in the affairs of Christendom,
and which many very reasonably believed might have proved
advantageous to the King. The Parliament had, as soon as
they had settled their commonwealth, and had no enemy they
feared, sent ambassadors[1] to their sister republic, the States of
the United Provinces, to invite them to enter into a stricter
alliance with them, and, upon the matter, to be as one commonwealth, and to have one interest. They were received in
Holland with all imaginable respect, and as great expressions March.
made as could be of an equal desire that a firm union might
be established between the two commonwealths; and for the
forming thereof persons were appointed to treat with the ambassadors; which was looked upon as a matter that would
easily succeed, since the prince of Aurange, who could have
given powerful obstructions in such cases, was now dead, and
all those who adhered to him discountenanced and removed
from places of trust and power in all the provinces, and his son
an infant, born after the death of his father, at the mercy of
the States even for his support; the two dowagers, his mother
and grandmother, having so great jointures out of the estate,
and the rest being liable for the payment of vast debts. In the
treaty, St. John, who had the whole trust of the embassy, being
very powerful in the Parliament, and the known confident of
Cromwell, pressed such a kind of union as must disunite them April 17
from all their other allies; so that for the friendship of England they must lose the friendship of all other princes, and yet
lose many other advantages in trade, which they enjoyed, and
which they saw the younger and more powerful commonwealth
would in a short time deprive them of. This they [the States]
could not digest[3], and used all the ways they could to divert
them from insisting upon so unreasonable conditions; and made
many large overtures and concessions, which had never been

1651
Feb. 1.

and
May 10[2].

---

[1] [Walter Strickland and Oliver St. John.]
[2] [Thurloe's *S. P.* i. 182.]   [3] [' disgest,' MS.]

1651 granted by them to the greatest kings, and were willing to quit some advantages they had enjoyed by all the treaties with the Crown of England, and to yield other considerable benefits which they always before denied to grant.

155. But this would not satisfy, nor [would] the ambassadors recede from any particular they had proposed: so that after some months' stay, during which time they received many affronts from some English and from others, they returned,
June 20 [1]. with great presents from the States, but without any effect by the treaty, or entering into any terms of alliance, and with the extreme indignation of St. John, which he manifested as soon as he returned to the Parliament; which, disdaining likewise to find themselves undervalued, that is, not valued above all the world beside, presently entered upon counsels how they might discountenance and control the trade of Holland and increase their own.

Oct. 9.   156. And hereupon they made that ordinance that inhibits all foreign ships from bringing in any merchandises or commodities into England but such as were the proceed or growth of their own country, upon the penalty of forfeiture of all such ships. This indeed concerned all other countries; but it did, upon the matter, totally suppress all trade with Holland, which had very little merchandise of the growth of their own country, but had used to bring in their ships the growth of all other kingdoms in the world; wine from France and Spain, spices from the Indies, and all commodities from all other countries; which they must now do no more. The Dutch ambassador expostulated this manner very warmly, as a breach of commerce and amity, which could not consist with the peace between the two nations, and that his masters could not look upon it otherwise than as a declaration of war. The Parliament answered him superciliously, that his masters might take it in what manner they pleased, but they knew what was best for their own State, and would not repeal laws to gratify their neighbours;

[1] [On this day they took leave at the Hague; arrived in London on June 26, and reported their negotiation to the House of Commons on July 2.]

and caused the Act to be executed with the utmost rigour and **1652** severity.

157. The United Provinces now discerned that they had raised an enemy that was too powerful for them, and that would not be treated as the Crown had been. However, they could not believe it possible that in the infancy of their republic, and when their government was manifestly odious to all the nobility and gentry of the kingdom, and the people generally weary of the taxes and impositions upon the nations for the support of their land-armies, the Parliament would venture to increase those taxes and impositions proportionably to maintain a new war at sea, at so vast an expense as could not be avoided; and therefore that they only made show of this courage to amuse and terrify them. However, at the spring they set out a fleet stronger than of course they used to do; which made no impression upon the English, who never suspected that the Dutch durst enter into a war with them, besides that they were confident no such counsel and resolution could be taken on a sudden, and without their having first notice of it, they having several of the States General, and more of the States of Holland, very devoted to them. And therefore they increased not their expense, but sent out their usual fleet for the guard of the coast at their season, and with no other instructions than they had been accustomed to.

158. The council of the admiralty of Holland, which governed the maritime affairs, without communication with the States General, gave their instructions to the admiral Van Trumpe, that when he met any of the English ships of war he should not strike to them, nor shew them any other respect than what they received from them; and if the English expostulated the matter, they should answer frankly, that the respect they had formerly shewed upon those encounters was because the ships were the King's, and for the good intelligence they had with the Crown, but they had no reason to continue the same in this alteration of government, except there was some stipulation between them to that purpose: and if this answer did not satisfy, but that force was used towards them, they should

1652 defend themselves with their utmost vigour. These instructions were very secret, and never suspected by the English commanders, who had their old instructions to oblige all foreign vessels to strike sail to them, which had never been refused by any nation.

159. It was about the beginning of May in the year 1652, that the Dutch fleet, consisting of above forty sail, under the command of Van Trumpe, rode at anchor in Dover road, being driven by a strong wind, as they pretended, from the Flanders May 19. coast, when the English fleet, under the command of Blake [1], of a much less number, appeared in view; upon which the Dutch weighed anchor and put out to sea without striking their flag; which Blake observing, caused three guns to be fired, without any ball. It was then observed that there was an express ketch came at the very time from Holland on board the admiral, and it was then conceived that he had by that express received more positive orders to fight; for, upon his arrival, he tacked about, and bore directly towards the English fleet; and the three guns were no sooner fired, but in contempt of the advertisement he discharged one single gun from his poop, and hung out a red flag, and came up to the English admiral, and gave him a broadside, with which he killed many of his men and hurt his ship. With which, though Blake was surprised, as not expecting such an assault, he deferred not to give him the same rude salutation; and so both fleets were forthwith engaged in a very fierce encounter, which continued for the space of four hours, and until the night parted them, after the loss of much blood on both sides. On the part of the Dutch, they lost two ships, whereof one was sunk and the other taken, with both the captains, and near two hundred prisoners. On the English side there were many slain, but more wounded; but no ship lost, nor officer of name. When the morning appeared, the Dutch were gone to their coast. And thus the war was entered into before it was suspected in England.

160. With what consideration soever the Dutch had em-

---

[1] [Clarendon spells the name here 'Blake,' but sometimes, as in the very next instance, 'Blague.']

barked themselves in this sudden enterprise, it quickly appeared 1652 they had taken very ill measures of the people's affections. For the news of this conflict no sooner arrived in Holland but there was the most general consternation amongst all sorts of men that can be imagined; and the States themselves were so much troubled at it, that with marvellous expedition they May 24, despatched two extraordinary ambassadors[1] into England; by O. S. whom they protested that the late unhappy engagement be- June 11. tween the fleets of the two commonwealths had happened without their knowledge, and contrary to the desire of the lords the States General: that they had received the fatal tidings of so rash an attempt and action with amazement and astonishment, and that they had immediately entered into consultation how they might best close this fresh bleeding wound, and to avoid the farther effusion of Christian blood, so much desired by the enemies of both States: and therefore they most earnestly desired them, by their mutual concurrence in religion, and by their mutual love of liberty, that nothing might be done with passion and heat, which might widen the breach, but that they might speedily receive such an answer that there might be no farther obstruction to the trade of both commonwealths.

161. To which this answer was presently returned to them: that the civility which they had always shewed towards the States of the United Provinces was so notorious, that nothing was more strange than the ill return they had made to them; that the extraordinary preparation which they had made of one hundred and fifty ships, without any apparent necessity, and the instructions which they had given to the seamen, had administered too much cause to believe that the lords the States General of the United Provinces had a purpose to usurp the known right which the English have to the seas, and to destroy their fleets, which, under the protection of the Almighty, are their walls and bulwarks, that so they might be exposed to the invasion of any powerful enemy: therefore they thought themselves obliged to endeavour, by God's assistance, to seek repa-

---

[1] [One, Adrian Pauw. Three others, G. Schaep, P. Van de Perre, and J. Catz, had been sent before, in Jan. 1652.]

1652 ration for the injuries and damage they had already received, and to prevent the like for the future : however, they should never be without an intention and desire that some effectual means might be found to establish a good peace, union, and right understanding between the two nations.

162. With this haughty answer they vigorously prosecuted their revenge, and commanded Blake presently to sail to the northward ; it being then the season of the year for their great fisheries upon the coasts of Scotland and the isles of Orkney, (by the benefit whereof they drive a great part of their trade over Europe ;) and where he now found their multitude of fishing boats, guarded by twelve ships of war ; all which, with the fish they had made ready, he brought away with him as good prize.

163. When Blake was sent to the north, sir George Askew was sent with another part of the fleet to the south ; who at July 3 his very going out met with thirty sail of their merchants between Dover and Calice, a good part whereof he took or sunk, and forced the rest to run on shore upon the French coast, which is very little better than being taken. And from thence he stood westward ; and near Plimmoth, in the middle of Aug 16. August, with thirty sail of men of war he engaged the whole Dutch fleet, consisting of sixty ships of war and thirty merchants. It was near four of the clock in the afternoon when both fleets began to engage, so that the night quickly parted them ; yet not before two of the Holland ships of war were sunk and most of the men lost ; the Dutch in that action applying themselves most to spoil the tackling and sails of the English ; in which they had so good success, that the next morning they were not able to give them farther chase till their sails and rigging could be repaired. But no day passed without the taking and bringing in many and valuable Dutch ships into the ports of England, which, [having] begun their voyages before any notice given to them of the war, made haste home without any fear of their security. So that there being now no hope of a peace by the mediation of their ambassadors, who could not prevail in any thing they proposed, they re-

turned; and the war was proclaimed on either side[1] as well as 1652
prosecuted.

164. The King thought he might very reasonably hope to
reap some benefit and advantage from this war, so briskly
entered upon on both sides; and when he had sat still till the
return of the Dutch ambassador from London, and that all
treaties were given over, he believed it might contribute to
his ends if he made a journey into Holland, and made such
propositions upon the place as he might be advised to: but
when he imparted this design to his friends there, who did
really desire to serve him, he was very warmly dissuaded from
coming thither; and assured that it was so far from being yet
seasonable, that it would more advance a peace than any thing
else that could be proposed, and would for the present bring
the greatest prejudice to his sister, and to the affairs of his
nephew the prince of Aurange, that could be imagined.

165. The King hereupon took a resolution to make an attempt which could do him no harm, if it did not produce the
good he desired. The Dutch ambassador then resident at Paris,
monsieur Boreel, who had been Pensioner of Amsterdam, was
very much devoted to the King's service, having been formerly
ambassador in England, and had always dependence upon the
princes of Aurange successively. He communicated in all
things with great freedom with the Chancellor [of the Exchequer,] who visited him constantly once a week, and received
advertisements and advices from him, and the ambassador
frequently came to his lodging. The King, upon conference
only with the marquis of Ormonde and the Chancellor, and
enjoining them secresy, caused a paper to be drawn up, in 1653
which he declared that he had very good reason to believe that Feb. 6.
there were many officers and seamen engaged in the service of
the English fleet, who undertook that service in hope to find a
good opportunity to serve his majesty; and that if the Dutch
were willing to receive him he would immediately put himself
on board their fleet, without requiring any command, except of

---

[1] [The declaration was passed in Parliament July 7, and published
July 9, O.S., and that of the States General on Aug. 2, N.S.]

1653 such ships only as upon their notice of his being there should repair to him out of the rebels' fleet; and by this means he presumed he should be able much to weaken their naval power, and to raise divisions in the kingdom, by which the Dutch would receive benefit and advantage. And having signed this paper, he sent the Chancellor with it open, to shew to the Dutch ambassador, and to desire him to send it enclosed in his letter to the States. The ambassador was very much surprised with it, and made some scruple of sending it, lest he might be suspected to have advised it. For they were extremely jealous of him for his affection to the King, and for his dependence upon the house of Aurange. In the end, he desired the King would enclose it in a letter to him, and oblige him to send it to the States General; which was

March 7. done accordingly; and he sent it by the post to the States.

166. The war had already made the councils of the States less united than [they[1]] had been, and the party that was known to be inclined to the prince of Aurange recovered courage, and joined with those who were no friends to the war, and when this message from the King was read magnified the King's spirit in making this overture, and wished that an answer of very humble thanks and acknowledgment might be returned to his majesty; and they said no means ought to be neglected that might abate the pride and the power of their enemy. And as soon as the people heard of it, they thought it reason to accept the King's offer. De Witt, who was Pensioner of Holland, and had the greatest influence upon their counsels, had no mind to have any conjunction with the King, which he foresaw must necessarily introduce the pretences of the prince of Aurange, to which he was an avowed and declared enemy. He told them, it was indeed a very generous offer of the King; but if they should accept it, they could never recede from his interest; which, instead of putting an end to the war, of which they were already weary, would make it without end, and would be the ruin of their State: that, whilst they were free from being engaged in any interest but their own, they might reasonably hope that both sides would be equally weary of the

[1] ['it,' MS.]

war, and then a peace would easily ensue; which they should **1653** otherwise put out of their own power. So that thanks were returned to the King for his good will; and they pursued their own method in their counsels, and were much superior to those who were of another opinion, desiring nothing so much as to make a peace upon any conditions.

167. Nor can it appear very wonderful that the Dutch made show of so much phlegm in this affair, when the very choler and pride of the French was at the same time so humbled by the spirit of the English, that, though they took their ships every day, and made them prize, and had now seized upon their whole fleet that was going to the relief of Dunkirk, that was 1652 Sept. 5 [1]. then closely besieged by the Spaniard, and by the taking that fleet was delivered into their hands, yet they [the French] would not be provoked to be angry with them, or to express any inclination to the King; but sent an ambassador [2], which they had not before done, to expostulate very civilly with them Dec. 21. for having been so unneighbourly, but in truth to desire their friendship upon what terms they pleased; the cardinal fearing nothing so much as that the Spaniard would make such a conjunction with the new commonwealth as should disappoint and break all his designs.

168. The insupportable losses which the Dutch every day sustained by the taking their merchants' ships and their ships of war, and the total obstruction of their trade, broke the hearts of all the Dutch, and increased their factions and divisions at home. All the seas were covered with the English fleets, which made no distinction of seasons, but were as active in the winter as the summer, and engaged the Dutch upon any inequality of number. In the month of February, the most dangerous season of the year, they having appointed a rendezvous of about one hundred and fifty merchantmen, they sent a fleet of above a hundred sail of men of war to convoy them; and Blake, with a fleet much inferior in number, engaged them in a very sharp battle from noon till the night parted them: 1653 Feb. 18–20. which only disposed them to endeavour to preserve themselves

---

[1] [*Cal. Dom. S. P.*, 1651–2, p. 504.]   [2] [Ant. de Bordeaux.]

1653 by flight; but in the morning they found the English had attended them so close, that they were engaged again to fight, and so unprosperously, that after the loss of above two thousand men, who were thrown overboard, besides a multitude hurt, they were glad to leave fifty of their merchantmen to the English, that they might make their flight the more securely.

March 18, N.S.
March 29, O.S.

169. This last loss made them send again to the Parliament to desire a peace; and they rejected the overture, as they pretended, for want of formality, (for they always pretended a desire of an honourable peace,) the address being made only by the States of Holland and West-Friesland, the States General being at that time not assembled[1]. It was generally believed that this address from Holland was not only with the approbation but by the direction of Cromwell, who had rather consented to those particulars which were naturally like to produce that war to gratify St. John, who was inseparable from him in all his counsels and was incensed by the Dutch, than approved the resolution. And now he found, by the charge of the engagements [which] had already passed on both sides, what an insupportable charge that war must be attended with. Besides, he well discerned that all parties, friends and foes, Presbyterians, Independents, Levellers, were all united as to the carrying on that war; which could proceed from nothing but that the excess of the expense might make it necessary to disband a great part of the land army, of which there appeared no use, to support the navy, which they could not now be without. Nor had he authority to place his own creatures there, all the officers thereof being nominated and appointed solely by the Parliament: so that when this address was made by the Dutch, he set up his whole rest and interest that it might be well accepted, and a treaty thereupon entered into; which when he could not bring to pass, he laid to heart, and deferred not long, as will appear, to take vengeance upon them with a witness, and by a way they least thought of.

170. Though he was exercised with these contradictions and

[1] [From this place to the end of book xiii the text is from the *Hist.*, pp. 24-28.]

vexations at home by the authority of the Parliament, he found 1653
not the least opposition from abroad. He was more absolute
in the other two kingdoms, more feared, and more obeyed, than
any king had ever been, and all the dominions belonging to the
Crown owned no other subjection than to the commonwealth
of England. The two isles of Guarnsy and Jarsy were reduced,
the former presently after the battle of Worcester[1], and the
other after the King's return to Paris, sir George Carteret
having well defended the same as long as he could; and being
so overpowered that he could no longer defend the island, he 1651
Oct. 27.
retired into Castle Elizabeth, which he had well fortified, and
provided with all things necessary for a siege; presuming that
by the care and diligence of the lord Jermin, (who was governor
thereof,) he should receive supplies of men and provisions, [as[2]]
he should stand in need of them, as he might easily have done
in spite of any power of the Parliament by sea or land. But
it had been the principal reason that Cromwell had hitherto
kept the better quarter with the cardinal, lest the bait of those
two islands, which the King could put into his hands when he
would, should tempt him to give him [the King] any assistance.
But the King was so strict and punctual in his care of the
interest of England, when he seemed to be abandoned by it,
that he chose rather to suffer those precious places to fall into
its power than to deposit them upon any conditions into their
hands who, he knew, would never restore them to the just
owner, what obligations soever they entered into.

171. When the castle had been besieged three months[3], and
the enemy could not approach nearer to plant their ordnance
than at least half an English mile, the sea encompassing it
round more than so far from any land, and it not being possible
for any of their ships to come within such a distance, they
brought notwithstanding mortar pieces of such an incredible

---

[1] [The island of Guernsey declared for the Parliament early in 1643, but
Castle Cornet, which was held by col. Roger Burgess, did not surrender
until the same day on which sir G. Carteret gave up Castle Elizabeth in
Jersey, Dec. 15, 1651.]

[2] ['and,' MS.]   [3] [less than two months.]

1651 greatness, and such as had never been before seen in this part
of the world, that from the highest point of the hill, near
St. Hillary's, they shot granadoes of a vast bigness into the
castle, and beat down many houses, and at last blowed up a
great magazine, where most of the provision of victual lay, and
killed many men. Upon which he [sir George Carteret] sent
an express to give the King an account of the condition he was
in, and to desire a supply of men and provisions; which being
impossible for his majesty to procure, he sent him orders to
1651 make the best conditions he could; which he shortly after did;
Dec. 15. and came himself to Paris, to give the King a larger information of all that had passed in that affair, and afterwards
remained in France, under many mortifications by the power
and prosecution of Cromwell, till the King's happy restoration.

172. All the foreign plantations had submitted to the yoke
without a blow, and indeed without any other damage or inconvenience than the having citizens and inferior persons put
to govern them, instead of gentlemen who had been intrusted
by the King in those places. New England had been too much
allied to all the conspiracies and combinations against the
Crown not to be very well pleased that men of their own principles had prevailed and settled a government themselves were
delighted with. The Barbados, which was much the richest
plantation, was principally inhabited by men who had retired
thither only to be quiet, and to be free from the noise and
oppressions in England, and without any ill thoughts towards
the King; many of them having served him with fidelity and
courage during the war, and, that being ended, made that island
their refuge from farther prosecutions. But having now gotten
good estates there, (as it is incredible to what fortunes men
raised themselves in few years in that plantation,) they were
more willing to live in subjection to that government at that
distance, than to return into England and be liable to the
penalties of their former transgressions; which, upon the arti-
1652 cles of surrender, they were indemnified for: nor was there any
Jan. 11. other alteration there than the removing the lord Willoughby
of Parham, (who was upon many accounts odious to the Par-

liament, as well as being governor there by the King's com- 1652
mission,) and putting an inferior mean person[1] in his place.

173. More was expected from Virginia, which was the most
ancient plantation, and so was thought to be better provided to
defend itself, and to be better affected. Upon both which sup-
positions, and out of confidence in sir William Berkely, the
governor there, who had industriously invited many gentlemen
and others thither, as to a place of security which he could
defend against any attempt, and where they might live plentifully, many persons of condition, and good officers in the war,
had transported themselves, with all the estate they had been
able to preserve; with which the honest governor, (for no man
meant better,) was so confirmed in his confidence, that he writ
to the King almost inviting him thither, as to a place that
wanted nothing. And the truth is, that, whilst the Parliament
had nothing else to do, that plantation in a short time was more
improved in people and stock than it had been from the beginning to that time, and had reduced the Indians to very good
neighbourhood. But, alas! they were so far from being in a
condition to defend themselves, all the industry having been
employed in the making the best advantage of their particular
plantations, without assigning time or men to provide for the
public security in building forts or any places of retreat, that
there no sooner appeared two or three ships from the Parliament than all thoughts of resistance were laid aside. Sir 1652
William Berkely, the governor, was suffered to remain there as $^{\text{May}\,2}$.
a private man, upon his own plantation; which was a better
subsistence than he could have found any where else. And in
that quiet posture he continued, by the reputation he had with
the people, till, upon the noise and fame of the King's restoration, he did as quietly resume the exercise of his former
commission, and found as ready an obedience.

174. We shall not in this place enlarge upon the affairs of
Scotland, which will be part of the argument of the next book,
and where Munke for the present governed with a rod of iron,
and found no contradiction or opposition to his good will and

---

[1] [col. Daniel Searle.]   [2] [*Calend. Clar. S. P.* ii. 133.]

1651 pleasure.   In Ireland, if that people had not been prepared and
ripe for destruction, there happened an alteration which might
have given some respite to it, and disposed the nation to have
united themselves under their new deputy, whom they had
themselves desired, under all the solemn obligations of obedience.   Shortly after the departure of the marquis of Ormonde,
Cromwell's deputy Ireton, who had married his daughter, died
1651 in Lymerick of the plague, which was gotten into his army,
Nov. 26. that was so much weakened by it, and there [were[1]] so great
factions and divisions amongst the officers after his sudden
death, that great advantages might have been gotten by it.
His authority was so absolute that he was entirely submitted
to in all the civil as well as martial affairs.   But his death was
thought so little possible, that no provision had been made for
that contingency.   So that no man had authority to take the
command upon him till Cromwell's pleasure was farther known,
who put the charge of the army under Ludlow[2], (a man of a
very different temper from the other), but appointed the civil
government to run in another channel; so that there remained
jealousy and discontent enough still between the council and
the officers to have shaken a government that was yet no better
established.

175. Ireton, of whom we have had too much occasion to
speak formerly, was of a melancholic, reserved, dark nature,
who communicated his thoughts to very few, so that for the
most part he resolved alone, but was never diverted from any
resolution he had taken; and he was thought often by his
obstinacy to prevail over Cromwell, and to extort his concurrence contrary to his own inclinations.   But that proceeded
only from his dissembling less; for he was never reserved in
the owning and communicating his worst and most barbarous
purposes; which the other always concealed and disavowed.
Hitherto their occurrence was very natural, since they had the

---

[1] ['was,' MS.]
[2] [Ludlow was temporarily nominated by the commissioners in Ireland
on Ireton's death, but Fleetwood was appointed by Parliament on July 9,
1652, upon the recommendation of the Council of State.]

same ends and designs. It was generally conceived by those 1651
who had the opportunity to know them both very well, that
Ireton was a man so radically averse from monarchy, and so
fixed to a republ[ican] government, that if he had lived he
would either by his counsel and credit have prevented those
tyrannical excesses in Cromwell, or publicly opposed and declared against them, and carried the greatest part of the army
against him ; and that Cromwell, who best knew his nature
and his temper, had therefore carried him into Ireland and left
him there, that he might be without his counsels or importunities when he should find it necessary to put off his mask,
and to act that part which he foresaw would be requisite to
do. Others thought his parts lay more towards civil affairs,
and were fitter for the modelling that government which his
heart was set upon, (being a scholar, conversant in the law, and
in all that learning which had expressed the greatest animosity
and malice against regal government,) than for the conduct of
an army to support it, his personal courage being never reckoned amongst his other abilities.

176. What influence soever his life might have had upon
the future transactions, certain it is his death had none upon
the state of Ireland to the King's advantage. The marquis of
Clanrickarde left no way unattempted that might apply the
visible strength and power of the Irish nation to the preservation of themselves and to the support of the King's government.
He sent out his orders and warrants for the levying of new
men, and to draw the old troops together, and to raise money;
but few men could be got together, and when they were assembled they could not stay together, for want of money to pay
them ; so that he could never get a body together to march
towards the enemy; and if he did prevail with them to march
a whole day with him, he found the next morning that half of
them were run away. And it quickly appeared that they had
only made those ample vows and protestations that they might
be rid of the marquis of Ormonde, without any purpose of
obeying the other. The greatest part of the clergy, and all
the Irish of Ulster, had no mind to have any relation to the

1651 English nation, and as little to return to their obedience to the Crown. They blamed each other for having deserted the nuncio, and thought of nothing but how they might get some foreign prince to take them into his protection. They first chose a committee, Plunkett and Browne, two lawyers, who had been eminent conductors of the rebellion from the beginning, and men of good parts, and joined others to them who were in France and Flanders. And then they moved the Lord Deputy to send these gentlemen into Flanders, to invite the duke of Lorrayne to assist them with arms, money, and ammunition, undertaking to have good intelligence from thence that the duke (who was known to wish well to the King) was well prepared to receive their desire, and resolved, out of his affection to the King, to engage himself cordially in the defence of that Catholic kingdom, his zeal to that religion being known to be very great.

177. The marquis [of Clanrickarde] had no opinion of the expedient, and less that the duke would engage himself on the behalf of a people who had so little reputation in the world, and therefore refused to give any commission to those gentlemen, or to any other to that purpose, without first receiving the King's order, or at least the advice of the marquis of Ormonde, who was known to be safely arrived in France. But that was looked upon as delay which their condition could not bear; and the doubting the truth of the intelligence and information of the duke of Lorrayne's being willing to undertake their relief was imputed to want of good will to receive it. And then all the libels and scandals and declarations which had been published against the marquis of Ormonde were now renewed, and with equal malice and virulency, against the marquis of Clanrickarde; and they declared that God would never bless his withered hand, which had always concurred with Ormonde in the prosecution and persecution of the Catholic Confederates from the beginning of their engagement for the defence of their religion; and that he had still had more conversation with heretics than with Catholics; that he had refused always to submit to the Pope's authority, and had treated his

nuncio with less respect than was due from any good Catholic ; 1651
and that all the Catholics who were cherished or countenanced
by him were of the same faction.   In the end, he could not
longer resist the importunity of the assembly of the Confederate Catholics, (which was again brought together,) and of the
bishops and clergy that governed the other, but gave his consent to send the same persons they recommended to him, and
gave them his credentials to the duke of Lorrayne; and required them punctually to observe his instructions, and not to
presume to depart from them in the least degree.   Their in- 1651
structions were, to give the marquis of Ormonde notice of their Apr. 12.
arrival, and to shew him their instructions, and to conclude
nothing without his positive advice, who he well knew would
communicate all with the Queen ; and that likewise, when they
came into Flanders, they should advise with such of the King's
Council as should be there, and proceed in all things as they
should direct.

178. What instructions soever the Lord Deputy prescribed
to them, the commissioner[s] received others from the council
and assembly of the clergy, which they thought more to the
purpose, and resolved to follow; by which they were authorized
to yield to any conditions which might prevail with the duke of
Lorrayne to take them into his protection, and to engage him
in their defence, even by delivering all they had of the kingdom into his hands.   Though they landed in France, they gave
no notice of their business or their arrival to the Queen or to
the marquis of Ormonde[1], but prosecuted their journey to June 12,
Bruxells, and made their address, with all secresy, to the duke N. S.
of Lorrayne.   There were, at the same time, at Antwerp, the
marquis of Newcastle, the Chancellor [of the Exchequer,] (who
was newly returned from his embassy in Spain,) and Secretary
Nicholas, all three of the King's Council; to neither of whom
they so much as gave a visit.   And though the duke of York

---

[1] [They wrote from Brussels to the Queen on June 19, N. S., and to
Ormonde on June 7 and 19, by lord Taaffe, who carried the letters. Clanricarde's *Memoirs*, 1757, part ii. pp. 31, 32.   But they did not communicate
the conditions they were about to propose to the duke of Lorraine.]

1651 during this time passed through Bruxells in his journey to Paris, they imparted not their negotiations to his highness [1].

179. The duke of Lorrayne had a very good mind to get a footing in Ireland; where he was sure there wanted no men to make armies enough, which were not like to want courage to
1651 defend their country and their religion. And the commis-
July 2. sioners very frankly offered to deliver up Galloway, and all the places which were in their possession, into his hands, with the remainder of the kingdom as soon as it could be reduced, and to obey him absolutely as their prince [2]. But he, as a reserve to decline the whole if it appeared to be a design fuller of difficulty than he then apprehended, discoursed much of his affection to the King, and his resolution not to accept any thing that was proposed without his majesty's privity and full approbation. But in the mean time, and till that might be procured, he was content to send the abbot of [St. Catharine's [3],] a Lorrayner, and a person principally trusted by him, as his
1651 ambassador into Ireland, to be informed of the true state of
Feb. that kingdom, and what real strength the Confederate Catholics were possessed of, and at what unity amongst themselves. And with him he sent about three or four thousand pistoles, to supply their present necessities, and some arms and ammunition. He writ to the Lord Deputy, the marquis of Clanrickarde, as the King's governor, and the person by whose authority all those propositions had been made to him by the commissioners.

180. The abbot upon his arrival (though he was civilly received) quickly found that the marquis knew nothing of what the commissioners had proposed or offered, and would by no means so much as enter upon any treaty with him, but disavowed all that they had said or done, with much vehemence,

---

[1] [They wrote to him from Brussels on June 15. Clanricarde's *Memoirs*, p. 32.]

[2] [*Ib.*, pp. 34–36.]

[3] [*Left blank in the MS.* His name was Stephen de Henin. His credentials were dated at Brussels, Dec. 31, 1650. Clarendon has represented the abbot's mission as following that of the Irish commissioners instead of preceding it.]

and with a protestation that he would cause their heads to 1651 be cut off, if they returned or came into his hands. And the Oct. 20 [1]. marquis did at the same time write very large letters both to the King and the marquis of Ormonde of their presumption and wickedness, and very earnestly desired that they might be imprisoned, and kept till they might undergo a just trial.

181. As the marquis expressed all possible indignation, so many of the Catholic nobility, and even some of the clergy, who never intended to withdraw their loyalty from the Crown of England, how weakly soever they had manifested it, indeed all the Irish nation but those of Ulster who were of the old septs, were wonderfully scandalized to find that all their strength was to be delivered presently up into the possession of a foreign prince, upon whose good nature only it must [be] presumed that [he] would hereafter restore it to the King. It was now time for the bishops and their confederates to make good what had been offered by the commissioners with their authority; which though they thought not fit to own, they used all their endeavours now in procuring to have consented to and ratified. They very importunately advised and pressed the Lord Deputy to confirm what had been offered, as the only visible means to preserve the nation, and a root out of which the King's right might again spring and grow up. And when they found that he was so far from yielding to what they desired, that if he had power he would proceed against them with the utmost severity for what they had done, that he would no more give audience to the ambassador, and removed from the place where they were to his own house and castle at Portumny to be secure from their importunity or violence, they barefaced owned all that the commissioners had propounded, as done by their order, who could make it good; and desired the ambassador to enter into a treaty with them; and [declared] that they would sign such articles with which the duke of Lorrayne should be well satisfied. They undervalued the power of the marquis of Clanrickarde, as not able to oppose any agreement they should make, nor able to make good any thing he should promise himself without their assistance.

[1] [See *Calend. Clar. S. P.* ii. 109 ; Clanricarde's *Memoirs, ut supra*, p. 37.]

1651 182. The ambassador was a wise man, and of phlegm enough; and though he heard all they would say, and received any propositions they would give him in writing, yet he quickly discerned that they were so unskilful as to the managery of any great design, and so disjointed amongst themselves, that they could not be depended upon to any purpose; and excused himself from entering upon any new treaty with them, as having no commission to treat but with the Lord Deputy. But he told them he would deliver all that they had, or would propose to him, to the duke his master, who, he presumed, would speedily return his answer, and proceed with [their] commissioners in such a manner as would be grateful to them. And April. so he returned in the same ship that brought him, and gave the duke such an account of his voyage and people that put an end to that negotiation, which had been entered into and prosecuted with less wariness, circumspection, and good husbandry, than that prince was accustomed to use.

183. When the ambassador was gone, they prosecuted the Deputy with all reproaches of ruining and betraying his country, and had several designs upon his person, and communicated whatever attempt was resolved to the enemy; yet there were many of the nobility and gentry that continued firm, and adhered to him very faithfully; which defended his person from any violence they intended against him, but could not secure him against their acts of treachery, nor keep his counsels from being betrayed. After the defeat of Worcester was known and published, they less considered all they did; and every one thought he was to provide for his own security that way that seemed most probable to him; and he that was most intent upon that, put on a new face, and application to the Deputy, and loudly urged the necessity of uniting themselves for the public safety, which was desperate any other way, whilst in truth every man was negotiating for his own indemnity with Ludlow, (who commanded the English,) or for leave to transport regiments; which kept the soldiers together, as if they had been the Deputy's army.

184. The Deputy had a suspicion of a fellow who was observed

every day to go out, and returned not till the next, and ap- 1652
pointed an officer of trust, with some horse, to watch him and
search him; which they did, and found about him a letter[1],
which contained many reproaches against the marquis and the
intelligence of many particulars, which the messenger was
carrying to Ludlow. They quickly discovered that the letter
was written by one father Cohogan[2], a Franciscan friar in Galloway, where the Deputy then was; but much of the intelligence
was such as could not be known by him, but must come from
some who [were[3]] in the most private consultations. The
Deputy caused the friar to be imprisoned, and resolved to proceed exemplarily against him, after he had first discovered his
complices. The friar confessed the letter to be of his writing,
but refused to answer to any other question, and demanded his
privilege of a churchman, and not to be tried by the Deputy's
order. The conclusion was, the bishops caused him to be taken
out of the prison; and sent to the Deputy, that if he would send
his evidence against the friar, who was an ecclesiastical person,
to them, they would take care that justice should be done[4].

185. This proceeding convinced the Deputy that he should
not be able to do the King any service in that company; nor
durst he stay longer in that town, lest they should make their
own peace by delivering up him and the town together, which they
would have made no scruple to have done. And from that time
he removed from place to place, not daring to lodge twice in the
same place together, lest he should be betrayed, and sometimes
without any accommodations; so that, having not been accustomed to those hardnesses, he contracted those diseases which
he could never recover. In this manner he continued till he
received commands from the King. As soon as he received
advertisement of the King's arrival at Paris, and it was very
evident by the behaviour of the Irish that they would be no
more applied to the King's service under his command than
under the marquis of Ormonde, he sent the earl of Castlehaven

---

[1] [Dated Feb. 4, 1652.]   [2] [Anthony Geoghegan.]   [3] ['was,' MS.]
[4] [He was examined before ecclesiastical authorities on Feb. 13. *Calend.
Clar. S. P.* ii. 122.]

1652 (who had been formerly a general of the Confederate Catholics, and remained with great constancy with the marquis of Clanrickarde as long as there was any hope) to the King, with so particular an account under his own hand of all that had passed from the time that he had received his commission from the marquis of Ormonde that it even contained almost a diurnal, and in which he made so lively a description of the proceedings of the Irish, of their overtures to the duke of Lorrayne and of their several tergiversations and treachery towards him, that any man might discern, especially they who knew the generosity of the marquis, his nature, and his custom of living, that he had submitted to a life very uncomfortable and melancholy; and desired his majesty's leave that he might retire, and procure a pass to go into England, where he had some estate of his own[1], and many friends, who would not suffer him to starve; which

1652 his majesty made haste to send to him, with as great a testi-
Feb. 10[2]. mony of his gracious acceptation of his service and affection as his singular merit deserved.

Oct. 11.   186. And thereupon he sent to Ludlow for a pass to go into England and render himself to the Parliament, which he pre-
1653 sently sent him; and so he transported himself to London;
March. where he was civilly treated by all men, as a man who had many friends, and could have no enemies but those who could not be friends to any. But by the infirmities he had contracted in Ireland by those unnatural fatigues and distresses he had been exposed to, he lived not to the end of a year[3], and had resolved upon the recovery of any degree of health to have transported himself to the King, and to attend his fortune. He left behind so full a relation of all material passages, as well from the beginning of that rebellion as during the time of his own ministration, that I have been the less particular in the account of what passed in the transactions of that kingdom, presuming that more exact work of his will in due time be communicated to the world[4].

[1] [Somerhill, near Tunbridge, Kent.]   [2] [Received 8 Aug.]
[3] [He lived four years longer, dying in July, 1657.]
[4] [The narrative and papers, extending from 1641 to 1643, and from

187. The affairs of the three nations being in this posture at 1653 the end of the year [1652 [1]], and there being new accidents and alterations of a very extraordinary nature in the year following, which were attended with much variety of success, though not with that benefit to the King as might have been expected naturally from those emotions, we shall here conclude this book, and reserve the other for the next.

1650 to 1652, were printed in folio at London in 1757. The papers of the three latter years had been previously printed in 8vo. in 1722.]

[1] ['1653,' MS.]

THE END OF THE THIRTEENTH BOOK.

BOOK XIV.

1. [1] IF God had not reserved the deliverance and restoration of the King to himself, and resolved to accomplish it when there appeared least hope of it and least worldly means to bring it to pass, there happened at this time another very great alteration in England, that, together with the continuance of the war with Holland, and affronts every day offered to France, might very reasonably have administered great hopes of a speedy change of government to the King. From the time of the defeat at Worcester, and the reduction of Scotland and Ireland to perfect obedience, Cromwell did not find the Parliament so supple and so much to observe his orders as he expected they would have been. The Presbyterian party, which he had discountenanced all he could, and made his army of the Independent party, were bold in contradicting him in the House, and crossing all his designs in the city, and exceedingly inveighed against the license that was practised in religion by the several factions of Independents, Anabaptists, Quakers, and the several species of these, who contemned all magistrates and the laws established. And all these, how contradictory soever to one another, Cromwell cherished and protected, that he might not be overrun by the Presbyterians, of whom the time was not yet come that he could make use; yet he seemed to shew much respect to some principal preachers of that party, and consulted much with them how the distempers in religion might be composed.

2. Though he had been forward enough to enter upon the war of Holland, that so there might be no proposition made for the disbanding any part of his army, which otherwise could not be prevented, yet he found the expense of it was so great, that the nation could never bear that addition of burden to the

[1] [*Life*, p. 461.]

other of the land-forces; which how apparent soever, he saw 1653
the Parliament so fierce for the carrying on that war, that they
would not hearken to any reasonable conditions of peace; which
the Dutch appeared most solicitous to make upon any conditions.   But that which troubled him most was the jealousy
that his own party of Independents had contracted against him;
that party that had advanced him to the height he was at, and
made him superior to all opposition, even his beloved Vane,
thought his power and authority to be too great for a commonwealth, and that he and his army had not dependence enough
on, or submission to, the Parliament.   So that he found those
who had exalted him now most solicitous to bring him lower;
and he knew well enough what any diminution of his power
and authority must quickly be attended with.   He observed
that those his old friends very frankly united themselves with
his and their old enemies, the Presbyterians, for the prosecution
of the war with Holland, and obstructing all the overtures
towards peace; which must in a short time exhaust the stock,
and consequently disturb any settlement in the kingdom.

3. In this perplexity he resorts to his old remedy, his army;
and again erects another council of officers, who, under the style,
first, of petitions, and then of remonstrances, interposed in
whatsoever had any relation to the army; used great importunity for the arrears of their pay, that they might not be compelled to take free quarter upon their fellow subjects, who
already paid so great contributions and taxes, which they were
well assured, if well managed, would abundantly defray all the
charges of the war and of the government.   The sharp answers
the Parliament gave to their addresses, and the reprehensions
for their presumption in meddling with matters above them,
gave them new matter to reply to, and put them·in mind of
some former profession they had made that they would be glad
to be eased of the burden of their employment, and that there
might be successive parliaments to undergo the same trouble
they had done.   They therefore desired them that they would
remember how many years they had sat; and though they had
done great things, yet it was a great injury to the rest of the

1653 nation to be utterly excluded from bearing any part in the service of their country, by their engrossing the whole power into
their hands; and thereupon besought them, that they would
settle a council for the administration of the government during
the interval, and then dissolve themselves, and summon a new
Parliament; which they told them would be the most popular
action they could perform.

4. These addresses [being] in the name of the army, and confidently delivered by some officers of it, and as confidently
seconded by others who were members of the House, it was
thought necessary that they should receive a solemn debate,
to the end that when the Parliament had declared its resolution
and determination, all persons might be obliged to acquiesce
therein, and so there would be an end put to all addresses of
this kind.

5. There were many members of the House, who, either from
the justice and reason of the request, or seasonably to comply
with the sense of the army, to which they foresaw they should
be at last compelled to submit, seemed to think it necessary, for
the abating the great envy which was confessedly against the
Parliament throughout the kingdom, that they should be dissolved, to the end the people might make a new election of such
persons as they thought fit to trust with their liberty and
property and whatsoever was dearest to them.

6. Mr. Martin told them, that he thought they might find
the best advice from the Scripture what they were to do in this
particular: that when Moyses was found upon the river, and
brought to Pharaoh's daughter, she took great care that the
mother might be found out, to whose care he might be committed to be nursed; which succeeded very happily. He said,
their commonwealth was yet an infant, of a weak growth and a
very tender constitution; and therefore his opinion was, that
nobody would be so fit to nurse it as the mother who brought
it forth, and that they should not think of putting it under any
other hands until it had obtained more years and vigour. To
which he added, that they had another infant too under their
hands, which was the war with Holland, which had thrived

wonderfully under their conduct; but he much doubted that it 1653
would be quickly strangled if it were taken out of their care
who had hitherto governed it.

7. These reasons prevailed so far, that, whatsoever was said to
the contrary, it was determined, that the Parliament would not
yet think of dissolving, nor would take it well that any persons
should take the presumption any more to make overtures to
them of that nature, which was not fit for private and particular
persons to meddle with. And[1], to put a seasonable stop to any
farther presumption of that kind, they appointed a committee
speedily to prepare an Act of Parliament, by which it should be
declared to be high treason for any man to propose or contrive
the dissolution of this Parliament, or to change the present
government settled and established. And this bill being prepared by the committee, they resolved to pass [it] with all possible expedition. And so Cromwell clearly discerned that by
this means they would never be persuaded to part with that
authority and power which was so profitable and so pleasant to
them. Yet the army declared they were not satisfied with the
determination, and continued their applications to the same
purpose, or to others as unagreeable to the sense of the House;
and did all they could to infuse the same spirit into all the
parts of the kingdom, to make the Parliament odious, as it was
already very abundantly; and Cromwell was well pleased that
the Parliament should express as much prejudice against the
army.

8. All things being thus prepared, Cromwell thought this a
good season to expose these enemies to peace to the indignation
of the nation; which he well knew was generally weary of the
war, and hoped if that were at an end that they should be eased
of the greatest part of their contributions and other impositions:
and thereupon, having adjusted all things with his chief officers
of the army, who were at his devotion, in the month of April
that was in the year 1653, he came into the House of Parlia- April 20.
ment, in a morning when it was sitting, attended with the officers
who were likewise members of the House, and told them that he

---

[1] [The rest of this section is from the *Hist.*, p. 25.]

1653 came thither to put an end to their power and authority, which
they had managed so ill that the nation could be no otherwise
preserved than by their dissolution, which he advised them,
without farther debate, quietly to submit unto.

9. And thereupon another officer, with some files of mus-
keteers, entered into the House, and stayed there till all members walked out; Cromwell reproaching many of the members
by name, as they went out of the House, with their vices and
corruptions, and amongst the rest, sir Harry Vane with his
breach of faith and corruption; and having given the mace to
an officer to be safely kept, he caused the doors to be locked up;
and so dissolved that assembly which had sat [almost [1]] thirteen
years, and under whose name he had wrought so much mischieve, and reduced three kingdoms to his own entire obedience
and subjection, without any example or precedent in the Christian world that could raise his ambition to such a presumptuous
undertaking, and without any rational dependence upon the
friendship of one man who had any other interest to advance
his designs but what he had given him by preferring him in
the war.

10. When he had thus prosperously passed this Rubicon, he
April 22. lost no time in publishing a Declaration of the ground and
reason of his proceeding, for the satisfaction of the people: in
which he put them in mind how miraculously God had appeared
for them in reducing Ireland and Scotland to so great a degree
of peace, and England to a perfect quiet; whereby the Parliament had opportunity to give the people the harvest of all their
labour, blood, and treasure, and to settle a due liberty in reference to civil and spiritual things, whereunto they were obliged
by their duty, engagements, and those great and wonderful
things God had wrought for them. That they had made so
little progress towards this good end, that it was matter of
much grief to the good people of the land, who had thereupon
applied themselves to the army, expecting redress by their
means; who, being very unwilling to meddle with the civil
authority, thought fit that some officers who were members of

---

[1] ['above,' MS.]

the Parliament should move and desire the Parliament to proceed vigorously in reforming what was amiss in the commonwealth, and in settling it upon a foundation of justice and
righteousness. That they found this and some other endeavours
they had used produced no good effect, but rather an averseness to the things themselves, with much bitterness and aversion
to the people of God and his Spirit acting in them: insomuch
as the godly party in the army was now become of no other use
than to countenance the ends of a corrupt party that desired to
perpetuate themselves in the supreme government of the nation.
That for the obviating these evils the officers of the army had
obtained several meetings with some members of the Parliament, to consider what remedies might properly be applied;
but that it appeared very evident unto them that the Parliament, by the want of attendance of many of their members, and
want of integrity in others who did attend, would never answer
those ends which God, his people, and the whole nation, expected from them, but that this cause which God had so greatly
blessed must needs languish under their hands, and by degrees
be lost, and the lives, liberties, and comforts of his people be
delivered into their enemies' hands. All which being seriously
and sadly considered by the honest people of the nation, as well
as by the army, it seemed a duty incumbent upon them, who
had seen so much of the power and presence of God, to consider
of some effectual means whereby to establish righteousness and
peace [in[1]] these nations. That after much debate it had been
judged necessary that the supreme government should be by the
Parliament devolved upon known persons, fearing God, and of
approved integrity, for a time, as the most hopeful way to countenance all God's people, reform the law, and administer justice
impartially; hoping thereby that people might forget monarchy,
and understand their true interest in the election of successive
parliaments, and so the government might be settled upon a
right basis, without hazard to this glorious cause, or necessity
to keep up armies for the defence thereof. That being resolved,
if possible, to decline all extraordinary courses, they had pre-

[1] ['to,' MS.]

1653 vailed with about twenty members of the Parliament to give them a conference, with whom they debated the necessity and justice of that proposition; but found them of so contrary an opinion, that they insisted upon the continuance of the present Parliament, as it was then constituted, as the only way to bring those good things to pass which they seemed to desire : that they insisted upon this with so much vehemence, and were so much transported with passion, that they caused a bill to be prepared for the perpetuating this Parliament, and investing the supreme power in themselves. And for the preventing the consummation of this act, and all the sad and evil consequences which upon the grounds thereof must have ensued, and whereby at one blow the interest of all honest men and of this glorious cause had been in danger to be laid in the dust, they had been necessitated (though with much repugnance) to put an end to the Parliament.

11. There needs not be any other description of the temper of the nation at that time, than the remembering that the dissolution of that body of men who had reigned so long over the three nations was generally very grateful and acceptable to the people, how wonderful soever the circumstances thereof had been; and that this Declaration, which was not only subscribed by Cromwell and his council of officers, but was owned by the admirals at sea, and all the captains of ships, and by the commanders of all the land-forces in England, Scotland, and Ireland, was looked upon as very reasonable. And the Declaration that issued thereupon, by which the people were required to live peaceably, and quietly to submit themselves to the government of the Council of State which should be nominated by the general, until such a time as a Parliament consisting of persons of approved fidelity and honesty could meet and take upon them the government of these nations, found an equal submission and obedience.

April 25.

12. And the method he pursued afterward for the composing a government, by first putting it into a most ridiculous confusion, and by divesting himself of all pretences to authority, and putting what he had no title to keep in the hands of men

so well chosen that they should shortly after delegate the power **1653**
legally to him for the preservation of the nation, was not less
admirable; and puts me in mind of what Seneca said of Pompey,
that he had brought the people of Rome to that pass, by magni-
fying their power and authority, *ut salvus esse non posset nisi
beneficio servitutis* [1]. And if Cromwell had not now made himself a tyrant, all bonds being broken, and the universal guilt
diverting all inclinations to return to the King's obedience,
they must have perished together, in such a confusion as would
rather have exposed them as a prey to foreigners than disposed
them to the only reasonable way for their preservation, there
being no man that durst mention the King or the old form of
government.

13. It was upon the [twentieth [2]] of April that the Parliament had been dissolved; and though Cromwell found that the
people were satisfied in it and the Declaration published thereupon, yet he knew it would be necessary to provide some other
visible power to settle the government than the council of officers, all whom he was not sure he should be able long entirely
to govern, many of them having clear other notions of a republic
than he was willing England should be brought to. A Parliament was still a name of more veneration than any other assembly of men was like to be, and the contempt the last was
fallen into was like to teach the next to behave itself with more
discretion. However, the ice was broken for dissolving them
when they should do otherwise; yet he was not so well satisfied
in the general temper as to trust the election of them to the
humour and inclination of the people.

14. He resolved therefore to choose them himself, that he
might with the more justice unmake them when he should
think fit; and therefore, with the advice of his council of officers
(for he made no other council of state,) he made choice of a
number of men, consisting of about one hundred and forty
persons, who should meet as a Parliament to settle the government of the nation. It can hardly be believed that so wild a
notion should fall into any man's imagination that such a people

---

[1] [*De beneficiis*, lib. v, cap. 16.]   [2] ['twenty-fourth,' MS.]

1653 should be fit to contribute towards any settlement, or from whose actions any thing could result, that might advance his particular design ; yet, upon the view and consideration of the persons made choice of, many did conclude that he had made his own scheme entirely to himself, and, though he communicated it with no man, concluded it the most natural way to ripen and produce the effects it did afterwards, to the end he proposed to himself.

15. There were amongst them some few of the quality and degree of gentlemen, and who had estates, and such a proportion of credit and reputation as could consist with the guilt they had contracted. But much the major part of them consisted of inferior persons, of no quality or name, artificers of the meanest trades, known only by their gifts in praying and preaching ; which was now practised by all degrees of men but scholars throughout the kingdom. In which number, that there may be a better judgment made of the rest, it will not be amiss to name one, from whom that Parliament itself was afterwards denominated, who was Praise-God (that was his Christen-name) Barebone, a leather-seller in Fleet-street, from whom (he being an eminent speaker in it) it was afterwards called Praise-God Barebone's Parliament. In a word, they were a pack of weak senseless fellows, fit only to bring the name and reputation of Parliament lower than it was yet.

16. It was fit these new men should be brought together by some new way ; and a very new way it was. For Cromwell by
June 8. his warrant, directed to every one of them, and telling them of the necessity of dissolving the late Parliament, and of an equal necessity that the peace, safety, and good government of the commonwealth should be provided for, and therefore that he had, by the advice of his council of officers, nominated divers persons fearing God, and of approved fidelity and honesty, to whom the great charge and trust of so weighty affairs was to be committed, and that having good assurance of his love to, and courage for, God, and the interest of his cause, and the good people of this commonwealth, concluded[1] in these words :

[1] ['he concluded,' MS.]

' I, Oliver Cromwell, captain general and commander in chief 1653 of all the forces raised, or to be raised, within this commonwealth, do hereby summon and require you personally to be and appear at the Council-chamber at Whitehall upon the fourth day of July next, then and there to take upon you the said trust. And you are hereby called and appointed to serve as a member for the county of,' &c. And upon this wild summons the persons so nominated appeared at the Council-chamber upon the fourth of July, which was near three months after the dissolution of the former Parliament.

17. Cromwell, with his council of officers, was ready to re- July 4. ceive them, and he made them a long discourse of the fear of God, and the honour due to his name, full of texts of Scripture; and remembered the wonderful mercies of God to this nation, and the continued series of providence by which he had appeared in carrying on his cause, and bringing affairs unto that present glorious condition wherein they then were. He put them in mind of the noble actions of the army in the famous victory of Worcester, of the applications they had made to the Parliament for a good settlement of all the affairs of the commonwealth, the neglect whereof made it absolutely necessary to dissolve it. He assured them by many arguments, some of which were urged out of Scripture, that they had a very lawful call to take upon them the supreme authority of the nation; and concluded with a véry earnest desire, that great tenderness might be used towards all conscientious persons, of what judgment soever they appeared to be.

18. And when he had finished his discourse, he delivered unto them an instrument, engrossed in parchment, and under his hand and seal, whereby, by the advice of his council of officers, he did devolve and intrust the supreme authority of this commonwealth into the hands of those persons therein mentioned; and declared that they, or any forty of them, were to be held and acknowledged the supreme authority of the nation, unto which all persons within the same, and the territories thereunto belonging, were to yield obedience and subjection to the third day of the month of November which

1653 should be in the year 1654, which was about a year and three
months from the time that he spake to them; and three months
before that time prescribed should expire, they were to make
choice of other persons to succeed them, whose power and
authority should not exceed one year, and then they were likewise to provide and take care for a like succession in the
government.   And being thus invested with this authority,
they repaired to the Parliament House, and made choice of one
July 5. Rouse[1] to be their Speaker, an old gentleman of Devonshire,
who had been a member of the former Parliament, and in that
time been preferred and made provost of the college at Eton,
which office he then enjoyed, with an opinion of having some
knowledge in the Latin and Greek tongues; of a very mean
understanding, but throughly engaged in the guilt of the times.

19. At their first coming together, some of them had the
modesty to doubt that they were not in many respects so well
qualified as to take upon them the style and title of a parliament.   But that modesty was quickly subdued, and they
were easily persuaded to assume that title, and to consider
themselves as the supreme authority in the nation.   These men
thus brought together continued in this capacity near six
months, to the amazement and even mirth of the people; in
which time they never entered upon any grave and serious
debate that might tend to any settlement, but generally expressed great sharpness and animosity against the clergy, and
against all learning, out of which they thought the clergy had
[grown] and still would grow.

20. There were now no bishops for them to be angry with;
they had already reduced all that order to the lowest beggary.
But their quarrel was against all who called themselves ministers, and who, by being called so, received tithes and respect
from their neighbours.   They resolved the function itself to be
antichristian, and their persons to be burdensome to the people,
July 15. and the requiring and payment of tithes to be absolute Judaism,
and they thought fit that they should be abolished altogether;
and that there might not for the time to come be any race of

---
[1] ['Rowze,' MS.]

people who might revive those pretences, they thought fit that 1653
all lands belonging to the Universities, and colleges in those
Universities, might be sold, and the monies that should arise
thereby to be disposed for the public service, and to ease the
people from the payment of taxes and contributions.

21. And when they had tired and perplexed themselves so Dec. 12.
long in such debates, as soon as they were met in the morning
upon the twelfth of December, and before many of them were
come who were like to dissent from the motion, one of them
stood up and declared that he did believe that they were not
equal to the burden that was laid upon them, and therefore
that they might dissolve themselves, and deliver back their
authority in[to] their hands from whom they had received it;
which being presently consented to, their Speaker, with those
who were of that mind, went to Whitehall, and re-delivered to
Cromwell the instrument they had received from him, acknowledged their own impotency, and besought him to take care of
the commonwealth.

22. And by this frank donation he and his council of officers
were once more possessed of the supreme sovereign power of
the nation. And in few days after, his council were too modest
to share with him in this royal authority, but declared, That
the government of the commonwealth should reside in a single Dec. 14.
person; that that person should be Oliver Cromwell, captain
general of all the forces in England, Scotland, and Ireland, and
that his title should be Lord Protector of the Commonwealth
of England, Scotland, and Ireland, and of the dominions and
territories thereunto belonging; and that he should have a
council of one and twenty persons to be assistant to him in the
government.

23. Most men did now conclude that the folly and sottish-
ness of this late assembly was so much foreseen, that from their
very first coming together it was determined what should
follow their dissolution. For the method that succeeded could
hardly have been composed in so short a time after by persons
who had not consulted upon the contingence some time before.
It was upon the 12th of December that the small Parliament

1653 was dissolved, when many of the members came to the House as to their usual consultations, and found that they who came before were gone to Whitehall to be dissolved, which the other Dec. 16. never thought of: and upon the 16th day, the commissioners of the Great Seal, with the Lord Mayor and aldermen, were sent for to attend Cromwell and his council to Westminster Hall, it being then vacation-time; and being come thither, the commissioners sitting upon their usual seat, and not knowing what they were sent for, the declaration of the council of officers was read, whereby Cromwell was made Protector; who stood in the court uncovered, whilst what was contained in a piece of parchment was read, [which [1]] was called the *Instrument of Government;* whereby it was ordained, That the Protector should call a Parliament once in every three years; that the first Parliament should be convened upon the third day of September following which would be in the year 1654, and that he should not dissolve any Parliament once met till they had sat five months; that such bills as should be presented to him by the Parliament, if they should not be confirmed by him within twenty days, should pass without him, and be looked upon as laws: that he should have a select council to assist him, which should not exceed the number of one and twenty, nor be less than thirteen: that immediately after his death the council should choose another Protector before they rose: that no Protector after him should be general of the army: that the Protector should have power to make peace and war: that, with the consent of his council, he should make laws, which should be binding to the subjects during the intervals of Parliament.

24. Whilst this was reading, Cromwell had his hand upon the Bible; and it being read, he took his oath that he would not violate any thing that was contained in that Instrument of Government, but would observe [it], and cause the same to be observed; and in all things, according to the best of his understanding, to govern the nations according to the laws, statutes, and customs, seeking peace, and causing justice and law to be equally administered.

[1] [' and,' MS.]

25. And this new invented ceremony being in this manner 1653 performed, he himself was covered, and all the rest bare; and Lambert, who was then the second person in the army, carried the sword before his highness (which was the style he took from thenceforth) to his coach, all they whom he called into it sitting bare; and so he returned to Whitehall; and immediately proclamation was made by a herald, in the Palace-yard at Dec. 19. Westminster, That the late Parliament having dissolved themselves and resigned their whole power and authority, the government of the commonwealth of England, Scotland, and Ireland, by a Lord Protector, and successive triennial Parliaments, was now established: and whereas Oliver Cromwell, captain general of all the forces of the commonwealth, is declared Lord Protector of the said nations, and had accepted thereof, publication was now made of the same; and all persons, of what quality and condition soever in any of the said three nations, were strictly charged and commanded to take notice thereof, and to conform and submit themselves to the government so established; and all shrieves, mayors, &c. were required to publish this proclamation, to the end that none might have cause to pretend ignorance therein. Which proclamation was at the same time published in Cheapside by the Lord Mayor of London, and with all possible expedition by the shrieves and other officers throughout England, Scotland, and 1654 Ireland. And in few days after the city of London invited Feb. 8. their new Protector to a very splendid entertainment at Grocers' Hall, the streets being railed, and the solemnity of his reception such as had been at any time performed to the King; and he, as like a king, graciously conferred the honour of knighthood upon the Lord Mayor at his departure.

26. And in this manner, and with so little pains, this extraordinary man, without any other reason than because he had a mind to it, and without the assistance, and against the desire, of all noble persons or men of quality, or of three men who in the beginning of the troubles were possessed of three hundred pounds land by the year, mounted himself into the throne of three kingdoms, without the name of king, but with a greater

1653 power and authority than had been ever exercised or claimed by any king; and received greater evidence and manifestation of respect and esteem from all the kings and princes in Christendom than had ever been shewed to any monarch of those nations: and which was so much the more notorious, in that they all abhorred him, when they trembled at his power and courted his friendship.

27. Though during this unsettlement in England Cromwell had, *ex plenitudine potestatis*, taken care that there was a good winter guard of ships in the Downs, yet the Dutch had enjoyed a very fruitful harvest of trade during that confusion and suspension of power, and had sent out their fleets of merchantmen under a convoy by the north of Scotland, and by the return of that convoy received their fleet from the Baltic with security; so that upon the hope that those domestic contentions of England would not be so soon composed, they began to recover their spirits again. But Cromwell was no sooner invested in his new dignity [1], but with great diligence he caused a strong fleet to be made ready against the spring, and committed the command thereof to three admirals jointly; Blake, a man well known, but not thought entirely enough devoted to Cromwell; Munke, whom he called out of Scotland as his own creature; and Deane, a mere seaman, grown from a common mariner to the reputation of a bold and excellent officer.

June 2.   28. This fleet, in the beginning of June [in the year 1653,] met with the Dutch about the middle seas over between Dover and Zealand, and made what haste they could to engage them. But the wind not being favourable, it was noon before the fight began, which continued very sharp till the night parted them, without any visible advantage to either side, save that Deane, one of the English admirals, was killed by a cannon-shot from June 3. the rear-admiral of the Dutch. But the next morning, the Dutch having the advantage of the small wind that was, the English charged so furiously upon the thickest part of them, without discharging any of their guns till they were at a very small distance, that they broke their squadrons; and in the end

[1] [not when made Protector, but in the previous year.]

forced them to fly, and make all the sail they could for their 1653 own coast, leaving behind them eleven of their ships which were all taken, besides six which were sunk. The execution on that part was very great, as was likewise the number of the prisoners, as well officers as soldiers. The loss of the English was greatest in their general Deane : there was beside him but one captain and about two hundred common seamen killed ; the number of the wounded was greater ; nor did they lose one ship, or were so disabled but that they followed with the whole fleet to the coast of Holland, whither the other fled ; and being got into the Fly and the Texell, the English for some time blocked them up in their own harbours, taking all such ships as came bound for those ports.

29. This great defeat so humbled the States that they made all possible haste to send four commissioners [1] into England to June. mediate for a treaty and a cessation of arms ; who were received very loftily by Cromwell, and with some reprehension for their want of wariness in entering into so unequal a contention ; yet he declared a gracious inclination to a treaty, till the conclusion whereof he would admit no cessation ; which being known in Holland, they would not stay so long under the reproach and disadvantage of being besieged and shut up in their ports, but made all possible haste to prepare another fleet, strong enough to remove the English from their coasts; which they believed was the best expedient to advance their treaty. And there cannot be a greater instance of the opulency of that people than that they should be able, after so many [losses,] and so late a great defeat, in so short a time to gather a fleet strong enough together to visit those who had so lately conquered them, and who at present shut them within their ports.

30. Their admiral Trumpe had with some of the fleet retired into the Weelings, at too great a distance from the other ports for the English fleet to divide itself. He had with marvellous industry caused his hurt ships to be repaired, and more severe punishment to be inflicted on those who had behaved themselves cowardly than had ever been used in that State. And

[1] [Beverning, Nieuport, Van de Perre, and Jongestall.]

1653 the States published so great and ample rewards to all officers and seamen who would in that conjuncture repair to their service, that[1] by the end of July, within less than two months after their defeat, he came out of the Weelings with a fleet of ninety and five men of war; which as soon as the English had notice of, July 29. they made towards them. But the wind rising they were forced to stand more to sea, for fear of the sands and shelfs upon that coast. Whereupon Van Trumpe all that night stood into the Texell, where he joined five and twenty more of their best ships, and with this addition, which made him one hundred and twenty sail, he faced the English, who kept still to the sea, and having got a little more room, and the weather being a little clearer, tacked about, and were received by the Dutch with great courage and gallantry.

July 31. 31. The battle continued very hot and bloody on both sides from six of the clock in the morning till one in the afternoon, when the Admiral of Holland, the famous Van Trumpe, whilst he very signally performed the office of a brave and bold commander, was shot with a musket bullet into the heart, of which he fell dead without speaking word. And this blow killed the courage of the rest; who, seeing many of their companions burned and sunk, and after having endured very hot service, before the evening fled, and made all the sail they could towards the Texell, the English not being in a condition to pursue them, but found themselves obliged to retire to their own coast, both to preserve and mend their maimed and torn ships, and refresh their wounded men.

32. This battle was the most bloody that had been yet fought, both sides rather endeavouring the destruction of their enemy's fleet than the taking their ships. On the Hollanders' part, between twenty and thirty of their ships of war were fired or sunk, and above one thousand prisoners taken. The victory cost the English dear too; for four hundred common men and eight captains were slain outright, and above seven hundred common men and five captains wounded. But they lost only one ship, which was burned; and two or three more, though carried home, were disabled for future service. The most

[1] ['so that,' MS.]

sensible part of the loss to the Dutch was the death of their 1653
admiral Van Trumpe, who, in respect of his maritime experience and the frequent actions he had been engaged in, might
very well be reckoned amongst the most eminent commanders
at sea of that age, and to whose memory his country is farther
indebted than they have yet acknowledged.

33. This was the last engagement at sea between the two
commonwealths : for as the Dutch were by this last defeat, and
loss of their brave admiral, totally dispirited, and gave their
commissioners at London order to prosecute the peace upon
any conditions, so Cromwell was weary enough of so chargeable
a war, and knew he had much to do to settle his government at
home, and that he might choose more convenient enemies
abroad, who would neither be able to defend themselves as well,
or to do him so much harm, as the Hollanders had [done] and
could do. And therefore, when he had drawn the Dutch to
accept of such conditions as he thought fit to give them, (among
which one was, that they would not suffer any of the King's
party, or any enemy to the commonwealth of England, to reside
within their dominions; and another, which was contained in a
secret article, to which the Great Seal of the State was affixed,
by which they obliged themselves never to admit the prince of
Aurange to be their Stateholder, general, or admiral, and likewise to deliver up the island of Poleroone in the East Indies,
which they had taken from the English in the time of King
James and usurped it ever since, into the hands of the East
India English company again, and to pay a good sum of money
for the old barbarous violence exercised so many years since at 1623
Amboyna, for which the two last Kings could never obtain
satisfaction and reparation,) about the middle of April 1654 he 1654
made a peace with the States General, with all the advantages April 5.
he could desire, having indeed all the persons of power and
interest there fast bound to him upon their joint interest.

34. And now having rendered himself terrible abroad, forced
the Portugal to send an ambassador to beg peace, and to submit
to expiate the offence they had committed in receiving prince 1654
Rupert by the payment of a great sum of money, and brought July 10.

1654 the two crowns of France and Spain to sue for his alliance, he suspended for a time to choose a new enemy, that he might make himself as much obeyed at home as he was feared abroad; and in order to that, prosecuted all those who had been of the King's party with utmost rigour; laid new impositions upon them, and upon every light rumour of a conspiracy clapped up all those whom he thought fit to suspect into close prisons, en-

1655
July 6 and
Oct. 25. joined others not to stir from their own houses, and banished all who had ever been in arms for the King from the city of London and Westminster; and laid other penalties upon them contrary to the articles granted to them when they gave up their arms, and to the indemnity upon making their compositions.

35. The discontent was general over the whole kingdom, and among all sorts of people, of what party soever. The Presbyterians preached boldly against the liberty of conscience, and the monstrous license that sprung from thence: and they who enjoyed that license were as unsatisfied with the government as any of the rest, talked more loudly, and threatened the person of Cromwell more than any. But into these distempers Cromwell was not inquisitive; nor would give those men an opportunity to talk, by calling them in question, who, he knew, would say more than he was willing any body should hear; but intended to mortify those unruly spirits at the charge of the King's party, and with the spectacle of their suffering upon any the most trivial occasion. And if, in this general license of discourse, any man who was suspected to wish well to the King let fall any light word against the government, he was sure to be cast in prison, and to be pursued with all possible severity and cruelty: and he could not want frequent opportunities of revenge this way. It was the greatest consolation to miserable men, who had in themselves or their friends been undone by their loyalty, to meet together and lament their condition; and this brought on invectives against the person of Cromwell; and wine, and the continuance of the discourse, disposed them to take notice of the universal hatred that the whole nation had of him, and to fancy how easy it would be to destroy him. And commonly

there was in all those meetings some corrupted person of the 1654
party, who fomented most the discourse, and for a vile recompense betrayed his companions, and informed of all, and more
than had been said; whereupon a new plot was discovered
against the commonwealth and the person of the Protector,
and a high court of justice was presently erected to try the June 13.
criminals, which rarely absolved any man who was brought
before them. But to this kind of trial they never exposed any
man but those of the King's party; the other, of whom they
were more afraid, had too many friends to suffer them to be
brought before such a tribunal; which had been first erected
to murder the King himself, and continued to root out all who
had adhered to him. No man who had ever been against the
King (except he became afterwards for him) was ever brought
before that extravagant power, but was remitted to the trial of
the law by juries, which seldom condemned any.

36. The very next month after the peace was made, for the
better establishment of his empire, a high court of justice was June 27.
erected for the trial of persons who were accused of holding
correspondence with Charles Steward, (which was the style they
allowed the King,) and for having a design against the life of
the Protector, to seize upon the Tower, and to proclaim the
King. And the chief persons they accused of this were, Mr.
Gerard, a young gentleman of a good family, who had been an June 30.
ensign in the King's army, but was not at present above 22
years of age, without any interest or fortune; the other, one
Mr. Vowell, who kept a school, and taught many boys about
Islington[1]. Mr. Gerard was charged with having been at
Paris, and having there spoken with the King; which he confessed, and declared that he went to Paris upon a business that
concerned himself, (which he named,) and when he had despatched it, and was to return for England, he desired the lord
Gerard, his kinsman, to present him to the King, that he
might kiss his hand, which he did in a large room, where were
many present; and that when he asked his majesty whether
he would command him any service into England, his majesty

---

[1] ['Islington' substituted in the MS. for 'Knitsbridge.']

1654 bad him to commend him to his friends there, and to charge them that they should be quiet, and not engage themselves in any plots, which must prove ruinous to them, and could do the King no good; which was very true; for his majesty had observed so much of the temper of the people at his being at Worcester, and his abode there after, the fear they were under, and how fruitless any insurrection must be, that he endeavoured nothing more than to divert and suppress all inclinations that way. However, this high court of justice received proof that Mr. Gerard and Mr. Vowell had been present with some other gentlemen in a tavern where discourse had been held how easy a thing it was to kill the Protector, and at the same time to seize upon the Tower of London, and that, if at the same time the King was proclaimed, the city of London would presently declare for his majesty, and nobody would oppose him.

July 6.   37. Upon this evidence these two gentlemen were con-
July 10. demned to be hanged; and upon the tenth of July, about two months after they had been in prison, a gallows was erected at Charing[1] Cross, whither Mr. Vowell was brought; who was a person utterly unknown to the King, and to any person intrusted by him, but very worthy to have his name and memory preserved in the list of those who shewed most magnanimity and courage in sacrificing their lives for the Crown. He expressed a marvellous contempt of death, which he said he suffered without having committed any fault. He professed his duty to the King, and his reverence for the Church; and earnestly and pathetically advised the people to return to their fidelity to both, which he told them that they would at last be compelled to do after all their sufferings. He addressed himself most to the soldiers; told them how unworthily they prostituted themselves to serve the ambition of an unworthy tyrant, and conjured them to forsake him and to serve the King, which he was sure they would at last do. And so, having devoutly recommended the King and the kingdom and himself to God in very pious prayers, he ended his life with as much Christian resolution as can be expected from the most composed conscience.

[1] ['Charon,' MS.]

38. The Protector was prevailed with to shew more respect 1654
to Mr. Gerard in causing him to be beheaded, who was
brought the afternoon of the same day to a scaffold upon the
Tower Hill.   But they were so ill pleased with the behaviour
of him who suffered in the morning, that they would not suffer
the other to speak to the people, but pressed him to discover
all the secrets of the plot and conspiracy.   He told them, that
if he had a hundred lives, he would lose them all to do the
King any service, and was now willing to die upon that suspicion; but that he was very innocent of that which was
charged against him ; that he had not entered into or consented to any plot or conspiracy, nor given any countenance to
any discourses to that purpose ; and offered again to speak to
the people, and to magnify the King; upon which they would
not suffer him to proceed ; and thereupon, with great and undaunted courage, he laid down his head upon the block.

39. The same day was concluded with another very exemplary piece of justice, and of a very different nature from the
other two.   The ambassador of Portugal had a very splendid
equipage, and in his company his brother don Pantaleon Sa,
a knight of Malta, and a man eminent in many great actions,
who out of curiosity accompanied his brother in this embassy,
that he might see England.   This gentleman was of a haughty
and imperious nature, and one day being in the new Exchange, 1653
upon a sudden accident and mistake, had a quarrel with that Nov. 21.
Mr. Gerard whom we now left without his head ; · who had
then returned some negligence and contempt to the *rodomontados*
of the Portuguese, and had left him sensible of receiving some
affront.   Whereupon he repaired thither again the next day, Nov. 22.
with many servants, better armed and provided for any encounter, imagin[ing] [1] he should find his former adversary, who
did not expect the visitation.   But the Portuguese not dis-
tinguishing of persons, and finding many gentlemen walking
there, and amongst the rest one he believed very like the
other, he thought he was not to lose the occasion ; he entered
into a new quarrel ; in which a gentleman utterly unacquainted

[1] ['imagined,' MS.]

1654 with what had formerly passed, and walking there accidentally, was killed, and others hurt; upon which, the people rising from all the neighbour places, don Pantaleon thought fit to make his retreat [1] to his brother's house; which he did, and caused the gates to be locked, and put all the servants in arms to defend the house against the people, which had pursued him, and flocked now together from all parts to apprehend those who had caused the disorder and had killed a gentleman.

40. The ambassador knew nothing of the affair, but looked upon himself as affronted and assaulted by a rude multitude, and took care to defend his house till the justice should allay the tumult. Cromwell was quickly advertised of the insolence, and sent an officer with soldiers to demand and seize upon all the persons who had been engaged in the action: and so the ambassador came to be informed of the truth of the story, with which he was exceedingly afflicted and astonished. The officer demanded the person of his brother, who was well known, and the rest of those who were present, to be delivered to him, without which he would break up the house, and find them wherever they were concealed. The ambassador demanded the privilege that was due to his house by the law of nations, and which he would defend against any violence with his own life and the lives of all his family; but finding the officer resolute, and that he should be too weak in the encounter, he desired respite till he might send to the Protector; which was granted to him. He complained of the injury that was done him, and desired an audience. Cromwell sent him word that a gentleman had been murdered, and many others hurt, and that justice must be satisfied; and therefore required that all the persons engaged might be delivered into the hands of the officer; without which, if he should withdraw the soldiers, and desist the requiring it, the people would pull down the house, and execute justice themselves, of which he would not answer for the effects. When this was done, he should have an audience and all the satisfaction it was in his power to give. The ambassador desired that his brother and the rest might remain in his

---

[1] ['retraight,' MS.]

house, and he would be responsible, and produce them before 1654
the justice as the time should be assigned.   But nothing would
serve but the delivery of the persons, and the people increased
their cry that they would pull down the house.   Whereupon
the ambassador was compelled to deliver up his brother and 1653
the rest of the persons, who were all sent prisoners to Newgate. Nov. 23.
The ambassador used all the instances he could for his brother,
being willing to leave the rest to the mercy of the law, but
could receive no other answer but that justice must be done. 1654
July 5.
And justice was done to the full, for they were all brought to
their trial at the sessions at Newgate, and there so many of
them condemned to be hanged as were found guilty.   And the July 6
rest of those who were condemned were executed at Tyburn ;
and don Pantaleon himself was brought to the scaffold on
Tower Hill as soon as Mr. Gerard was executed, where he lost July 10.
his head, with less grace than his antagonist had done.

41. Though he [the Protector] had nothing now to do but
at home, Holland having accepted peace upon his own terms,
Portugal bought it at a full price and upon an humble submission, Denmark contented with such an alliance as he
was contented to make with them, and France and Spain
contending by their ambassadors which should render themselves most acceptable to the Protector; Scotland lying under
a heavy yoke by the severe government of Munke, who after the
peace with the Dutch was sent back to govern that province,
which was reduced under the government of the English laws, Apr. 12.
and their Kirk and kirkmen entirely subdued to the obedience
of the State without reference to assemblies or synods ; Ireland
[being[1]] confessedly subdued, [and] no opposition made to the
Protector's commands, so that commissions were sent to divide
all the lands which had belonged to the Irish, or to those
English who had adhered to the King, amongst those adven-
turers who had supplied money for the war, and the soldiers
and officers, who were in great arrears for their pay, and who
received liberal assignations in lands, a whole province being
reserved for a demesne to the Protector ; and all these divisions

[1] ['was,' MS.]

1654 made under the government of his younger son, Harry Crom-
1657 well, whom he sent thither as his Lieutenant of that kingdom,
Nov. 17. and who lived in the full grandeur of the office : notwithstanding all which, England proved not yet so towardly as he
expected. Vane, and the most considerable men of the Independent party, from the time [he [1]] had turned them out of the
Parliament, and so dissolved it, retired quietly to their houses
in the country, poisoned the affections of their neighbours
towards the government, and lost nothing of their credit with
the people; yet carried themselves so warily, that they did
nothing to disturb the peace of the nation, or to give Cromwell any advantage against them upon which to call them in
question.

42. There were another less wary, because a more desperate,
party, which were the Levellers; many whereof had been
the most active Agitators in the army, who had executed his
orders and designs in incensing the army against the Parliament, and had been at that time his sole confidents and bed-
fellows; who from the time that he assumed the title of Protector, which to them was as odious as that of King, professed
a mortal hatred to his person. And he well knew both these
people had too much credit in his army, and with some principal officers of it. And of these men he stood in more fear
than of all the King's party; of which he had in truth very
little apprehension, though he coloured many of the preparations
which he made against the other, as if provided against the
dangers which were threatened from them.

43. But the time drew near now when he was obliged, by
the Instrument of Government and upon his oath, to call a
Parliament, which seemed to him the only means left to compose the minds of the people to an entire submission to his
June 9. government. And in order to this meeting, though he did
not observe the old course in sending writs out to all the little
boroughs throughout England which use to send burgesses,
(in which there is so great an inequality that some single counties
send more members to the Parliament than six other counties

[1] ['they,' MS.]

do,) he seemed to take a more equal way, by appointing more **1654** knights for every shire to be chosen and fewer burgesses, whereby the number of the whole was much lessened, and yet, the people being left to their own election, it was not thought an ill temperament, and was generally looked upon as an alteration fit to be more warrantably made and in a better time. And so, upon the receipts of his writs, elections were made accordingly in all places, and such persons for the most part chosen and returned as were believed to be least affected to the present government and to those who had any authority in it; there being strict order given, that no person who had ever been against the Parliament during the time of the civil war, or the sons of any such persons, should be capable of being chosen to sit in that Parliament; nor was any such person made choice of.

44. The day for their meeting was the third of September Sept. 3. in the year 1654, within less than a year after he had been declared Protector; when, after they had been at a sermon in the abbey at Westminster, they all came into the Painted Sept. 4. Chamber, where his highness made them a large discourse; and told them, That that Parliament was such a congregation of wise, prudent, and discreet persons, that England had scarce seen the like; that he should forbear relating to them the series of God's providence all along to that· time, because it was well known to them, and only declare to them, that the erection of his present power was a suitable providence to the rest, by shewing what a condition these nations were in at its erection: that then every man's heart was against another's, every man's interest divided against another's, and almost every thing grown arbitrary: that there was grown up a general contempt of God and Christ, the grace of God turned into wantonness, and his Spirit made a cloak for all wickedness and profaneness; nay, that the axe was even laid to the root of the ministry, and swarms of Jesuits were continually wafted over hither to consume and destroy the welfare of England: that the nation was then likewise engaged in a deep war with Portugal, Holland, and France; so that the whole nation was one heap of con-

1654 fusion: but that this present government was calculated for the people's interest, let malignant spirits say what they would; and that, with humbleness towards God and modesty towards them, he would recount somewhat in the behalf of the government. First, it had endeavoured to reform the law; it had put into the seat of justice men of known integrity and ability; it had settled a way for probation of ministers to preach the gospel; and besides all this, it had called a free Parliament: that, blessed be God, they that day saw a free Parliament. Then, as to wars, that a peace was made with Denmark, Sweden, the Dutch, and Portugal, and was likewise near concluding with France. That these things were but entrances and doors of hopes; but now he made no question to enable them to lay the top stone of the work, recommending to them that maxim, that peace, though it were made, was not to be trusted farther than it consisted with interest. That the great work which now lay upon this Parliament was, that the government of England might be settled upon terms of honour: that they would avoid confusions, lest foreign states should take advantage of them: that, as for himself, he did not speak like one that would be a lord over them, but as one that would be a fellow-servant in that great affair: and concluded, that they should go to their House, and there make choice of a Speaker; which they presently did, and seemed very unanimous in their first act, which was the making choice of William Lenthall to be their Speaker. Which agreement was upon very disagreeing principles; Cromwell having designed him for luck sake, and, being well acquainted with his temper, concluded that he would be made a property in this as well as he had been in the Long Parliament, when he always complied with that party that was most powerful; and the other persons, who meant nothing that Cromwell did, were well pleased, out of hope that the same man's being in the chair might facilitate the renewing and reviving the former House; which they looked upon as the true legitimate Parliament, strangled by the tyranny of Cromwell, and yet that had life enough left in it.

45. And he was no sooner in his chair, than it was proposed

that they might in the first place consider, by what authority 1654
they came thither, and whether that which had convened them
had a lawful power to that purpose. From which subject the
Protector's creatures, and those of the army, endeavoured to
divert them by all the arguments they could. Notwithstanding
which, the current of the House insisted upon the first clearing
that point, as the foundation upon which all their counsels
must be built: and as many of the members positively enough
declared against that power, so one of them, more confident
than the rest, said plainly that they might easily discern the
snares which were laid to entrap the privileges of the people,
and for his own part, as God had made him instrumental in
cutting down tyranny in one person, so now he could not endure to see the nation's liberties shackled in another, whose
right to the government could not be measured otherwise than
by the length of his sword, which had been only that which
emboldened him to command his commanders. And this spirit
prevailed so far, that for eight days together those of the Sept. 6–11.
council and officers and others, who were called the Court
party, could not divert the question from being put, Whether
the government should be by a Protector and a Parliament, any
other way than by lengthening the debate, and then adjourning
the House when the question was ready to be put, because they
plainly saw that it would be carried in the negative.

46. The continuance of this warm debate in the house, in
which the Protector's own person was not treated with much
reverence, exceedingly perplexed him, and obliged him once
more to try what effect his sovereign presence would produce
towards a better composure. And so he came again to the
Painted Chamber, and sent for his Parliament to come to him; Sept. 12.
and then told them that, The great God of heaven and earth
knew what grief and sorrow of heart it was to him to find them
falling into heats and divisions; that he would have them take
notice of this, that the same government made him a Protector
that made them a Parliament; that as they were intrusted in
some things, so was he in others; that in the government were
certain fundamentals which could not be altered, to wit, that

1654 the government should be in a single person and a Parliament, that Parliaments should not be perpetual and always sitting, that the militia should not be trusted into one hand or power, but so as the Parliament might have a check on the Protector and the Protector on the Parliament; that in matters of religion there ought to be liberty of conscience, and that persecution in the Church was not to be tolerated. These, he said, were unalterable fundamentals. As for the rest of the things in the government, they were examinable and alterable as the state of affairs did require: that for his own part he was even overwhelmed with grief to see that any of them should go about to overthrow what was settled, contrary to the trust they had received from the people, which could not but bring very great inconveniences upon themselves and the nation. When he had made this frank declaration unto them what they were to trust to, the better to confirm them in their duty, he appointed a guard to attend at the door of the Parliament House, and there to restrain all men from entering into the House who refused to subscribe this following engagement: 'I do hereby promise and engage to be true and faithful to the lord Protector of the commonwealth of England, Scotland, and Ireland; and shall not (according to the tenor of the indenture whereby I am returned to serve in Parliament) propose or give my consent to alter the government as it is settled in one person and a Parliament.'

47. This engagement the major part of the members utterly refused to sign, and called it a violation of the privilege of Parliament, and an absolute depriving of them of that freedom which was essential to it. And so they were excluded, and restrained from entering into the House: and they who did subscribe it, and had thereupon liberty to sit there, were yet so refractory to any proposition that might settle him in the government in the manner he desired it, that, after the five months spent in wrangling and useless discourses, (during which he durst not attempt the dissolution of them by his **1655.** Instrument of Government,) he took the first opportunity he **Jan. 22.** could to dissolve them; and upon the [twenty-second[1]] of

¹ ['tenth,' MS.]

January, with some reproaches, he let them know he could do 1655
the business without them; and so dismissed them, with much
evidence of his displeasure: and they again retired to their
habitations, resolved to wait another opportunity of revenge,
and in the mean time to give no evidence of their submitting
to his usurpation by undertaking any employment or office
under his authority; and he as carefully endeavouring and
watching to find such an advantage against them as might
make them liable to the penalty of the laws. And yet even his
weakness and impotency upon such a notorious advantage
appeared in two very notable instances, which happened about
that time in the cases of two persons whose names were then
much taken notice of upon the stage of affairs, John Wildman
and John Lilborne.

48. The former had been bred a scholar in the university of
Cambridge, and being young, and of a pregnant wit, in the beginning of the rebellion, meant to make his fortune in the war, and
chose to depend upon Cromwell's countenance and advice when
he was not above the degree of a captain of a troop of horse
himself, and was much esteemed and valued by him, and made
an officer, and was so active in contriving and fomenting
jealousies and discontents, and so dexterous in composing or im-
proving any disgusts, and so inspired with the spirit of praying
and preaching when those gifts came into request and became
thriving arts, that about the time when the King was taken
from Holmeby, and it was necessary that the army should enter
into contests with the parliament, John Wildman grew to be one
of the principal Agitators, and was most relied upon by Cromwell
to infuse those things into the minds of the soldiers, and to
conduct them in the managery of their discontents, as might
most advance those designs he then had; and quickly got the
reputation of a man of parts, and, having a smooth pen, drew
most of the papers which first kindled that fire between the
Parliament and the army that was after extinguished but in the
ruin of both. His reputation in those faculties made him quit
the army, where he was become a major, and where he kept still
a great interest, and betake himself to civil affairs, in the soli-

1655 citation of suits depending in the Parliament or before committees, where he had much credit with those who had most
power to do right or wrong, and so made himself necessary to
those who had need of such protection from the tyranny of the
time.   And by these arts he thrived, and got much more than
he could have done in the army, and kept and increased his
credit there by the interest he had in the other places.   When
Cromwell declined the ways of establishing the commonwealth,
Wildman, amongst the rest, forsook him, and entered warily
into any counsels which were like to destroy him : and upon
the dissolution of this last Parliament, having less phlegm, and
so less patience, than other men, to expect another opportunity,
and in the mean time to leave him to establish his greatness, he
did believe he should be able to make such a schism in the
army as would give an opportunity to other enraged persons to
take vengeance upon him.

49. Cromwell knew the man and his undermining faculties ;
knew he had some design in hand, but could not make any such
discovery as might warrant a public prosecution, but appointed
some trusty spies (of which he had plenty) to watch him very
narrowly, and, by being often with him, to find his papers, the
spreading whereof he knew would be the preamble to any conspiracy of his.   Shortly after the dissolution of that Parliament,
Feb. 10. these instruments of [Cromwell[1]] surprised him in a room
where he thought he had been safe enough, as he was writing a
Declaration, and seized upon the papers ; the title whereof was,
' A Declaration, containing the reasons and motive which oblige
us to take up arms against Oliver Cromwell ;' and though it
was not finished, yet in that that was done there was all venom
imaginable expressed against him, and a large and bitter narra-
tion of all his foul breach of trust and perjuries, enough to
have exposed any man to the severest judgment of that time,
and as much as he could wish to discover against him or any
man whom he most desired to destroy[2].   The issue was, the
man was straitly imprisoned, and preparations made for his

---

[1] [' his,' MS.]
[2] [Printed in Whitlocke's *Memorials* under date of Feb. 13, 1655.]

trial, and towards his execution, which all men expected. But **1655** whether Cromwell found that there were more engaged with him than could be brought to justice or were fit to be discovered, (as many men believed,) or that Wildman obliged himself for the time to come not only to be quiet but to be a spy for him upon others, (as others at that time suspected, and had reason for it afterwards,) but after a short time of imprisonment the man was restored to his liberty, and resorted, with the same success and reputation, to his former course of life, in which he thrived very notably.

50. The case of John Lilborne was much more wonderful, **1653** and administered more occasion of discourse and observation. This man before the troubles was a poor bookbinder, and for procuring some seditious pamphlets against the Church and State to be printed and dispersed, had been severely censured **1638** in the Star Chamber, and received a sharp castigation, which **Feb. 13.** made him more obstinate and malicious against [them [1];] and, as he afterwards confessed, in the melancholique of his imprisonment, and by reading the Book of Martyrs, he raised in himself a marvellous inclination and appetite to suffer in the defence, or for the vindication, of any oppressed truth, and found himself very much confirmed in that spirit; and in that time diligently collected and read all those libels and books which had anciently as well as lately been written against the Church; from whence, with the venom, he had likewise contracted the impudence and bitterness of their style, and by practice brought himself to the faculty of writing like them; and so, when that license broke in of printing all that malice and wit could suggest, he published some pamphlets in his own name, full of that confidence and virulency which might asperse the government most to the sense of the people and to their humour. When the war began, he put himself into the army, and was taken prisoner by the King's forces in that engagement at Brayneford shortly after the battle of Edgehill, and then being a man much known and talked of for his qualities above mentioned, he was not so well treated in prison as was like to reconcile them: and being

---

[1] ['it,' MS.]

1653 brought before the Chief Justice, to be tried for treason by a commission of oyer and terminer, (in which method the King intended then to have proceeded against the rebels which should be taken,) he behaved himself with so great impudence in extolling the power of Parliament, that it was manifest he had an ambition to have been made a martyr for that cause. But as he was liberally supplied from his friends at London, and the 1642 Parliament in express terms declared that they would inflict Dec. 17. punishment upon the prisoners they had of the King's party in the same manner as Lilborne and the rest should suffer at Oxford, so he did find means to corrupt the marshal who had the custody of him, and so made his escape into the Parliament quarters, where he was received with public joy, as a champion that had defied the King in his own court.

51. And from this time he was entertained by Cromwell with great familiarity, and in his contests with the Parliament was of much use and privacy to him. But he began then to find him of so restless and unruly a spirit, and to make those advances in religion against the Presbyterians before he thought it seasonable, that he dispensed with his presence in the army, where he was an officer of name, and made him reside in London, where he wished that temper should be improved. And when the Parliament was so much offended with his seditious humour, and the pamphlets he published every day in religion with reflections upon their proceedings, that they resolved to have proceeded 1645 against him with great rigour, towards which the Assembly of July. Divines, which he had likewise provoked, contributed their desire and demand, Cromwell writ a very passionate letter to the Parliament, that they would not so much discourage their army that was fighting for them as to censure an officer of it for his opinion in point of conscience; for the liberty whereof, and to free themselves from the shackles in which the bishops would enslave them, that army had been principally raised. Upon which, all farther prosecution against him was declined at that time, though he declined not the farther provocation, and continued to make the proceedings of the Parliament as odious as he could. But from the time that Cromwell had dispersed the

Parliament, and made himself Protector, and was in possession 1653
of the sovereign power, Lilborne withdrew his favour from him,
and thought him now an enemy worthy of his displeasure; and
both in discourses and writings, in pamphlets and invectives,
loaded him with all the aspersions of hypocrisy and lying and
tyranny, and all other imputations and reproaches which either
he deserved or the malice and bitterness of his nature could
suggest to him, to make him the most universally odious that a
faithless perjured person could be.

52. The Protector could bear ill language and reproaches
with less disturbance and concernment than any person in
authority had ever done; yet the persecution this man exercised him with made him plainly discern that it would be
impossible to preserve his dignity, or to have any security in
his government, whilst his license continued; and therefore,
after he had set spies upon him to observe his actions and
collect his words, and upon advice with his counsel at law was
confidently informed that as well by the old established laws as
by new ordinances he [Lilborne] was guilty of high treason,
and had forfeited his life, if he were prosecuted in any court of
justice, he caused him to be sent to Newgate, and at the next 1653
June 16.
sessions to be indicted of high treason; all his judges being pre- July 13.
sent, and his counsel at law to enforce the evidence, and all care
being taken for the return of such a jury as might be fit for the
importance of the case. Lilborne appeared undaunted, and, with
the confidence of a man that was to play a prize before the
people for their own liberty, he pleaded not guilty, and heard
all the charge and evidence against him with patience enough,
save that by interrupting the lawyers at some time who prosecuted him, and by sharp answers to some questions of the judges,
he shewed that he had no reverence for their persons nor any
submission to their authority. The whole day was spent in his
trial; and when he came to make his defence, he mingled so
much law in his discourse to invalidate the authority of Cromwell, and to make it appear so tyrannical that neither their
lives, liberties or estates were in any degree secure whilst that
usurpation was exercised, and answered all the matters objected

1653 against him with such an assurance, making them to contain
nothing of high treason, and Cromwell to be a person against
whom high treason could not be committed ; and, telling them
that all true born Englishmen were obliged to oppose this
tyranny, as he had done purely for their sake, and that he had
done it only for their sakes, and to preserve them from being
slaves, contrary to his own profit and worldly interest, he told
them how much he had been in his [Cromwell's] friendship :
that he might have received any benefit or preferment from him
if he would have sat still and seen his country enslaved ; which
because he would not do, he was brought thither to have his
life taken from him by their judgment, which he apprehended
not : he defended himself with that vigour, and charmed the
jury so powerfully, that, against all the direction and charge
the judges could give them, (who assured them that the words
and actions fully proved against the prisoner were high treason
by the law, and that they were bound by all the obligation of
conscience to find him guilty,) after no long consultation between themselves they returned with their verdict that he was
July 20. not guilty, nor could be persuaded by the judges to change or
recede from their judgment : which infinitely enraged and perplexed the Protector, who looked upon it as a greater defeat
than the loss of a battle would have been ; and would never
suffer the man to be set at liberty, as by the law he ought to
have been, but sent him from prison to prison, and kept him
enclosed there till he [himself] died. These two instances of
persons not otherwise considerable were thought pertinent to be
inserted, as an evidence of the temper of the [nation [1]], and how
far the spirits of that time were from paying a submission to
that power, when nobody had the courage to lift up their
hands against it.

53. Whatever uneasiness and perplexity Cromwell found in
his condition at home, the King found no benefit from it abroad,
from the friendship or the indignation of other princes : they
had all the same terrible apprehension of his power as if he had
been landed with an army in any of their dominions, and looked

[1] ['nature,' MS.]

upon the King's condition as desperate, and not to be supported. 1653
The treaty between France and England proceeded very fast,
and every day produced fresh evidence of the good intelligence
between Cromwell and the cardinal. The ships and prisoners
which had been taken when they went to relieve Dunkirk, and
by the taking whereof Dunkirk had been lost, were now restored
and set at liberty; and such mutual offices performed between
them, as, with the frequent evidences of aversion from the King
and his interest, made it very manifest to his majesty that his
residence would not be suffered to continue longer in France
after the alliance should be published with Cromwell; which
was not yet perfected, by the cardinal's blushing to consent to
some propositions without which the other's fast friendship was
not to be obtained, and he was not willing that modesty should
be conquered at once, though every body knew it would quickly
be prostituted.

54. There could be no doubt but that the King was heartily
weary of being in a place where he was so ill treated, and where
he lived so uncomfortably, and from whence he foresaw that he
should soon be driven. But as he had no money to enable him
to remove, or to pay the debts he owed there, so he knew not
to what place to repair where he might find a civil reception.
Holland was bound not to admit him into their dominions, and
by their example had shewed other princes and states what
conditions they must submit to who would be allies to Cromwell. The King of Spain was at the same time contending
with France for his [Cromwell's] friendship, and thought he
had some advantage by the residence his majesty had there [in
France:] and so there could be no thought of repairing into
Flanders, and that he could be admitted to stay there. The
Protestants, in all places, expressed much more inclination to
his rebels than to him ; and the Roman Catholics looked upon
him as in so desperate a condition, as that he would in a short
time be necessitated to throw himself into their arms by changing his religion, without which they all declared they would
never give him the least assistance. In this distress he resumed
the consideration he had formerly entered upon, of sending to

1653 the Diet, which was summoned by the Emperor to meet shortly at Ratisbon, to make choice of a King of the Romans; [as to] which, Germany being then in peace, the Emperor made little doubt of finding a concurrence in the choice of the King of Hungary, his eldest son, to be made King of the Romans, and thereby to be sure to succeed him in the empire. And he had long promised the lord Wilmott to send him on that errand, to try what the Emperor and princes of Germany [would do] in such a conjunction, towards the uniting all other princes with themselves, in undertaking a quarrel they were all concerned in, to restore so injured and oppressed a prince by so odious a rebellion; and in the mean time, of which there seemed to be more hope, what contribution they would make towards his support; and likewise, upon this occasion, some fit place might be found in the nearest parts of Germany for the King to repair to, and where he might attend his better destiny.

55. Though it was more suitable to the occasion, and the necessity of the King's condition, that this affair should be despatched in as private a way as was possible, and with as little expense, it being impossible to send an ambassador in such an equipage as, at such an illustrious convention of all the princes of the empire, was necessary if he pretended to that character, [yet[1]] Wilmott pressed very much for the character, that he might the more easily accomplish his being made an earl, for which he had obtained the King's promise in a fit season. And he took great pains to persuade the King that this was a proper season, and very much for the advancement of his service: and that if he had the title of an earl, which would be looked upon as a high qualification, he would not assume the character of ambassador, though he would carry such a commission with him, but make all his negotiation as a private envoy; of which he promised the King wonderful effects, and pretended to have great assurance of money, and of making levies of men for any expedition. The King, rather to comply with the general expectation, and to do all that was in his power to do, than out **1652** **Dec. 13.** of any hope of notable advantage from this agitation, was con-

---

[1] ['and,' MS.]

tented to make him earl of Rochester, and gave him all such com- **1653** missions and credentials as were necessary for the employment; **1652** and sent him from Paris in the Christmas time, that he might ^{Dec. 21.} be at Ratisbon at the meeting of the Diet, which was to meet in the beginning of April following; means having been found to procure so much money as was necessary for that journey out of the assignment that had been made to the King for his support: of which there was a great arrear due, and which the cardinal caused at this time to be supplied, because he looked upon this sending to Ratisbon as a preparatory for the King's own remove.

56. Though Scotland was vanquished, and subdued to that degree that there was nor place nor person who made the least show of opposing Cromwell, who by the administration of Munke made the yoke very grievous to the whole nation, yet the preachers kept their pulpit license, and, more for the affront that was offered to Presbytery than the conscience of what was due to majesty, many of them presumed to pray for the King, and generally, though secretly, exasperated the minds of the people against the present government. The Highlanders, by the advantage of their situation, and the hardiness of that people, made frequent incursions in the night into the English quarters, and killed many of their soldiers, but stole more of their horses : and where there was most appearance of peace and subjection, if the soldiers straggled in the night, or went single in the day, they were always knocked in the head, and no inquiry could discover the malefactors.

57. Many expresses were sent to the King, as well from those who were prisoners in England as from some lords who were at liberty in Scotland, that Middleton might be sent into the Highlands with his majesty's commission; but in the mean time the earl of Glengarne, a gallant gentleman, if he were authorized by the King, would draw a body of horse and foot together in the Highlands, and infest the enemy, and be ready to submit to Middleton as soon as he should arrive there with a supply of arms and ammunition. And accordingly the King **1653** had sent a commission to the earl of Glengarne, who behaved March 4 [1].

---

[1] [*Calend. Clar. S. P.* ii. 319. The paper has no date of year, and is wrongly placed under 1654.]

1653 himself very worthily, and gave Munke some trouble. But he
pressing very earnestly that Middleton might be sent over, to
compose some animosities and emulation which were growing
up to the breaking of that union without which nothing could
succeed, his majesty, about the time that the earl of Rochester
1654 was despatched for Ratisbon, sent likewise Middleton into Scot-
Feb. land, with some few officers of that nation, and such a poor
supply of arms and ammunition as, by the activity and industry
of Middleton, could be gotten upon the credit and contribution
of some merchants and officers in Holland of that nation, who
were willing to redeem their country from the slavery it was in.
And with this very slender assistance he transported himself in
the winter into the Highlands; where, to welcome him, he found
the few whom he looked to find in arms more broken with
faction amongst themselves than by the enemy, nor was he able
to reconcile them. But after Glengarne had delivered his thin
unarmed troops to Middleton, and condescended to fight a duel
with an inferior officer who provoked him to it[1], after he was
out of his command, whether he was troubled to have another
command over him who, upon the matter, had no other men to
command but what were raised by him, (though he had exceedingly pressed his [Middleton's] being sent over to that purpose[2],)
or whether convinced with the impossibility of the attempt, he
retired first to his own house, and then made his peace with
Munke that he should live quietly; and retained still his affection and fidelity to the King, which he made manifest afterwards in a more favourable conjuncture ; and at the same time
excused himself to the King for giving over an enterprise which
he was not able to prosecute, though Middleton sustained it a
full year afterwards.

58. The truth is, the two persons who were most concerned
in that expedition had no degree of hope that it would be attended with any success, the King and Middleton ; who had both
seen an army of that people, well provided with all things necessary, not able to do any thing when they fought upon terms
more advantageous than people now drawn together by chance,

---

[1] [Sir George Monro.]   [2] [Cf. *Calend. Clar. S. P.* ii. 393-4.]

half armed and disciplined, were now like to contend [in] with **1654**
victorious troops, which wanted nothing, and would hardly part
with what they got. But his majesty could not refuse to give
them leave to attempt what they believed they could go through
[with;] and the other, who had promised them to come to them
when he was promised to be enabled to carry over with him two
thousand men and good store of arms, thought himself obliged
to venture his life with them who expected him, though he
could carry no more with him than is mentioned; and by his
behaviour there, notwithstanding all discouragements, he manifested how much he would have done if others had performed
half their promises.

59. It will not be amiss in this place to mention an adventure **1653**
that was made during his being in the Highlands, which de-
serves to be recorded for the honour of the undertakers. There
was attending upon the King a young gentleman, one Mr. Wogan,
a beautiful person, of the age of three or four and twenty. This
gentleman had, when he was a boy of fifteen or sixteen years,
been, by the corruption of some of his nearest friends, engaged
in the Parliament service against the King; where the emi-
nency of his courage made him so much taken notice of that he
was of general estimation, and beloved of all, but so much in
the friendship of Ireton, under whom he had the command of a
troop of horse, that no man was in so much credit with him.
By the time of the murder of the King he was so much improved in age and understanding, that, by that horrible and
impious murder, and by the information and advice of sober
men in his conversation, he grew into so great a detestation of
all that people that he thought of nothing but to repair his own
reputation by taking vengeance of those who had cozened and
misled him; and in order thereunto, as soon as the marquis of
Ormonde resumed the government of Ireland again for the King,
(which was the only place then where any arms were borne for
his majesty,) captain Wogan repaired thither to him, and behaved
himself with such signal valour, that the marquis of Ormonde
gave him the command of his own guards, and every man the
testimony of deserving it. He came over with him [the marquis]

1653 into France, and being restless to be in action, no sooner heard of Middleton's being arrived in Scotland than he resolved to find himself with him; and immediately asked the King's leave, not only for himself, but for as many of the young men about the Court as he could persuade to go with him, declaring to his majesty that he resolved to pass through England. The King, that had much grace for him, dissuaded him from the undertaking, for the difficulty and danger of it, and denied to give him leave. But neither his majesty nor the marquis of Ormonde could divert him; and his importunity continuing, he was left to follow his inclinations: and there was no news so much talked of in the Court as that captain Wogan would go into England, and from thence march into Scotland to general Middleton; and many young gentlemen, and others, who were in Paris, listed themselves with him for the expedition. He went then to the Chancellor [of the Exchequer,] who during the time of the King's stay in France executed the office of Secretary of State, to desire the despatch of such passes, letters, and commissions, as were necessary for the affair he had in hand. The Chancellor had much kindness for him; but, having heard by the common talk of the Court and from the loose discourses of some of those who resolved to go with him, presented the danger of the enterprise to himself, and the dishonour that would reflect upon the King for suffering men under his pass and with his commission to expose themselves to inevitable ruin: that it was now the discourse of the town, and would without doubt be known in England and to Cromwell before he and his friends could get thither, so that they would be apprehended the first minute in which they set their foot on shore; and how much his own particular person was more liable to danger than other men he knew well; and, upon the whole matter, very positively dissuaded him from proceeding farther.

60. He answered most of the particular considerations with contempt of the danger and confidence of going through with it, but with no kind of reason (which was a talent that did not abound in him) to make it appear probable. Whereupon the Chancellor expressly refused to make his despatches till he

could speak with the King; whom, he said, he would do the **1653** best he could to persuade to hinder his journey; with which the captain was provoked to so great passion that he broke into tears, and besought him not to dissuade the King ; and seemed so much transported with the resolution of the adventure as if he would not outlive the disappointment. And this passion so far prevailed with the King, that he caused all his despatches to be made and delivered to him. And the very next day he and his companions, being seven or eight in number, went out of Paris together, and took post for Calice.

61. They landed at Dover, continued their journey to London, walked the town, stayed there above three weeks, till they had bought horses, which they quartered at common inns, and listed men enough[1] of their friends and acquaintance to prosecute their purpose. And then they appointed their rendezvous at Barnet, marched out of London as Cromwell's soldiers, and from Barnet marched full fourscore horse, well armed and appointed, and quartered that night at St. Alban's ; and from thence, by easy journeys, but out of the common roads, marched safely into Scotland ; and then beat up some quarters which lay in their way, and without any misadventure joined Middleton[2] in the Highlands ; where poor Wogan, after many brave actions performed there, received upon a party an ordinary flesh wound, which for want of a good surgeon proved mortal to him, to the very great grief of Middleton and all who knew him. Many of the troop, when they could stay no longer there, found their way again through England, and returned to the King.

62. In the distress which the King suffered during his abode **1652.** in France, the Chancellor [of the Exchequer]'s part was the most uneasy and grievous. For though all who were angry with him were as angry with the marquis of Ormonde, who lived in great friendship with him, and was in the same trust with the King in all counsels which were reserved from others, yet [the marquis's] quality, and great services he had per-

[1] [fifty. *Calend. Clar. S. P.* ii. 286.]
[2] [Wogan arrived in Scotland in Dec. 1653, and was killed in Jan. 1654, before Middleton's arrival. See Whitlocke's *Memorials*, under dates of Jan. 24 and Feb. 17.]

1652 formed, and great sufferings he underwent for the Crown, made
him above all their exceptions; and [they] believed his aversion
from all their devices to make marriages, and to traffic in religion, proceeded most from the credit the other had with him.
But the Queen's displeasure was so notorious against the Chancellor, that after he found that she would not speak to him,
nor take any notice of him when she saw him, he forbore being
in her presence; and for many months did not see her face,
though he had the honour to lodge in the same house, the Palais
Royale, where both their majesties kept their Courts; which
encouraged all who desired to ingratiate themselves to her
majesty to express a great prejudice to the Chancellor, at least
to withdraw from his conversation; and the Queen was not
reserved in declaring that she did exceedingly desire to remove
him from the King, which nothing kept him from desiring too,
in so uncomfortable a condition, but the conscience of his duty,
and the confidence his majesty had in his fidelity.

63. This disinclination towards him produced at one and
the same time a conspiracy of an odd nature, and a union
between two very irreconcilable[1] factions, the Papists and the
Presbyterians: which was discovered to the King by a false
brother before the Chancellor had any intimation of it. The
lord Balcarris, with Dr. Frayzar, and some other Scots about
the Court, thought themselves enough qualified to undertake in
the name of the Presbyterians; and caused a petition to be
prepared, in which they set out that the Presbyterian party had
great affections to serve his majesty, and much power to do it,
and that they had many propositions and advices to offer to his
majesty for the advancement thereof, but that they were dis-
couraged and hindered from offering the same by reason that
his majesty intrusted his whole affairs to the Chancellor of the
Exchequer, who was an old known and declared enemy to all
their party, and in whom they could repose no trust; and
therefore they besought his majesty that he might be removed
from his counsels, at least not be suffered to be privy to any
thing that should be proposed by them; and they should then

[1] ['irreconcilable,' MS.]

make it appear how ready and how able they were in a very **1652**
short time to advance his majesty's affairs.

64. The petition prepared in the name of his majesty's
Catholic subjects said, that all his majesty's party which had
adhered to him were now totally suppressed, and had for the
most part compounded with his enemies, and submitted to their
government; that the church-lands were all sold, and the
bishops dead, except very few, who durst not exercise their
function, so that he could expect no more aid from any who
were concerned to support the government of the Church as
it had been formerly established: that by the defeat of duke
Hambleton's army first, and then by his majesty's [ill] success
at Worcester, and the total reduction of the kingdom of Scotland afterwards by Cromwell, his majesty might conclude what
greater aid he was to expect from the Presbyterian party.
Nothing therefore remained to him of hope for his restoration
but from the affection of his Roman Catholic subjects, who, as
they would never be wanting as to their persons, and their
estates which were left, so they had hope to draw from the
Catholic princes, and the Pope himself, such considerable assistance both in men and money, that his majesty should owe his
restitution, under the blessing of God, to the sole power and
assistance of the Catholics. But they had great reason to fear
that all these hopes would be obstructed and rendered of no
use, not only by there being no person about his majesty in
whom the Catholics could have any confidence, but by reason that
the person most trusted by him, and through whose hands all
letters and despatches must pass, is a known enemy to all Catholics; and therefore they besought his majesty that that person,
the Chancellor of the Exchequer, might be removed from him;
whereupon he should find great benefit to accrue to his service.
They concluded, that when these two petitions should be weighed
and considered, the Queen would easily convince his majesty, that
a person who was so odious to all the Roman Catholics, from
whose affections he had most reason to promise himself relief, and
to all Protestants who could contribute to his assistance or subsistence, could not be fit to be continued in any trust about him.

1652   65. When matters were thus adjusted, which were the longer in preparation because the persons concerned could not without suspicion and scandal meet together, but were to be treated with by persons mutually employed, one Mr. Walsingham, (a person very well known to all men who at that time knew the Palais Royale,) who had been employed in the affair, came to the King, and, whether out of ingenuity, and dislike of so foul a combination, or as he thought the discovery would be grateful to his majesty, informed [1] him of the whole intrigue, and gave a copy of the petitions to the King, who shewed them to the marquis of Ormonde and to the Chancellor, and informed them of the whole intrigue. And from this time his majesty made himself very merry with the design, and spake of it sometimes at dinner when the Queen was present, and asked pleasantly when the two petitions would be brought against the Chancellor; which being quickly known to some of the persons engaged in the prosecution, they gave it over, and thought not fit to proceed any farther in it; though both factions continued their implacable malice toward him, nor did he find any ease or quiet by the giving over that design, one breaking out after another as long as the King remained in France; the Queen taking all occasions to complain to the Queen Regent of the King's unkindness, that she might impute all that she disliked to the Chancellor, who [the Queen Regent] was like to be very tender in a point that so much concerned herself, that any man should dare to interpose between the mother and the son.

66. And there was an accident fell out that administered some argument to make those complaints appear more reasonable. The cardinal de Retz had always expressed great civilities towards the King, and a desire to serve him; and upon some occasional conference between them, the cardinal asked the King whether he had made any attempt to draw any assistance from the Pope, and whether he thought that nothing might be done that way to his advantage. The King told him nothing had been attempted that way by him, and he was better able to judge whether the Pope were like to do any thing to a man

[1] ['and informed,' MS.]

of his faith. The cardinal, smiling, said, he had no thought of speaking of his faith; yet, in short, spake of any overtures of the change of religion like a wise and an honest man, and told him it became him as a cardinal to wish his majesty a Catholic for the saving his soul, but he must declare too, that if he did [change his religion] he would never be restored to his kingdoms. But he said he did believe, though the Pope was old, and much decayed in his generosity, (for Innocent [X] was then living,) that if some proper application were made to the princes of Italy, and to the Pope himself, though there would not be gotten wherewithal to raise and maintain armies, there might be somewhat considerable obtained for his more pleasant support, wherever he should choose to reside. He said he had himself some alliance with the Great Duke, and interest in other Courts and in Rome itself, and if his majesty would give him leave, and trust his discretion, he would write in such a manner in his own name to some of his friends as should not be of any prejudice to his majesty if it brought him no convenience. The King had reason to acknowledge the obligation, and to leave it to his own wisdom what he would do. In the conclusion of the discourse, the cardinal asked his majesty a question or two of matter of fact, which he could not answer, but told him he would give a punctual information of it the next day in a letter; which the cardinal desired might be as soon as his majesty thought fit, because he would upon the receipt of it make his despatches into Italy. And the things being out of the King's memory, as soon as he returned, he asked the Chancellor concerning them; and having received a punctual account from him, he writ a letter the next day to the cardinal, and gave him information as to those particulars. Within very few days after this, the cardinal coming one day to the Louver to see the Queen [Regent,] he was arrested by the captain of the guard, and sent prisoner to the Bastille; and in one of his pockets, which they searched, that letter which the King had sent to him was found, and delivered to the Queen Regent, who presently imparted it to the Queen of England; and after they had made themselves merry with some

1652 improprieties in the French, the King having, for the secrecy, not consulted with any body, they discovered some purpose of applying to the Pope and to other Catholic princes ; and that his majesty should enter upon any such counsel without first consulting with the Queen his mother could proceed only from the instigation of the Chancellor.

67. And her majesty, with a very great proportion of sharpness, reproached the King for this neglect, and gave him his letter. The King was exceedingly sensible of the little respect the Queen mother had shewed towards him in the communicating his letter in that manner to his mother, and expostulated with her for it, and took that occasion to enlarge more upon the injustice of his mother's complaints than he had ever done. And from that time the Queen mother (who was in truth a very worthy lady) shewed much more kindness to the King. And a little time after, there being a masque at the Court that the King liked very well, he persuaded the Chancellor to see it ; and vouchsafed, the next night, to carry him thither himself, and to place the marquis of Ormonde and him next the seat where all their majesties were to sit. And when they entered, the Queen [Regent] asked who that fat man was who sat by the marquis of Ormonde ? The King told her aloud, that was the naughty man who did all the mischieve, and set him against his mother : at which the Queen herself was little less disordered than the Chancellor was, who blushed very much. But they within hearing laughed so much, that the Queen was not displeased ; and somewhat was spoken to his advantage, whom few thought to deserve the reproach.

1653 68. At this time the King was informed by the French Court, that prince Rupert, who had been so long absent, having gone with the fleet from Holland before the murder of the late March. King, and had not been heard of in some years, was now upon the coast of France, and soon after at Nantes[1], in the province of Bretagne[1], with the Swallow, a ship of the King's, and with three or four lesser ships : and that the Constant Reformation, another of the King's, in which prince Morrice had been, was

[1] [' Nance,' ' Britayne,' MS.]

cast away in the Indies near two years before; and that prince **1653**
Rupert himself was returned with very ill health. The King
sent presently to welcome him, and to invite him to Paris to
attend his health; and his majesty presumed that by the arrival
of this fleet, which he thought must be very rich, he should
receive some money that would enable him to remove out of
France, of which he was as weary as it was of him.

69. Great expectation was raised in the Court that there
would be some notable change upon the arrival of this prince,
and though he had professed much kindness to the Chancellor
when he parted from Holland, yet there was hope that he would
not appear now his friend, the rather for that he had left Ireland with some declared unkindness towards the marquis of
Ormonde. And all men knew that the Attorney General, (who
was unsatisfied with every body,) would have most influence
upon that prince, and that he could not be without credit
enough with the King to introduce him into business; which
they thought would at least lessen the Chancellor. In order to
which, it was no sooner known that prince Rupert was landed
in France but the lord Jermin visited and made great court to
sir Edward Harbert, between whom and him there had been
greater show of animosity than between any two of the nation
who were beyond the seas, they having for some years seldom
spoken to, never well of, each other; and Harbert, who was of
a rude and proud nature, declared publicly that he would have
no friendship with any man who believed the other to be an
honest man. Between these two a great friendship is suddenly
made; and the Attorney is every day with the Queen, who had
shewed a greater aversion from him than from any man, not
only upon the business of the duke of York but upon many
other occasions, but now she commended him to the King as a
wise man, of great experience, and of great interest in England.

70. From the death of sir Richard Lane[1], who had been
Keeper of the Great Seal under his late majesty, and afterwards

---

[1] [In Jersey, in 1650; probably in April or May, a letter from him dated
April 16 being endorsed by E. Nicholas as 'My Lord Keeper Lane's last
letter to me.' *Cal. Dom. S. P.* 1650, p. 111.]

1653 under this King, there had not only been no officer in that place, but from the defeat at Worcester the King had been without any Great Seal, which had been there lost. But he had lately employed a graver to prepare a Great Seal, which he kept himself, not intending to confer that office whilst he remained abroad. But now the Queen pressed the King very earnestly to make the Attorney General Lord Keeper of the Great Seal, which was a promotion very natural, men ordinarily rising from one office to the other. The King knew the man very well, and had neither esteem or kindness [for][1] him; yet he well foresaw that when prince Rupert came to him he should be pressed both by his mother and him so importunately that he should not with any ease be able to refuse it. Then he believed that if the man were himself in good humour, he would be of great use in composing any ill humour that should arise in the prince, to which he apprehended he might be apt to be inclined. And therefore he thought it best (since nobody dissuaded him from the thing) to oblige him frankly himself before the prince came, and so called him to his councils, and made him Keeper 1653 April. of the Great Seal, with which he seemed wonderfully delighted, and for some time lived well towards everybody; though as to anything of business, he appeared only in his old excellent faculty of raising doubts, and objecting against any thing that was proposed, and proposing nothing himself; which was a temper of understanding he could not rectify, and in the present state of affairs did less mischieve than it would have done in a time when any thing had been to have been done.

71. Before the prince came to Paris he gave the King such an account as made it evident that his majesty was to expect no money: what treasure had been gotten together, (which he confessed had amounted to great value,) had been all lost in the ship in which himself was, that sprung a plank in the Indies, when his highness was miraculously preserved, and in the boat 1651 Sept. 30. carried to another ship, when that, (the Antelope,) with all the men, and all that had been gotten, sunk in the sea; and much of 1652 Sept. 14. their other purchase had been likewise cast away in the ship in

[1] ['from,' MS.]

which his brother perished, which was after his own misfortune: **1653**
so that all that was brought into Nantes[1] would scarce pay off 1653
the seamen, and discharge some debts at Toulon[1] which the March.
prince had contracted at his former being there, during the time
that the King had been in Holland : [and] the ships were all so
eaten with worms, even the Swallow itself, that there was no
possibility of setting them out again to sea.   And this was all
the account the King could receive of that whole affair when
the prince himself came to Paris ; with which though the King April.
was not satisfied, yet he knew not how to remedy it, the prince
taking it very ill that any account should be required of him ;
and the Keeper quickly persuaded his highness that it was only
the Chancellor's influence that disposed the King with so much
strictness to examine his account.

72.   There was another design now set on foot, by which they
concluded they should sufficiently mortify the Chancellor, who
still had too much credit with his master.   When the King
went into Scotland, Mr. Robert Longe, who hath been mentioned before, was Secretary of State ; who, having been always
a creature of the Queen's, and dependent upon the lord Jermin,
had so behaved himself towards them during his short stay in
Scotland, (for he was one of those who was removed from the
King there, and sent out of that kingdom,) that when his
majesty returned from Worcester to Paris they would by no
means suffer that he should wait upon his majesty, and accused
him of much breach of trust and dishonesty, and amongst the
rest that he should say, which could be proved, that it was impossible for any man to serve the King honestly and to preserve
the good opinion of the Queen and keep the lord Jermin's
favour.   The truth is, that gentleman had not the good fortune
to be generally well thought of, and the King did not believe
him faultless, and therefore was contented to satisfy his mother, 1652
and would not permit him to execute his office, or to attend in Jan.
his councils.   Whereupon he left the Court, and lived privately
at Rouen ; which was the reason that the Chancellor had been
commanded to execute that place, which entitled him to so

[1] ['Nance,' 'Toloone,' MS.]

1653 much trouble. Upon this conjunction between the lord Jermin and the Keeper, the last of whom had in all times inveighed against Mr. Longe's want of fidelity, they agreed that there could not be a better expedient found out to lessen the Chancellor's credit than by restoring him again to the execution of the Secretary's function. Whereupon they sent for him, and advised him to prepare a petition to the King, that he might be again restored to his office and attendance, or that he might be charged with his crimes, and be farther punished if he did not clear himself and appear innocent. And this petition was presented to the King, when he was in Council, by the Queen, who came thither only for that purpose, and desired that it might be read; which being done, the King was surprised, having not in the least received any notice of it, and said, that her majesty was the principal cause that induced his majesty to remove him from his place, and that she then believed that he was not fit for the trust. She said, she had now a better opinion of him, and that she had been misinformed. The King thought it unfit to receive a person into so near a trust against whose fidelity there had been such public exception, and his majesty knew that few of his friends in England would correspond with him, and therefore would not be persuaded to restore him. This was again put all upon the Chancellor's account, and to the influence he had upon the King.

1654
Jan. 12. 73. Thereupon Mr. Longe accused the Chancellor of having betrayed the King, and undertook to prove that he had been over in England, and had private conference with Cromwell: which was an aspersion so impossible, that everybody laughed at it: yet because he undertook to prove it, the Chancellor pressed that a day might be appointed for him to produce his proof. And at that day the Queen came again to the Council that she might

Jan. 13. be present at the charge. There Mr. Longe produced Massonett, a man who had served him, and afterwards been an under-clerk for writing letters and commissions during the time of the King's being in Scotland, and had been taken prisoner at Worcester, and, being released with the rest of the King's servants, had been employed from the time of the King's return in the same

service under the Chancellor; the man having before the troubles **1654**
taught the King and the duke of York and the rest of the King's
children to write, being indeed the best writer in Latin as well as
English, for the fairness of the hand, of any man in that time [1].

74. He said, that after his release from his imprisonment,
and whilst he stayed in London, he spake with a maid who had
formerly served him, that knew the Chancellor very well, and
who assured him that one evening she had seen the Chancellor
go into Cromwell's chamber at Whitehall, and, after he had been
shut up with him some hours, she saw him conducted out again.
And Mr. Longe desired time, that he might send over for this
woman, who should appear and justify it. To this impossible
discourse, the Chancellor said he could make no other defence,
than that there were persons then in the town who, he was confident, would avow that they had seen him once every day from
the time he returned from Spain to the day on which he attended
his majesty at Paris; as indeed there [were [2];] and when he
had said so, he offered to go out of the room; which the King
would not have him to do. But he told his majesty that it was
the course, and that he ought not to be present at the debate
that was to concern himself; and the Keeper, with some warmth,
said it was true; and so he retired to his own chamber. The
lord Jermin, as soon as he was gone, said, he never thought the
accusation had any thing of probability in it, and that he believed the Chancellor a very honest man; but the use that he
thought ought to be made of this calumny was, that it appeared
that an honest and innocent man might be calumniated, as he
thought Mr. Longe had likewise been; and therefore they ought
both to be cleared. The Keeper said he saw not ground enough
to condemn the Chancellor, but he saw no cause neither to
declare him innocent; that there was one witness which declared only what he had heard, but he [Longe] undertook also
to produce the witness if he might have time, which in justice
could not be denied; and therefore he proposed that a com-

---

[1] [He was created M.D. at Oxford, by desire of Charles I, as being sub-
tutor to the Duke of York, April 8, 1646. *Convoc. Reg.* S 25. f. 103.]

[2] ['was,' MS.]

1654 petent time might be given to Mr. Longe to make out his proof, and that in the mean time the Chancellor might not repair to the Council. With which proposition the King was so offended, that, with much warmth, he said, he discerned well the design, and that it was so false and wicked a charge that if he had no other exception against Mr. Longe than this foul and foolish accusation, it was cause enough never to trust him. And therefore he presently sent for the Chancellor, and as soon as he came in commanded him to sit in his place, and told him he was sorry he was not in a condition to do more justice than to Jan. 13. declare him innocent; which he did do, and commanded the clerk of the Council to draw up a full order for his vindication, which his majesty himself would sign[1].

75. The Keeper could not contain himself from appearing very much troubled, and said, if what he heard from a person of honour, who he thought would justify it, were true, the Chancellor had aspersed the King in such a manner, and so much depraved him in point of his honour, that he was not fit to sit there. The Chancellor was wonderfully surprised with the charge, and humbly besought his majesty that the Lord Keeper might produce his author, or be looked upon as the contriver of the scandal. He answered, that if his majesty would appoint an hour the next day for the Council to meet, he would produce the person, who he was confident would justify all he had said.

76. The next day, the King being sat in Council, the Keeper desired that the lord Gerard might be called in; who presently appeared, and being asked whether he had at any time heard the Chancellor of the Exchequer speak ill of the King, he answered, 'Yes.' And thereupon he made a relation of a conference that had passed between the Chancellor and him a year before, when the King lay at Chantilly; that one day after dinner the King took the air, and being in the field his majesty alighted out of his coach, and took his horse with other of the lords to ride into the next field to see a dog set partridge; and that he, the lord Gerard, and the Chancellor remained in the coach, when he entered into discourse of the King's condition,

[1] [*Cal. Clar. S. P.* ii. 299, mis-dated Jan. 14. *Cal. Dom. S. P.* 1653–4, p. 359.]

and said he thought his majesty was not active enough, nor did **1654** think of his business, and that the Chancellor, who was known to have credit with him, ought to advise him to be active, for his honour and his interest ; otherwise his friends would fall from him ; but that it was generally believed that he, the Chancellor, had no mind that his majesty should put himself into action, but was rather for sitting still ; and therefore it concerned him, for his own justification, to persuade the King to be active, and to leave France, where he could not but observe that every body was weary of him. To all which the Chancellor took great pains to purge himself from being in the fault, and said that nobody could think that he could take delight to stay in a place where he was so ill used, but laid all the fault upon the King, who, he said, was indisposed to business, and took too much delight in pleasures, and did not love to take pains ; for which he was heartily sorry, but could not help it ; which, he [Gerard] said, he thought was a great reproach and scandal upon the King, from a man so obliged and trusted, who ought not to asperse his master in that manner.

77. The Chancellor was a little out of countenance, and said, he did not expect that accusation from any body, less that the lord Gerard should discover any private discourse that had passed a year before between them two, and which appeared by his relation to have been introduced by himself and by his own freedom ; that whosoever believed that he had a mind to traduce the King, would never believe that he would have chosen the lord Gerard, (who was known to be none of his friend,) to have communicated it to. He said, he did very well remember that the lord Gerard did, at that time when they two remained alone in the coach, very passionately censure the King's not being active, and blamed him, the Chancellor, for not persuading his majesty to put himself into action, and that he was generally believed to be in the fault. Upon which he had asked him what he did intend by being active, and what that action was, and where, to which he wished the King should be persuaded. He answered with an increase of passion and addition of oaths, that rather than sit still in France his majesty ought to go to every

1654 Court in Christendom ; that, instead of sending an ambassador
who was not fit for any business, he should have gone himself
to the Diet at Ratisbon, and solicited his own business, which
would have been more effectual; and that if he could not find
any other way to put himself into action, he ought to go into
the Highlands of Scotland to Middleton, and there try his
fortune. To all which, he [the Chancellor] said, he did remember
that he said he believed the King was indisposed to any of that
action he proposed: and though he did not believe that he had
used those expressions, of the King's delighting in pleasures, and
not loving business so well as he ought to do, if the lord Gerard
would positively affirm he had, he would rather confess it, and
submit himself to his majesty's judgment, if he thought such words
proceeded from any malice in his heart towards him, than, by
denying it, to continue the debate; and then he offered to retire,
which the King forbad him to do ; upon which the Keeper was
very angry, and said, the words amounted to an offence of a high
nature, and that he was sorry his majesty was no more sensible
of them : that for any man, especially a councillor, and a man
in so near trust, to accuse his master of not loving his business,
and being inclined to pleasures, was to do all he could to persuade all men to forsake him ; and proceeding with his usual
warm[th] and positiveness, the King interrupted him, and said,
he did really believe the Chancellor had used those very words,
because he had often said that, and much more, to himself, which
he had never taken ill : that he did really believe that he was
himself in fault, and did not enough delight in his business,
which was not very pleasant; but he did not know that such
putting himself into action, which was the common word, as the
lord Gerard advised, was like to be attended with those benefits
which, he was confident, he wished. In fine, he declared he
was very well satisfied in the Chancellor's affection, and took
nothing ill that he had said : and directed the clerk of the
Council to enter such his majesty's declaration in his book ; with
which both the Keeper and the lord Gerard were very ill satisfied. But from that time there were no farther public attempts
against the Chancellor during the time of his majesty's abode in

France.   But it may not be unseasonable to insert in this place, **1654**
that after the King's return into England there came the woman
to the Chancellor who had been carried over to Rouen by Massonett, and importuned by Mr. Longe to testify that she had
seen the Chancellor with Cromwell, for which she should have
a present liberal reward in money from him and a good service
at Paris ; which when the woman refused to do, he gave her
money for her journey, and so she returned : of which the
Chancellor informed the King.   But Mr. Longe himself coming
at the same time to him, and making great acknowledgments,
and asking pardon, the Chancellor frankly remitted the injury,
and would make no more words of it ; which Mr. Longe seemed
to acknowledge with great gratitude ever after.

78.   The King, wearied with these domestic vexations, as well
as with the uneasiness of his entertainment, and the change he
every day discovered in the countenance of the Court to him,
grew very impatient to leave France ; and though he was totally
disappointed of the expectation he had to receive money by the
return of prince Rupert with that fleet, he hoped that when the
prizes should be sold, and all the seamen discharged, and prince
Rupert satisfied his demands, which were very large, there
would be still left the ships and ordnance and tackling, which
(though they required great charge to be fitted out again to sea,)
he presumed would yield a good sum of money to enable him to
remove, and support him some time after he was removed ; for
there [were[1],] beside the ship itself, fifty good brass guns on
board the Swallow, which were very valuable.   His majesty
therefore writ to prince Rupert, (who was returned to Nantes[2],
to discharge some seamen who still remained, and to sell the
rest of the prizes,) that he would find some good chapmen to
buy all the ships and ordnance and tackle, at the value they
were worth : which was no sooner known at Nantes[2] than there
appeared chapmen enough, besides the marshal of Melleray, who,
being governor of that place and of the province, had much
money still by him to lay out on such occasions.   And the
prince writ the King word, that he had then a good chapman,

[1] ['was,' MS.]   [2] ['Nance,' MS.]

1654 who would pay well for the brass cannon, and that he should
put off all the rest at good rates.   But he writ again the next
week, that, when he had even finished the contract for the brass
cannon, there came an order from the Court that no man should
presume to buy the brass cannon, and to marshal Melleray to
take care that they were not carried out of that port.

79. The prince apprehended that this unexpected restraint
proceeded from some claim and demand from Cromwell, and
then expected that it would likewise relate to the Swallow
itself, if not to all the other ships ; and the marshal contributed
to and cherished this jealousy, that the better markets might be
made of all the rest, himself being always a sharer with the
merchants who made any purchases of that kind ; as he had
from the time that his highness first came into that port always
insinuated into him, in confidence, and under great good-will
and trust, that he should use all expedition in the sale of the
prizes, lest either Cromwell should demand the whole, (which
he much doubted,) or that the merchants, owners of the goods,
should, upon the hearing where they were, send and arrest the
said ships and goods, and demand restitution to be made of
them in a course of justice ; in either of which cases, he said,
he did not know, considering how things stood with England,
what the Court would determine ; though he promised he would
extend his authority to serve the prince, as far as he could with
his own safety, and defer the publishing and execution of any
orders he should receive till the prince might facilitate the despatch ; and by this kind advice very good bargains had been
made for those goods which had been sold ; of which the marshal had an account to his own desire.

80. But when upon this unwelcome advertisement the King
made his address to the cardinal to revoke this order, and, as
the best reason to oblige him to gratify him, told him that the
money which should be raised upon the sale of these cannon was
the only means he had to remove himself out of France, which
he intended shortly to do, and to go to the hither parts of Germany, and that his sister, the Princess of Aurange, and he had
some thoughts of finding themselves together, in the beginning

of the summer, at the Spaw (which indeed had newly entered 1654 into the King's consideration, and had been entertained by the Princess Royal) the cardinal, being well pleased with the reason, told his majesty that this order was not newly made, but had been very ancient, that no merchants or any private subjects should buy any brass ordnance in any port, lest ill use might be made of them; and that the order was not now revived with any purpose to bring any prejudice to his majesty, who should be no loser by the restraint, for that he himself would buy the ordnance, and give as much for them as they were worth; in order to which, he would forthwith send an agent to Nantes[1] April. to see the cannon, and, upon conference with a person employed by the King, they two should agree upon the price, and then the money should be all paid together to his majesty in Paris; intimating that he would dispute the matter afterwards with Cromwell, as if he knew or foresaw that he would make some demand.

81. It was well for the King that this condition was made for the payment of this money in Paris, for of all the money paid or received at Nantes[1], as well for the ships, tackle, and ordnance, as for the prize-goods, not one penny ever came to the King's hands, or to his use, but what he received at Paris from the cardinal for the brass guns which were upon the Swallow, for the valuing whereof the King sent one thither to treat with the officer of the cardinal. All the rest was disposed, as well as received, by prince Rupert, who when he returned to Paris gave his majesty a confused account, and averred that the expenses had been so great that there was not only no money remaining in his hands but that there was a debt still due to a merchant, which he desired his majesty to promise to satisfy.

82. The King's resolution to go into Germany was very grateful to every body, more from the weariness they had of France than from the foresight of any benefit and advantage that was like to accrue by the remove. But his majesty, who needed no spurs for that journey, was the more disposed to it by the extraordinary importunity of his friends in England, who, observing the strict correspondence that was between the

[1] ['Nance,' MS.]

1654 cardinal and Cromwell, and [knowing[1]] that the alliance between them was very near concluded, and [being[2]] informed that
there were conditions agreed upon which were very prejudicial
to the King, did really apprehend that his majesty's person
May. might be given up; and thereupon they sent Harry Seymour,
who, being of his majesty's bedchamber, and having his leave to
attend his own affairs in England, they well knew would be believed by the King, and being addressed only to the marquis of
Ormonde and the Chancellor [of the Exchequer,] he might have
opportunity to speak with the King privately and undiscovered,
and return again with security, as he and all messengers of that
kind frequently did.   He was sent by the marquis of Hartford
and the earl of Southampton, with the privity of those few who
were trusted by them, to be very importunate with the King
that he would remove out of France, and to communicate all
which they received from persons who were admitted into many
of the secret resolutions and purposes of Cromwell.   And because they well knew in what straits the King was for money,
they found some means at that time to send him a supply of
about three thousand pounds, which the King received and kept
with marvellous secresy[3].   And they sent him word likewise,
that, wherever he should choose to reside out of France, they
were confident his servants in England (under what persecution
soever they lay) would send him some supply, but whilst he remained in France nobody would be prevailed with to send to
him.   The King was glad to be confirmed in the resolution he
had taken by his friends' advice, and that they had in some degree enabled him to prosecute it; which was the more valuable
because it was known to none.   Yet his debts were so great in
Paris, and the servants who were to attend him in so ill a condition, and so without all conveniences for a journey, that if the
cardinal, over and above the money for the cannon, (which he
did not desire to receive till the last,) did not take care for the
payment of all the arrears which were due upon the assignment
they had made to him, he should not be able to make his journey.

---

[1] ['knew,' MS.]   [2] ['were,' MS.]
[3] [See *Calend. Clar. S. P.* ii. 361.]

83. But in this he received some ease quickly; for when the 1654 cardinal was satisfied that his majesty had a full resolution to be gone, which he still doubted till he heard from Holland that the Princess Royal did really provide for her journey to the Spaw, he did let the King know, that, against the time that his majesty appointed his remove, his arrears should be either entirely paid, or so much of his debts secured to his creditors as should well satisfy them, and the rest should be paid to his receiver for the charge of the journey; and likewise assured his majesty that for the future time the monthly assignation should be punctually paid to whomsoever his majesty would appoint to receive it. And this promise was better complied with than any other that had been made, until, some years after [1], the King thought fit to decline the receiving thereof; which will be remembered in its place [2].

84. All things being in this state, he declared his resolution to begin his journey as soon as he could put himself into a capacity of moving upon the receipt of the money he expected, and all preparations were made for enabling the family to be ready to wait upon his majesty, and for the better regulating and governing it when the King should be out of France; there having never been any order put in it whilst he remained there, nor could be, because his majesty had always eaten with the Queen, and her officers had governed the expense; so that by the failing of receiving the money that was promised, and by the Queen's officers receiving all that was paid, to carry on the expense of their majesties' table, which the King's servants durst not inquire into, very few of his majesty's servants had received any wages from the time of his coming from Worcester to the remove he was now to make. Nor was it possible now to satisfy them what they might in justice expect, but they were to be contented with such a proportion as could be spared, and which might enable them without reproach and scandal to attend and leave Paris. And they were all modest in their desires, hoping that they should be better provided for in another place. But now the King met with an obstruction that he least ex-

[1] [two years after.] [2] [book xv. § 69.]

1654 pected, from the wonderful narrowness of the cardinal's nature, and his over good husbandry in bargaining. The agent he had sent to Nantes [1] to view the cannon made so many scruples and exceptions upon the price, and upon the weight, that spent much time, and at last offered much less than they were worth, and than the other merchant had offered when the injunction came that restrained him from proceeding. The King knew not what to propose in this. The cardinal said he understood not the price of cannon himself, and therefore he had employed a man that did, and it was reasonable for him to govern himself by his conduct, who assured him that he had offered as much as they could reasonably be valued at. It was moved on the King's behalf that he would permit others to buy them, which he said he could not do, because of the [French] King's restraint; and if any merchant or other person should agree for them, Cromwell would demand them wherever they should be found; and there were not many that would dispute the right with him. In conclusion, the King was compelled to refer the matter to [the cardinal] himself, and to accept what he was content to pay; and when all was agreed upon according to his own pleasure, he required new abatements in the manner of payment of the money, as, allowance for paying it in gold, and the like, fitter to be insisted on by the meanest merchant than by a member of the sacred college, who would be esteemed a prince of the Church.

85. Whilst the King was preparing for his journey, he received news that pleased him very well, and looked like some addition of strength to him. After the duke of York had made his escape from St. James', where he and the rest of the royal family that remained in England were under the care and tuition of the earl of Northumberland, the Parliament would not suffer, nor did the earl desire, that the rest should remain longer under his government. But the other three, two princesses [2] 1649 and the duke of Gloster, were committed to the countess of May 24. Leicester, to whom such an allowance was paid out of the treasury as might well defray their expenses with that respect that

[1] ['Nantz,' MS.]   [2] [One, the princess Elizabeth.]

was due to their birth: which was performed towards them as **1654** long as the King their father lived. But as soon as the King was murdered, it was ordered that the children should be removed into the country, that they might not be the objects of respect, to draw the eyes and application of people towards them. The allowance was retrenched, that their attendants and servants might be lessened, and order was given that they should be treated without any addition of titles, and that they should sit at their meat as the children of the family did, and all at one table. Whereupon they were removed to Penshurst, a house of **1649** the earl of Leicester's in Kent, where they lived under the **June 11.** tuition of the same countess, who observed the order of the Parliament with obedience enough; yet they were carefully looked to, and treated with as much respect as the lady pretended she durst pay to them.

86. There, by an act of Providence, an honest man [1], who had been recommended to teach the earl of Sunderland, whose mother was a daughter of the house, became likewise tutor to the duke of Gloster; who was by that means well taught in that learning that was fit for his years, and very well instructed in the principles of religion and the duty that he owed to the King his brother: all which made the deeper impression in his very pregnant nature by what his memory retained of those instructions which the King his father had, with much fervour, given him before his death. One of the princesses died at Penshurst [2], and shortly after the other princess and the duke of Gloster were removed from the government of the countess of Leicester, and sent into the Isle of Wight to Carisbrooke Castle, where Mildmay was captain, and the care of them committed to him, **1650** with an assignation for their maintenance, which he was to **July 29.** order, and which in truth was given as a boon to him; and he was required strictly that no person should be permitted to kiss their hands, or that they should be otherwise treated than as the children of a gentleman; which Mildmay observed very exactly,

---

[1] [R. Lovell.]
[2] [A strange mistake; there was no other princess in custody besides the princess Elizabeth.]

1654 and the duke of Gloster was not called by any other style than 'Mr. Harry.' The tutor was continued, and sent thither with him; which pleased him very well. And here they remained

1650 at least two or three years. The princess died in this place,
Sept. 8. and, according to the charity of that time towards Cromwell, very many would have it believed to be by poison; of which there was no appearance, nor any proof ever after made of it.

87. But whether this reproach and suspicion made any impression in the mind of Cromwell, or whether he had any jealousy that the duke of Gloster, who was now about fourteen years of age, and a prince of extraordinary hopes, both from the comeliness and gracefulness of his person and the vivacity and vigour of his wit and understanding, which made him much spoken of, might at some time or other be made use of by the discontented party of his own army to give him trouble, or whether he would shew the contempt he had of the royal family, by sending another of it into the world to try his fortune, he did declare one day to his council, that he was well content that the son of the late King who was then in Carisbrooke Castle should have liberty to transport himself into any parts beyond the seas as he should desire; which was at that time much wondered at, and not believed, and many thought it a presage of a worse inclination; and for some time there was no more speech of it. But notice and advice being sent to the duke by those who wished his liberty that he should prosecute the obtaining that order and release, he, who desired most to be out of restraint, sent his tutor, Mr. Lovell, to London, to be advised by friends what he should do to procure such an order and warrant as was necessary for his transportation. And he, by the advice of those who wished well to the affair, did so dexterously solicit it, that he

1653 did not only procure an order from the council that gave him
Jan. 17. liberty to go over seas with the duke, and to require Mildmay to permit them to embark, but likewise five hundred pounds from the commissioners of the treasury, which he received to defray the charges and expenses of the voyage[1]; being left to
Feb. 11. provide a ship himself, and being obliged to embark at the Isle

[1] [and £500 afterwards: *Cal. Dom. S.P.* 1653, p. 103.]

of Wight, and not to suffer the duke to go on shore in any other part of England [1]. **1654**

88. And this was so well prosecuted, that, at the time when the King was making his preparations ready to leave France, he received advertisement from his sister in Holland that the duke of Gloster was arrived there, and would be the next day with her; which was no sooner known than the Queen very earnestly desired that he might be presently sent for to Paris, that she might see him; which she had never done since he was three months [2] old; for within such a short time after he was born the troubles were so far advanced that her majesty made her voyage into Holland, and from that time had never seen him. The King could not refuse to satisfy his mother in so reasonable a desire, though he did then suspect that there might be a farther purpose in that design of seeing him than was then owned; and therefore he despatched presently a messenger to the Hague, that his brother might make all possible haste to Paris; his majesty having nothing more in his resolution than that his brother should not make any stay in France, but that he should return again with him into Germany; and with this determination of the King's he was presently sent for, and came safely to Paris, to the satisfaction of all who saw him. **1653 March.**

May 21, N.S.

89. All expedition was used to provide for the King's remove, so generally desired of all; and the future charge of governing the expenses of the family, and of payment of the wages of the servants, and indeed of issuing out all moneys, as well in journeys as when the Court resided any where, was committed to Stephen Fox, a young man bred under the severe discipline of the lord Percy, who was now Chamberlain of the King's household, and very well qualified with languages and all other parts of clerkship, honesty, and discretion, that were necessary for the discharge of such a trust; and indeed his great industry, modesty, and prudence did very much contribute to the bringing the family, which for so many years had been under no government, into

---

[1] [He was allowed to land at Dover on Feb. 14. *Cal. Dom. S. P.* 1652-3, p. 164.]

[2] [about eighteen months.]

1654 very good order ; by which his majesty, in the pinching straits of
his condition, enjoyed very much ease from the time he left Paris.

90. Prince Rupert was now returned from Nantes[1], and
finding that he should receive none of the money the cardinal
was to pay for the brass ordnance, and being every day more
indisposed by the chagrin[2] humour of the Keeper, (who endeavoured to inflame him against the King, as well as against
most other men, and thought [his highness] did not give evidence
enough of his concernment and friendship for him except he fell
out with everybody with whom he was angry,) resolved to leave
the King ; wrought upon, no doubt, beside the frowardness of
the other man, by the despair that seemed to attend the King's
fortune ; and told his majesty that he was resolved to look after
his own affairs in Germany, and first to visit his brother in the
Palatinate, and require what was due from him for his appanage,
and then to go to the Emperor, to receive the money that was
due to him upon the treaty of Munster, which was to be all paid
by the Emperor : from the prosecution of which purpose his
majesty did not dissuade him, and possibly heard it with more
indifferency than the prince expected ; which more raised his
natural passion ; insomuch as, the day when he took his leave,
that nobody might imagine that he had any thoughts ever to
return to have any relation to or dependence upon the King,
he told his majesty, that, if he pleased, he might dispose of the
place of the Mastership of the Horse, in which he had been
settled by the last King ; and his present majesty had, to pre-
1653 serve that office for him, and to take away the pretence the lord
May[3]. Percy might have to it by his having had that office to the Prince
1653 of Wales, recompensed him with the place of Chamberlain, though
Oct. 23, not to his full content.   But the King bore this resignation like-
N. S.[4] wise from the prince with the same countenance as he had done
his first resolution ; and so, towards the end of April or the be-
1654 ginning of May, his highness left the King, and began his journey
June 5, for the Palatinate.
N. S.[5]
91. Shortly after the prince was gone, the King began to

---

[1] ['Nantz,' MS.]   [2] ['shaggringe,' MS.]
[3] [*Calend. Clar. S. P.* ii. 206.]   [4] [*Ibid.* 265.]   [5] [*Ibid.* 364.]

think of a day for his own departure, and to make a list of his 1654
servants which he intended should wait upon him.   He foresaw
that the only end of his journey was to find some place where
he might securely attend such a conjuncture as God Almighty
should give him, that might invite him to new activity, his
present business being to be quiet; and therefore he was wont
to say, that he would provide the best he could for it by having
only such about him as could be quiet.   He could not forget
the vexation the Lord Keeper had always given him, and how
impossible it was for him to live easily with any body, and so,
in the making the list of those who were to go with him, he left
his name out; which he [the Keeper] could not be long without Saturday,
knowing, and thereupon he came to the King, and asked him May 30,
whether he did not intend that he should wait upon him.   His N. S.[1]
majesty told him, 'No,' for that he resolved to make no use of
his Great Seal; and therefore that he should stay at Paris, and
not put himself to the trouble of such a journey which he himself intended to make without the ease and benefit of a coach:
which in truth he did, putting his coach-horses into a waggon,
wherein his bed and clothes were carried, nor was he owner of
a coach in some years after.   The Keeper expostulated with
him in vain upon the dishonour that it would be to him to be
left behind; and the next day brought his Great Seal, and Monday,
delivered it to him, and desired that he would sign a paper, June 1,
in which his majesty acknowledged that he had received again N. S.[2]
his Great Seal from him; which the King very willingly
signed; and he immediately removed his lodging, and left the
Court, and never after saw his majesty; which did not at all
please the Queen, who was as much troubled that he was to
stay where she was as that he did not go with the King.

92. The Queen prevailed with the King, at parting, in a
particular in which he had fortified himself to deny her, which
was, that he would leave the duke of Gloster with her; which
she importuned him so much, that, without very much dis-
obliging her, he could not resist.   She desired him to consider
in what condition he had been bred, without learning either

[1] [*Clar. S. P.* iii. 245.]   [2] [*Ibid.* 246; *Calend. Clar. S. P.* ii. 365.]

1654 exercise or language, or having ever seen a Court or good
company; and being now in a place, and he at an age, that
might be instructed in all these, to carry him away from all
these advantages, to live in Germany, would be interpreted by
all the world not only to be want of kindness towards his
brother but want of all manner of respect to her. The reason-
ableness of this discourse, together with the King's utter disability to support him in the condition that was fit for him,
would easily have prevailed, if it had not been the fear that the
purpose was to pervert him in his religion; which when the
Queen had assured the King was not in her thought, and that
she would not permit any such attempt to be made, his majesty
consented to it.

93. And now the day being appointed for his majesty to
begin his journey, the King desired that the Chancellor [of the
Exchequer] might likewise part in the Queen's good grace, at
least without her notable disfavour, which had been so severe
towards him that he had for some months not presumed to be
in her presence: so that though he was very desirous to kiss
her majesty's hand, he knew not how to make any advance
towards it. But the day before the King was to be gone, the
lord Percy, who was directed by his majesty to speak in the
affair, and who in truth had kindness for the Chancellor, and
knew the prejudice against him to be very unjust, brought him
word that the Queen was content to see him, and that he would
accompany him to her in the afternoon. And accordingly at
the hour appointed by her majesty they found her alone in her
private gallery; and the lord Percy withdrawing to the other
end of the room, the Chancellor told her majesty, that now she
had vouchsafed to admit him into her presence, he hoped she
would let him know the ground of the displeasure she had conceived against him; that so, having vindicated himself from
any fault towards her majesty, he might leave her with a
confidence in his duty, and receive her commands with an
assurance that they should be punctually obeyed by him. The
Queen, with a louder voice and more emotion than she was
accustomed to, told him, that she had been contented to see

him, and to give him leave to kiss her hand, to comply with the **1654**
King's desires, who had importuned her to it; otherwise, that
he lived in that manner towards her, that he had no reason to
expect to be welcome to her: that she need not assign any
particular miscarriage of his, since his disrespect towards her
was notorious to all men; and that all men took notice that he
never came where she was, though he lodged under her roof,
(for the house was hers,) and that she thought she had not seen
him in six months before, which she looked upon as so high
affront that only her respect towards the King prevailed with
her to endure it.

94. When her majesty made a pause, the Chancellor said
that her majesty had only mentioned his punishment, and
nothing of his fault: that how great soever his infirmities
were, in defect of understanding or in good manners, he had
yet never been in Bedlam, which he had deserved to be if he
had affected to publish to the world that he was in the Queen's
disfavour, by avoiding to be seen by her: that he had no kind
of apprehension that they who thought worst of him would
ever believe him to be such a fool as to provoke the wife of his
dead master, the greatness of whose affections to her was well
known to him, and the mother of the King, who subsisted by
her favour; and all this in France, where himself was a banished
person, and she at home, where she might oblige or disoblige
him at her pleasure. So that he was well assured that nobody
would think him guilty of so much folly and madness as not to
use all the endeavours he possibly could to obtain her grace and
protection: that it was very true he had been long without the
presumption of being in her majesty's presence, after he had
undergone many sharp instances of her displeasure, and after
he had observed some alteration and aversion in her majesty's
looks and countenance upon his coming into the room where
she was and during the time he stayed there; which others
likewise observed so much, that they withdrew from holding
any conversation with him in those places out of fear to offend
her majesty: that he had often desired, by several persons, to
know the cause of her majesty's displeasure, and that he might

1654 be admitted to clear himself from any unworthy suggestions which had been made before her majesty, but could never obtain that honour; and therefore he had conceived that he was obliged, in good manners, to remove so unacceptable an object from the eyes of her majesty by not coming into her presence, which all who knew him could not but know to be the greatest mortification that could be inflicted upon him; and therefore he most humbly besought her majesty at this audience, which might be the last he should receive of her, she would dismiss him with the knowledge of what he had done amiss, that he might be able to make his innocence and integrity appear, which he knew had been blasted by the malice of some persons, and thereby misunderstood and misinterpreted by her majesty. But all this prevailed not with her majesty, who, after she had, with her former passion, objected his credit with the King, and his endeavours to lessen that credit which she ought to have, concluded, that she should be glad to see reason to change her opinion; and so, carelessly extended her hand towards him, which he kissing, her majesty departed to her chamber.

95. It was about the beginning of June[1] in the year 1654 that the King left Paris; and because he made a private journey the first night, and did not join his family till the next day, which administered much occasion of discourse, and gave occasion to a bold person[2] to publish amongst the amours of the French Court a particular that reflected upon the person of the King, with less license than he used towards his own sovereign, it will not be amiss in this place to mention a preservation God then wrought for the King, little inferior to the greatest that is contained in the bundle of his mercies vouchsafed to him, and which shews the wonderful liberty that was then taken to promote their own designs and projects at the price of their master's honour and the interest of their country, or the sense they had of that honour and interest.

[1] [in July. *Cal. Clar. S. P.* ii. 382. July 10, N. S. Thurloe's *S. P.* ii. 418.]
[2] ['Bussy Rabutin;' bishop Warburton's note. The reference is to the 'Hist. d'Angelie et de Ginotic' in *Hist. amoreuse des Gaules.*]

96. There was at that time in the Court of France, or 1654
rather in the jealousy of that Court, a lady of great beauty [1],
of a presence very graceful and alluring, and a wit and behaviour that captivated those who were admitted into her
presence; her extraction was very noble, and her alliance the
best under the Crown, her fortune rather competent than
abounding for her degree, being the widow of a duke of an
illustrious name, who had been killed fighting for the King 1649
[of France] in the late troubles, and left his wife childless Feb. 8.
and in her full beauty. The King had often seen this lady,
with that esteem and inclination which few were without,
both her beauty and her wit deserving the homage that was
paid to her. The earl of Bristol, who was then a lieutenant
general in the French army, and always amorously inclined,
and the more inclined by the difficulty of the attempt, was
grown powerfully in love with this lady, and, to have the more
power with her, communicated those secrets of state which
concerned her safety, and more the prince of Condé, whose
cousin german she was, and the communication whereof was
of benefit or convenience to both; yet, though he made many
romantic attempts to ingratiate himself with her, and such as
would neither have become, or been safe to, any other man than
himself, who was accustomed to extraordinary flights in the air,
he could not arrive at the high success he proposed. At the
same time, the lord Crofts was transported with the same
ambition; and though his parts were very different from the
other's, yet he wanted not art and address to encourage him
in those attempts, and could bear repulses with more tranquillity of mind and acquiescence than the other could. When
these two lords had lamented to each other their mutual in-
felicity, they agreed generously to merit their mistress's favour
by doing her a service that should deserve it, and boldly proposed to her the marriage of the King, who, they both knew,
had no dislike of her person : and they pursued it with his
majesty with all their artifices. They added the reputation
of her wisdom and virtue to that of her beauty, and that she

[1] [The duchesse de Chastillon.]

1654 might be instrumental to the procuring more friends towards his restoration than any other expedient then was in view; and at last prevailed so far with the King, who no doubt had a perfect esteem of her, that he seriously made the overture to her of marriage ; which she received with her natural modesty and address, declaring herself to be much unworthy of that grace, and beseeching and advising him to preserve that affection and inclination for a subject more equal to him, and more capable to contribute to his service ; using all those arguments for refusal which might prevail with and inflame him to new importunities.

97. Though [these lords] made themselves upon this advance sure to go through with their design, yet they foresaw many obstructions in the way. The Queen, they knew, would never consent to it, and the French Court would obstruct it, as they had done that of mademoiselle; nor could they persuade the lady herself to depart from her dignity, and to use any of those arts which might expedite the design. The earl of Bristol therefore, that the news might not come to his friend the Chancellor by other hands, frankly imparted it to him, only as a passion of the King that had exceedingly transported him ; and then magnified the lady, as a person that would exceedingly cultivate the King's nature, and render him much more dexterous to advance his fortune : and therefore he professed that he could not dissuade his majesty from gratifying so noble an affection, and used many arguments to persuade the Chancellor to think very well of the choice. But when he found that he was so far from concurring with him, that he reproached his great presumption for interposing in an affair of so delicate a nature as by his conduct might prove the ruin of the King, he seemed resolved to prosecute it no farther, but to leave it entirely to the King's own inclination, who, upon serious reflections upon his own condition, and conference with those he trusted most, quickly concluded that such a marriage was not like to yield much advantage to his cause, and so resolved to decline any farther advance towards it. Yet the same persons persuaded him that it was a necessary generosity to take his last farewell of her ; and so, after he had

taken leave of his mother, he went so much out of his way as to 1654
visit her at her house, where those lords made their last effort;
and his majesty, with great esteem of the lady's virtue and
wisdom, the next day joined his family, and prosecuted his
journey towards Flanders; his small step out of the way having
raised a confident rumour in Paris that he was married to that
lady.

98. Though the King had received a pass from the archduke
for his passing through Flanders, so warily worded that he could
not but take notice that it was expected and provided for that
he should by no means make any unnecessary stay in his journey,
yet he found the gates of Cambray shut when he came thither,
and was compelled to stay long in the afternoon before they
were opened to receive him; which they excused by reason that
they understood the enemy was at hand, and intended to sit
down before that city; of which there appeared in the face of all
the people, and the governor himself, a terrible apprehension.
But upon recollection, his majesty was well received by the
governor, the conde of [   ][1] and treated and lodged that July 14,
night by him in his house, who was the better composed by his N.S.
majesty's assuring him that the French army was at a great
distance from him, and that his majesty had passed through it
the day before, (when marshall Turynn had drawn up the army
to receive his majesty, the duke of York having there likewise
taken his leave of the King,) and by the march that they then
appeared to make there was great reason to conclude that they
had no design upon Cambray; which good information made
the King's presence the more acceptable. But besides the
civility of that supper, and lodging that night, his majesty had
not the least address from the archduke, who was within four
or five leagues with his army, but passed without the least notice
taken of him through those provinces; so great a terror possessed
the hearts of the Spaniard, lest their shewing any respect to
the King in his passage through their country should incense
Cromwell against them, whose friendship they yet seemed to
have hope of.

[1] [*blank in MS.*]

99. His majesty intended to have made no stay, having received letters from the Hague that his sister was already in her
journey for the Spaw.　But when he came to Mons [1], he found
two gentlemen there [2] who came out of England, with letters
and instructions from those of his friends there who retained
their old affections, and recovered new courage from the general
discontent which possessed the kingdom, and which every day
increased by the continual oppressions and tyranny they sustained.　The taxes and impositions every day were augmented,
and Cromwell and his council did greater acts of sovereignty
than ever King and Parliament had attempted.　All gaols were
full of such persons who contradicted their commands, and were
suspected to wish well to the King ; and there appeared such a
rent amongst the officers of the army, that the Protector was
compelled to displace many of them, and to put more confiding
men in their places.　And [3] as this remedy was very necessary
to be applied for his security, so it proved of great reputation to
him, even beyond his own hope, or at least his confidence.　For
the license of the common soldiers, manifested in their general
and public discourses, censures, and reproaches of him and his
tyrannical proceedings, (which liberty he well knew was taken
by many that they might discover the affections and inclinations
of other men, and for his service,) did not much affect him, or
was not terrible to him, otherwise than as they were soldiers of
this or that regiment, and under this or that captain, whose
officers, he knew well, hated him, and who had their soldiers so
much at their devotion that they could lead them upon any
enterprise : and he knew well that this seditious spirit possessed
many of the principal officers both of horse and foot, who hated
him now in the same proportion that they had heretofore loved
him, above all the world.　And this loud distemper grew the
more formidable to him in that he did believe that the fire was
kindled and blown by Lambert, and that they were all conducted

---

[1] [' Monts,' MS. here, and in several instances below, from the Latin
form of the name, *Montes.*]

[2] [Col. John Stephens and ' Fa.' (Rich. Fanshawe ?) *Calend. Clar. S. P.* ii.
383–4.]

[3] [*Hist.* p. 29.]

and inspired by his melancholic and undiscerned spirit, though 1654
yet all things were outwardly very fair between them. Upon
this disquisition he saw hazard enough in attempting any reformation, (and which the army thought he durst not undertake to
do alone, and they feared not his proceeding by a council of war,
where they knew they had many friends,) but apparent danger,
and very probable ruin, if he deferred it. And so, trusting only
and depending upon his own stars, he cashiered ten or a dozen
officers, though not of the highest command and those whom he
most apprehended, yet of those petulant and active humours
which made them for the present most useful to the others and
most pernicious to him. And by this experiment he found the
example wrought great effects upon many who were not touched
by it, and that the men who had done so much mischieve, being
now reduced to a private condition and like other particular
men, did not only lose all their credit with the soldiers, but
behaved themselves with much more wariness and reservation
towards all other men. And this gave him more ease than
he had before enjoyed, and raised his resolution how to
proceed hereafter upon the like provocations, and gave him
great credit and authority with those who had believed
that many officers had a greater influence upon the army than
himself.

100 [1]. It was very evident that he had some war in his purpose ; for from the time that he had made a peace with the
Dutch, he took greater care to increase his stores and magazines
of arms and ammunition, and to build more ships, than he had
ever done before ; and he had given order to make ready two
great fleets against the winter, under officers who should have
no dependence upon each other ; and landmen were likewise appointed to be levied, some principal officers whereof
made great professions of duty to the King, and made tender
of their service to his majesty by these gentlemen. It
was thought necessary to make a day's stay at Mons, to
despatch those gentlemen, who were very well known, and
worthy to be trusted. Such commissions were prepared for

[1] [*Life,* p. 488.]

them, and such instructions, as were desired by those who employed them.

101. And his majesty gave nothing so much in charge to the messengers, and to all his friends in England with whom he had correspondence, as that they should live quietly, without making any desperate or unseasonable attempt, or giving advantage to those who watched them to put them into prisons and to ruin their estates and families. He told them the vanity of imagining that any insurrection could give any trouble to so well a formed and disciplined army, and the destruction that must attend such a rash and uncounsellable attempt: that as he would be always ready to venture his own person with them in any reasonable and well formed undertaking, so he would with patience attend God's own time for such an opportunity; and in the mean time he would sit still in such a convenient place as he should find willing to receive him; of which he could yet make no judgment: however [1], it was very necessary that such commissions should be in the hands of discreet and able men, in expectation of two contingencies which might reasonably be expected; the one, such a schism in the army as might divide it, upon contrary interests, into open contests and declarations against each other, which could not but produce an equal schism in the Parliament; [the other,] the death of Cromwell, which was conspired by the Levellers under several combinations; and if that fell out, it could hardly be imagined that the army would remain united to the particular design of any single person, but that the Parliament, which had been with so much violence turned out of doors by Cromwell, and which took itself to be perpetual, would quickly assemble again together, and take upon themselves the supreme government. Lambert, who was unquestionably the second person in the command of the army, and was thought to be the first in their affections, had had no less hand than Cromwell himself in the odious dissolution of that Parliament, and was principal in raising him to be Protector under the Instrument of Government; and so could never reasonably hope to be trusted and employed by them in the

[1] [*Hist.* p. 29.]

absolute command of an army that had already so notoriously 1654
rebelled against their masters.   Then Munke, who had the absolute command in Scotland, and was his rival already, under a
mutual jealousy, would never submit to the government of
Lambert, if he had no other title to it than his own presumption;
and Harry Cromwell had made himself so popular in Ireland,
that he would not probably be commanded by a man whom he
knew to be his father's greatest enemy.   These considerations
had made that impression upon those in England who were the
most wary and averse from any rash attempt, that they all
wished that commissions and all other necessary powers might
be granted by the King, and deposited in such good hands as
had the courage to trust themselves with the keeping them, till
such a conjuncture should fall out as is mentioned, and of which
few men thought there was reason to despair.

102[1]. The King having in this manner despatched those
messengers, and settled the best way he could to correspond
with his friends, he continued his journey from Mons to Namur[3], July 18,
where he had a pleasant passage by water to Liége; from N.S.[2]
whence, in five or six hours, he reached the Spaw the next day
after the Princess Royal, his beloved sister, was come thither,
and where they resolved to spend two or three months together;
which they did, to their singular content and satisfaction.   And
for some time the joy of being out of France, where his majesty
had enjoyed no other pleasure than being alive, and the delight
in the company he was now in, suspended all thoughts of what
place he was next to retire to.   For as it could not be fit for
his sister to stay longer from her own affairs in Holland than
the pretence of her health required, so the Spaw was a place
that nobody could stay longer in than the season for the waters
continued, which ended with the summer.

103. The King no sooner arrived at the Spaw than the earl
of Rochester returned thither to him from his negotiation at June 21,
Ratisbon, where he had wisely remained during the Diet with- N.S.[4]

[1] [*Life*, p. 488.]   [2] [Thurloe's *S. P.* ii. 451.
[3] ['Nemours,' MS., from a Latin form of the name, *Nemurcium*.]
[4] [*Calend. Clar. S. P.* ii. 385.]

1654 out owning the character he might have assumed, yet performed
all the offices with the Emperor and the other princes, with less
noise and expense, and with the same success as he could have
expected from any qualification.   The truth is, all the German
princes were at that time very poor ; and that meeting for the
choosing a King of the Romans was of vast expense to every
one of them, and full of faction and contradiction ; so that they
had little leisure, and less inclination, to think of any business
but what concerned themselves : yet in the close of the Diet, by
the conduct and dexterity of the Elector of Mentz, who was
esteemed the wisest and most practical prince of the empire,
and who out of mere generosity was exceedingly affected with
the ill fortune of the King, it was prevailed with to grant a
subsidy of four *Römer* months, which is the measure of all taxes
and impositions in Germany ; that is, by the *Römer* months,
which every prince is to pay, and cause it to be collected from
their subjects in their own method.   And this money was to be
paid towards the better support of the King of Great Britain.
And the Elector of Mentz, by his own example, persuaded as
many of the princes as he had credit with forthwith to pay
their proportions to the earl of Rochester, who was solicitous
enough to receive it.   The whole contribution, if it had been
generously made good, had not amounted to any considerable
sum upon so important an occasion.   But the Emperor himself
paid nothing, nor many other of the princes, amongst whom
were the Elector of Heydleburgh and the Lan[d]grave of Hesse
Cassell, both who had received great obligations both from King
James and the last King his son : so that the whole that was
ever paid to the King did not amount to the sum of ten thousand pounds sterling ; a great part whereof was spent in the
negotiation of the earl, and in the many journeys he made to
the princes, being extremely possessed with the spirit of being
the King's general, which he thought he should not be except
he made levies of men ; for which he was very solicitous to
make contracts with old German officers, when there was neither
port in view where he might embark them, nor a possibility of procuring ships to transport them, though Cromwell

had not been possessed of any naval power to have resisted. **1654**
So blind men are, whose passions are so strong, and their
judgments so weak, that they can look but upon one thing
at once.

104. That part of the money that was paid to his majesty's
use was managed with very good husbandry, and was a seasonable support to his well ordered family, which, with his own
expenses for his table and his stable, and the board-wages with
which all his servants from the highest to the lowest were well
satisfied, according to the establishment he made after he left
France, amounted not to above six hundred pistoles a month ;
which expense was not exceeded in many years, even until his
coming into Holland in order to his return into England. And
as this method in the managery gave the King great ease, so it
contented and kept the family in better order and humour than
could reasonably have been expected ; all which was then imputed to the care and industry of the Chancellor, and was the
more satisfactory by the no care and order that had been observed during all the residence the King had made in France.

105. The King stayed not so long at the Spaw as he meant
to have done, the small-pox breaking out there ; and one of the
young ladies who attended upon the Princess Royal, being
seized upon by it, died: so that his majesty and his sister
upon very sudden thoughts removed from the Spaw to [Aachen [1]], end of
or Aquisgrane, an imperial and free town, governed by their   Aug.[2]
own magistrates, and where the King of the Romans ought to
receive his first iron crown, which is kept there. It is famous
for its hot baths, whither many come after they have drunk the
cold waters of the Spaw, and was a part of the prescription
which the physicians had made to the Princess, after she should
have finished her course in the other place. And upon that
pretence, and for the use of those baths, the Courts removed
now thither, but in truth with a design that the King might
make his residence there, the town being large, and the country

---

[1] [Here and in following instances Hyde writes ' Acon,' or ' Acen,' as his
form for ' Aachen.']
[2] [Thurloe's *S. P.* ii. 547.]

1654 about it pleasant, and within five hours (for the journeys in those countries are measured by hours) of Ma[e]stricht, the most pleasant seat within the dominions of the United Provinces. The magistrates received the King so civilly, that his majesty, who knew no other place where he was sure to be admitted, resolved to stay there; and in order thereunto contracted for a convenient house, which belonged to one who was called a baron; whither he resolved to remove, as soon as his sister, who had taken the two great inns of the town for [her] [1] and the King's accommodation, should return into Holland.

106. Here the good old Secretary Nicholas, who had remained in Holland from the time that upon the treaty of Breda the King had transported himself into Scotland, presented himself to his majesty, who received him very graciously as a person of great merit and integrity from the beginning of the troubles, and always entirely trusted by the King his father. And to him the King gave his signet; which for three years had been kept by the Chancellor out of friendship, that it might be restored him, and had therefore refused in France to be admitted into the Secretary's office, which he executed, because he knew that they who advised it did it rather that Nicholas might not have it than out of any kindness to him. And he held himself obliged by the friendship that had ever been between them to preserve [it] for him; and as soon as he came to [Aachen], desired the King to declare him to be his Secretary; which was done, and by which he had a fast friend added to the Council and of general reputation [2].

107. Whilst the King remained at [Aachen] he received many expresses out of England, who informed [him] of the renewed courage of his friends there; that the faction and animosity which every day appeared between the officers of the army, and in the council upon particular interest, raised a general opinion and hope that there would be an absolute rup-

[1] ['hers,' MS.]
[2] [Here is omitted a long passage 'not pertinent to the public history of that time,' relative to the preferment of Hyde's daughter in the household of the Princess of Orange, which is printed in the *Life*.]

ture between them, when either party would be glad to make a **1654**
conjunction with the King's; and in order thereunto, there was
an intelligence entered into throughout the kingdom, that they
might make use of such an occasion. And they sent now to
the King, to be directed by him how they should behave themselves upon such and such contingencies, and sent for more commissions of the same kind as had been formerly sent to them.
The King renewed his commands to them not to flatter themselves with vain imaginations, not to give too easy credit to
appearances of factions and divisions, which would always be
counterfeited, that they might the more easily discover the
agitations and transactions of those upon whom they looked as
inveterate and irreconcilable[1] enemies to the government.

108. News came from Scotland that Middleton had some **June.**
successes in the Highlands, and the Scots' lords who were
prisoners in England assured the King that there was now so
entire a union in that nation for his service, that they wished
his majesty himself would venture thither; and the lord Balcarris, who was with the King, and intrusted by that people,
used much instance with him to that purpose; which, how unreasonable soever the advice seemed to be, men knew not how
to contradict by proposing any thing that seemed more reasonable; and so underwent the reproach of being laish[2] and un-
active, and unwilling to submit to any fatigue, or to expose
themselves to any danger; without which, his majesty could not
expect to be restored to any part of his sovereignty.

109. The Chancellor one day representing to the King the
misery of his condition, and the general discourses of men, and
that it was his majesty's misfortune to be thought by many not
to be active enough towards his own redemption, and to love his
ease too much, both for his age and his fortune, desired him to
consider, upon this news and importunity from Scotland,
whether in those Highlands there might not be such a safe
retreat and residence, that he might reasonably say that, with

---

[1] ['irreconciliable,' MS.]
[2] [altered to *lazy* in previous editions. Cf. book v. § 448, and vii. § 264,
note 2.]

1654 the affections of that people which had been always firm both to his father and himself, he might preserve himself in safety, though he could not hope to make any advance or recover the lower part of that kingdom possessed by the enemy; and if so, whether he might not expect the good hand of Providence by some revolution more honourably there, than in such corners of others' dominions as he might be forced to put himself into. His majesty discoursed very calmly of that country, part whereof he had seen; of the miserable poverty of the people, and their course of life, and how impossible it was for him to live there with security or with health : that if sickness did not destroy him, which he had reason to expect from the ill accommodation he must be there contented with, he should in a short time be betrayed and given up. And in this debate he told him that melancholic conclusion which David Lashly made at Warrington Bridge, which is mentioned before[1], when he told the King that those men would never fight; which his majesty had never, he said, told to any body before. However, he said, if his friends would advise him to that expedition, he would transport himself into the Highlands, though he knew what would come of it, and that they would be sorry for it, which stopped the Chancellor from ever saying more to that purpose. And it was not long after, before news came of Middleton's having been like to be given up to the enemy by the treachery of that people, and of some defeat his troops had received, and that he would be at last forced to quit that miserable country, which, however, he resolved to endure as long as should be possible.

110. The season of the year now began to approach that would oblige the Princess Royal to return to the Hague, lest the jealous States, from her long absence, might be induced to contrive some prejudicial act to her and her son ; which she was the more liable to, from the unkind differences which were between her and the princess dowager, mother of the deceased Prince of Orange, a lady of great cunning and dexterity to promote her own interest. The air of [Aachen[2]] and the ill smell of the baths made that place less agreeable to the King than at first he

---

[1] [book xiii. § 62.]   [2] ['Acen,' MS., here and in following instances.]

believed it to be, and he wished to find a better town to **1654**
reside in, which he might be put to endure long. The city
of Cullen was distant from [Aachen] two short days' journey,
and had the fame of an excellent situation. But the people
were reported to be of a proud and mutinous nature, always in
rebellion against their bishop and prince, and of so much bigotry
in religion that they had expelled all Protestants out of their
city, and would suffer no exercise of religion but of the Roman
Catholic. So that there seemed little hope that they would
permit the King to reside there; the rather, because it was the
staple for the wines of that country, and maintained a good intelligence and trade with England. If the King should send
thither to provide a house, and declare his purpose to stay there,
and they should refuse to receive him, it might be of a very ill
consequence, and fright any other place, and [Aachen] itself
from permitting him to return thither; and therefore that adventure was to be avoided. At last it was concluded that the
Princess Royal should make Cullen her way into Holland, which
was reasonable enough, by the convenience of the river for the
commodious transportation of her goods and family; and the
King, accompanying her so far, might make a judgment, upon
his observation, whether it would be best for him to stay there
or to return to [Aachen], where he would leave his family, as
the place where he had taken a house, and to which he meant in
few days to return. With this resolution they left [Aachen]
about the middle of September, and lodging one night at Juliers, Oct. 15,
(a little dirty town upon a flat, not worthy to have made a quarrel N.S.[1]
between all the princes of Europe, nor of the fame it got by the
siege,) they came the next day to Cullen; where they were received Oct. 16.
with all the respect, pomp, and magnificence that could be expected, or [the city[2]] could perform. The house, which the har-
bingers of the Princess had taken for her reception, served likewise
to accommodate the King; and the magistrates performed their
respects to both with all possible demonstration of civility.

111. Cullen is a city most pleasantly situated upon the banks
of the Rhine; of a large extent, and fair and substantial build-

---

[1] [Thurloe's *S. P.* ii. 646.]   [2] ['they,' MS.]

1654 ings; and encompassed with a broad and excellent wall, upon which are fair walks of great elms, where two coaches may go on breast, and for the beauty of it is not inferior to the walls of Antwerp, but rather superior, because [this[1]] goes round the town. The government is under the senate and consuls, of whom there was one then consul who was descended from father to son of a patrician Roman family, that had continued from the time the colony was first planted there. It had never been otherwise subject to the bishop than in some points which refer to his ecclesiastical jurisdiction, which they sometimes endeavouring to enlarge, the magistrates always oppose; which gives the subject of the discourse of jealousies and contests between their prince and them, which are neither so frequent nor of that moment as they are reported to be. The Elector never resides there, but keeps his court at the castle of Bon[n]e, near four miles from thence. And that Elector, who was of the House of Bavaria, and a melancholic and peevish man, had not then been in the city in very many years. The number of churches and religious houses is incredible, insomuch as it was then averred that the religious persons and churchmen made up a full moiety of the inhabitants of the town; and their interest and authority so far prevailed, that some few years before the King came thither they expelled all those of the Protestant religion, contrary to the advice of the wisest of the magistrates, who confess that the trade of the town was much decayed thereby, and the poverty thereof much increased. And it is very possible that the vast number and unskilful zeal of the ecclesiastical and religious persons may at some time expose that noble city to the surprise of some powerful prince, who will quickly deprive them of their long enjoyed privileges. And there was in that very time of the King's stay there a design by the French to have surprised it, [S]chomberg lying many days in wait there to have performed that service, which was very hardly prevented. The people are so much more civil than they were reported to be, that they seem to be the most conversable[2], and to understand the laws of society and conversation better than any other people

---

[1] ['they,' MS.]   [2] ['conversible,' MS.]

of Germany. To the King they were so devoted, that when **1654** they understood that he was not so fixed to the resolution of residing at [Aachen] but that he might be diverted from it, they very handsomely made tender to him of any accommodation that city could yield him, and of all the affection and duty they could pay him; which his majesty most willingly accepted; and, giving order for the payment of the rent for the house he had taken at [Aachen], which he had not at all used, and other disbursements which the master of the house had made to make it the more convenient for his majesty, and likewise sending very gracious letters to the magistrates of that town for the civility they had expressed towards him, he sent for that part of his family which remained there, to attend him at Cullen, where he declared he would spend that winter.

112. As soon as the King came to Cullen, he sent to the neighbour princes, by proper messages and insinuations, for that money which by the grant of the Diet, that is, by their own concession, they were obliged to pay to his majesty, which, though it amounted to no great sums, yet [was]¹ of great conveniency to his support. The Duke of Newburgh, whose court was at Disseldorp, a small day's journey from Cullen, and by which the Princess Royal was to pass if she made use of the river, sent his proportion very generously, and with many expressions of great respect and duty, and with insinuation that he would be glad to receive the honour of entertaining the King and his sister in his palace as she returned. However, he forebore to make any solemn invitation, without which they could not make the visit, without some ceremonies were first adjusted; upon which that nation is more punctual and obstinate than any other people in Europe. He who gave the intimation, and came only with a compliment to congratulate his majesty's and her royal highness's arrival in those parts, was well instructed in the particulars; of which there were only two of moment, and the rest were only formalities, upon which they might recede if those two were not consented to. The one was, that the King, at their first meeting, should at least once treat

¹ [' were,' MS.]

1654 the Duke with *Altesse*; the other, that the Duke might salute the
Princess Royal; and without consenting to these two there could
be no meeting between them. Both the King and his sister
were naturally enough inclined to new sights and festivities, and
the King thought it of moment to him to receive the respect and
civility of any of the German princes; and amongst them there
were few more considerable in their dominions, and none in their
persons, than the Duke of Newburgh, who reckoned himself
upon the same level with the Electors. And the King was informed that the Emperor himself always treated him with
Altesse, and therefore made no scruple of giving him the same.
The matter of saluting the Princess Royal was of a new and
delicate nature; and that dignity had been so punctually preserved from the time of her coming into Holland, that the old
Prince of Aurange, father of her husband, would never pretend
to it : yet that ceremony depending only upon the custom of
countries, (and every marshal of France having the privilege in
that kingdom to salute the daughters of the King,) and the Duke
of Newburgh being a sovereign prince, inferior to none in
Germany, and his ambassador always covering before the Emperor, the King thought fit, and her royal highness consented,
that the Duke should salute her. And so all matters being
adjusted without any noise[1], the King about the middle of
October accompanied his sister by water to Disseldorp; where
they arrived between three and four of the clock in the afternoon; and found the Duke and his duchess waiting for them on
the side of the water; where, after having performed their
mutual civilities and compliments, the King and the Princess
Royal and the Duke and the duchess went into the Duke's coach,
and the company into the coaches which were provided for them,
and alighted at the castle, that was very near; where his majesty
was conducted into his quarter, and the Princess into her's, the
Duke and the duchess immediately retiring into their own
quarters; where they new dressed themselves, and visited not
the King again till about half an hour before supper, and after
the King and Princess had performed their devotions.

Oct. 29,
N. S.[2]

---

[1] [See *Calend. Clar. S. P*. ii. 411.]   [2] [Thurloe's *S. P*. ii. 684.]

113. The castle is a very princely house, having been the seat 1654 of the duke of Cleve, which duchy, together with that of Juliers, having lately fallen to heirs females, (whereof the mothers of the Elector of Brandenburgh and Duke of Newburgh were two,) when all the pretenders seizing upon that which lay most convenient to them, this of Disseldorp, by agreement, afterwards remained still to Newburgh; whose father, being of the Reformed religion, in the late contention found the House of Brandenburgh too strong for him by having the prince of Aurange and the States his fast friends; and thereupon that he might have a strong support from the Emperor and King of Spain, became 1614 Catholic, and thereby had the assistance he expected. And at the same time he put his son, who was then very young, to be bred under the Jesuits, by which education the present Duke was with more than ordinary bigotry zealous in the Roman religion.

114. He was a man of very fine parts of knowledge, and in his manners and behaviour much the best bred of any German. He had the flowing civility and language of the French, enough restrained and controlled by the German gravity and formality; so that altogether he seemed a very accomplished prince, and became himself very well, having a good person and graceful motion, which that nation seldom attain to. He was at that time above thirty, and had been married to the sister of the 1642 former and the then King of Poland; who leaving only a daughter, he was now newly married to the daughter of the 1653 Lan[d]grave of Hesse D'Armstad[t], who upon her marriage Aug. 24. became Catholic. She had no eminent features of beauty, nor the French language and vivacity to contribute to the entertainment; so that she was rather a spectator of the festivity than a part of it, and confirmed the King in his aversion from ever marrying a German lady. The entertainment was very splendid and magnificent, in all preparations, as well for the tables which were prepared for the lords and the ladies, as that where his majesty and his sister and the duke and the duchess only sat: the meals, according to the custom of Germany, very long, with several sorts of music, both of instruments and voices, which if not excellent was new, and differed much from what his majesty

1654 was accustomed to hear. There was wine in abundance, but no man so much as wished to drink if he called not for it, and the duke himself an enemy to all excesses.

115. After two days spent in this manner, in which time the King made a great friendship with the Duke, which always Oct. 31, continued, they parted; and there being near the river, distant
N. S. another short day's journey, a handsome open town of good receipt, called Santoinge [1], belonging to that part of the duchy of Cleve which was assigned to the Elector of Brandenburgh, the King resolved to accompany his sister [thither;] where having spent that night, the next morning her royal highness, after an unwilling farewell, prosecuted her journey to Holland, Nov. 5, and his majesty returned by horse to Cullen, where the same
N. S. house was prepared for him in which he and his sister had inhabited whilst she stayed there. And by this time the end of October was come, which in those parts is more than the entrance into winter. The magistrates of the city renewed their civilities and professions of respect to the King; which they always made good; nor could his majesty have chosen a more convenient retreat in any place; and he, being well refreshed with the divertisements he had enjoyed, betook himself with great cheerfulness to compose his mind to his fortune, and with a marvellous contentedness prescribed so many hours in the day to his retirement in his closet, which he employed in reading and studying both the Italian and French languages; and at other times walked much upon the walls of the town, § 91. (for, as is said before, he had no coach, nor would suffer his sister to leave him one,) and sometimes rode into the fields; and in the whole spent his time very well.

116. The nuncio of the Pope resided in that city, and performed all respects to his majesty: he was a proper and grave man, an Italian bishop, who never made the least scruple at his majesty's enjoying the liberty of his chapel and the exercise of

---

[1] [Xancten. See *Calend. Clar. S. P.* ii. 417. The stay there was apparently for more than one night, as the King and his sister are said in a letter in Thurloe's *S. P.* ii. 694, to have parted on Wednesday, which was Nov. 4.]

his religion, though it was very public. So that in truth his 1654 majesty was not without any respect that could be shewed to him in those parts, save that the Elector never came to see him, though he lived within little more than an hour; which he excused by some indisposition of health, and unwillingness to enter into that city; though it proceeded as much from the sullenness and morosity of his nature, unapt for any conversation, and averse from all civilities; which made him for a long time to defer the payment of his small quota, which had been granted to the King by the Diet, and which was at last extorted from him by an importunity unfit to have been pressed upon any other prince or gentleman[1]. And this Elector's defect of urbanity was the more excusable, or the less to be complained of, since the Elector of Heydlebergh, so nearly allied to the Crown, and so much obliged by it, did not think fit to take any notice of the King's being so near him, or to send a messenger to salute him.

117. Within a short time after his majesty's return to Cullen, he received news that exceedingly afflicted him, and the more, that he knew not what remedy to apply to the mischieve which he saw would befall him. From Paris, he heard that the Queen had put away the tutor he had left to attend his brother the duke of Gloster, who remained at Paris upon her majesty's desire that he might learn his exercises. The Queen had con- Nov. 6. ferred with him upon the desperateness of his condition, in respect of the King his brother's fortune, and the little hope that appeared that his majesty could ever be restored, at least if he did not himself become Roman Catholic, whereby the Pope and other princes of that religion might be united in his quarrel, which they would never undertake upon any other obligation: that it was therefore fit that the duke, who had nothing to support him, nor could expect any thing from the King, should be instructed in the Catholic religion; that so, becoming a good Catholic, he might be capable of those advantages which her majesty should be able to procure for him: that the Queen of France would hereupon confer abbeys and

---

[1] [In June, 1655. Thurloe's *S. P.* iii. 561.]

1654 benefices upon him, to such a value as would maintain him in that splendour as was suitable to his birth; that in a little time the Pope would make him a cardinal, by which he might be able to do the King his brother much service, and contribute to his recovery; whereas without this he must be exposed to great necessity and misery, for that she was able no longer to give him maintenance. She found the duke more obstinate than she expected from his age; he was so well instructed in his religion, that he disputed against the change; urged the precepts he had received from the King his father, and his dying in the faith he had prescribed to him; put her majesty in mind of the promise she had made to the King his brother at parting; and acknowledged that he had obliged himself to his majesty that he would never change his religion; and therefore besought her majesty that she would not farther press him, at least till he should inform the King of it. The Queen well enough knew the King's mind, and thought it more excusable to proceed in that affair without imparting it to him; and therefore took upon her the authority of a mother, and removed his tutor from him, and committed the duke to the care of the abbot Mountague her almoner, who having the pleasant abbey at Pontoise entertained his highness there, sequestered from all resort of such persons who might confirm him in his averseness from being converted.

118. As soon as the King received this advertisement, which both the duke and his tutor made haste to transmit to him, he was exceedingly perplexed. On the one hand, he knew the reproaches which would be cast upon him by his enemies, who took all the pains they could to persuade the world that he himself had changed his religion; and though his exercise of it was so public wherever he was that strangers resorted to it, and so could bear witness of it, yet their impudence was such in their positive averment, that they persuaded many in England, and especially of those of the Reformed religion abroad, that his majesty was in truth a Papist; and his leaving his brother behind him in France, where it was evident the Queen would endeavour to pervert him, would be an argument that he

did not desire to prevent it. On the other side, he knew well **1654** the little credit he had in France, and how far they would be from assisting him in a contest of such a nature with his mother. However, that the world might see plainly that he did all that was in his power, he sent the marquis of Ormonde with all possible expedition into France, who he very well knew would steadily execute his commands. He writ a letter of complaint to the Queen of her having proceeded in that Nov. 10. manner in a matter of so near importance to him, and conjured her to discontinue the prosecution of it, and to suffer his brother the duke of Gloster to repair with the marquis of Ormonde to his presence. He commanded the duke not to consent to any propositions which should be made to him for the change of his religion, and that he should follow the advice of the marquis of Ormonde and accompany him to Cullen. And he directed the marquis of Ormonde to let Mr. Mountague, and whosoever of the English who should join with him, know, that they should expect such a resentment from his majesty, if they did not comply with his commands, as should be suitable to his honour and to the affront they put upon him.

119. The marquis behaved himself with so much wisdom and resolution, that though the Queen was enough offended with him, and with the expostulation the King made with her, and imputed all the King's sharpness and resolution to the counsel he received from the marquis and the Chancellor, yet she thought not fit to extend her power in detaining the duke both against the King's and his own will; and the duke, upon receipt of the King's letter, declared that he would obey his majesty; and the abbot found that he must enter into an absolute defiance with the King if he persisted in advising the Queen not to comply with his directions: so that after two or three days deliberation, the Queen, expressing very·much displeasure at the King's proceeding, and that she should be wholly divested of the power and authority of a mother, told the marquis that the duke might dispose of himself as he pleased, Nov. 29. and that she would not concern herself farther, nor see him any more. And thereupon the duke put himself into the hands of

1654
Dec. 1. the marquis, who immediately removed him from Pontoise to the house of an English lord[1] who lived then in Paris; where he remained for some days, until the marquis could borrow money (which was no easy matter) to defray the journey to the King, and then they quickly left Paris, and shortly after came to the King[2], who was infinitely delighted with the marquis his negotiation and success, and kept his brother always with him till the time that he returned into England, the Queen remaining as much unsatisfied.

1655
Jan. 7. 120. Innocent the Tenth was now dead, who had outlived the understanding and judgment he had been formerly master of, and lost all the reputation he had formerly gotten, and, as Jehoram, he *departed without being desired*[3]. He fomented the rebellion in England by cherishing that in Ireland, whither he had sent a light-headed nuncio[4], who did much mischieve to his majesty's service, as hath been touched before[5]. The world was in great expectation who should succeed him, when one day the Duke of Newburgh sent a gentleman to the King to
April 7. bring him the news that cardinal Guighy [Chigi] was chosen Pope, of which the Duke said his majesty had great cause to be glad; which the King understood not. But the next day the Duke himself came to the King, and told him that he came to congratulate with his majesty for the election of the new Pope, who called himself Alexander the Seventh, and who, he said, he was confident would do him great service; and thereupon related a discourse that had passed between him and the new Pope when he was nuncio at Cullen, some years before; when they two conferring together (as, he said, there was great confidence and friendship between them) of the rebellion in England, and of the execrableness of the murder of the late King, the nuncio brake out into a great passion, even with tears, and said it was a monstrous thing that the two Crowns should weary and spend each other's strength and spirits in so unjust

---

[1] [lord Hatton. See *Calend. Clar. S.P.* ii. 434.]
[2] [In May, 1655, after the duke had fallen ill at Antwerp, and had stopped in Holland for some time with his sister.]
[3] [2 Chron. xxi. 20.]
[4] [Jo. Bapt. Rinuccini.]　　　　　　　[5] [book xi. § 148.]

and groundless a war, when they had so noble an occasion to 1655
unite all their power to revenge that impious murder, in which
the honour, and the life, of all kings was concerned; and he
said the Pope was concerned never to let either of them to be
quiet till he had reconciled them, and obliged all Christian
kings and states, without consideration of any difference in
religion, to join together for the restoration of the King, which
would be the greatest honour the Pope could obtain in this
world. All which, he said, he spake with so much warmth and
concernment, that he could not doubt but that, now God had
raised him to that chair, (he hoped for that end,) he would
remember his former opinion, and execute it himself, being, he
said, a man of the most public heart, and the most superior to
all private designs, that the world had; the Duke taking great
delight to remember many of his discourses, and describing him
to be such a man as he was generally believed to be for the
first two years of his reign, till he manifested his affections
with more ingenuity. The Duke desired his majesty to consider
whether there might not be somewhat which he might reasonably wish from the Pope; and if it were not fit to be proposed
as from his majesty, he would be willing to promote it in his
own name, having, he thought, some interest in his holiness.
And he said he was resolved to send a person purposely to
Rome with his congratulation, and to tender his obedience to
the Pope, and that he would instruct that person in whatsoever
his majesty should wish; and though he could not hope that
any great matter could be done towards his majesty's restoration till the peace should be effected between the two Crowns,
(which he knew the Pope would labour in till he had brought it
to pass,) yet he could not doubt but that, out of the generosity
of his holiness, his majesty would receive some supply towards
his better support, which for the present was all that could be
expected: that the person whom he intended to send was a
Jesuit, who was at that present in Newburgh, but he had or
would send for him: that though he was a religious man, yet
he was a person of that experience, temper, and wisdom, that
he had intrusted him in affairs not only of the greatest

1655 secresy, but in negotiations of the greatest importance, in
which he had always behaved himself with singular prudence
and judgment : and he assured his majesty he was equal to any
trust ; and if, upon what he had said and offered, his majesty
thought he might be of use to him in this journey, he would
send him to Cullen as soon as he came, that he might attend
upon his majesty, and receive any commands he would vouchsafe to impose upon him.

121. Though the King had in truth very little hope that the
new Pope would be more magnanimous than the old, and did
believe that the maxim with which Innocent had answered
those who would have disposed him to supply the King with
some money, that he could not with a good conscience apply
the patrimony of the Church to the assistance and support of
heretics, would be as current divinity with Alexander and all
his successors, yet he could not but be abundantly satisfied with
the kindness of the Duke of Newburgh, and could not conclude
how far his interposition might prevail upon a temper and
constitution so refined, and without those dregs which others
had used to carry about them to that promotion : therefore,
after those acknowledgments which were due for the overtures,
his majesty told him that he would entirely commit it to his
wisdom to do those offices with the new Pope which he thought
fit, since he could expect nothing but upon that account ; and
that he would do any thing on his part which [was [1]] fit for
him to do, and which should be thought of moment to facilitate
the other pretences.   Whereupon the Duke told him, that the
bloody laws in England against Catholic religion made a very
great noise in the world ; and that his majesty was generally
understood to be a prince of a tender and merciful nature,
which would not take delight in the executing so much cruelty;
and therefore he conceived it might be very agreeable to his
inclination to declare and promise, that when it should please
God to restore his majesty to his government he would never
suffer those laws to be executed, but would cause them to be
repealed ; which generous and pious resolution made known to

[1] ['were,' MS.]

the Pope, would work very much upon him, and dispose him **1655**
to make an answerable return to his majesty. The King
answered, that his highness might very safely undertake on his
behalf, that if it should be in his power it should never be in
his will to execute those severe laws; that it was not in his
power absolutely to repeal them; and it would be less in his
power to do it, if he declared that he had a purpose to do it:
therefore that must be left to time; and it might reasonably
be presumed that he would not be backward to do all of that
kind which he should find himself able to do; and the declaration which he then made, his majesty said that he would be
ready to make to the person the Duke meant to send, if he came
to him: which was acknowledged to be as much as could be
desired [1].

122. Germany is the only part of the world where the
Jesuits are looked upon to have the ascendant over all other men
in the deepest mysteries of state and policy, insomuch as in no
prince's court a man is held to be a good courtier, or to have a
desire to be thought a wise man, who hath not a Jesuit to his
confessor; which may be one of the reasons that the policy of
that nation is so different from, and so much undervalued by, the
other politic parts of the world. And therefore it is the less to
be wondered at that this Duke, who had himself extraordinary
qualifications, retained that reverence for those who had taught
him when he was young, that he believed them to grow and to be
improved as fast as he, and so to be still abler to inform him.
Without doubt he did believe his Jesuit to be a very wise man,
and, it may be, knew that he would think so to whom he was
sent: and as soon as he came to him, he sent him to the King,
to be instructed and informed of his majesty's pleasure. The
man had a very good aspect, and less vanity and presumption
than that society use to have, and seemed desirous to merit
from the King by doing him service, but had not the same
confidence he should do it as his master had. And when he
returned from Rome, he brought nothing with him from the
Pope but general good wishes of the King's restoration, and

[1] [See *Calend. Clar. S. P.* iii. 19.]

sharp complaints against cardinal Mazaryne for being deaf to all overtures of peace ; and that till then, all attempts to serve his majesty would be vain and ineffectual : and concerning any supply of money, he told the Duke that the Pope had used the same adage that his predecessor had done ; and so that intrigue was determined.

123. The rest and quiet that the King proposed to himself in this necessitated retreat was disturbed by the impatience and activity of his friends in England, who, notwithstanding all his majesty's commands and injunctions not to enter upon any sudden and rash insurrections, which could only contribute to their own ruin without the least benefit or advantage to his service, were so pricked and stung by the insolence of their enemies and the uneasiness of their own condition and fortune, that they could not rest. They sent expresses every day to Cullen for commissions and instructions, and made an erroneous judgment of their own strength and power, and concluded that all who hated the present government would concur with them to overthrow it, at least would act no part in the defence of it. They assured the King that they had made sufficient provision of arms and ammunition, and had so many persons engaged to appear upon any day that should be assigned that they only desired that his majesty would appoint that day ; and that they were so united, that even the discovery before the day, and the clapping up many persons in prison, (which they expected) should not break the design. The King knew well enough that they would be deceived, and that though the persons who sent those expresses were very honest men, and had served well in the war, and were ready to engage again, yet they were not equal to so great a work. Yet it was not fit to discountenance or dishearten them ; for as many of his party were too restless and too active, so there were more of them remiss and lazy, and even abandoned to despair. And the truth is, the unequal temper of those who wished very well, and the jealousy, at least the want of confidence in each other, made the King's part exceeding difficult. Very many who held correspondence with his majesty, and those he assigned to that office, would not

trust each other ; every body chose their own knot with whom
they would converse, and would not communicate with any
body else; for which they had too just excuses from the
discoveries which were [made] every day by want of wit as
much as want of honesty; and so men were cast into prison,
and kept there, upon general jealousies. But this reservation,
since they could not all resolve to be quiet, proved very
grievous to the King ; for he could not convert and restrain
those who were too forward by the counsel of those who stood
in a better light and could discern better what was to be done,
because they could not be brought together to confer ; and they
who appeared to be less desperate were by the others reproached with being less affectionate, and to want loyalty as
much as courage : and so they who were undone upon one and
the same account, were oppressed and torn in pieces by one
and the same enemy and could never hope for recovery but by
one and the same remedy, grew to reproach and revile one
another, and contracted a greater animosity between themselves
than against the common adversary. Nor could the King
reconcile this distemper, nor preserve himself from being invaded by it.

124. Though the messengers who were sent were addressed
to the King himself and to the Chancellor, and were so carefully
concealed that no notice was taken or advertisement sent by the
many spies who were suborned to give intelligence of any one
express that was sent to Cullen, yet they had commonly some
friend or acquaintance in the Court with whom they conferred ;
and ever returned worst satisfied with those who made objections
against what they proposed, or seemed to doubt that they would
not be able to perform what they so confidently promised; and
it was thought a very reasonable conviction of a man who liked
not the most extravagant undertaking, if he were not ready to
propose a better : so that his majesty thought fit often to seem
to think better of many things promised than in truth he did.
The messengers which were sent this winter to Cullen, (who, I
say still, were honest men, and sent from those who were such,)
proposed to the King, (which they had formerly done), that, when

1655 they were in arms, and had provided a place where his majesty
might land safely, he[1] would then be with them, that there
might be no dispute upon command : and in the spring they
sent to him that the day was appointed, the 18th of April, when
the rising would be general, and many places seized upon, and
some declare for the King, which were in the hands of the army :
for they still pretended, and did believe, that a part of the
army would declare against Cromwell at least, though not for
the King : that Kent was united to a man ; Dover Castle would
be possessed, and the whole county in arms upon that day ; and
therefore that his majesty would vouchsafe to be in some place
concealed upon the sea-coast, which it was very easy for him to
be, on that day ; from whence, upon all being made good that
was undertaken, and full notice given to his majesty that it was
so, he might then, and not before, transport himself to that
part which he thought to be in the best posture to receive him,
and might give such other directions to the rest as he found
necessary. And[2] even all these particulars were communicated
in confidence by the messengers to their friends who were near
the King, and who again thought it but reasonable to raise the
spirits of their friends by letting them know in how happy a
condition the King's affairs were in England, and that his
friends were in so good a posture throughout the kingdom, that
they feared not that any discovery might be made to Cromwell,
being ready to own and justify their counsels with their swords :
so that it quickly became more than whispered throughout the
Court that the King was only expected to be nearer England,
how disguised soever, that he might quickly put himself into
the head of the army that would be ready to receive him,
whereby all emulations about command might be prevented, or
immediately taken away ; and if his majesty should now neglect
this opportunity, it might easily be concluded, that either he
was betrayed, or that his counsels were conducted by men of
very shallow capacities and understanding.

125. [3] How weakly and improbably soever these preparations
were adjusted, the day was positively appointed, and was so

---

[1] ['that he,' MS.]   [2] [*Hist.* p. 29.]   [3] [*Life*, p. 498.]

near at the time when his majesty had notice of it that it was **1655**
not possible for him to send orders to contradict it; and he
foresaw that if any thing should be attempted without success,
it would be imputed to his not being at a distance to countenance it.   On the other. hand, it was neither difficult nor hazard-
ous to his majesty to remove that reproach, and to be in a place
from whence he might advance if there were cause, or retire to
Cullen if there were nothing to do ; and all this with so little
noise, that his absence should scarce be taken notice of.   Hereupon the messenger returned with the King's approbation of
the day, and direction that as soon as the day should be past an
express should be directed to Flushing, and at the sign of the
City of Rouen, (a known harbour in that town,) to enquire for an
Englishman, (whose name was given him,) who should be able to
inform him whither he should repair to speak with the King.

126. Before the messenger's departure, or the King's resolution was taken, the earl of Rochester, who was always jealous
that somebody would be general before him, upon the first news
of the general disposition and resolution to be in arms, desired
the King that he would permit him to go over in disguise, to
the end that, finding the way to London, which was very easy,
he might, upon advising with the principal persons engaged, of
whom there was none who had not been commanded by him,
or was [not] inferior to him in command, assist [1] them in their
enterprise, and make the best of that force which they could
bring together : and if he found that in truth they were not
competently provided to sustain the first shock, he might by
his advice and authority compose them to expect a better conjuncture, and in the mean time to give over all inconsiderate
attempts ; and there would be little danger in his withdrawing
back again to his majesty.

127. And in this errand he left Cullen, under pretence of
pursuing his business with the German princes upon the dona-
tive of the Diet, in which he used to make many journeys; and
nobody suspected that he was gone upon any other design.   But
when he came into Flanders, he was not at all reserved ; but in

[1] ['he might assist,' MS.]

1655 the hours of good fellowship, which was a great part of the day and night, communicated his purpose to any body he did believe would keep him company and run the same hazard with him ; and finding sir Jo[seph] Wagstaffe, who had served the King in the last war very honestly, and was then watching at the sea-coast to take the first opportunity to transport himself as soon as he should hear of the general insurrection, (which all letters to all places mentioned as a matter resolved on,) Rochester

March 1. frankly declared what he was going about; and so they hired a bark at Dunkirk, and without any misadventure found them-selves in safety together at London : but many of those who should have been in arms were seized upon, and secured in several prisons.

128. The messenger being despatched, the King at the time appointed, and that he might be sure to be near at the day, left Cullen very early in the morning, attended only by the marquis of Ormonde and one groom to look to their horses : nor was it known to any body but to the Chancellor and the Secretary (Nicholas,) whither the King was gone, they making such relations to inquisitive people as they thought fit. The day before the King went, sir John Mennes and John Nicholas, eldest son to the Secretary, were sent into Zealand, to stay there till they should receive farther orders ; the former of them being the person designed to be at the sign of the *Rouen* in Flushing, and the other to be near to prepare any thing for the King's hand that should be found necessary, and to keep the ciphers ; both of them persons of undoubted fidelity.

129. There was a gentleman who lived in Middleborough [1] and of one of the best families and best fortune there, who had

---

[1] [Apparently one called in a letter to Thurloe in 1657 'baronet Krin-son,' to whose son the King stood as godfather (*Calend. Clar. S. P.* iii. 231) ; and 'Monsieur Croinson' in a letter from Manning to the same, written from Middleburg in 1655 (Thurloe's *S. P.* iii. 301) ; and Sir Will. Crinston in a letter of Hyde's of March 27, 1658. Lord Wentworth writing to Nicholas from the same place in 1658 encloses a letter from 'Lady Quirinsen ;' *Calend. Dom. S. P.* 1657-8, p. 298. And she and her husband, 'Geleyn Quirinssen,' write letters to Ormonde on Nov. 18, 1659, which are in Carte MS. (Bodl. Libr.) ccxiii, ff. 431, 435. No mention of him, however, is found in any list of the baronets created by Charles II.]

married an English lady, who had been brought up in the court 1655
of the Queen of Bohemia, and was the daughter of a gentleman
of a very noble family, who had been long an officer in Holland.
The King had made this Dutchman a baronet; and some who
were nearly acquainted with him were confident that his majesty
might secretly repose himself in his house, without any notice
taken of him, as long as it would be necessary for him to be
concealed.   And his majesty being first assured of this, made
his journey directly thither in the manner mentioned before; March.
and being received as he expected in that house, he gave present
notice to Sir John Mennes and Mr. Nicholas, that they might
know whither to resort to his majesty upon any occasion.   And
upon his first arrival there, he received intelligence that the
messenger who had been despatched from Cullen met with cross
winds and accidents in his return, which had been his misfortune likewise in his journey thither, so that he came not so
soon to London as was expected; whereupon some conceived
that the King did not approve the day, and therefore excused
themselves from appearing at the time; others were well content with the excuse, having discerned, with the approach of
the day, that they had embarked themselves in a design of
more difficulty than was at first apprehended; and some were
actually seized upon and imprisoned, by which they were incapable of performing their promise.   Though this disappointment confirmed the King in his former belief that nothing solid
could result from such a general combination, yet he thought it
fit, now he was in a post where he might securely rest, to expect
what the earl of Rochester's presence, of whose being in London
he was advertised, might produce.   And by this time the Chancellor, according to order, was come to Breda; from whence he March 24.
every day might hear from and send to the King.

130. There cannot be a greater manifestation of the universal
prejudice and aversion in the whole kingdom towards Cromwell
and his government, than that there could be so many designs
and conspiracies against him, which were communicated to so
many men, and that such signal and notorious persons could
resort to London and remain there, without any such informa-

1655 tion or discovery as might enable him to cause them to be
apprehended; there being nobody intent and zealous to make
any such discoveries but such whose trade it was, for great
wages, to give him those informations; and they seldom care
whether what they inform be true or no.   The earl of Rochester
consulted with great freedom in London with the King's friends,
and found that the persons imprisoned were only taken upon
general suspicion, and as being known to be of that party, not
upon any particular discovery of what they designed or intended
to do, and that the same spirit still possessed those who were at
liberty.   The design in Kent appeared not reasonable, at least
not to begin upon; but he was persuaded (and he was very
credulous) that in the north there was a foundation of strong
hope, and a party ready to appear powerful enough to possess
themselves of York, nor had the army many troops in those
parts.   In the west likewise there seemed to be a strong combination, in which many gentlemen were engaged, and their
agents were then in London, and were exceedingly importunate
to have a day assigned, and desired no more than that sir Joseph
Wagstaffe might be authorized to be in the head of them, who
had been well known to them; and he was as ready to engage
with them.   The earl of Rochester liked the countenance of the
north better, and sent [Marma]duke Darcy, a gallant gentleman,
and nobly allied in those parts, to prepare the party there;
appointed a day and place for the rendezvous, and promised to
be himself there; and was contented that sir Joseph Wagstaffe
should go into the west, who, upon conference with those of that
country, likewise appointed their rendezvous upon a fixed day,
to be within two miles of Salisbury.   And it was an argument
that they had no mean opinion of their strength, that they
appointed to appear that very day when the judges were to keep
their assizes in that city, and where the shrief and principal
gentlemen of the county were obliged to give their attendance.
And of both these resolutions the earl of Rochester, who knew
where the King was, took care to advertise his majesty, who
from hence had his former faint hopes renewed; and in a short
time after they were so improved, that he thought of nothing

more than how he might with the greatest secresy transport 1655
himself into England; for which he did expect a sudden
occasion.

131. Sir Joseph Wagstaffe had been formerly major general
of the foot in the King's western army, a man generally beloved; and though he was rather for execution than counsel, a
stout man, who looked not far before him, yet he had a great
companionableness[1] in his nature, which exceedingly prevailed
with those who in the intermission of fighting loved to spend
their time in jollity and mirth. He, as soon as the day was
appointed, left London, and went to some of his friends' houses
in the country, near the place, that he might assist the preparations as much as was possible. Those of Hampshire were not
so punctual at their own rendezvous as to be present at that
near Salisbury at the hour; however, Wagstaffe and they of
Wiltshire appeared to expectation. Penruddocke, a gentleman March 8.
of a fair fortune and great zeal and forwardness in the service,
Hugh Grove, and other persons of condition, were there, with
a body of near two hundred horse well armed, which they presumed would every day be improved upon the access of those
who had engaged themselves in the western association, especially if the fame of their being up, and effecting any thing,
should come to their ears. They accounted that they were
already strong enough to visit Salisbury in all its present lustre,
knowing that they had many friends there, and reckoning that
all who were not against them were for them, and that they
should there increase their numbers both in foot and horse,
with which the town then abounded: nor did their computation
and conjecture fail them. They entered the city about five of March 12[2].
the clock in the morning: they appointed some officers, of
which they had plenty, to cause all the stables to be locked up,
that all the horses might be at their devotion; others to break
open the gaols, that all there might attend their benefactors.
They kept a good body of horse upon the market-place, to
encounter all opposition; and gave order to apprehend the
judges and the shrief, who were yet in their beds, and to bring

---

[1] ['companiableness,' MS.]   [2] [Thurloe's *S. P.* iii. 370.]

1655 them into [the][1] market-place with their several commissions, resolving or not caring to seize upon the persons of any others.

132. All this was done with so little noise or disorder as if the town had been all of one mind. And they who were within doors, except they were commanded to come out, stayed still there, being more desirous to hear than to see what was done; very many being well pleased, and not willing that others should discern it in their countenance. When the judges were brought out in their own robes, and humbly produced their commissions, and the shrief likewise, Wagstaffe resolved, after he had caused the King to be proclaimed, to cause them all three to be hanged, who were half dead already, having well considered, with the policy which men in such actions are naturally possessed with, how he himself should be used if he were under their hands, and therefore choosing to be before-hand with them. But having not thought fit to deliberate this beforehand with his friends, whereby their scrupulous consciences might have been confirmed, many of the country gentlemen were so startled with this proposition that they pro-tested against it; and poor Penruddocke was so passionate to preserve their lives, as if works of this nature could be done by halves, that the major general durst not persist in it, but was prevailed with to dismiss the judges, and, having taken their commissions from them, to oblige them upon another occasion to remember to whom they owed their lives, resolving still to hang the shrief[2], who positively, though humbly and with many tears, refused to proclaim the King; which being otherwise done, they likewise prevailed with him rather to keep the shrief alive, and to carry him with them to redeem an honester man out of the hands of their enemies. This was an ill omen to their future agreement and submission to the commands of their general; nor was the tender-heartedness so general but that very many of the gentlemen were much scandalized at it, both as it was a contradiction to their commander in chief, and as it would have been a seasonable act of severity to have cemented

[1] ['their,' MS.]   [2] [col. John Dove.]

those to perseverance who were engaged in it, and kept them **1655**
from entertaining any hopes but in the sharpness of their
swords.

133. The noise of this action was very great both in and out
of the kingdom, whither it was quickly sent. And without
doubt it was a bold enterprise, and might have produced wonderful effects, if it had been prosecuted with the same resolution,
or the same rashness, it was entered into. All that was reasonable in the general contrivance of insurrection and commotion
over the whole kingdom was founded upon a supposition of the
division and faction in the army, which was known to be so
great that Cromwell durst not draw the whole army to a general
rendezvous, out of apprehension that when they should once
meet together he should no longer be master of them. And
thence it was concluded, that, if there were in any one place
such a body brought together as might oblige Cromwell to
make the army, or a considerable part of it, to march, there
would at least be no disposition in them to fight to strengthen
that authority which they abhorred. And many did at that
time believe that if they had remained with that party at
Salisbury for some days, which they might well have done
without any disturbance, that their numbers would have much
increased, and their friends farther west must have been prepared to receive them, when their retreat had been necessary
by a stronger part of the army's marching against them.
Cromwell himself was amazed; he knew well the distemper of
the kingdom and in his army, and now when he saw such a
body gathered together without any noise, that durst in the
middle of the kingdom enter into the chief city of it, when his
judges and all the power of that county was in it, and take
them prisoners, and proclaim the King in a time of full peace,
and when no man durst so much as name him but with a
reproach, he could not imagine that such an enterprise could
be undertaken without a universal conspiracy, in which his
own army could not be innocent; and therefore knew not how
to trust them together. But all this apprehension vanished,
when it was known that within four or five hours after they

1655 had performed this exploit they left the town with very small increase or addition to their numbers.

134. The truth is, they did nothing resolutely after their first action, and were in such disorder and discontent between themselves, that without staying for their friends out of Hampshire, (who were, to the number of two or three hundred horse, upon their way, and would have been at Salisbury that night,) upon pretence that they were expected in Dorsetshire, they left the town, and took the shrief with them, about two of the clock in the afternoon; but were so weary of their day's labour, and their watching the night before, that they grew less in love with what they were about, and differed again amongst themselves about the shrief, [whom [1]] many desired should be presently released; and that party carried it in hope of receiving good offices afterwards from him. And in this manner they continued on their march westward. They from Hampshire and other places, who were behind them, being angry for their leaving Salisbury, would not follow, but scattered themselves; and they who were before them, and heard in what disorder they had left Wiltshire, likewise dispersed. So that after they had continued their journey into Devonshire, without meeting any who would join with them, horse and man were so tired for want of meat and sleep that one single troop of horse, inferior in number, and commanded by an officer of no credit in the war, being [2] in those parts by chance, followed them at a dis-

March 14 [3]. tance, till they were so spent that he rather entreated than compelled them to deliver themselves. Some, and amongst those Wagstaffe, quitted their horses, and found shelter in some honest houses, where they were concealed till opportunity served to transport them into the parts beyond the seas, where they arrived safely. But Mr. Penruddocke, Mr. Grove, and most of the rest, were taken prisoners, upon promise given by the officer that their lives should be saved; which they quickly found he had no authority to make good, for Cromwell no

March 23 [4]. sooner heard of his cheap victory, than he sent judges away

---

[1] ['which,' MS.]   [2] ['which being,' MS.]
[3] [Thurloe's *S. P.* iii. 263.]   [4] [*Ibid.* 296.]

with a new commission of oyer and terminer, and order to 1655
proceed with the utmost severity against the offenders. But
Roles, his chief justice, who had so luckily scaped at Salisbury,
had not recovered the fright, and would no more look those
men in the face who had dealt so kindly with him, but expressly
refused to be employed in the service, raising some scruples in
point of law whether the men could be legally condemned; upon
which Cromwell shortly after turned him out of his office, June 7.
having found others who executed his commands. Penruddocke
and Grove lost their heads at Exciter, and others were hanged May 16.
there, who, having recovered the faintness they were in when
they rendered, died with great courage and resolution, professing
their duty and loyalty to the King. Many were sent to Salisbury, and tried[1] and executed there, in the place where they
had so lately triumphed; and some who were condemned, where
there were fathers and sons and brothers, that the butchery
might appear with some remorse, were reprieved, and sold, and
sent slaves to the Barbadoes; where their treatment was such
that few of them ever returned into their own country[2]. And
thus this little fire, which probably might have kindled and
inflamed all the kingdom, was for the present extinguished in
the west, and Cromwell secured without the help of his army;
which he saw, by the countenance it then shewed when they
thought he would have use of them, it was high time to reform;
and in that he resolved to use no longer delay.

135. The design of the north, which was thought to be much
better prepared and provided for, made less noise, and expired
most peaceably. The earl of Rochester, who saw danger at a
distance with great courage, [but] looked upon it less resolutely
when it was nearer, made his journey from London, with a
friend or two, into Yorkshire at the time appointed, and found
such an appearance of gentlemen upon the place as might very
well have deserved his patience. It appeared that there had
been some mistake in the notice that had been given, and they

[1] [April 11. The list of prisoners tried and condemned is given in
Thurloe's *S. P.* iii. 365.]
[2] [See Tho. Burton's *Diary*, iv. 256-9.]

1655 who did appear undertook for many who were absent that if he would appoint another short day for the rendezvous he should be well attended. [Marma]duke Darcy had spent his time very well amongst them, and found them well disposed, and there could be no danger in staying the time proposed, many of them having houses where he might be well concealed; and the country generally wished well to the King, and to those who concerned themselves in his affairs. But he took many exceptions; complained as if they had deceived him; and asked many questions, which were rather reasonable than seasonable, and which would have furnished reasons against entering upon the design, which were not to be urged now when they were to execute, and when indeed they had gone too far to retire. He had not yet heard of the success at Salisbury, yet did not think the force which the gentlemen were confident they could draw together, before they could meet with any opposition, sufficient to enter upon an action that was like to be dangerous in the end, and so he resolved to stay no longer; the gentlemen being as much troubled that he had come at all, they parted with little good will to each other, the earl returning through by-roads to London, which was the securest place, from whence he gave the King notice of the hopelessness of affairs. If he had not been a man very fortunate in disguises, he could never have escaped so many perambulations; for as he was the least wary in making his journeys in safe hours, so he departed very unwillingly from all places where there was good eating and drinking, and entered into conferences with any strangers he met or joined with.

March 20. 136. When he returned from the north, he lodged at Ayles-bury, and having been observed to ride out of the way, in a large ground not far from the town, of which he seemed to take some survey, and had asked many questions of a country fellow who was there, (that ground in truth belonging to his wife,) the next justice of peace had notice of it; who, being a man devoted to the government, and all that country very ill affected always to the King, and the news of Salisbury, and proclamations thereupon, having put all men upon their guard, came himself to the inn where he was; and being informed **1655** that there were only two gentlemen above at supper, (for sir Nicholas Armorer was likewise with the earl, and had accompanied him in that journey,) he went into the stable; and upon view of the horses found they were the same which had been observed in the ground. He commanded the keeper of the inn, one Kilby, (who, besides that he was a person notoriously affected to the government, was likewise an officer,) that he should not suffer those horses, nor the persons to whom they belonged, to go out of house, till he, the said justice, came thither in the morning, when he would examine the gentlemen, who they were, and from whence they came. The earl was quickly advertised of all that passed below, and enough apprehensive of what must follow in the morning. Whereupon he presently sent for the master of the house, and, nobody being present but his companion, he told him he would put his life into his hands, which he might destroy or preserve; that he could get nothing by the one, but by the other he should have profit, and the good will of many friends who might be able to do him good. Then he told him who he was; and, as an earnest of more benefit that he might receive hereafter, he gave him thirty or forty Jacobuses, and a fair gold chain, which was more worth to be sold than one hundred pounds. Whether the man was moved by the reward, which he might have possessed without deserving it, or by generosity, or by wisdom and foresight, for he was a man of a very good understanding, and might consider the changes which followed after, and in which this service proved of advantage to him, he [1] did resolve both to permit and contrive their escape; and though he thought fit to be accountable to the justice for their horses, yet he caused two other, as good for their purpose, of his own, to be made ready by a trusty servant in another stable, who about midnight conducted them into London-way, which put them in safety. The inn-keeper was visited in the morning by **March 21.** the justice, whom he carried into the stable, where the horses still stood, he having still kept the key in his own pocket, not

---

[1] ['but he,' MS.]

1655 making any doubt of the persons whilst he kept their horses; but he confessed they were escaped out of his house in the night, how or whither he could not imagine. The justice threatened loud; but the inn-keeper was of that unquestionable fidelity, and gave such daily demonstration of his affection to the commonwealth, that Cromwell more suspected the connivance of the justice, who ought not to have deferred the examination of the persons till the morning, than the integrity of a man so well known as the inn-keeper was[1]. The earl remained in London whilst the inquiry was warm and im-
June. portunate, and afterwards easily procured a passage for Flanders, and so returned to Cullen.

137. As soon as the King received advertisement of the ill successes in England, and that all their hopes were for the present blasted there, he left Zealand, and, returning by Breda, stayed in a dorp near the town till the Chancellor at-
April 9, tended him, and then returned with all speed to Cullen;
N. S.[2] where his little Court was quickly gathered together again, and better disposed to sit still and expect God's own time. His majesty was exceedingly afflicted for the loss of so many honest gentlemen in England, who had engaged themselves so desperately, not only without but expressly against his majesty's judgment: and he was the more troubled, because he was from several of his friends from thence advertised that all his counsels were discovered, and that Cromwell had perfect intelligence of whatsoever he resolved to do, and of all he said himself, so that it would not be safe for any body to correspond with him, or to meddle in his affairs and concernments: that his coming into Zealand, and his continuance there, was known to Cromwell, with all the particulars of his motion; that many persons of condition were seized upon and imprisoned for having a design to possess themselves of some towns and places of strength, which intelligence could not be given but from Cullen; implying that the miscarriage in all the late designs proceeded wholly from the treason of some

---

[1] [For the account of the escape, cf. Thurloe's *S. P.* iii. 335-6, where it is said 'the inn-keeper is a very untoward fellow.'] [2] [*Ibid.* 339.]

persons near his majesty. He did not at all wonder that Cromwell and his instruments took great pains to make it generally to be believed that they knew all that was resolved or thought of at Cullen; but that any men who were really devoted to his service, and who had kindness and esteem for all those who were trusted by his majesty, should be wrought upon to believe those reports, very much disturbed him.

138. Whilst he was in this agony, and immediately after his return to Cullen, a discovery was made of a villainy that made him excuse his friends in England for their jealousy, and yet composed his own mind from any fear of being betrayed, being an imposture of such a nature that was dangerous and ridiculous together. There was one Manning, a proper young gentleman, bred a Catholic in the family of the marquis of Worcester, whose page he had been. His father, of that religion likewise, had been a colonel in the King's army, and was slain at the battle of Al[re]sford, where this young man, being then a youth, was hurt, and maimed in the left arm and shoulder. This young gentleman came to Cullen shortly after the King came thither first, and pretended that he had sold the incumbered fortune his father had left him, upon which he had enough to maintain him, and resolved to spend it in waiting upon the King, till his majesty should be able to raise an army, in which he hoped to have an opportunity to revenge his father's blood; with many discourses of that nature; and he brought a letter to Dr. Earles from his uncle Manning, who was well known to him, to commend his nephew to his conversation. He was a handsome man, had store of good clothes, and plenty of money; which, with the memory of his father, easily introduced him, and made him acceptable to the company that was there. He knew most of the King's party in England, and spake as if he were much trusted by them, and held correspondence with them, and had every week the *Diurnal* and the news of the town, which seldom came so far as Cullen. He associated himself most with the good fellows, and eat in their company, being well provided for the expense. By degrees he insinuated himself with the earl of Rochester, and

1655 told him that all the King's party looked upon him as the general who must govern and command them, and for which they were very impatient; that he himself would be ready to run his fortune, and attend him into England; and that he had two hundred good men listed, who would appear well mounted and armed whenever he should require them; and that he knew where good sums of money lay ready to be applied to that service. The earl was ravished with this discourse, and looked upon him as a man sent from heaven to advance his designs, and asked him whether he had been with the Chancellor, and communicated all this to him. He said he had at his first coming to town waited upon the Chancellor, and intended to have spoken of this and much more than he had spoken yet, if he had been vacant, or willing to hear, but he seemed to him so reserved; which he imputed then to some business that possessed him, and therefore made him a second visit, when he found him with the same wariness, and without any desire to be informed by him concerning the affairs of that kingdom; so that he resolved to visit him no more.

139. In the end, he told the earl that he would impart a secret to him of the last importance, and which he had not yet had opportunity to inform the King of, and he did believe it would be the same thing to impart it to his lordship as to his majesty himself: the sum was [1], that he was trusted by the earl of Pembroke, who retained his affection entire for his majesty, to assure the King of the same; and that though it would not be safe for him to appear in the head and beginning of an insurrection, he would advance it as much as if he were there in person; and because he knew the west was better prepared to begin the work than any other part of the kingdom, he had caused £3000 [2] to be laid aside, and kept ready at Wilton, which should be delivered to any man who in the King's name should require it of such a man, naming a person who was known to be much trusted by that earl, upon delivery of a private token which he produced out of his pocket, which was a clean piece of paper sealed with three impressions of an

[1] [See *Calend. Clar. S. P.* iii. 80.] [2] [£5000; *ib.*]

antique head in hard wax, which, he said, the earl required 1655 him to present to the King when he thought it might be seasonable. He added, that he would be glad to be himself in that first engagement, and so to be present when that token should be delivered; yet he considered that he was not enough known to have such a secret imparted to him as the time of such an action ought to be; and therefore, if it pleased the King, he would presently deliver that token into his lordship's hands, who he was confident would be the first that would have opportunity to employ it.

140. The earl had the journey then in his head which he made shortly after, and thought such a treasure as this would infinitely advance the service. He made haste to inform the King of the whole, that he might have his approbation to receive the token. And to that purpose he brought the man to the King, who had never before taken other notice of him than for his bringing the *Diurnal* constantly to be read to his majesty after dinner or supper, as he received it. He made a large relation to the King of what the earl [of Pembroke] had commanded him to say, and presented the token to his majesty for the three thousand pounds; the manner of his discourse being such, that he [the King] had not the least suspicion of the truth of it. As soon as he left the King, the earl brought him to the Chancellor, conjuring him to use him with great kindness, and gently reproaching him for his want of courtesy to him before; which he wondered at; for it was very true that he [Manning] had visited him twice before, and it was as true that he had received him with as much civility as was possible, having known his father and most of his family, and was glad to see him frequently at prayers, well knowing that he had been bred a Roman Catholic; and the young man had seemed much pleased with the reception he had given him. But from that time that he made that relation concerning the earl of Pembroke, which he repeated over to him as he had related it to the King, the Chancellor always suspected him, and could not prevail with himself to have any familiarity with him; which the other complained heavily of, and the Chancellor was

1655 much reproached for not treating a person of so much merit, who had lost his father and had been himself maimed in the King's service, with more openness; for he did always use him with all necessary civility. But his [the Chancellor's] knowledge of the earl of Pembroke, and of the humour that then possessed him, and of the uneasiness of his own fortune, which did not make him at that time master of much money, besides [that] he believed that if the thing were true he should have received advertisement sooner of it from a person who was most trusted by the earl, and who corresponded very constantly with the Chancellor, [made him distrust him]. And therefore he told the King, that he doubted he [Manning] had made that part of the story to make himself the more welcome; which his majesty did not think was a reasonable jealousy, but wished him to use all the means he could to discover the truth. But the Chancellor had no farther suspicion of him, nor the least apprehension that he was a spy.

141. When it was discovered that the King was absent from Cullen, at that time that he made his journey to Zealand, in the manner that is mentioned before, the earl of Rochester being departed from thence some time before, Mr. Manning appeared wonderfully troubled, and complained to some that he, being intrusted by all the King's friends, who would not credit any orders but such as should pass through his hands, the King was now gone without imparting it to him; which would be the ruin of his design. He went to the Chancellor, and lamented himself that there should be any sword drawn in England before his; his father's blood boiled within him, and kept him from sleep. He desired him therefore that he would so far communicate the design to him, that he might only know to what part of England to transport himself, that he might be in action as soon as should be possible. He could draw nothing from the Chancellor, who told him that he knew of no probability of any action, and therefore could give no advice. Upon which he complained much of the Chancellor's want of kindness to him; but he lost no time in following the King; and having great acquaintance with Harbert Price, a man much trusted by

the earl of Rochester, and that affected to know, or to be thought 1655
to know, the greatest secrets, he prevailed with him, upon bearing
his charges, to accompany him, that they might find out where
the King was, at least that they might be ready on the sea-
coast to transport themselves into England upon the first
occasion. Whether by accident, or that the earl of Rochester
had made any mention of Zealand to Mr. Price, thither [1] they
both came; and seeing sir John Mennes and Mr. Nicholas
there, they believed there might likewise be others of their
Cullen friends. Harbert Price, as he was a man of a very
inquisitive nature, watched so narrowly, that he found an
opportunity to meet the King in an evening, when he used to
walk to take a little air after the day's confinement; and the
King, since he was discovered, thought it best to trust him,
and charged him not only to make no discovery but to remove
out of the island, lest his being seen there might raise suspicion
in other men. He did very importunately desire the King
that he might bring Manning to speak with him, as not only an
honest man, (as no doubt he thought him to be,) but a man
of that importance and trust as might contribute much to his
present service. But the King would by no means admit him,
nor did he see him; yet afterwards upon this reflection, his
majesty concluded that Cromwell came to be informed of his
being in Zealand, without any reproach to Mr. Price's fidelity;
which was not suspected, though his presumption and importunity were always very inconvenient.

142. Shortly after the King's return to Cullen, Manning
likewise came thither with his accustomed confidence; and in
this time the Chancellor received advertisement from England
that he had no kind of trust from the earl of Pembroke, but on
the contrary had been turned out of his service upon matter of
dishonesty, and that he was a loose person, of no reputation;
and his majesty was informed by others from Antwerp that
every post brought many letters for him, which were taken up
there and transmitted to Cullen, and that he had letters of
credit upon a merchant at Antwerp for good sums of money.

[1] ['but thither,' MS.]

1655 All this raised a suspicion in the King, who gave direction to
a trusty person, who was purposely sent thither, to take up all
those letters at Antwerp which were sent thither from England
for him, it being known under what cover they came, and
likewise those which were sent from Cullen by him, his address
being likewise discovered. By this means the party returned
with great packets both from and to him, which being opened
and read administered matter of great amazement. There were
letters from Thurlow, (Cromwell's secretary and principal
minister,) containing the satisfaction the Protector received in
the particular intelligence he received from him, with short
instructions how he should behave himself. The person employed had been so dexterous, that he brought with him
Manning's letters of three posts, all full of the most particular
things done at Cullen, and the particular words said by the
King and others, that must needs affect those who should receive the intelligence; but of all which there was nothing true;
no such action had been done, no such word spoken.

143. In one letter, after such information as he thought
fit, he said that by the next he should send such advice as was
of much more moment than he had ever yet sent, and above
what he had given from Zealand, and by which they might see
that there was nothing so secret at Cullen of which he could
not be informed if he had money enough, and therefore desired
the bill for the thousand crowns might be despatched. And
together with this, the letter of the subsequent post was likewise seized upon; and by his method, which was afterwards
discovered, it was very probable that they were both sent at
one and the same time, and by the same post, though they were
of several dates. That of the later date was very long, and in
it was enclosed an overture or design for the surprise and
taking of Plimmoth; in which there was a very exact and true
description of the town and fort and island, and the present
strength and force that was there; then a proposition, that a
vessel with 500 men (there were no more desired) should come
to such a place, (a creek described,) and upon a sign then
given, such a place in the town should be first seized upon,

whilst others should possess both the fort and island. The 1655 names of the persons who undertook to do both the one and the other were likewise set down; and they were all men known to be well affected to the King, and who, with the assistance of that five hundred men, might indeed be able to master the place. For the better going through the work when it was thus begun, there was an undertaking that sir Hugh Pollard, and other persons named, who were all notable men for their zeal to the King's service, should be ready from the Devonshire side, as colonel Arrundell and others from Cornwall, to second and support what was to be done.

144. The letter informed, that when the King delivered that paper to the Council, (which, he said, he had received from a very good hand,) it was twice read; and then the marquis of Ormonde made this and this objection, and others found this and that difficulty in the execution of the enterprise, all which the Chancellor answered very clearly, and the King himself said very much of the easiness in the undertaking : there was one difficulty urged that the King himself appeared to be startled at, and looked upon the Chancellor, who rose from his place and went to the King's chair, and whispered somewhat in his ear; whereupon his majesty told the lords that he had indeed forgot somewhat that the Chancellor put him in mind of, and for that particular they should refer the care of it to him, who would take it upon him ; and so the matter was resolved, and the earl of Rochester undertook for the five hundred men and their transportation. He [Manning] concluded, if he had money they should know constantly how this design should be advanced, or any other set on foot. Every -body was exceedingly amazed at this relation, in which there was not one syllable of truth. There had never such a proposition been made, nor was there any such debate or discourse[1]. There were [in his letter] many vain insinuations of his interest, as if he were never out of the King's company. Two of the King's servants were sent to seize upon his person Dec. 5 N. S.[2]

---

[1] [See *Calend. Clar. S. P.*, iii. 69, 77.]
[2] [Thurloe's *S. P.*, iv. 249.]

1655 and his papers; who found him in his chamber writing, and his cipher and papers before him; all which they possessed themselves of, without any resistance. There were several letters prepared and made up with the dates proper for many posts to come, with information and intelligence of the same nature as the former.

145. The Secretary of State and one of the lords of the Council were sent to examine him; to whom he confessed, without any reserve, that the necessity of his fortune had exposed him to that base condition of life ; and to make himself fit for it he had dissembled his religion; for, he said, he remained still a Catholic : that he was sent over by Thurlow to be a spy wherever the King should be, and had constantly sent him intelligence, for which he had received good sums of money; yet that he had been so troubled in mind for the vileness of the life he led, that he was resolved, by raising great expectations in them, to draw a good sum of money from them, and then to renounce farther correspondence, and to procure the King's pardon, and faithfully to serve him. Being asked why he made such relations which had no truth in them, he answered, that if he had come to the knowledge of any thing which in truth had concerned the King, he would never have discovered it; but he thought it would do no prejudice to the King if he got money from the rebels by sending them lies which could neither do them good nor hurt his majesty ; and therefore all his care was to amuse them with particulars which he knew would please them; and so, when he was alone, he always prepared letters containing such things as occurred to his invention, to be sent by the succeeding posts, and that he had never written any thing that was true, but of his majesty's being in Zealand, which he believed could produce no prejudice to him [1].

146. The King now discerned from whence all the apprehensions of his friends proceeded, and that they had too much

---

[1] [Manning was shortly after shot in a wood near Cologne, in the same month of December, by Sir James Hamilton and W. Armorer. See *Calend. Clar. S. P.*, iii. 77 ; and Thurloe's *S. P.*, iv. 718.]

ground for their jealousies; for though none of his counsels had **1655** been discovered, they who had received those letters might reasonably think that none of them were concealed, and might well brag to their confidents of their knowing all that the King did. And by this means such particulars were transmitted to the King's friends as could not but very much amuse them, and no doubt was the cause of the commitment of very many persons, and of some who had no purpose to suffer for their loyalty. His majesty took care to publish the transactions of this man, with the method of the intelligence he gave; by which his friends discerned with what shadows they had been affrighted, and his enemies likewise discovered what current ware they had received for their money : yet they endeavoured to have it believed that he was not a man sent over by them, but a secretary in great trust about some person employed, whom they had corrupted : in which men were likewise quickly undeceived, and knew that he was a man without any dependence or relation to, or countenance from, the Court.

147. As the King's hopes were much eclipsed in England by the late unseasonable attempt and the loss of so many gallant persons as perished or were undone in it, so Cromwell advanced his own credit, and was infinitely enriched by it, and more confirmed with those who were of doubtful faith towards him. He lay before under the reproach of devising plots himself, that the commonwealth might be thought in danger, to the end he might have excuse to continue so vast forces still in pay ; whereas it now appeared how active and confident the King's party still was, and that they would not have had the presumption to make so bold an attempt in the middle of the kingdom if they had not had good assurance of being seconded ; and therefore they were to look upon the fire as only raked up, not extinguished. The success and triumph of a few desperate persons at Salisbury, that had produced such a consternation throughout the kingdom, and would have endangered the security of the whole west if there had not happened some accidental confusion amongst the undertakers, was evidence enough that there was not yet force sufficient to provide for

1655 the safety of the kingdom, and therefore that it was necessary
to make better provision for the quiet of every county, that it
might not be endangered by every bold attempt; and the
charge that this necessary defence would cause should in justice
be borne by those who were the occasion of the expense.

148. Thereupon he made by his own authority and that of
Sept. 21. his council an order, that all those who had ever borne arms for
the King, or had declared themselves to be of the royal party,
should be decimated, [that is], pay a tenth part of all that
estate which they had left, to support the charge which the
commonwealth was put to by the unquietness of their temper
and the just cause of jealousy which they had administered.
And that the public might lose nothing of what he had so frankly
given to it, commissioners were appointed in every county to
value what that tenth part of every such estate did amount to ;
and that no man might have too good a bargain of his own,
every man was obliged to pay as much as those commissioners
judged fit ; and till he paid it, besides imprisonment, which was
a judgment apart, and inflicted once or twice a year, as the
jealousies wrought, his whole estate was sequestered.   And in
this decimation there was no consideration taken of former
compositions, of any articles of war, or of any acts of pardon
and indemnity which had been granted under their great seal,
and without inquiry into their actions, or so much as accusing
any of them of any crime or guilt, or of having any correspondence with the King or any body trusted by him, or that they
were in any degree privy to the late designs or insurrection.

149. And that this order might be submitted to and executed,
Oct. 31. he published a Declaration to make the justice as well as the
necessity of that proceeding appear [1]; and in which he did not
only set down the grounds of his present proceeding against
the royal party, but the rules by which he meant to proceed
against any other party that should provoke or give him trouble.
It was a declaration worded and digested with much more

---

[1] [From this point to the end of the book the text is found in the MS. of
the *Hist.* p. 30, of which the latter part of § 150 is found also in the MS.
of the *Life*, but is there struck out.]

asperity against all who had served the King than had ever **1655** been before published. Great caution had been hitherto used, as if nothing more had been desired than to unite the whole nation in the joint defence of their common interest, and as if a resolution had been taken to have abolished all marks of dis-union and distinction of parties, and that all men, of what con-dition soever, (except those who had been always excepted by name,) who would submit to the government, should be admitted to have shares and to act parts in the administration and defence of it. But now, notice was taken of such an inherent malignity and irreconcilableness [1] in all those who from the beginning had adhered to the King and opposed the proceedings of the Parlia-ment, towards all those who had served their country and vindicated the interest of the people and nation, that they declined the common rules of civility, and would have no con-versation with them ; and, that the same malice and animosity might descend to their posterity, they would not make marriages, or any friendship or alliance, with those who had been separated or divided from them in those public contentions ; and therefore they were not hereafter to wonder or complain, if they were looked upon as a common enemy, which must be kept from being able to do mischieve, since they would always be willing to do all they could ; and that they were not to expect to be prosecuted like other men, by the ordinary forms of justice, and to have their crimes to be proved by witnesses before they should be concluded to be guilty, if any desperate attempts were undertaken by any of that party to disturb the public peace; that it would be reasonable to conclude that they all wished well to it, though they appeared not to own it ; that all conspiracies of that nature were acted in secret, and were deeds of darkness, and men might justly be suspected and proceeded against as privy to them, by their common discourses, by the company they usually kept, and by their very looks; with many other expressions of such an unusual nature in the disquisition of justice and legal proceedings, that they might reasonably conclude, that they had nothing left that they could call their

[1] ['irreconciliableness,' MS.]

own, but must expect a total extirpation, either by massacre or transplantation.

150. But then it [the Declaration] took notice likewise of the factions in the army, that would not acquiesce in the government established, but would have another found out, and formed according to their levelling humours; all which distractions, to what other ends soever directed, must so weaken the kingdom, if not wisely prevented, as it must in the end be exposed as a prey to their inveterate enemies; and therefore, that the same remedies must be applied to them as to the others; with intimation clear enough, that the connivance they had formerly received, and even the pardons that had been granted for their former mutinies and transgressions, were of no more validity than the articles, promises, and acts of indemnity, which had been granted to the royal party, all which were declared to be void and null, upon any succeeding delinquency: so that all discontented people who liked not the present government, what part soever they had acted in the pulling down the old, Presbyterian, Independent, or Leveller, were left to consider of the consequence of those maxims which were laid down, and might naturally conclude that they were in no better condition of security for what they enjoyed, and had purchased dearly, than those who by their help were brought to the lowest misery; though, for the present, none but that party underwent that insupportable burden of decimation; which brought in a vast incredible sum of money into his [Cromwell's] coffers, the greater part whereof was raised (which was a kind of pleasure, though not ease, to the rest) upon those who never did, nor ever would have given, the King the least assistance, and were only reputed to be of his party because they had not assisted the rebels with a visible cheerfulness, or in any considerable proportion, and had proposed to themselves to sit still as neuters, and not to be at any charge with reference to either party; or such who had sheltered themselves in some of the King's garrisons for their own conveniency.

151. This Declaration was quickly sent to Cullen; where the King caused such an answer to be made to it, upon the grounds

that were laid down in it, as[1] if it were made by one who had 1655 been always of the Parliament side and who was well pleased to see the cavaliers reduced to that extremity; but with such reflections upon the tyranny that was exercised over the kingdom, [and] the foulness of the breach of trust that the Protector was guilty of, that obliged all the nation to look upon him as a detestable enemy that was to be removed by any way that offered itself: many of which arguments were made use of in the next Parliament that he called; which was not long after[2].

[1] ['and as,' MS.]

[2] [The following is a version of this paragraph which is struck out in the MS. of the *Life*, p. 507. 'This declaration as soon as printed was sent over to Cullen, and the Chancellor was commanded by the King to write some discourse upon it, to awaken the people, and to shew them their concernment in it, which he did by way of a letter to a friend ; which was likewise sent into England, and there printed ; and when Cromwell called his next Parliament ; it was made great use of to inflame the people, and make them sensible of the destruction that attended them, and was thought then to produce many good effects. And so we conclude this part. Montpelier, 27 May, 1670.' The original MS. of this Letter is preserved among Clarendon's papers : see *Calend. Clar. S. P.* iii. 79, and *pref.* vi–ix. The Letter was printed in 1656 under the title of *A letter from a true and lawful member of Parliament . . . to one of the lords of his Highnesse councell.*]

THE END OF THE FOURTEENTH BOOK.